Married to a Mafia Princess

A True Love Story

Linda Robinson

2024

This book is a work of nonfiction although for privacy reasons some names, locations, and identifying characteristics have been changed.

Cover designed by Linda Robinson

ISBN: 979-8-35094-310-8

Married to a Mafia Princess

Dedication
In memory of
Albert and Georgann Volpe

Linda Robinson

Prologue

When I was nineteen, I fell in love with a beautiful, Italian girl from The Bronx. She was charming, smart, and sweet - she was also the favorite daughter of a family connected to the Mafia. I had to wait to tell this story until most of the bad players had died -- unfortunately, that included me. I changed the names of some of the people in the book to protect the innocent although there are very few in this story. What I am about to relate is all true, no embellishments, just the story, and it really happened. Really!

This is me talking to you from the grave. Before you begin to read my love story, I'm telling you right up front, there are no happy endings.

Part One

1

Background

Stay with me ....Although this chapter is not part of the love story, it is my story – a second generation Italian boy growing up in The Bronx.

I was Albert N. Volpe, Jr. (no relation to any Mafia person real or fictional) born on March 19, 1945 - solid baby boomer. Until I was six, my parents and I lived in a three room, fifth floor walk-up in Melrose, a primarily Italian section of the South Bronx. This was before the area established its Latino roots and way before Father Gigante started the area on the road to gentrification in the early 1980's. (History lesson – look it up). In 1951, my mother's parents purchased a two-family house in the northeast section of The Bronx, and, of course, we moved in with them because multi generation Italian families always lived together.

As first generation Italians, my parents were hard-working, honest people. Like me, my father, Albert, was an only child. He was a quiet man without vices or excesses who worked for thirty-five years making bread in a commercial bakery in Long Island City. His slight build, thinning blond hair and pale blue eyes were unmemorable. He could enter and leave a crowded room without anyone recalling whether he had been there. To this day, I barely remember what he looked like although I see my father's clear, blue eyes every time I look in the mirror.

My mother, Caterina, worked as a seamstress at the Liberty Lace Mill in The Bronx. She had an older brother, my favorite uncle Augie, and a younger sister, Aunt Theresa. Like my father, my mother was tall and slender; I inherited her thick, black hair, aquiline nose and stubborn nature. I never heard my parents fight or say a harsh word to each other, and they never raised a hand to me.

As an only child, I was spoiled rotten by my parents and grandparents. I don't think my feet ever touched the ground until I was three and too big to be carried around. When you grow up in an extended Italian family, life is orderly; everyone co-exists without chaos, confusion or conflict; each has a defined role in the household pecking order. Parents are parents, not your friends; and they lived with their parents who were the major caregivers of children if both parents worked. Life was simple; life was good.

(This is the relevant part of the story.) I was raised to believe that there was a significant difference between northern and southern Italians; beliefs based primarily on perceived stereotypes - some having a measure of validity but none of them very complimentary. The worst versions of the stereotypes are that the terrone - southern Italians - are lazy, ignorant and criminal while the polentone - polenta eating northern Italians - are selfish and racist. Some northern Italians even make the assertion that a southern Italian is anyone who claims naissance south of Florence, and they are pretty snooty about it. Some northerners don't even deign to call Sicilians Italians at all! Through intermarriage, these distinctions have lost most of their stigma, but to my grandparents and parents, they were significant. Although we were Italian, the Mafia was only something my family knew existed but knew nothing much about. We weren't those 'kind' of Italians aka Mafia aka Sicilians or as my grandmother called them sfaccim – scum. I would learn plenty about the Mafia in the years to come. (Spoilers)

When I was twelve, my Uncle Augie built me a fancy, shoeshine box so I could go into business for myself. I bought supplies and practiced shining my grandfather's and father's shoes until I wore out the leather. Finally, I was ready. I set up next to the big boys on the corner of Gun Hill Road and White Plains Avenue. Three of the biggest (and ugliest) boys came over to my spot. They glared down at me for a few minutes before telling me to get lost - this was their corner. When I refused to move, they slapped me around and broke my shoeshine box. I picked up my broken kit and went home, but I didn't cry until I closed the door to my room, threw myself on the bed and muffled my sobs into my pillow. That was my first lesson in Business 101. The competition can put a serious hurt on sales. I repaired my box. The next Sunday, I found my own corner. I did well and discovered that I liked earning my own money. During my teenage years, I had many part time jobs, and I never asked my parents for an allowance again.

I found time for fun, too. One summer night when I was sixteen some friends and I 'borrowed' a '59 Buick Special for a little joy ride. No one had a license yet so our driving skills were a little sketchy. I was at the wheel and driving under the Third Avenue el heading west on Gun Hill Road. Bending to light a cigarette with my new Zippo, I took my eyes off the road for just a second - I swear, just a second - got too close to the iron upright of the el and had to swerve to miss it. Unfortunately, I swerved a little too much and ran into the upright on the opposite side of the street denting in the front of the Buick. None of us was hurt, but we couldn't put the borrowed car back with its hood crushed in so we pushed it over the side of the embankment into The Bronx River. There it lies still, rusting in its watery grave.

In 1962, my father decided to purchase his first new car. He always took the subway to Long Island City to his job. Because he knew nothing about cars, I went along with him to the Chevrolet dealership on Gun Hill Road as his automotive consultant. We walked into the showroom, wise-guy me swaggering as my father stared in confusion at the shiny, new cars. Looking around, I saw a guy sitting in the corner of the showroom with his feet propped up on a desk. In his mid-thirties and already combing his sparse, greasy hair over a bald spot, he looked more like a snake oil peddler than a new car salesman. He was reading a newspaper. We walked over to him.

"Are you looking for a new car?" he asked without raising his head from the newspaper. My father nodded, and I said, "Yeah."

"Is there any particular car you are interested in?" Slowly, he took his feet off the desk, folded his newspaper paying more attention to exacting its creases than to us and placed it on the corner of his desk before asking my father. "What kind of car would fit your needs?"

My father sat in the metal folding chair by the salesman's desk, and I stood behind him. "Write down these specs," I said and pointed to a yellow pad on the desk. I gave him the description I read in a car magazine."My father here wants a 1962 Chevy Impala with a 409 cube engine, two four-barrel carburetors, and a 4-speed transmission. It needs to have spinner hubcaps, a shifter plate, power steering, power brakes, air conditioning, an AM radio, front fender birds, grill and bumper guards, dual outside mirrors, dual rear antenna, and white sidewall tires."

"Got it. Is that all?" he said hiding a grin.

"One more spec. It needs to be black with a red stripe and black interior. That's it."

The salesman filled out the sales forms, had my father sign them, shook our hands - I wiped my hand on my jeans - and walked us to the showroom door.

Weeks later, the car arrived. My father and I took the bus to the dealership to pick it up. In the garage, the same salesman asked my father if he knew how to drive a 4-speed with Hurst shifter. My father nodded. He went over the operating features before giving my father the keys.

He slapped my father on the back and said, "You're all set. Take her away!"

My father got courageously behind the wheel. As soon as he started the engine, his face turned deathly pale. The 409-cubic-inch engine with the two four-barrel carburetors roared into life sending reverberations throughout the big garage. The ride home was harrowing. At each stoplight, when the light turned green my father would lightly touch the gas pedal and burn rubber taking off. We were both scared stiff by the time we got home. I felt really sorry for what I had done to this gentle man.

My father continued to take the subway to work in Queens and never once used his new car. Me, I had a ball drag racing it all over The Bronx.

By the time I turned eighteen, I had saved enough money to buy my own car. My pride and joy was a 1955 Ford Crown Victoria - black on black, rolled and pleated interior with header pipes. I had the dashboard scripted in gold leaf with the name 'Big Bluffer,' because I thought it was way cooler than its common nickname, Vickie. Gag. The car looked fast but didn't run too great. I joined a car club called The Strokers who treated their cars better than their girlfriends. The guys in the club loved fixing cars so they kept my Vickie (I couldn't help reverting to her common name) running for me. As soon as I got my own car, my father traded in his 409 NASCAR for a Chevy Nova losing money on the deal, but he never once said a recriminating word to me.

If we were alive today, I would kiss him. His memory brings to mind what a sweet man my father was and the hell I put my parents through during my teenage years. My mother would never acknowledge the ball-buster I was growing up to be. "Not my Junior!"

I was Albert N. Volpe, Jr. - arrogant, vain, know it all - a punk.

And now, the love story.

2

Love

In 1962, I graduated from Evander Childs High School. My parents hoped I'd get a job with security and a pension, but I knew I wasn't a 9-to-5er kind of guy. I had other plans for my life but not much clue what they might be. Since computer programming appeared to be the wave of the future, I decided to enroll in a six-month course in computer programming at Monroe Business School in The Bronx.

At that time, computers were in their infancy. Before any computations could be made, all the data had to first be entered onto little cards by key punch operators before feeding the cards into a computer bigger than a refrigerator. The programming part I was learning involved placing little wire plugs into circuit boards. This seemed like tedious, boring work to me. Instead of going to class, I spent a lot of time in the poolroom across the street from Monroe. By graduation, I had learned to shoot a decent game of pool but not much about making a living in the computer age. While many of my classmates went on to lucrative careers in computer programming, I still had to figure out what I was going to do with my life besides becoming the next Minnesota Fats. I wasn't too bright.

After class, a group of us from Monroe met at Saul's Luncheonette on 172nd Street. I was sipping a coke at the counter when I first set eyes on Georgann Marino who was taking a secretarial course at Monroe. Georgann really stood out from the other girls. She was tall and slender but still curvy; her dark brown hair was frosted and teased high in the style of the day. Her big, brown eyes with their tiny flecks of gold that glinted in the sunlight drew me like a moth to a flame. She accented her long lashes with lots of mascara and when she fluttered them at me my heart skipped a beat. Her nose was a bit too wide but her luscious mouth, out of which came only softly spoken words, had me hanging on them like a puppet on a string. She was my dream girl.

Soon Georgann and I sat together at Saul's shutting out the rest of the group as if they didn't exist. If we passed each other in the hall at Monroe, she would lower her head; look up at me through those long lashes and whisper a soft, 'Hi, Al." My knees would buckle. I fell for Georgann hard. Even before we had our first date, it was too late for me to cut my emotions and run.

Georgann and I both graduated at the same time from Monroe. She got a job as a teller with County Trust Bank in Mt. Vernon and I found work as a clerk n a law firm in Ardsley, NY - just until I found a real job. Since computers were not my cup of espresso, I decided to enroll in night courses at Fordham University's Business School. I never intended to get a degree - that would have required more work, discipline, and time than I wanted to expend - but I figured it couldn't hurt to learn something about management and balance sheets, since I intended to have my own business someday. My adolescent shoe shine business spurred my entrepreneurial aspirations.

A few weeks after graduation, Georgann and I decided it was time for us to become 'steadies' and date exclusively. We made plans to go on our first real date as a couple.

"Al, pick me up at my house at 6:00 on Saturday. I want you to meet my parents."

"How about I just beep my horn and you come out."

"No, Al, you have to meet my parents. They have to approve of you."

"What are you talking about, Georgann? This is 1962, not 1862 and we live in The Bronx, not Italy. Since when does a girl need her parents' permission who to date?"

"You don't know my parents. They would give me nothing but grief if they didn't meet you and give their okay."

"How are they going stop me from seeing you? Have me whacked?" I was joking, because, at the time, I didn't know how close I was to the truth. Still, I couldn't help laughing at Georgann's old fashioned notions - until she explained her reasons.

"I never told you much about my family, Al, because I didn't want to scare you off."

"What are they ax-murderers?" I was so hilarious.

"Of course they aren't, Al. Don't be silly. But, my father's line of work is not exactly legitimate, or at least, I don't think so. He works for the Gambino family as some kind of union representative. I don't know much about what else he does, but he's gone a lot. My mother doesn't have a job, but I know her two brothers are part of the same Colombo crime family her father belonged to. He died a number of years ago, but I was never told the cause of his death, and I wasn't allowed to attend his funeral. I never ask my uncles what they do for the Colombo family. It isn't my place not that they'd tell me. Now that you know my family is involved with the Mafia, do you still want to see me?"

I knew the Gambino and Colombo families were big Mafia, but my knowledge came from what I read in the papers, not from personal experience.

"Your family doesn't scare me, Georgann. It's you I want to be with, not them. Don't worry your pretty head. Your parents are going to love me. I'll charm the daylights out of them. I'll pick you up at 6." I said this with the same bravado I felt, because at nineteen, I wasn't very smart.

The Marinos lived on Mace Avenue in the northeast section of The Bronx, a residential neighborhood off Pelham Parkway where many southern Italians - aka Mafia - lived. The Marinos house was a red-brick, two-story colonial with a small, neatly tended front lawn sporting the obligatory statue of the Madonna. A short brick path led to a five step stoop. The house was modest looking on the outside - like all Mafia houses - to avoid notifying the IRS that the occupants might be living beyond their means or have a different source of income they reported on their tax returns. Inside was another story - plush furniture (covered in plastic, of course), lots of gold leaf, top of the line appliances, custom made suits and designer clothes in all the closets, and a Cadillac in the single car garage.

At two minutes to six, I pulled my Ford Vicky to the curb in front of the Marino house. Dropping the visor, I smoothed back the sides of my hair with my hands, checked my teeth for food, and practiced my 'you-gotta-love-me' grin in the mirror before getting out of the car. I had more than my fair share of vanity. I was 6'1" with a 32" waist, broad shoulders, lots of thick, black hair slicked straight back from a forehead that was maybe a little too Neanderthal, clear blue eyes, a small, aquiline nose, and enough lip to produce a first-class sneer when needed. I was hip.

I got out of Vicky, pulled my Hawaiian shirt closed but not buttoned over my 'wife beater' undershirt, hiked up my black chinos and sauntered over to the house. I ran up the steps taking two at a time and rang the bell. I stood on the step smiling with my best shit-eating grin frozen on my face. Georgann's mother answered the door. Her smile was a red slash that didn't go past her lips which were pursed as narrow as the squint of her eyes. Mrs. Marino was an attractive woman, slender, fortyish, and almost as tall as Georgann with the same dark hair teased and sprayed stiff by her weekly trips to the hair dresser. Her forehead was high and smooth except for the two deep lines between her eyes - a result of the narrow, unblinking stare she used to view the world and which she now directed at me. The memory of those piercing, dark eyes would send involuntary shivers up my spine for the rest of my life. She was dressed in a stylish blue and white shirtwaist dress and wore high heeled pointy toed shoes matching the blue in her dress. She stood blocking the entrance, hand on one hip. I could tell that her appealing looks masked a coarser side as soon as she opened her mouth.

"Hi, Mrs. Marino," I said, "I'm Al Volpe, and I'm here to pick up Georgann. It's a pleasure to meet you."

"Oh, yeah," she answered looking me up and down with a flinty, fish-eyed stare. "Georgann," she screamed into the house, "there's some guy here who says he's here to get you. I guess you're expecting him." Her voice was deep and raspy after years of smoking unfiltered Camels. No 'nice to meet you' from this lady.

Georgann came bouncing down the stairs, smiling at me as she put her arm around her mother's shoulders "This is Al, Ma. He's a business major and computer expert."

My hoodlum haircut, loud Hawaiian shirt, and hot rod car didn't fit that profile. It was obvious that Mrs. Marino's first impression of me wasn't one of warmth and welcome. She didn't say anything, just continued to stare at me through narrowed eyes.

Then, with a crooked smile minutely lifting one corner of her red lips, she said, "Your father's not home yet, Georgann, but I'll be sure to tell him all about Al." She said my name as if I was a rat whose neck was snapped in a trap waiting for her husband to dump in the trash when he got home. I could've filled a book with the unspoken words her sneer conveyed.

"Bye, Ma, I'll be home by one."

Georgann rushed through the door sweeping us both down the front steps. Mrs. Marino came out on the stoop. As we walked to the car, I hunched up my shoulders feeling Mrs. Marino's stare stabbing me in the back like daggers. If I believed in malocchio - the evil eye - I swear she was putting a curse on me. I peeled away from the curb wanting to put some distance between me and that strega - evil witch. I glanced in the rear view mirror to see Mrs. Marino rooted in the same spot watching us as we sped away. It took me a long time that night to shake that scary image.

The longer Georgann and I dated, the more I learned about her family. Her father, Silvio, was a tough piece of work - union organizer, loan shark, and known criminal with a considerable rap sheet of felonies. In his late forties and a couple of inches under six feet, Silvio looked more like an aging Marcello Mastroianni than a mid-level thug. His brown, wavy hair already streaked with silver was combed straight back from a wide forehead. His mustache was trimmed pencil thin enhancing full lips. The dentures he kept neon white made the smile he flashed only for a second even scarier. Silvio never talked much about his family preserving the age old Mafia tradition keeping his personal life to himself. He was a man who spoke little, but when he did everyone, including me, straightened up and listened.

Marie, on the other hand, did nothing but talk in a volume just slightly lower than boom box and nobody listened. Marie's older brother, James Vingo, aka 'Crazy Vinnie,' had been a light weight prize fighter in the late '40's winning six out of his eight bouts before retiring from the ring to enter the more lucrative field of vicious underworld enforcer who, at times, bent mob rules to suit his whims. Don't confuse Crazy Vinnie with Carmine 'Bingo' Vingo, a legit heavy weight boxer whose biggest claim to fame was that he was knocked out by Rocky Marciano in the sixth round of a fight in 1949. As a result, Bingo sustained brain injury resulting in paralysis on his left side which ended his fight career.

Marie's younger brother, Ralph - aka Sonny - Vingo, was a 260-pound hairdresser. Although married with two kids, his proclivity might have remained with the male sex. (Even hinting he might be gay was unthinkable and terminal.) Besides running a hair salon on Long Island, he was also an antique expert, wannabe crooner, and a bullshit artist whose heart was both scheming and made of gold. He preferred to pursue legitimate activities to those of The Family. He was the only member of the Marino family who liked me.

(Some complicated Mafia history) Silvio was a member of the Gambino crime family, one of New York City's Five Families that dominated the New York area's organized underworld activities since the early 1900's. The five Families were the Genovese, Mangano/Gambino, Profaci/Colombo, Lucchese, and Bonanno families – aka the Cosa Nostra aka The Mafia. The five Families divvied up New York City and for a time existed somewhat amicably. Carlo Gambino was capo dei capi - boss of all bosses – of the Gambino contingent from 1957 until 1976 when, at age seventy-four; he died of a heart attack in New Jersey. Silvio never met Gambino face to face. His low status as an associate didn't allow such chumminess, but Silvio knew The Family was aware of him, and he made sure he kept his criminal nose clean.

Marie's brothers, Jimmy and Sonny, followed in their father's footsteps beginning their Mafia alignment with the Profaci crime family. Joe Gallo was an enforcer for Profaci and, in 1957, under Profaci's orders; was presumed to have killed Albert Anastasia, the current capo of the Mangano Family, to make way for Carlo Gambino who renamed that contingent after himself when he took over as capo. Anastasia's death initiated a war among the Gambino and Profaci factions. The gang war continued until Gallo's arrest in 1961 and Joe Profaci's death of liver cancer in 1962. Joe Colombo was installed as capo dei capi after Profaci's death whose reign in the underworld began in 1963 and was ended in 1971 by several bullets which left him paralyzed. Gallo, after serving ten years in prison, returned to the Colombo Family, but his enforcer status was short lived - he was shot dead in Umberto's Clam house in Little Italy in 1972. Carmine Persico, although serving thirty two years in Federal prison, assumed the official capo leadership of the Colombo family in 1973 and ruled behind bars until his death in 2019 at age eighty-five. By 1965, when I met Georgann, the internal strife among the members of the Five Families still existed.

Because of the lack of strong leadership, the Colombo Family was considered the weakest of the Five Families by their counterparts. Silvio, remaining loyal to mob opinion, had little respect for anyone whose mob affiliation was with the Colombo family; therefore, he had no business dealings with Marie's brothers - both stronziatini - bullshitters. I never knew how Marie and Silvio ended up married. These mixed marriages are always complicated.

As a small time thug, Silvio was not yet a made-man or a fully initiated member of the Gambino Family. In those years, a potential initiate, besides being of Sicilian descent, was required to personally carry out a contract killing, known as 'making your bones,' as well as taking the oath of omertá - never telling anyone about the family business even under threat of losing one's life. When I first met him, being a soldier or made-man was not a major goal for Silvio. As an associate, he did what he was told but only had to give the capos a share of what he criminally made. Silvio wasn't ready to kick in a bigger share of his illicit earnings to The Family as part of his dues as a soldier. But, in his old age he became sentimental. (More about Silvio's ambitions later on in the story.)

Although Marie was not directly involved in the crime scene, she was equally as corrupt as other members of her family. Since Mafia rule dictated that Family business was not shared with one's personal family, Marie endearingly used the expression 'away at college' as a euphemism for someone doing time in prison. By the time I met them, Silvio had received his Bachelor's degree and Jimmy was then finishing up his Master's. Sonny, who was living a semi-normal life, had managed to avoid any college credits. If Silvio couldn't attend a parent-teacher conference or school function, Georgann told her classmates and teachers at the exclusive Villa Maria Girls Academy elementary school in the Country Club section of The Bronx that her father was away at college. She was so young and innocent then; she believed Marie was telling her the truth. What a sweetheart!

That's enough of the Marino Mafia background.

Over the next year, Georgann and I dated casually and had some crazy times in my Vickie. One night, after fun on the rides at Rye Playland which was situated in a quiet, residential neighborhood in Westchester, we were leaving the parking lot when the roar of the header pipes motivated a local cop to arrest me for violating the noise ordinance. (To impress Georgann, I might have provoked him a little by giving him some wise guy lip.) I was handcuffed and put in the back of the patrol car. Georgann followed me in the Vicky to the police station. At the precinct, while I was cooling off in a cell, Georgann was pleading my case with the desk sergeant to please release me and not impound my car. Those soft, brown eyes and the Marino name did the trick. Because I had no prior arrests, I was let off with a warning and a handful of tickets including one for disturbing the peace.

We sat in silence on the drive home. At a stop light, Georgann turned to me and gave me what I would from then on dub 'the look' - a shake of her head, a slow blink then a roll of her big eyes, followed by a little grin that turned into her beautiful smile. We burst out laughing! Hey, I was lucky. I was sitting next to the most wonderful girl in the world instead of spending the night in jail.

More than once (maybe five or six times), I brought Georgann home from a date in a taxi. Once or twice we sat in the front seat of the tow truck hauling my Vickie to the Strokers garage. Somehow, Georgann always laughed about it. Vicky was not a reliable car. You think?

Although my parents loved Georgann, they didn't love the idea that I was involved with someone whose family was Sicilian. To them Sicilian meant Mafia, and my parents had a good reason to be concerned for my welfare. God forbid I married Georgann. With Sicilians, marriage meant a package deal that included her parents, uncles, cousins, etc. and even zio Vincenzo who at ninety and living in Palermo still retained his capo status. Unlike my reserved, northern Italian parents who would never consider interfering in my life, it was a given that Georgann's relatives would stick their 'two lire' into our business whether asked for or not. What's more, my parents had no real understanding of what it meant to be part of a 'connected' family. In fact, I had no idea myself, because if I had, I would have run for the hills. What did I say, not too smart.

It didn't take long for me to realize that Georgann's parents did not approve of my dating Georgann but not for the same reasons my parents disapproved. Georgann's parents wanted her to marry Manny, the builder's son who she had been dating when we first met. Manny's father was a successful contractor whose big money contracts with New York City bought him a big house, big cars and a flashy lifestyle. Silvio saw that corrupt money could be made from such a marriage liaison, and Marie saw a gentile or more cultured status for her daughter and for herself by association. I was the son of a baker who wasn't even Sicilian!

If I telephoned Georgann and Marie answered she would tell me that Georgann was out on a date with someone else. If I waited on the steps for Georgann instead of in my car, Marie stood silently behind the screen door arms crossed over her chest and glared menacingly at me. Silvio pretended I was invisible. And, that was when they were being nice!

The Marinos became so hostile to me that I stopped picking Georgann up at her house. We pre-arranged our dates. She would sneak out to see me telling her parents she was with a girlfriend. Sometimes, I would get a friend of mine to pretend he was her date and pick her up at her house. Georgann's parents might be controlling, but they weren't stupid. A girl as attractive as Georgann had to have a date once in a while. I waited at a safe distance for Georgann or for my friend to bring Georgann over to me in the new Ford Galaxy I bought after selling my cherished Vicky so the Marinos wouldn't hear me coming. For some reason, I could never get a friend to go back to the Marino house a second time. They didn't want to talk about it.

Considering the environment in which she grew up, Georgann was amazingly well adjusted. Even though she knew her parents had ties to the Mafia, her behavior was always respectful and loving to both of them, but especially to her mother. Even though the sun rose and set on Georgann, her parents were not above using violent means to break us up, and Georgann knew this. This knowledge cast an ugly shadow over our dating.

Sometimes I would suggest that it might be a good idea to meet with her parents to discuss our relationship. She would just say, "Soon, Al. It's not the right time yet."

We dated exclusively over the next two years and continued to meet on the sneak to avoid arousing her parents' attention and giving her grief. After picking Georgann up at the corner one night, I said, "This sneaking around is not working for me anymore. I'm running out of friends who will stand in for me once they meet your mother. It's time to go public. I'm going to have a talk with your parents."

"I don't think that's such a good idea. Let's wait a little longer."

"Everything will be fine. I'll talk nice to your parents and get them to understand that we're serious about each other. I'm making decent money at the bank, and I have some ideas about doing better. Hey, I'm every mother's dream date for her daughter." Call me naïve, definitely stupid, but I felt it was the right thing to do.

On the night I designated for the meeting with Georgann's parents, she met me at the corner and got into the car. She begged me once more to wait until a better time, but I stubbornly refused. I decided to speak with her parents alone while Georgann waited for me in the car. I got out, hiked up my chinos, buttoned my shirt and headed for the Marino house.

After I rang the doorbell, I stood on the front steps rehearsing what I was going to say. Marie opened the front door but kept the screen door shut. If she was surprised to see me, her icy stare gave no indication.

"Evening, Mrs. Marino. Can I come in and talk to you and Mr. Marino?"

"What for?

"About me and Georgann."

Not taking her reptilian eyes off me and shaking her thumb in my direction, she yelled into the house, "Silvio, come out here! Al's here, and he wants to talk to us about him and Georgann."

Through the screen, I watched him slowly saunter down the hallway. He pushed open the screen door bellowing, "What the fuck do you want? Get the fuck out of here! You got nothin' to say I wanna hear."

I started to say, "Mr. Marino," and bam! He punched me in the chest. I staggered back a couple of inches, shook it off and tried again, "Please, Mr. Marino, can I…." Bam! He sucker punched me in the face; I went down on one knee, nose bleeding.

I got up, begging this time, "Mr. Marino, please..." He swung again. This time I blocked his punch with my left arm, grabbed his hand with my right, and pushed it down to his side. We locked eyes for ten seconds, mine showing neither aggression nor fear which seemed to shock him to immobility. Without a word, I let his hand go, turned and walked slowly down the steps.

I was 6'1" to his 5'10", more than twenty years his junior and outweighed him by at least thirty pounds. After his initial, cheap shots, I could easily have fought back and hurt him, but I never raised a hand to him. I'd done what was right. Where's the honor in beating up my girlfriend's father? I doubt Georgann would think I was such a great guy after I cold-cocked her father even if he did pull the first punch. It was in that moment that I realized there would be no talking to these people. Reason just wasn't part of their gene pool.

I ran my hand over my face and, without realizing it, smeared blood from the nose bleed. When she saw my bloodied face, Georgann began to cry, "Oh my God, what did they do to you?"

In the car, I looked at my face in the rear view mirror. I knew it looked a lot worse than it was.

Georgann pulled some tissues out of her purse and wiped my face repeating over and over, "Oh my God, oh my God."

I said, "Stop crying, it's only a nose bleed. I'm okay. Let's get out of here."

She calmed down when she realized I wasn't going to die. We drove to a gas station, and she ran into the bathroom to get some wet paper towels to wipe my face. When she came back to the car, I sat staring out the windshield as she tenderly cleaned the blood off my face. "I'm so sorry my father did this to you."

"What are you sorry for? It's not your fault you were born into that madhouse. I love you." Those three little words spilled out before I even knew what I was saying.

She whispered back, "I love you, too."

"Will you marry me?" I was on an emotional roll.

Through her tears, she smiled and whispered, "Yes!"

In that moment, we knew we were meant to spend the rest of our lives together. We had no idea where that life would take us, but love is not only blind; it's dumb as a bowl of yesterday's cold ravioli.

Mangia bene!

3

Elopement

Two years before, Big John, a friend of mine from the neighborhood, was in a big hurry to get married and eloped to Maryland with his girlfriend. Since planning wasn't my forte, this sounded like a good idea to me, too, plus, the timing couldn't be better.

"If you really love me, Georgann, let's get married right away." I told her about Big John going to Maryland.

Fueled with love, the thrill of the adventure, as well as those female hormones that kick in whenever marriage is mentioned, Georgann said, "Let's go tonight. I can't wait to be Mrs. Albert Volpe."

I went into the gas station and bought a road map. On October 25, 1965, Georgann and I headed for Maryland following Big John's lead. After forty five minutes (it felt like three hours) we were over the George Washington Bridge and on the Jersey Turnpike. We decided to stop for gas and something to eat at the Molly Pitcher rest stop in southern New Jersey. I opened my wallet to audit our finances.

"I have $230 in my wallet and seventy cents in my pocket. How much do you have, Georgann?"

"I only have four dollars. I never needed to carry any money when I was with you." Ah, her trust in me was charming.

"Nothing like starting our future on firm, financial grounds," I said.

In the parking lot of the rest stop we ran into a guy I knew from The Strokers car club. His name was Mitch and he was driving back from Atlantic City after a string of good luck. We did some catch up talking in front of my car. He admired the chrome rims on the Ford Galaxie.

"Hey, Al, you got some sweet rims on that baby."

Half-joking, I said, "If you give me $300 and pay to have the gas station attendant to switch the rims they're yours." I didn't think he would go for it, but he did.

"I'll give you $250."

"Deal," I said. We shook hands on it. "Georgann, we just doubled our bankroll in that transaction." She laughed and gave me a big kiss on the cheek. That kiss was worth more than fancy chrome wheels.

While we waited for the rim switch, Georgann decided to call her cousin, Maryann who was Sonny's daughter and like a big sister to Georgann. As her aunt and uncle, Maryann was well acquainted with the personalities of Marie and Silvio. Maryann also knew my parents, because she came with Georgann to dinner at my house a few times. My parents liked her and she liked them. We headed for the bank of telephone booths in the cafeteria. I stood outside the booth as she called but only heard Georgann's side of the conversation.

"Maryann, Al and me are on our way to Maryland to get married. No, I am not pregnant. Okay, okay, but we love each other. Because my parents never approved of us dating and hate him, that's why. Yes, I know. Silvio is going to kill him, but by time my father finds us, we'll be married. He wouldn't try anything with Al after because it would upset me. Don't worry. It's fine. I'll call you tomorrow."

I thought about calling my mother but decided not to. She would only torture herself with notions of what the Marino family would do to me if we got caught putting her nerves into a higher state of frenzy. I imagined I could hear her hysterical crying all the way from The Bronx to South Jersey. I'd wait until after we got married to call my parents. I'm not big on confrontation even if it's only over the phone and with my mother. I figured it would be best if both Georgann and I faced our parents together and in person. It couldn't be soon enough for me to have Georgann begin her new role as buffer to spare my sensitive nature the agita when facing a bad situation. (Spoilers – that role would continue for almost thirty years.)

It was late at night when we arrived in Maryland with no idea where to go. We stopped at an all-night diner for some burgers and to make some plans. Two state troopers sitting at the counter. I went up to them.

"Excuse me officers for interrupting your dinner but maybe you can help us? My girlfriend and I just drove down from New York City and want to get married."

The two of them looked over their shoulders at Georgann who smiled back at them from the booth giving them a finger wave.

"So you two kids want to get married." He winked at his partner.

"Yes, sir."

He pulled out his notepad. "Here are the directions to the town hall. It doesn't open until 9:00." He jotted them down and ripped off the page handing it to me. "Good luck," he said before returning to his pie. I thanked him.

"What did the officer say?" asked Georgann.

"He gave me directions to the town hall, but we have to wait until nine for it to open."

"As long as I'm with you, I can wait forever," said Georgann giving my hand a squeeze. Was she terrific or what?

We lingered as long as we could in the diner drinking too many coffee refills, then drove to the beach to watch the sunrise. We were in front of the Town Hall by eight. As soon as the doors opened, holding hands, we walked into the clerk's office and up to the desk. A matronly woman around fifty with tightly curled, salt and pepper hair and friendly eyes looked up from her paperwork over glasses perched on the tip of her nose.

"May I help you?" she said giving us a motherly smile. She knew why we were there having seen hundreds of couples with the same dreamy, dopey looks on their faces.

"We want to get married right away," I said.

"I'm sure you do," she answered, "I can see you two are very much in love."

"Yes, we are," said Georgann blushing and squeezing my hand even tighter.

"First, you have to fill out these forms," she said handing me a bunch of papers. "After I verify the information, you will have to wait three days to fulfill Maryland's residency requirement for a marriage license. Come back in three days, and the justice of peace will perform the ceremony."

I looked at Georgann; she stared back at me. Now what? Clutching the forms, we left the town hall in a state of confusion. Not knowing what else to do, Georgann found a phone booth and called Maryann.

"What should we do, Maryann? We can't wait three days! I'm sure my father already has some of his cronies out looking for us. I don't know what they will do to Al if they find us."

"Come back home, Georgann. Your mother called me. When I told her you eloped with Al, she went ballistic. She insisted I tell her where Al's parents live to confront them. She thinks they helped you two elope. Marie can be really brutal so I raced over to Al's house to prepare his parents for Marie's onslaught. She showed up, pushed her way into the house screaming that she was going to have Al's legs broken when she finds the two of you. Al's mother fainted. Marie had sense enough to storm back out before your father called the police. Come back. You can stay at my house until we figure out what to do next. Tell Al to go home and stay there until he hears from me.

"Ask Maryann how's my mother doing," I said.

"Al's mother is worried sick. She does nothing but cry. Al's father just sits on the couch holding his head in his hands and rocking back and forth. Come back. The longer you two stay away, the more fuel you are putting on Marie's bonfire."

Georgann and I decided to take Maryann's advice. Our elopement in defiance of the wishes of both our families was proof enough how much we loved each other. We had no idea what was waiting for us when we got back to New York; we just knew we could face it together.

Georgann sat close to me with her head on my shoulder the whole way back to The Bronx. I dropped her at Maryann's before heading home. I was physically and emotionally drained after driving to Maryland and back in twenty four hours without any sleep to achieve – nothing - no, not nothing. We now knew our commitment to each other was real.

As soon as I walked through the door, my mother bombarded me with questions. My head was throbbing so much I didn't understand a word she said.

I pleaded, "Ma, please, I got a headache. Leave me alone for now. I'll tell you everything later."

In the bathroom, I grabbed the aspirin bottle, swallowed down a bunch, went into my room, threw myself on the bed, hid my head under the pillow and was instantly asleep. Hours later, my mother woke me. Georgann was on the phone. She was calling me from Maryann's. I shook the sleep from my fuzzy head before taking the phone; I felt as if I had dreamt the last twenty four hours. As soon as I heard Georgann's voice, I knew it had been real.

"How are you?" Georgann whispered.

I mumbled, "I'm okay, just tired. Have you spoken to your parents yet?" I asked.

"Yes. I told them that I was so angry at Daddy for punching you and giving you a bloody nose. I just wanted to get back at the both of them for treating you so badly and knew running away with you to get married would be the best way to hurt them. I told them that I love you very, very much and there was nothing they could do to keep us apart. That's why we eloped."

This was the kind of twisted revenge Silvio could understand. He didn't protest. "Before I could hang up with my parents, Maryann took the phone from me. She said to them, 'Aunt Marie, Uncle Silvio, I want assure you that although Georgann loves you both, she loves Al, too. But, and this is a big but, she is not going home. Let me finish, Aunt Marie. Georgann is not going to budge on this so there's no use you yelling at me. Uncle Silvio, don't try to threaten or bribe Al into leaving Georgann alone or you may never see your daughter again. Georgann is going to stay at my house until I can arrange a meeting between you and the Volpes. Until then, the only contact you will have with Georgann will be through me. Capisce?'

They understood.

4

Wedding

Five days later, Maryann presided over a tense but civil meeting with our families at a local restaurant (a public place to avoid a scene or a hit). Once everyone was seated, Georgann rose to speak.

"First, I want to thank all of you for coming tonight. Al and I really appreciate it." She turned to look at her parents. "Mom, Dad, I love you very much. I know you wish only the best for me. I have always tried to be a good daughter always doing what you asked of me; but this time, I have to do what I want. I'm sorry I made you worry by running off with Al. Believe me when I say I am not trying to hurt you even now, but you can't stop me from marrying Al. I love him. If we can't get married with your blessing, then we'll get married without it."

She turned to my parents. "Mr. and Mrs. Volpe, I love your son. I want you to know that I will make him a good wife. I hope you will look upon me as the daughter you never had. Al would tell you the same if his voice didn't crack from being so nervous." Georgann bowed her head, gave my hand a squeeze and sat down.

My mother, tears welling up in her eyes, reached across the table and squeezed Georgann's hand. "Bravisima, bella." My father patted my mother's shoulder and nodded to Georgann; no other words were needed.

Silvio's eyes darted to me - we locked stares. Silvio was a tough guy, but he had to maintain a certain demeanor when it came to family. It was okay for him to break my nose if I wasn't related to him, but becoming his son-in-law made me part of the family. Neither he nor Marie said a word. Me neither. I could tell that Marie was having a hard time controlling herself by the magenta color of her face.

I was proud of how diplomatically Georgann handled the situation. Me, I couldn't wait to get through the ordeal. I didn't realize it at the time, but this meeting was a forerunner of how all our family problems would be solved - Georgann taking charge and me shrinking in the shadows.

The meeting went as well as could be expected. Our families knew we were serious about getting married; the warning not to interfere was understood. Because Georgann was the only stable female member of his household, Silvio wanted to keep on her good side. Marie knew that she would lose Georgann, her princess, if she opposed our marriage. My parents just wanted me to be happy.

Maryann signaled for the waiters to bring the food. After several glasses of wine were raised to toast the engaged couple, the tension between the families eased, and the conversation turned to the meal. Marie and my mother talked about shopping on Arthur Avenue, the men made small talk about the food and wine; Georgann and I left before dessert.

Now that our relationship was out in the open, we could breathe easier. The threat that one of her father's associates would catch us together and rat us out to Silvio no longer hung over us. My parents still lived in hope that ours was just an infatuation that would end in a break up. Marie just hoped I would die, but she managed to keep her mouth shut.

Once we set the wedding date, Marie became a frenzied wedding planner arranging everything with or without Georgann's input. Her daughter was going to have the biggest, best wedding Silvio could afford - spare no expense. It was all about the spectacle. Out of our earshot, she told everyone that the marriage wouldn't last a year.

I was on my best behavior when I was with the Marinos. I attempted, though I knew it was futile, to ingratiate myself with Georgann's parents. Marie would blush like a school girl if I fussed over her cooking or told her how she looked more like Georgann's sister than her mother. Georgann would roll her eyes at my phony praise. Because he never said much, I wasn't able to discern how Silvio felt toward me - dislike or indifference - and didn't know how to get in better with him. I counted myself lucky for his silence.

My matriculation into Georgann's family enabled me to observe the extent of Marie's love/hate pendulum behavior. To my face, she acted like I was the greatest, but I knew what she really thought of me - less than dog shit. At times, her behavior morphed before my eyes. A loving, caring, mother and wife would, for no apparent reason, turn into a vile, abusive, raging shrew. Most of the time, her rages were directed at Silvio. Sometimes, if she got too violent, Silvio would smack her around a couple of times until she calmed down. Maybe her family was inured to her behavior, but she scared the crap out of me. Marie was probably bipolar, (my opinion) but her family blamed her unstable behavior on pills and alcohol. Georgann, bless her heart, just felt sorry for her mother.

Georgann's younger sister, Donna, was a self-absorbed nitwit who took every opportunity to gossip about everything and everyone. When she wasn't trying to instigate trouble, she was whining about her imaginary problems. She looked a little like Georgann but favored more her Grandma Vingo's looks - without the mustache. At 5'3", she was a little overweight with short legs and a big bust; her eyes were mud brown and her curly hair mousy brown. She tried to give the impression of being smart by quoting from some magazine article or TV program, but she had neither common sense nor people skills. Donna didn't work much, because she couldn't keep a job for very long. She mostly sat around the house in hair curlers watching television.

Is it any wonder why Georgann was her parent's favorite daughter, the Mafia Princess? (There, I said it.)

On April 23, 1966, we were married in Our Lady of Pity, a Catholic church on East 151st Street in the Melrose section of The Bronx. Everyone oohed and ahhed as Georgann made her way to the altar looking radiant as she walked down the aisle on Silvio's arm. Sonny's two little daughters spread rose petals and held up the long train to her bridal gown. I stood at the altar rubber legged and sweating bullets. If my grandparents were alive they would have been in their own church saying a novena for God's intervention to stop the wedding.

The reception was held at the Glen Island Harbor Club on the waterfront in New Rochelle. It was a sumptuous affair. Silvio went all out to impress. He hired a ten piece dance band, the waiters kept champagne flowing, and the three foot flower arrangements on each table could have been modeled after a royal wedding. There were over three hundred guests in attendance. A lot of heavyweight Mafiosi from both the Gambino and Colombo families showed up. Of course, they were seated on opposite sides of the hall with my family and friends seated in the middle as a buffer.

Uncle Augie was my best man. He walked around the reception hall like it was his wedding going to each table smiling, shaking everyone's hand and having his picture taken with them. A few of the guests mistakenly slipped envelopes with cash - the busta - to Augie thinking he was the groom. I mistook a member of the Gambino family for a waiter and asked him to bring more wine .... he did. Marie's brother, Sonny grabbed the microphone and sang all the popular tunes, plus the old, Italian favorites. (Marie's brother Jimmy was away in college getting his masters) Everyone, even Grandma Vingo, Marie's mother, danced the tarantella. She did a pretty lively step, too.

It was a classic mob wedding with all the pomp, pageantry and ritual. Everyone was either a 'friend of ours' meaning he was member of the same Family or a 'friend of mine' meaning 'don't talk business with this guy but act nice.' Financially, Georgann and I made out great. Uncle Augie called our wedding the great train robbery - whatever that meant. Before we left the hall, I checked all his pockets to make sure he turned over all the busta.

We went to Europe for our three week honeymoon - Madrid, Lisbon, the French Riviera, Monte Carlo, Nice and Majorca. We had a ball.

Honeymoon over, we returned home to settle into our new apartment in Yonkers. Georgann went to work at the Franklin National Bank on Baychester Avenue in The Bronx, two blocks from her parent's house. I was between jobs (unemployed) but we still had plenty of money from the busta, so I wasn't worried about finances. I was ready to start a new chapter of my life. Unfortunately, the chapter was written by Uncle Sam.

Home only two weeks from our honeymoon, I received a letter informing me that it was turn to serve my country. I was to report for basic Army training at Fort Jackson, South Carolina. A week later, I found myself sleeping on a metal bunk surrounded by strangers and being yelled at by mean men wearing Smokey the Bear hats. It was hard for me to believe that just a few weeks before the horrific reality busted in on my utopia, I had been munching croissants and sunbathing on the French Riviera.

C'est la vie!

5

Army

How did I wind up at Fort Jackson? As required by Federal law, a few days after my eighteenth birthday in 1963, I went with Benny LoPresti, a buddy of mine from the neighborhood, to 39 Whitehall Street in Manhattan to register with the Selective Service System.

In 1961, President John F. Kennedy began escalating American involvement in Vietnam. After Kennedy's assassination in 1963, President Lyndon Johnson continued the escalation efforts by instituting the draft in 1964. I saw the writing on the wall and this Bronx boy did not look forward to sleeping in a soggy tent in a mosquito infested jungle with a bunch of guys. As more and more men were drafted and sent to Vietnam, I had to figure out how I could keep my butt out of the monsoons without becoming a draft dodger. In fact, National Guard and Reserve soldiers were not being deployed to Vietnam. With that in mind, in 1965 Benny and I high-tailed it to the nearest Army National Guard office in The Bronx and signed up. It took the government a year to catch up to me, but one fine day in early May of '66, I was boarding the bus at Penn Station with the other Bronx boys and heading south. Benny was on the bus, too.

I had only been out of New York City twice in my life - the Maryland elopement and my honeymoon. South Carolina was not like another country; it was like another planet. Fort Jackson was, and still is, the largest basic training center in the U.S. Army pulling in recruits for the Army, Army Reserve, and Army National Guard from all around the country. I had to endure ten weeks of basic training which meant I was going to have to eat, sleep, march, and shit with these guys. Because they didn't speak Bronxese, half the time I couldn't even understand what they were saying although I knew it was English. And, I certainly didn't relate to their hick ways. Talk about culture shock! I was the cool guy from New York City, not some yokel from Bumfuck, USA.

The first days were the worst. As soon as I got off the bus, a Drill Sergeant screamed in my face to line up with the other recruits - double file and do it quickly. Dropping our duffels where we stood, the DS marched us to the mess hall for dinner where I was given a half hour to swallow some swill that didn't resemble any food I had ever eaten. After mess, we picked up our duffels and double timed to supply for bedding after which were shuffled in some semblance of a march to our quarters.

In 1964, Fort Jackson began a construction project which included replacing the wooden barracks with permanent steel and concrete buildings. My unit was bunked in one of the old wooden barracks built in the '40s. We didn't have assigned bunks so I scrambled with the rest of the guys to get a lower bunk. I was told to make up the bed, undress, put what I brought from home into the locker at the foot of bed and then stand at ease in my underwear in front of the locker. The DS started shouting at all of us. I couldn't understand all his words, but I got the gist - something about owning us for the next ten weeks, putting us through mental and physical hell, making us into real men instead of sissy mommas boys, blah, blah, blah after which we all screamed, "Yes, sir," all of us having seen a couple of army movies and thinking that was the correct response. (It wasn't.)

The next day, after a fitful night's sleep on a lumpy bed accompanied by a lot of snoring and farting, we dressed in our civies and were taken to the Reception Station to get shots, baldy haircuts, and our uniform-issue, maybe not in that order, but no one was paying much attention to details. This also included a lot of waiting.

Basic training hasn't changed much over the years so I won't describe all the exhausting, humiliating, grueling and mind deadening exercises the military deems essential to create a physically and mentally disciplined fighting machine ready to take up arms in defense of his (or her) country. Those interested can find any number of sites on the internet which go into more detail than I care to remember. My military experience was more re-markable.

As I said, Fort Jackson trains recruits from all around the country. My barracks was filled with fifty guys from Oklahoma, Mississippi, Michigan, South Carolina and most any other state. I was the only guy from The Bronx. Benny had been assigned to another barracks.

In the second week of training, I was on a break from one of the courses in Army Core Values. I went back to the barracks to grab a pack of cigarettes. As soon as I got there, I saw this Okie from Muskogee with his head in my foot locker.

"Hey, Clyde" I yelled. I think his real name was Harold. "Whadya think you're doing goin' through my shit?"

He jumped up, a guilty look spread across his broad, freckled face. He was 6'4" and had about forty pounds of hayseed brawn on me.

"Nothin'," he said, "I was just looking for my razor and someone told me the greaser from The Bronx took it. I want it back, greaser." He took a few steps toward me.

I got in his face, "I never touched your fucking razor. Nobody touches my shit and nobody calls me greaser." I shoved him with all I had.

He swayed about a tenth of an inch and raised a ham sized fist ready to hit me. As he lunged, I stepped sideways to avoid his punch. He swerved past me with his follow through and lost his balance. Before he could regain it and come at me again, I lowered my head and ran full speed at him ramming him in the stomach and knocking the air out of him. Bent over holding his stomach, he staggered back, slammed into the barracks window and took it with him frame and all as he flew out of the building and onto the concrete pavement. For ten seconds, I looked down at him through the hole in the barracks wall. He was dazed but trying to get up. I ran out the door, straddled him and began punching him left and right in the head. I was still pummeling him when I realized I had an audience. Some of the guys from the platoon were watching the fight. Nobody was saying a word nor did anyone make an attempt to pull me off, because the Drill Sergeant was also part of the audience.

I stopped in mid-punch, stood up and came to attention. I figured I was about to spend the rest of my life in the brig. I was actually grateful that the Drill Sergeant had showed up or I might have killed Clyde-Harold.

"At ease, soldier," he said. "What seems to be the problem here?"

I'm no snitch so I said, "We had a little disagreement, Drill Sergeant. I might have gotten a little carried away arguing my point."

The Drill Sergeant bent over Clyde-Harold and slapped his face a couple of times. There was no response.

"Oh, shit," I thought, "he's dead. I'm a goner."

After making sure Clyde-Harold was still breathing, the Drill Sergeant straightened up and walked over to me. Putting his face about two inches from mine and said, "Son, I've been looking for a soldier like you. You're the new platoon leader."

Turning to the guys standing around, he pointed to a couple of them. "You two get this soldier up and into the barracks before someone runs him over." They threw some cold water on Clyde-Harold, and he came around enough to stagger into the barracks with the help of the two soldiers holding him under the arms. He was okay after a couple hours. Fortunately for me, Clyde-Harold never remembered the whole story. Somehow he landed outside the barracks on the ground and had a big headache.

My new status as Platoon Leader designated by a special arm band I had to wear was a big surprise to me until I learned why I got the job. The Drill Sergeant wanted someone who the other guys would be afraid of crossing. What better choice could there be than the crazy greaser from The Bronx who could throw a giant like Clyde-Harold out a window and then try to kill him! I was his man.

As second in command, it was my job to make the Drill Sergeant's life easier by taking on some of the responsibilities for the smooth running of the platoon. Clyde-Harold was both afraid and in awe of me and became my puppy dog shadow. He was mostly the reason I kept any kind of order in the barracks - no one back-talked me with Clyde-Harold standing by my side.

After ten weeks, the whole platoon managed to graduate from basic training. Because the army placement tests we had been given showed that I was a good typist and had some math ability, I went to Advanced Individual Training assigned to Supply Clerk School. I graduated as a supply clerk, Military Occupational Specialty (MOS) after two months. While most of my platoon was deployed to parts unknown, my permanent duty assignment was at Fort Jackson as Private First Class Specialist in Supply doing stock room stuff for the next two months.

This is what a military supply clerk is supposed to do: receive, inspect, catalog, load, unload, organize, store, issue, deliver, and turn-in installation supplies and equipment; maintain the supply system for accounting of organizational and installation supplies and equipment; issue and receive small arms; secure and control weapons and ammunition in security areas; and schedule and perform preventive and organizational maintenance on weapons.

This is what I did: sat in my office reading magazines, napping, talking on the phone to Georgann and my family as well as a string of southern girlfriends. How was I able to shirk my military duties? Well you should ask. I had the great good fortune to be assigned to Supply Clerk duty with PFC Charlie Johnson.

Johnson was a career soldier from Biloxi, Mississippi who had joined up when he was twenty to escape being a career welfare recipient. His 5'10", 160 lb frame was toned muscle; his shiny, espresso-brown skin stretched taut over high cheek bones made his marble black eyes bug out and his big, white teeth protrude. Although he had been in the service for almost fifteen years, we had the same rank due to some unfortunate incidents in his military career. After he had served for thirteen years, Johnson was assigned to Fort Jackson as Staff Sergeant managing soldiers pay and supervising administrative issues for non-coms. Being somewhat of a hot-head, he had received two Article 15s or non-judicial punishments for insubordination and a third for striking an officer. That last one landed him sixty days in the brig and loss of rank which is why we now had the same rank. Only five years away from retirement from the military, Charlie was keeping his fleshy, black nose clean.

Charlie knew everything about being a supply clerk. Because I lacked much if any interest in supplies, weapons or anything military, whenever I decided to do my job, I screwed it up. It took Charlie more time to fix my fuck-ups than if he had done the job himself.

"Al, you just let me handle things from now on," he told me. I let him.

I had leave every weekend and spent most of my time in Columbia, the capital of South Carolina. I had some worry-free, fun times on these weekends, because I knew Charlie had supply well in hand. I looked cool in my uniform and had no trouble attracting southern belles. A month before my stint in the army was to end, I narrowed my skirt chasing to Carol Sue who I had met a couple of months before in the bar at the Howard Johnson's in Fort Jackson.

Carol Sue was a leggy redhead with sparkling green eyes, a pert, upturned nose, milky white skin chock-full of freckles, and pouty lips she painted Poison Pink. At twenty five, she had been married and divorced twice - no children. I didn't worry I was taking advantage of her nor was I interested in unproven territory. Georgann was the only virgin I ever dated, and I made sure I married her!

On our third weekend together and after some pretty good sex, I was enjoying a cigarette. I was leaning against the headboard of the motel room bed thinking 'life is good' when Carol Sue turned to me and said, "Al, you are just about the most wonderful man I ever met. I love you."

In the whirlwind of our short romance I had neglected to tell her I was married. What should I do? The manly thing was to tell her the truth and risk a slap and a walk out. I followed the wise old adage that women give sex to get love and men give love to get sex and said the first thing that came into my mind. "I love you, too, Carol Sue." My stint was almost up; I didn't want to chance finding another hot, willing babe like Carol Sue.

"I'm so happy, Al. I can't wait to get to New York so we can be together forever."

Gulp! "Sure, honey, me either."

Now you're thinking, 'He's in deep doodoo.' Right? No Siree. I never told her where I lived in New York nor gave her a phone number where she could reach me. Since the internet was far in the future, she couldn't Google me, either. On top of that, I hadn't told her when my time was up at Fort Jackson. I wasn't called Slick Al for nothing. Well, nobody ever called me Slick Al, but hey, I just needed to keep up the pretence of adoring suitor for another week. Piece of torrone! Now, you're thinking what a lying piece of adulterous crap I was. You would be right.

Hallelujah! My last week at Fort Jackson! I deemed it appropriate to take a little vacation from all the hard work I had been doing. I persuaded Carol Sue to take time off from her job, rented a room at the Holiday Inn for five days and told Charlie to cover for me. As usual, he did a superb job. If an officer came into supply looking for me, Charlie told him 'he's in the can', or 'you just missed him', or 'he went for coffee', etc. No one was the wiser as long as Charlie kept doing my job.

Sunbathing around the pool, sex whenever, and steak dinners were what I called a well deserved vacation. The next week, I packed up all my gear, shook Charlie's hand good bye and went home.

I wonder what ever happened to Carol Sue.

6

Chinese Food

Georgann didn't want to stay alone in an empty apartment when I was in South Carolina. She moved back with her parents but continued to pay the rent on our apartment. Marie was ecstatic to have Georgann back home. She probably prayed every night that I'd drown in a Carolina swamp so Georgann would stay with her permanently. Marie's fondest fantasy was that I would die, Georgann would act the grieving widow for six months and then marry Manny, the builder's son - happy ending for all. To Marie's disappointment, after six and half months of army training, I came back.

Georgann and I were finally able to settle into our new home as newlyweds. Marie had to adjust to living without her beloved daughter near her, but it wasn't much of an adjustment. We ate dinner with the Marinos at least a couple of times a week, and Georgann had lunch with Marie every weekday.

I continued to learn more about the dynamics of the Marino marriage. If Silvio came home for dinner, Marie would pick a fight with him; if he didn't come home, Georgann and I were subjected to listening to her bad mouth him. If Silvio told her about someone who got whacked, Marie would lament, "Why can't I be the lucky one to wear black?" But, Marie didn't mean it. Raised in a Mafia household where men were dominant and often violent, she saw confrontation as a sign of affection and took every opportunity to anger Silvio into showing his love by either physically or verbally abusing her.

By December, I landed a job as a salesman at Wallach's Clothing Store in White Plains. At Wallach's, I met another salesman, Frankie Convertino, fated to become my future partner and friend. (Much, much more about Frankie later on in the book.) We'd both gone to Evander Childs High School. Although we hadn't crossed paths, we were from the same neighborhood and our Italian backgrounds were similar, but that's where it ended. Frankie was a year older than me, five inches shorter, fifty pounds lighter and about forty IQ points dumber. His narrow shoulders were slightly stopped, and he had a thin, weasely face with skinny eyes and narrow lips, but he was a 'goombah'. We found that we had a lot in common like inventing new and better ways to goof off without the manager finding out.

Frankie and his wife, Phyllis, came to our apartment at least a couple times a month for Georgann's famous fondue parties, an in-thing in the '60s.

Phyllis, also an Italian girl from The Bronx, had a very sweet nature. She was tiny, no more than five feet but with a Betty Boop figure that quivered all over when she laughed. The four of us became fast friends.

It was Christmas season at Wallach's and Frankie and I were working day and night piling up a lot of overtime. During our dinner break on Christmas Eve, we decided to celebrate and got drunk. The store manager caught us hiding in the back room and threatened to fire us. With youthful indiscretion and stupidity fueled by liquor, we both told him to fuck off and quit. That was my present to Georgann our first Christmas together. She made me promise not to drink like that again – a promise I never broke.

Walking out of Wallach's was no big deal for either Frankie or me. I continued to look for another job and finally landed the kind of job I was looking for with R. J. Reynolds Tobacco Company as a sales-rep starting in the New Year. I was given a company car, a regular route, and an expense account. Frankie and Phyllis had saved enough money to buy the little dress shop in The Bronx where his mother worked. We four remained friends and a few years later, Frankie and I became partners in several clothing stores.

The apartments in our Yonkers building were built over the parking garage. The tenants were assigned one parking place in the garage and one place in the parking lot behind the building. I kept my RJR company car in the garage, because it had been broken into twice parked in the lot to steal the cartons of cigarette samples I kept on the back seat. Georgann was driving my old Ford Galaxy and parked it in the spot behind the building. I parked the new Galaxy I bought with the remainder of the 'busta' anywhere I could find a spot on the street, sometimes blocks away from the apartment.

It took some time for me to adjust to married life, but Georgann took to her role as my wife as if she were born to it naturally shifting her devotion from her parents to me thereby driving another AI thorn into Marie's side.

Although Georgann was a sweetheart, there was an incident that gave me good reason to keep a low profile with her. I was out with Frankie one night doing a little drinking at a club in Queens. Phyllis phoned Georgann to ask if she had heard from me, because Frankie told her he was getting together with me for advice about his clothing store. It was late and she was getting worried. Phyllis was wise that Frankie was always on the lookout for a little side action and used a lot of excuses to cover his philandering. She put a bug in Georgann's ear that I was doing the same - no better company for misery than having someone with whom to share it. When I came home late that night, Georgann was already asleep. I went to bed and enjoyed the sleep of the innocent.

Next morning, after the breakfast, I kissed Georgann goodbye and went down to the garage only to discover the company car had a broken windshield. I ran back upstairs to tell Georgann and to call the police.

Georgann was sitting at the kitchen table drinking coffee. She didn't look up when I came in. When I saw a baseball bat at her side, I stopped in mid sentence. Slowly, she put down her coffee cup, and, still not looking up, said, "Al, if I ever catch you with another woman, it won't be the windshield that gets broken."

I didn't say a word. I just nodded and backed out of the kitchen. I told Reynolds that a truck tossed up a rock and broke the windshield. The truth was that Phyllis was right. Frankie and me did meet a couple of women at the bar that night and shared a few intimate moments with them before going home. I never went out with Frankie again. I made sure, so I believed, that Georgann would never find out about my extracurricular activities. Word of advice – wives are smarter than that.

In the early spring, we planned our first Sunday dinner with Georgann's parents and Grandma Vingo. The date was set. We had been visiting friends the night before and got home late. Rather than search for a parking spot on the street, I parked my Galaxy in the parking plaza next to our apartment building in front of a Chinese food take-out. The take-out was the only store in the plaza open on Sunday. I planned to move the car before they opened at four. Georgann and I were so busy with preparations for Sunday dinner; I forgot to move my car.

The Marinos arrived with Grandma Vingo at 1:00. Marie even brought her miniature schnauzer, Pepe, whom I hated and who hated me. That nasty dog bit me more than a few times. I swear it had Marie's temperament. Silvio parked his caddy in the plaza lot near my Galaxy. Despite Pepe, who continued to nip at my ankles, we had a nice lunch and a fun visit. Around 4:00, we said our good-byes. About ten minutes after they left, I was relaxing in my slippers in front of the TV when I heard Pepe barking and Marie cursing. Looking out the window, I saw Silvio and Marie fighting in front of my car in the parking lot with a bunch of men from the Chinese take-out.

I told Georgann, "Stay here!" and dashed downstairs still wearing my slippers. I ran over to the fighting mob. Without thinking, I jumped up on the hood of my car and, like Tarzan, did a swan dive into the middle of the melee punching anything in white. Silvio was stomping a downed Chinese cook while Marie beat another on the head with her shoe. Pepe nipped at the cooks as they tried to crawl away. Grandma Vingo threw a rock and broke the storefront window, and an old Chinese lady leaning against the building with her hands raised over her head, was screaming at the top of her lungs.

Welcome to the neighborhood!

This is what happened minutes before I joined the fight. Silvio and Marie were walking to their car in the parking lot when they saw one of the cooks from the take-out slap a big 'No Parking' sticker on my car.

Marie said to Silvio, "That's Al's car."

She took the wet sticker off my window and stuck it on the take-out's front door. When the same old Chinese lady came out of the take-out yelling in Chinglish, Marie slugged her. Then, two cooks waving cleavers and two waiters came out and the free for all was off and running. Cleavers or not, they were no match for the Marinos – and Grandma Vingo. Holding their hands over their heads to ward off the blows, the cooks dropped their cleavers, and Grandma Vingo kicked them under my car before throwing the rock at the storefront window.

We all froze when we heard police sirens in the distance. I stopped in mid-punch. I told Silvio to take off because his yellow sheet was considerable plus he might have some outstanding warrants. Silvio and Marie ran to their car, Grandma Vingo picked up Pepe, still yapping, and threw him into the back seat before getting in. They turned the corner just as a police cruiser and paddy wagon screeched to a halt in front of me.

An anonymous phone call to the precinct said a gang war or racial riot was taking place in the plaza parking lot. The police got out of the cruiser, and a swat team wearing riot gear and carrying some nasty guns got out of the wagon. The bloodied cooks and waiters had already scrambled inside the take-out and shut the door putting a closed sign in the broken window. I was left standing alone in the parking lot - in my slippers. I lit a cigarette and leaned nonchalantly against my car, a look of pure innocence on my face. The old Chinese lady was still in front of the take-out pointing at me and ranting in Chinglish. Nobody could understand a word she said. The police and swat team looked around and wondered where the riot they were called to put down had disappeared. The swat team left.

Turning to me, a cop asked, "What's this all about?"

"Officer, I'm not really sure. I was coming down from my apartment to move my car onto the street when I saw a cook from the take-out putting a No Parking sticker on my windshield. I yelled out, 'Hey, don't do that, I'm moving my car,' but he ignored me and stuck that big, wet sticker on my window. I tore it off and put it on their window. That's when maybe five or six Chinese guys came out of the take-out and attacked me. When they heard the police siren, they ran away."

The cop, stifling a laugh, said, "You gotta' be kiddin'! That's it?" "You fought off these guys all by yourself?"

"Yep. In self defense," I said with straight face.

When questioned, the Chinese from the take-out pretended they didn't speak English, and the police were unable to find any other witnesses. The cop had to take my word for the incident. He brokered a 'no charges or counter charges' deal with me. He probably thought I was some kind of Kung-Fu expert and never learned that it was Marie who bloodied the head of one cook with her high-heeled shoe or that it was Silvio who kicked them when they were down. The cop never asked me how the store window got broken. Little Grandma Vingo lives to ride again!

Back in the apartment, Georgann gave me 'the look' before saying, "Come over here, Tarzan," and put an ice pack on my swollen hand.

I never parked my car in the plaza again. If we wanted Chinese take-out, I got my neighbor down the hall to order and pick it up for me. If those Chinese knew the food was for me, they'd have poisoned it.

Ah so.

7

Destiny Decisions

Two years after we married, Georgann and I had saved enough money to buy our first house - it was next door to my in-laws on Mace Avenue. Ok, you're saying, 'He must have been out of his mind,' but I thought it was a good idea at the time. (Why break my track record for stupidity?) Georgann was now head teller at the bank, and I was climbing the corporate ladder with R. J. Reynolds Tobacco Co. as one of their lead salesmen. Marie was ecstatic that Georgann would now be living only a stone's throw away. Not only did Georgann have lunch with her every day, but we were both eating dinner almost every night of the week with Marie. My only consolation was that Marie was a great cook. As usual, Silvio rarely came home for dinner.

Believe it or not, we actually had some fun times living next door to my in-laws. We went with them to lavish union functions, vacationed with them in Puerto Rico or the Caribbean, and had dinner every Friday night at Ann & Tony's on Arthur Avenue - all on Silvio's tab. Marie had a membership in a mob country club in Westchester and took Georgann with her to sit by the pool or play cards with the other Mafia wives.

Silvio and I had guy weekends hunting and fishing. We got along fine. The punching incident on his front step when Georgann and I were dating somehow created a bond between us. He saw me as a stand-up guy who could be relied on to keep his eyes open and mouth shut. I looked good, made his daughter happy, and became a willing ally in some of his shady deals.

In 1969, Silvio and I purchased ten acres of land in northern Westchester subdividing it into two five-acre building sites. The price was right; I never asked Silvio how we got it so cheap. The plan was that we would each build a home on the adjoining lots. Being a punk with street smarts didn't make me a candidate for Mensa. More on that deal later.

I made my own hours at R.J. Reynolds which afforded me some free time to dabble in Silvio's world. As I told you, not all Italians are mob connected. Although I thought of myself as a shrewd operator, Silvio was my mentor in the life of the underworld, albeit only on the periphery. Keep in mind that Silvio was only an associate and not a made-man. He moved on the fringes of the Mafia himself. Because he was useful to the Gambino Family, he was given a territory for loan sharking and allowed to keep most of the money from collections for himself. He also did general dog body work for thugs higher up on The Family ladder. Silvio considered himself slick in hiding some of the criminal earnings from The Family business - so he believed. As long as his private dealings were penny-ante The Family left him alone.

Silvio gave me entrée into the underworld on a very restricted basis, and, at the same time, fed my fascination with it. There were occasions when I learned more than I wanted. One night, early in our marriage, Georgann and I were having dinner at the Marinos when Silvio made an unusual appearance.

After dinner, Silvio said, "Come on, Al, let's take a ride." During the drive, he explained, "I'm gonna' show you how we discourage someone who's late with his vig payment to make sure it doesn't happen a second time."

This was before the informative Godfather and Scorsese movies, and I had no firsthand knowledge about underworld violence. After all, I wasn't that 'kind' of Italian. Also, as a confirmed chicken shit, I would never resort to anything physical unless I knew I had the upper hand. But, I still went along for the ride that night, insincerely telling Silvio, "Sure, I'm always ready to learn."

We drove to 156th Street and Fox Avenue in the Hunts Point section of the South Bronx and parked in front of an abandoned storefront - the one the infamous Savage Skulls gang eventually made their clubhouse. Hunts Point in the '60s was a pretty dangerous neighborhood known for its drug pushers, prostitution, crumbling buildings, and dark streets laden with filth and derelict cars. You won't find that Hunts Point today, thank God. Burned out buildings and rubble-filled lots have been replaced with high rise apartment buildings, restored single family houses, and commercial real estate.

We sat in the car for a few minutes until a '66 caddy pulled up and parked across the street from us. The driver sat hunched over in his seat.

Silvio got out of the car. "Follow me, Al." He walked around to the rear of our car, popped open the trunk and pulled out a tire iron. Then, he strolled over to the caddy, me on his heels, opened the door and dragged the driver out the car.

"Hello, Danny. Nice caddy. Did you buy it with my money?"

"No, man, my father-in-law lent me the money."

"Like I give a shit, Danny. Where's my money? Since you're late with the payment, you owe me twice this time."

Before the guy, a scrawny white dude in his mid-thirties whose sunken eyes and loose fitting three-piece suit said he wasn't sleeping or eating too well, could open his mouth; Silvio punched him in the stomach. The guy screamed and doubled over clutching his middle. Silvio grabbed the tire iron with two hands and smashed it onto the guy's back. He went down and stayed there.

Silvio said, "Al, pick him up."

I grabbed him under the arms and hauled up his limp body, his head hanging down on his chest. Silvio bent over him and whispered in his ear,

"The next time you're late, Danny, I won't be so nice. And, don't call me 'man'." Silvio stood up, smoothed back his hair and said, "Throw the bum back in his car, Al."

I picked the guy up by the scruff of his neck with one hand, opened the back door of the caddy with my other hand and flung him onto the back seat. He was blubbering like a baby and had pissed himself. It all happened so fast; it took me a couple of minutes for it to sink in what had just happened. When it did, I started to shake from head to foot. I ran behind the caddy and threw up.

"Come on, Al," said Silvio, "let's go home." He pretended not to have seen me puke, but realized I was not in any shape to drive. He got behind the wheel sneaking a peek at me a few times to make sure I wasn't going to throw up again. He said, "I think Marie made cannoli," as if we had just taken an after dinner stroll to work up an appetite for dessert. One thing about hoods, they don't let business interfere with their stomachs.

After that, whenever Silvio asked me to go with him, he made sure it was an easy vig pick-up. He didn't want to chance ruining the leather interior of his caddy. Most of the time, Silvio did all the talking while I stood next to him nodding and grinning like an asshole trying to look like Big Al - the nickname I gave myself.

Six months after we moved into our new house, Georgann was still working as a teller in the bank. One night at dinner she said, "This good looking guy came to my window today. When he saw my name tag he asked me if I had a brother named Al. I told him you were my husband. I think he was disappointed I wasn't your sister," she said winking at me. "His name is Dennis Weigart and he seemed really nice. He said he knew you. Do you remember him?"

"Yeah, we were in junior high school together, but we were never what I would call friends. He wasn't my kind of hang-out buddy. He lived a couple of blocks down the street from me, but I don't remember him being handsome, just a nothing kind of guy." He wasn't Italian, so how could he be good looking. Georgann, really!

"He still lives there with his parents," said Georgann. "I was thinking you know who he would go for?"

"Donna!" Great minds think alike. Georgann always tried to look out for her sister. She even managed to get Donna hired at the bank, but that didn't last long, because Donna couldn't keep a job or her mouth shut. I saw the match up as a way to rid us of Donna.

The next time Dennis came into the bank, Georgann invited him for dinner to meet Donna. Because Donna looked somewhat like Georgann, we counted on the resemblance to appeal to Dennis. We also hoped that once she opened her mouth, he wouldn't dash out the door.

Dennis worked at Kennedy Airport for TWA in the baggage and freight handling department. Between living at home, his union salary, overtime and stealing from TWA, Dennis had plenty of cash; he presented a nice package. Since Dennis loved to work as much as he loved to steal, and Donna loved to do nothing, they were a perfect match. He would fit right in with Marino standards.

Dinner went off like a charm. Dennis showed up in his new, white Mustang. Donna got the door and was greeted (in her mind) by a blond, blue eyed spectacle of Teutonic pulchritude. He saw a cute, shorter version of Georgann in a tight red dress showing about of mile of cleavage. It was love at first sight. We hoped that Dennis wouldn't learn that Donna was nothing like her sister until it was too late. Dumb as a meatball, he never did.

They got married the following year and moved into a big, new house in Dix Hills, Long Island. Donna stayed home pissing away Dennis' money on beauty care products while he continued to engage in his two favorite sports, working overtime and pilfering. I discounted Donna as sub-human; Dennis I barely tolerated.

By early 1970, Georgann was pregnant with our first child. After three years of trying we were overjoyed. Georgann was having an easy pregnancy, but, in her eighth month, R. J. Reynolds offered me the promotion I had been waiting for. I was hoping it would be in the New York area, but no such luck. If I wanted the promotion, I and my new family would have to relocate to Dayton, Ohio. Reynolds wanted me to take the position immediately with the assurance that they would fly me back to New York when Georgann was ready to deliver. I insisted on waiting until after the baby was born. Reynolds was so desperate to have me on the job they capitulated.

If you wanted to climb the corporate ladder, you went where the company told you to go. At twenty-seven, I was the youngest salesman ever to be offered a division manager position although I really wasn't the corporate type. I relied on street smarts and establishing good business relationships with key vendors rather doing business in accordance with company policy. My senior managers couldn't figure out how I raked in the sales, but they left me alone because whatever I was doing worked for their quotas.

Neither Georgann nor I wanted to relocate. New York City and The Bronx were part of our DNA, but, lacking a college degree, I had to rely on work experience to beef up my resume. If I wanted to use the Reynolds job as a stepping stone toward a more lucrative industrial sales job in New York, I needed to add management skills to my resume. Georgann and I formulated a plan; I'd go to Ohio, get some management experience, stall the relocation as long as possible, and then resign.

Nikol was born at 5:30 pm on October 1, 1970 at Miseriacordia Hospital in The Bronx. When she went into labor, Georgann called her doctor, Sam

Rosen, who alerted the hospital to be ready for our arrival. She also called her parents and mine. I didn't do anything. I barely managed to make the ten minute drive to the hospital without getting into an accident. As soon as we pulled in front of the hospital, I ran inside but had to run back to the car to get Georgann. I held Georgann by the elbow as we walked up to the reception desk. An orderly pushing a wheelchair rushed over to Georgann and took her to delivery. I signed Georgann in, and, after chain smoking about ten cigarettes in front of the hospital before finally going up to the maternity ward

I held Georgann's hand as they were about to wheel her into the delivery room. The delivery nurse asked me, "Are you coming in to witness the birth, Mr. Volpe? As the husband you are permitted."

I was too shocked to say anything. Eyes bulging, I stared back at the nurse before shaking my head hoping it wasn't compulsory that I witness the birth. Ugh.

Georgann laughed, "Don't let him in. He'll faint."

I smiled weakly at the nurse inwardly thanking Georgann for her wise assessment of my courage. I took my place outside the delivery room. There were no complications and Georgann delivered like a pro. The nurse came out and pulled me into the room.

"Hold your new baby daughter, Mr. Volpe," she said handing me the baby. "Mrs. Volpe told me her name is Nikol."

I held out shaking hands as she put this bread sized bundle wrapped in a pink cocoon into my arms. I stared down at Nikol's tiny, red face surrounded by pitch-black hair; she looked like a little bird.

Georgann exclaimed, "Isn't she beautiful!"

I just smiled and lied. "Sure, Georgann, gorgeous." Nikol was so ugly I was tempted to throw her in the waste pail with the afterbirth.

The nurse took Nikol from me to clean her up before bringing her back to Georgann. I ran down to the cafeteria where our parents were waiting. We all jammed into the elevator to the nursery, my mother and Marie both asking, "Is the baby beautiful?" I just smiled, silence seeming the better alternative to telling the truth.

The new grandmothers pushed ahead of me to the nursery window and began their 'oohing and ahhing'. "Al, she looks just like Georgann," Marie said.

I couldn't see the resemblance to anything human let alone Georgann. All the other babies were pink and pudgy-faced. None were hairy and red faced like Nikol. I was glad my mother didn't say she looked like me.

We hired a live-in nurse the first week Nicky was home, but she lasted only two days before quitting. When I came home to find her gone, Marie was hovering over the baby's crib. I asked, "Where's the nurse?"

"I didn't like her," said Marie not taking her eyes off Nicky. "You don't need a stranger touching my granddaughter. I'm here."

She sure was - all the time.

Georgann was resting in our bedroom. "How come the nurse left?" I asked.

"All my mother did was criticize her every move. According to my mother, the nurse was doing everything wrong with Nicky. She warned her she'd better be careful with her only grandchild. You know my mother, Al; she made her words sound more like a threat than a warning. The nurse packed up and left without even asking for her two days pay."

The nurse shouldn't have taken it personally. Marie nagged at me, too. 'Wash your hands, Al. Don't touch the baby, Al. Don't breathe your cigarette smoke breath on her. Be careful, Al.'

Georgann gave her mother free rein with Nikol, bowing to Marie's motherly experience. The two of them were so wrapped up in Nikol that I felt totally superfluous and invisible in my own home. A week after Nicky's birth, I booked a flight to Dayton to start my new job.

According to plan, I arrived in Dayton with a typed resignation tucked into my briefcase. The first evening there, I had dinner at the home of the man I was replacing. His name was Philip Durning. He was only forty-eight, but the stress of working twenty years with Reynolds had wreaked havoc on his handsome face and once athletic body evidenced by the slouch in his shoulders, a slight paunch over his belt and a receding hairline. He, his wife and two teenage daughters had built a good life in Dayton. They did not want to move to Springfield, Massachusetts.

After dinner, Phil and I went into his den for a private talk. Getting passed the usual rah-rah company bullshit, he told me that, like it or not, he had no choice but to uproot his family again and move clear across the country. According to Phil, R.J. Reynolds used re-location as a guarantee that an employee's career took priority over family and community.

"Al, this is my second move with Reynolds. I was with the company only five years when they transferred me to Dayton right after my second daughter was born. After twelve years, I realized the company pretty much owned my soul. I can't start all over again at my age not with two children ready to go to college." His hang dog expression was alarming. He stood up, shook my hand and said, "I wish you a lot of luck, Al." He walked me to the door shutting it quietly behind me. I swore to myself that I would never let what happened to Phil happen to me.

I was living in a great hotel and eating gourmet meals on the company tab, but, after five months, it was getting old fast. Georgann left Nicky with her mother and came to Dayton a few weekends, and I made the trip back to The Bronx several times, but I was home sick. Although Georgann and I enjoyed sightseeing and checking out the beautiful homes in the Dayton area, we were fish out of water. I wasn't cut out to be a company man and Georgann wasn't a corporate, gadabout wife. Our Italian roots were too embedded in us to abandon the motherland - The Bronx.

To assure my commitment to Reynolds, as part of the deal Georgann and I had to put our house in The Bronx on the real estate market as soon as I took my position with the company. We never did. I put Reynolds off by telling them we couldn't find a buyer. After five months of stalling, the company finally offered to buy our house. Out of reasons to hold them off it was time to tender my resignation. I called headquarters in Winston-Salem and told my regional manager, Bob Harrison, that I was resigning.

Bob didn't believe me. "Al, nobody gets promoted and then resigns after only five months. You're just overwhelmed with a new baby, a new job and the relocation. Tell you what. I'm going to fly to Dayton this weekend. We can talk about it face to face."

True to his word, Bob showed up at my hotel that Friday night. Over dinner in the hotel restaurant, Bob said, "Al, you've done a great job these past five months. Your division is tops in sales in the mid-Western division. You have a great career ahead of you with Reynolds. Down the road, after some management courses the company will pay for, you could be in line for my job."

"Bob, I really appreciate your confidence in me, but my mind is made up. Georgann and I don't want to leave New York. I know I may be making a big mistake but, unless you have the same job for me in New York, I have to quit."

"Sorry, Al, there aren't any management openings in the Eastern division. It's Dayton or nothing."

His big pep talk fell on deaf ears. I figured that if I could get this far at Reynolds in such a short time, I was positive I could do as well or even better with another company in New York. This was a destiny decision that would determine my future and my family's. I didn't realize, given the extent of my ego, that the result of this decision would haunt me for the rest of my life. (Spoilers)

"Bob, I guess this is where Reynolds and me part ways. Thanks any-way, for coming here to talk to me."

I said my good-byes to the good people of Dayton and headed back to New York. Georgann welcomed me home with a big hug and a smile so radiant that quitting Remolds was worth the sacrifice. I held my precious daughter who, in the months I was in Dayton, had become a beautiful little baby with Georgann's big brown eyes, soft curly, brown hair and melting smile. The pitch-black hair and pinched red face were gone. I returned home with no job, a 6-month old baby, a mortgage, and living next door to my in-laws.

Buona Fortuna!

8

Heart Trouble

A week after my return from Dayton, Georgann and Marie took Nicky to the pediatrician for her routine, six-month check-up. During the exam, the doctor believed he heard something irregular in Nicky's heartbeat and suggested we have her examined by a specialist. Nikol's pediatrician recommended Dr. Yuan (not his real name), a cardiologist affiliated with Albert Einstein Hospital in The Bronx, only a couple of miles from our house. We made an appointment with him for the following week.

Dr. Yuan was tall, just about my height, in his early forties with slightly stooped, narrow shoulders. His black hair was straight neatly parted on the left side and slicked back from his wide forehead. After an extensive examination, Dr. Yuan determined that Nicky was born with a congenital cardiac defect - a hole in her heart – which would require a cardiac catheterization sometime before her first birthday to aid Dr. Yuan in his determination of how well her blood vessels were supplying her heart.

Dr. Yuan explained the procedure. "In the operating room, Nicky will be sedated and strapped to a movable table. A thin, flexible tube or catheter will then be inserted into a vein or artery in her groin and threaded to her heart. Contrast dye injected through the catheter into the blood vessel will create x-ray images of valves, coronary arteries and the chambers of the heart on a special x-ray machine. During the procedure, I will be able to measure the pressure inside the heart chambers and blood vessels to determine whether blood was mixing correctly between the two sides of the heart as well as to observe the extent of the heart defect. Although the procedure is considered very safe, I must emphasize that precautions need to taken into consideration with a child as young and as small as Nicky. In next few months, I will continue to evaluate when Nicky will be able to have the catheterization."Dr. Yuan smiled and nodded to us as if he explained it so well.

He hadn't, but. I was too overwhelmed by his flood of incomprehensible medical-speak to take in any impression of him as a surgeon. His direct gaze behind heavy, black frames gave me some assurance he knew what he was talking about based on long experience. What did I know? I accepted his diagnosis as correct. From that day on, I left Nicky's care and scheduling of doctor visits to Georgann and Marie. My duty was to earn enough money to support my family.

I may have not know anything about medical procedures, but I did know that Nicky's need for specialists and possible multiple surgeries would require a great deal of money. Georgann had quit her job at the bank when Nicky was born and me leaving R.J. Reynolds left us without health insurance. We could end up in deep financial trouble. For the insurance alone, I took a no-show sales job with a food brokerage firm that my friend John got for me. (not Big John - I never saw him again). John assigned me to a territory no one ever checked. (As with dealings with Silvio, I deemed it best not to ask how he did this.) My only responsibility was to show up for the Friday afternoon sales meetings, collect a paycheck and split it with John.

Silvio got me a job working midnight to four making bagels at a mob-run bagel shop on the upper west side of Manhattan. (Obviously, a front for money laundering, but I didn't care - I was being paid under the table.) In the meantime, I continued to interview for jobs in industrial sales. Using the lame excuse that I needed the money, I was drawn more and more into Silvio's world of loan sharking and union organizing - mostly as Silvio's bag man.

I kept separate wardrobes in the trunk of my car to compliment my different careers – a suit for interviews, jeans and t-shirt for making bagels, and black shirt and slacks for mob stuff.

Two months into the bagel job, I was taking a cigarette break outside the store. It was about four am, almost time for my shift to end. Leaning against the front of the building next door, I saw a big, black Lincoln Town Car with tinted windows pull up in front of the bagel shop. I lifted myself off the building, put out my cigarette and started over to the car to ask if I could help them. Fortunately, I stopped before they saw me, because I saw the rear window roll down and the long barrel of a machine gun poke out. I dropped to the ground and crawled into the adjacent store's doorway as bullets ripped through the bagel store's front windows tearing up the counter and showering everything with glass and bagels.

I hid in the shadows until the Lincoln pulled away. I waited a few more minutes to make sure the Lincoln wasn't coming back before crawling out of the doorway and standing up. I went over to the bagel store to survey the damage. The plate glass windows on either side of the entrance were completely shattered, but the front door was still intact. If I had been inside, I might be looking at my body riddled with bullets and covered with bloody, cinnamon bagels. I opened the door, went into the back room, got my coat, hung my baker's apron on a hook, and went out the front door locking it, never looking back nor intending ever to return.

There was no need for me to discuss the incident with Silvio. He already knew. One of the rival families had a problem with the owner of the bagel shop and resolved it by established mob procedures. I was only the bagel maker - none of my business.

It was time for me to concentrate on getting a real job - one that wouldn't put me in the line of mob fire. Working on commission, I took a position as an executive recruiter for a headhunter that specialized in retail sales positions. I felt sorry for some of the men who came in. They once had held high paying sales jobs but were now resigned to taking anything. I can't tell you how many men broke down and cried in front of me, but my sympathy was for me first. I only took the job to get first dibs on any position that came across my desk that looked like a good fit for me. Eventually, it panned out. I recruited myself into a sales job in the pharmaceutical department of Revlon whose corporate headquarters were in midtown Manhattan. Revlon must have been really anxious to get someone on the job because, after a short training period, they gave me my own route and sent me out to sell drugs.

After three months on the job, I was moving along well in pharmaceutical sales when I got a big break - Revlon transferred me to their wholesale cosmetic department where big money could be made. I didn't know anything about makeup or beauty products, but I did know how to schmooze the cosmetic account buyers who were mostly women. Who could resist me - 6'1", no flab, full head of thick, black hair always impeccably cut, custom tailored three piece suits, and a glib tongue that would make an Irishman jealous - Adonis with a Bronx accent.

While I was scrambling to keep a roof over our heads, Georgann was devoting most of her time caring for our daughter. Marie's presence was oppressive. Neither Georgann nor her mother ever left Nicky alone in fear that her heart would stop. Although Nicky slept in her crib in our bedroom, Georgann would still get up a half dozen times a night just to make sure she was still breathing.

Shortly after Nikol's first birthday, Dr. Yuan arranged for her cardiac catheterization surgery at Albert Einstein Hospital. Georgann, Marie, and I arrived at the hospital at 6:00 am on October 15, 1971; Nicky still half asleep in Marie's arms. After checking in at the front desk, we took the elevator to the surgical floor. The attending surgical nurse met us at the nurse's station. After introducing herself, she held out her arms to take Nikol from Marie in order to prep her for surgery.

"I'll take her," said Marie holding Nicky tighter. "She needs her grand-mother now, not some stranger in green scrubs. You tell me what to do."

"I'm sorry, Mrs. Marino, but that is against hospital rules. We can't allow you in the operating room," said the nurse as gently as she could, realizing that this was not a woman easily reasoned with.

"I go or she don't," insisted Marie.

"Please, Ma, don't make a scene." said Georgann. "Let the nurse do her job and take Nicky. We can wait in outside the operating room and watch the procedure

"Okay," said Marie reluctantly handing Nicky over to the nurse. "For your sake, it better go all right," she said giving the nurse one of her malevolent looks.

Unfortunately, all right was not to be. The procedure did not go as planned. Nicky was sedated with a general anesthesia usually used with children that young. The surgeon made a small incision in her groin, inserted the catheter, fed it into the vein and moved it to her heart. All was going well until a gear in the movable table seized up. They halted the procedure to allow the technician time to fix the table, but the doctors couldn't abort the procedure because any slight movement might prove fatal. Nicky's sedation wore off. We stood outside the operating room listening to Nicky screaming as she lay strapped down on the table.

Marie went berserk, "Nicky's screaming! Those mother-fuckin' doctors and asshole technician are killing her! Yuan is a dead man. Get out of my way, I'm going in there."

Georgann and I managed to grab hold of Marie in time to prevent her from barging into the operating room. When security arrived, Marie turned even uglier. She continued to scream obscenities as she flailed out at the two guards. She managed to kick one in the knee and slam the other in the head with her purse. The guards were finally able to restrain Marie by seizing her by her arms and holding her far enough away so she couldn't kick them. They escorted her to a containment area in the basement.

The technician finished fixing the table; the anesthesiologist sedated Nicky again and the procedure concluded safely. We watched as Nicky was taken to recovery before heading to the basement to check on. OMG, if Marie had gotten into the operating room and grabbed Nicky, she might have killed her!

Marie was seething, but when we told her Nicky was all right, she insisted we take her to her granddaughter immediately. We took Marie to the waiting room and managed to curtail her enthusiasm long enough for Dr. Yuan to show up.

He said, "The cardiac catheterization procedure revealed what I expected. Nicky was born with an atrial septal defect or a hole in the wall between her two upper heart chambers. It is a common birth defect."

Marie burst in, "Is she going to die?" Georgann began to cry leaning against me for support.

"Of course not, Mrs. Marino," said Dr. Yuan. "We are going to take very good care of your granddaughter." He patted Marie on the shoulder whispering soothing words quietly to her as if she were a child. I couldn't hear what he was saying, but I was sure he heard about the incident in the hall and was making an effort to get on Marie's good side. Personally, I think he was taking care to watch his back with this certifiable lunatic. I didn't blame him.

"Eventually, Nicky will require open heart surgery," Dr. Yuan continued. Georgann almost passed out when she heard that, and Marie began to blubber. "Don't be alarmed, ladies. I have performed hundreds of such operations, and all the children are doing very well. There is no imminent need to do the surgery at this time. I would rather wait until Nicky is older. In the meantime, I want to perform pulmonary artery banding on Nicky before she is two. This is a technique of surgical therapy used by pediatric heart surgeons as a defensive measure until surgery can be performed more safely when she is older."

At that time, an atrial septal defect could only be treated with open-heart surgery. Today, during the cardiac catheterization procedure the hole is usually closed with an expandable disk positioned in the heart by use of a catheter.

As soon as Nicky recovered from the procedure, we took her home. Marie insisted on staying overnight and didn't move from her station at the baby's crib, not even for dinner.

Over the next ten months, we never let out a full breath where Nicky was concerned. I threw myself into building my sales territory with Revlon while Georgann and Marie continued their constant vigil. Although I was worried, too, Nicky appeared to be a very normal little girl as far as I could tell.

Before Nicky's second birthday, we brought her to Albert Einstein for the banding surgery. Dr. Yuan placed a Teflon band around her pulmonary artery to control the blood flow to her heart. It was accomplished without a problem.

Dr. Yuan cautioned us to watch for tell tale signs such as a visible bluish tinge around Nicky's upper lip as a warning that the band had be-come too restrictive on her growing heart at which time open heart surgery would be necessary to correct the defect. This medical nightmare would overshadow our lives for the next five years.

9

Tot Boutique

Marie was the most doting of grandmothers. Besides spending all her waking hours at our house on Nicky watch, she was forever buying expensive baby stuff like hand knit ensembles from Italy and carriages from England. She always bought two of everything; one for us and one for Nicky's bedroom in her house. Most of it never got used. It was a running joke among family and friends, "You guys could open a store with all that stuff."

My sales job at Revlon was going well. I was only required to commute to the office in Manhattan one day a week for the weekly sales meeting. The rest of the time I created my own schedule of appointments. Best of all, Revlon offered a really good health plan I did not have to pay into, and I was able to quit the no-show job with John. Running errands for Silvio - cash under the table - gave me some extra money to invest. Silvio and I had put any plans for the Westchester property on hold for the time being.

When we ran out of storage space at my house for Nicky purchases, the idea of opening a baby store became less of a joke. Georgann needed something else to occupy her time other than dwelling on Nicky's health problems; a store might provide the right diversion. For good measure, Marie would be included in the package. Because Silvio wanted Georgann to be happy and Marie to leave him alone, we both put up money required to open a fancy, baby boutique. We located a vacant store on 233rd Street in The Bronx next door to Danielle's Fashions, one the two clothing stores Frankie now owned. We had the place renovated to create a beautiful store we named Nikol's Tot Boutique. It opened in June 19, 1972, the day after Father's Day, because Silvio and I were the most excellent of fathers.

Georgann and Marie had a ball making the rounds of wholesale houses in Manhattan buying high-end baby clothes and accessories. They would buy ten items of everything - nine for the store and one for Nicky. Buying merchandise was one thing, but it soon became apparent that neither of them knew nor cared about running a retail business. The excitement (and shopping) for the store waned; it interfered with Georgann wanting to spend most of her time with Nikol, and Marie just wanting to be near Georgann. Busy with other ventures in his life, Silvio had no interest in the store.

Eventually, after only two months, Georgann and Marie stopped going to the store at all. To keep it open and not lose my entire investment, I had to take over the responsibility for running the place. I hired a sales staff and a merchandise buyer to replace Georgann and Marie. I set up a private office in the back room of the store to continue talking to Revlon clients and setting appointments with them by phone. My nights, if I wasn't running errands with Silvio, I stayed home going over the baby store accounts. I was exhausted, but, amazingly the place began to turn a profit!

Another retail opportunity near the Tot Boutique and Frankie's store presented itself. A successful women's store went up for sale, because the owners were retiring. Frankie and I made a deal. We were able to buy the store without involving Silvio, and, in 1973, Frankie and I became partners. The store already had a steady clientele, and because of Frankie's retail experience, I left him to manage the place alone. I already had enough on my plate. It did well.

As I dabbled in the three distinct worlds of legitimate business owner, corporate salesman, and underworld poser, I confused myself at times. For my sales job, I had a good income, a company car, health insurance and an expense account. As the owner of two successful clothing stores, I attained status as an entrepreneur. Traveling in Silvio's world, I experienced some of the perks of Mafia criminality. I never had to put a hand in my pocket whenever my family was with my in-laws. We stayed in the best hotels during vacations, ate in four star restaurants, and saw all the big shows. For example, on April 11, 1976, the four of us had a center table toward the back of the 3,500 seat Westchester Premier Theater in Tarrytown, NY. Frank Sinatra was entertaining a packed house for free in return for a favor he owed to Carlo Gambino for getting him into the Knights of Malta, an exclusive Christian order created in the middle ages. (Note: By 1982, the theater was bankrupt and razed, because greed knows no bounds when it comes to how much wise guys can skim off the top.)

Silvio lived the underworld trinity of manipulation, intimidation and domination. He knew nothing else. For him, corruption demanded obligation - the 'you owe me' mind-set. To Silvio, I owed him. I'd witnessed horrors that left me shaking which he took for business as usual. The beatings with baseball bats and black-jacks, guys pleading for their lives, and chasing shitheads through back alleys was getting really old for me. I had the greed but not the heart or the balls to continue in Silvio's way of life.

Outwardly, my life looked great, but between my involvement with Silvio's illicit dealings, the stress of managing two stores, maintaining accounts with Revlon, and worry about Nicky, I was unraveling inwardly.

As far as my marriage was concerned, it looked great on the outside too, except for the fact that Georgann and I had no personal life. Marie was always at our house. Her smothering was becoming a contagion in our household and our marriage, but Georgann didn't appear to be bothered by Marie's constant presence or by my resentment. If I suggested that Marie spend more time in her own house rather than ours, I was met with looks of incredulity and exasperation from Georgann. To her, my input lacked any authority. I was beginning to feel unneeded, unloved, and unwanted in my own home.

Silvio was rarely home, and I began to follow suit. Disengaging from Marie's meddling into our lives became a weak justification for my actions and indiscretions. The sales job with Revlon gave me an excuse to stay out late. Georgann believed me when I said I closed many deals over a steak and martini dinner. In truth, the only deals I ever closed were arranging a good price for the hotel room I was taking with a female companion after dinner - on the expense account. If I told Georgann I was with Silvio or running some errand for him, he backed me up. I knew too much about his goumare for him to rat me out. Georgann was too preoccupied with Nicky to question my whereabouts, and I always made sure I slept in my own bed each night with Georgann at my side.

I was the model husband!

10

Muddied Waters

There's a difference between people with a problem and people who are the problem. As far as I was concerned, Marie was both. Georgann relied on her mother's support with Nicky. The more she was at my house, the more I stayed away. My increasing absenteeism gave Marie inroad to promote suspicion about my activities.

"Georgann, sweetheart, Al comes home late a lot doesn't he? Let me tell you, he isn't always doing something for Silvio as he says. I know 'cause Silvio tells me everything." (Note: Silvio never told Marie anything.)

"He has an important job at Revlon, Ma. He told me he makes his best sales over dinner. He's home every night, even if it's very late."

Marie stared at Georgann for half a minute before saying, "Sure, sure, I know he's home every night, but that doesn't mean he's always with a client. You need to protect yourself."

"Protect myself from what?

"I'm just saying, that's all. You need to do what I been doing for years with your father. Here's the plan. Today, after Nicky gets up from her nap, we're going to the bank and open up a checking account in your name only. We won't tell Al. Every now and then ask Al for a little extra spending money and put that into your account."

"Won't he wonder why I need more money?"

"Nah, he's too busy spending money on himself to question you. If he did, that would give you a chance to grill him on where his money goes. He ain't goin' to say a word to you. Just say it's for Nicky. I got another way to get you more money. Al gave you a bunch of credit cards, right?"

"Yes, the bills come in and he pays them each month. He hardly ever asks me about the charges I make."

"That's what I figured. Ok, so you'll buy some stuff he wouldn't question and then return the merchandise to the store. Instead of having them take it off the charge card, ask for the cash. (Back then, you could do this.) Don't tell Al you brought the stuff back. This way you can build up more money in your account. We'll also get you some credit cards in your name only."

"Al sees all the bills. What if he asks me about them?"

"No, he won't see them because the second thing we're going to do today after we go to the bank is to get you a post office box. You put the PO address on the credit cards, and he will never see the bills. It's none of his business anyway. You can't trust men, Georgann. It's always good for a wife to have a little nest egg of her own just in case."

"In case of what, Ma?"

"I don't know. He might get hit by a bus if you're lucky or run off with one of his bimbos. I know he's cheatin' on you."

Georgann did not try to refute her mother's accusations. She did what her mother advised and opened up a bank account in her name and acquired a post office box. In the next few weeks, she got herself a couple of new credit cards. Marie was right on the money where I was concerned. Georgann loved to shop, but I never questioned her about her spending as long as it wasn't too much, and as long as she didn't question me about mine. (Spoilers: I didn't find out about Georgann's new financial plan until years later.)

Marie's big dream, other than seeing me dead, was for Silvio to build her a house on the Westchester property in New Paltz and for me to build Georgann one on the adjoining property. By 1974, she began filling Georgann's head with notions that it would be wonderful to get out of The Bronx; to move from that cramped, crummy little house her cheapskate husband was making her live in. Georgann deserved a home that reflected her special style.

"Georgann, The Bronx is no place to raise kids anymore. Nicky can't even go out to play without you or me watching her. She might get run over by a car or, God forbid, kidnapped and held for ransom."

"I don't think that will happen," said Georgann laughing. "It's not that bad, Ma. After all, I grew up here."

"Yeah, and look how you ended up. If you had married Manny the builder's son like I wanted, you'd be living in a nice, big house in Scarsdale instead of this dump. If Silvio builds me a house, it's only right that Al should do the same for you. They both got the money."

"I'll talk to Al about it tonight and see what he thinks."

"Forget about what Al thinks, sweetheart," Marie said fondly patting Georgann on her shoulder and nodding sagely, "You're father will take care of everything."

After dinner, once Nicky was asleep in her crib, Georgann asked me what I thought about us starting to build a house on our property in New Paltz. I put her off. "This isn't the right time," I said, "I just got some big accounts at Revlon and beginning to make good money. Frankie and me are turning a small profit with our stores. Wait a little longer, sweetheart, and I promise I'll get you your dream house."

Georgann didn't broach the topic of the house with me again, but I would catch her and Marie whispering to each other. The only words I heard were 'dream house,' and 'Al is a piker,' but I could put together the gist of their conversations. To appease her, I told Georgann that she could have some preliminary design plans drawn up. I didn't care what the house looked like, I just made one stipulation - the total building budget could not exceed $50,000. (about 250k 2017 dollars)

Georgann and her mother were off and running. The following week, they made an appointment with the highly respected architect Bruce Helmes who, as a lifelong resident of Katonah, NY could be depended upon to build a house that would suit both Georgann and the area.

Seated in front of Mr. Helmes, Marie began, "We want you to design two houses, one for me and one for my daughter on our adjoining lots. I know what I want. We can discuss my ideas later, but I want to make sure that you give Georgann everything she wants."

Georgann leaned over to her mother and whispered, "Ma, Al said we can only spend $50,000."

As if she hadn't heard Georgann, Marie repeated to Helmes, "Like I said, give my daughter everything she wants. Money is no object."

Helmes had heard what Georgann said about the building cap.

In the months that followed their meeting with Helmes, whenever I was around the dream house talk became very hush-hush. Assuming plans were being drawn up with a building ceiling of $50,000, I didn't ask. One afternoon, I stopped home to pick up some sales quotes I had left on my desk. No one was home. On my way to the kitchen to get a cup of coffee, I passed through the dining room and saw blueprints lying on table. I took a peek. I stared in amazement at the plans. I couldn't believe that an architect could design a house this elaborate on a $50,000 budget! They looked like plans for the White House, columns and all. I left the plans where they were. When I got home that evening, they had disappeared off the table.

The next day, without telling Georgann, I took a ride to the Helmes' office. I needed some answers directly from the architect himself. Experience told me Georgann and Marie had already concocted a story to explain the plans if I saw them.

As soon as the receptionist picked up the phone to announce me, Mr. Helmes came rushing out from his office. He grabbed my hand and shook it vigorously. "Mr. Volpe, what a great pleasure to finally meet you. Let's go into my office."

In his office, he gestured for me to take a seat in front of his big, oak desk. He was a tall, scarecrow of a man whose tweed jacket hung loosely on his broad shoulders. His blue eyes, magnified behind gold frames, were clear and bright, his wide smile engaging. I didn't let that deter me from my mission.

"Mr. Helmes," I began, "I saw the plans you drew up for my new house. You must be some kind of a miracle worker to create such an architectural masterpiece on a $50,000 budget."

Leaning back in his leather chair, he clasped his hands across his chest before saying, "Yes, I recall Georgann saying something about a $70,000 budget, but her mother told me to ignore that ceiling on the building costs as long as the design was to her daughter's liking. I just assumed that she and Mr. Marino were going to pick up the remainder of the costs for the construction."

"What are the costs?"

"Since you already own the property, I think we can keep the building costs down to just a little over $150,000." (About $750,000 in 2017 dollars)

"I see," I said keeping a poker face. I got to my feet, "I need time to go over the plans to give you my input. Don't do anything more on the plans till I get back to you. You can tell my mother-in-law and wife that I am now personally involved in the project and that nothing further will be done without my consent." I stood, shook his hand again and left him with a confused look on his face. I had kept my temper; it wasn't his fault, but I was fuming.

I confronted Georgann that evening.

"I took a ride to Helmes' office today." She blanched. "Georgann, what were you thinking? We can't afford a house that big, and you know your parents aren't putting up the money for the difference. I'm calling Helmes in the morning and tell him to can the plans and draw us up some new ones within our budget."

Defiantly and jutting out her chin, Georgann said, "My mother will not appreciate your interference now that the plans are done. If it was so important to you, why didn't you take more interest before? It's not about what I want is it, Al? It's all about the money."

"I'm taking an interest now. And, yes, it is all about the money. We can't afford it! Call your mother and tell her we changed our minds about the kind of house we - you and me - want. Tell her that from now on, I make all the decisions."

Georgann didn't like it, but she agreed.

The useless blueprints cost us $3,500. A new set of realistic plans cost us another $1,100. All this money wasted because of Marie's high-handed conviction that her daughter should live like a princess.

After the blueprint fiasco, things went from bad to worse. Marie convinced Georgann that giving Silvio all our savings to start building the house was good strategy. I don't know where my head was when I agreed to this.

"With your father's connections and calling in some favors, he'll get things done for next to nothing," she told Georgann.

I have to admit, this sounded great to me, too. Cheapskate Al, remember? That was until I learned that Silvio's 'contractors' were inner-city illegals used to working with shovels and wheelbarrows. They knew nothing about clearing virgin land, or about foundations, or septic systems, or restricted wetlands or much else. Their only job-site qualification was that their boss, John Corso, owed Silvio big money, and Silvio was calling in the debt.

Beginning in August of '74, 8:00 am each day, sitting in the bed of a beat-up pick-up truck Corso drove the workers up from The Bronx. Using the bulldozer I rented, they destroyed everything in its path. Twice, at eight hundred bucks a pop, I had to hire a wrecker to pull the dozer out of the mud. One of the workers nearly drowned in the mud when he fell off the dozer. Another time when they were knocking down trees, one snapped in the middle and fell onto the dozer. Good thing the driver escaped harm because insurance and disability were not part of their job perks.

Corso continued to sweat these poor bastards, because Silvio was giving him a discount on his vig payments. I didn't know if Silvio and I shared equally in the job costs; I only knew that he kept our money. With Silvio, it was just business - friend, enemy or family - everybody pays.

When the job-site failed its first inspection for excavation work, the town building inspector and Wetlands Committee shut it down. By the spring of 1975, our savings and worthless blueprints were sunk in the mud of this 5-acre wasteland. The job site looked more like a trench in a World War I battlefield after repeated bombardment than an excavation for luxury housing. I refused to borrow any money from the bank to sink into this mud-hole. Silvio came up with bupkis.

"Please Georgann," I begged, "let it go for now. I promise we will start up again after Nicky's heart surgery." With all the stress I had to cope with, I didn't need to deal with construction bullshit, too.

However, Marie continued to serenade Georgann with, "Don't worry, sweetheart, you'll have your dream house."

After all, every princess deserves a castle.

11

I Get Out

Around the same time as the house-in-the swamp disaster, Dennis' brother, Joe, was found dead in his garage. Joe's death was ruled a suicide, but everyone knew Joe was a mob hit.

Silvio had a partner, Mongo, a well known neighborhood thug. As his name implied, Mongo was a bull of a man – thick neck, meaty shoulders, expressionless face, and not much brain between his ears. He and Silvio had taken over a bar on the corner of Gun Hill and White Plains Roads in The Bronx to use as a front for their loan sharking activities. They hired Joe as their bar tender, and, because he was good with numbers, put him in charge of keeping their bank to record the daily take. One morning, Joe's wife found him sitting in his car in the garage with the motor running - dead. There was no reason for Joe to have killed himself.

Dozens of elderly people from the neighborhood showed up for Joe's funeral at the East End Funeral Home, but no one seemed to know or care why they were there. Although this seemed strange to me too, The Family members who came to the funeral didn't think anything of it – just a bunch of old farts with nothing else to do.

Joe was a sweetheart, and I really liked him. After the funeral, I decided to nose around on the QT. I found out that Joe had been helping needy, old people during the time he was working at the bar. He bought them TVs, paid their rent and gave them food money. Unfortunately, Joe was using Silvio's and Mongo's bank money for his charity work. In other words, Joe was stealing from them - an offense no Family member could let go unpunished if he wanted to save face. Goodbye Joe.

Although I was a Mafia novice, I'd seen enough to know it was easier to stay out of the life rather than get out once it had its grip on you. Somehow, I had to distance myself from Silvio's corrupt hook before it took over my life. First, I told Silvio that my Revlon job and running the clothing stores didn't give me much time to be his errand boy. Legitimate employment was an excellent front to Silvio, and he cut me some slack. He stopped asking me to go with him on vig collections - my touch wasn't persuasive enough. He used me only for vig pick-ups that didn't require a rough hand. Using more excuses,

I was able to get out of all the collections except one. Because Clara's Luncheonette was on my way home from the baby store, I couldn't figure how to get out of picking up Silvio's loan sharking payment from Clara.

Each Tuesday night, I'd stop by the luncheonette to get Silvio's $200 weekly vig payment. Clara knew Silvio as Charlie and me as Frankie, because, following the age old Mafioso tradition, you never gave your real name. Clara feared Charlie but liked me. Too any times I had to listen to her sorry excuses why she could only make a partial payment that week. (Father Al) I'd take what she gave me with a warning that she had better have the rest of the vig by Friday. Sometimes, I'd wind up laying out money from my own pocket to avoid hearing Silvio's bullshit but mostly to keep him from getting the payment from Clara his way.

Although almost sixty, Clara was a hard worker putting in fifteen-plus hour days at the luncheonette. Her chocolate skin was still smooth, her round, raisin-black eyes crinkled, and her generous mouth broke into a broad smile when she saw me come through the door. She always wore a red bandanna tied over her curly, salt and pepper hair, but she was no Aunt Jemima. Her husband, Ed, worked for the subway system as a rail cleaner. He helped out in the luncheonette at night after his shift. At 6'4" and well over 400 pounds, Ed was obviously a big guy, but little Clara, no more than 5"1" and about ninety pounds, ruled the roost.

I got a kick out of Clara's southern black humor. After picking up the payment, she would hand me a container of coffee saying, "Here you go, Frankie. I put a little something extra in the cup. If the coffee tastes a mite bitter, don't you fret, it'll just make you regular." Giving me a wink she and Ed would laugh each time.

One week, I stopped by on the usual Tuesday for the payment, but it was short. I had to go back on Friday to get the last $50.

At that time Clara said, "Frankie, I'm going to North Carolina to visit my family next week."

"What about the vig, Clara?"

"Don't you worry, Frankie, Ed will pay you on Tuesday just like always."

I smiled, "Clara, don't jive me, I mean it."

"Would I jive you, sugar?"

I believed her. Why should I be mad at Clara, because my life was falling apart? The following Tuesday, I went to collect. Ed was there in a white shirt, pants, and apron and paper hat. He looked like an overstuffed Michelin Tire man in black face. The luncheonette was narrow with enough room for a few red checkered, oilskin-covered tables and a long counter with rickety bar stools. Two stand-up soda display coolers at one end of the counter served as dividers to the back room. A couple of men were drinking coffee at the counter. I walked past them toward the back room to get the payment from Ed. They didn't look up.

"Where's my money, Ed?"

Ed tried to blow me off, "Clara said to come back next week."

I got up close to him, poked him in the chest and whispered so the guys at the counter couldn't hear me, "Clara told me she'd have the money for me today." I knew she kept her cash in an old stove in the back room. I pushed past Ed to get to it.

"Hey, you can't go back there," he protested. I ignored him.

Behind the coolers, the back room was littered with bundles of newspapers and crates of empty, glass soda bottles stacked five deep. I walked up to the stove, opened the oven door, and took out a manila envelope. Ed was surprised that I knew where Clara kept the weekly receipts.

Grabbing it out of my hand, he yelled, "Clara said I got to pay the electric with that money."

I got in his face, "Give me my money, Ed. I don't care what Clara told you. I don't want to hear any more of your bullshit."

"No. Clara said…"

Before he could finish the sentence, the thug part of my brain kicked in. I grabbed an empty bottle out of the crate next to the soda machine and whacked him in the head with it. He fell backward, and the impact of his massive body tilted the coolers. Before they could right themselves, soda bottles in the cooler flew out the front, some exploding as they hit the tile floor. Ed lay moaning on the floor, legs splayed out. Blood from the gash where I hit him in the head began seeping through the paper hat now stuck to his head and mixed with Coke from the broken soda bottles on the floor. I looked down at him but didn't attempt to help him up. I grabbed the envelope, counted out $200, and threw the envelope on top of him. I walked past the men at the counter, heads still bent over their coffee cups pretending to be both deaf and blind.

When I got into my car, I thanked God I hadn't killed Ed. On the drive home, the awareness of what my life had become hit me; I had become as uncaring an animal as Silvio. This epiphany struck me like a jackhammer and scared me straight; I began to tremble. I pulled over, and, sitting in the dark, I cried.

After fifteen minutes, I managed to pull myself together enough to drive to Silvio's. After I gave him the money, I said, "Tonight is my last pickup at Clara's. I'm not gonna' be your bagman anymore. I resign."

"You can't resign, Al. It don't work that way. I tell you when you can resign," he said poking my shoulder with his forefinger emphasizing the word 'resign' with an extra hard poke.

"Come on, Silvio, gimme a break. I'm working my ass off at Revlon and trying to keep both stores going since Marie and Georgann got bored and backed out of the baby store. Georgann wants me home at night to spend more time with Nicky. She's worried Nicky isn't gonna make it. Can't you get someone else to make the pickup, at least, until Nicky gets better?" I threw in the last bit about Nicky knowing that it would get to Silvio, who, despite his brutality toward everyone who wasn't Family, loved his granddaughter. I never said a word about what had happened at Clara's.

"Ok, Al, you can take a little time off, but don't think you're out of it."

The next week, Silvio went to Clara's to collect his money. After giving Silvio the vig, Clara told him, "Charlie, I don't want Frankie coming here no more."

"Why not, Clara? I thought you liked Frankie." It wasn't Silvio's game to let a mark dictate how to run his business.

Clara exclaimed, "Look what Frankie did to my Ed!" Ed waddled out from the back room, his head wrapped in a turban of bandages. "He almost killed my husband!"

"Ok, ok, Clara. Frankie won't come here again unless you're late with your vig. Understand?" Silvio never missed an opportunity to squeeze or threaten a mark.

"Sure, Charlie. I won't be late ever again; just don't send that maniac Frankie here."

Silvio didn't understand my reticence. Given his world view, beating up Ed was something to boast about, not hide. The next day, he went to my house to have a talk with Georgann before I got home.

"Georgann," he asked, "Is something bothering Al? Is he taking drugs or drinking a lot?

"Of course not," she laughed. "Al can hardly drink of few glasses of red wine without falling asleep in front of the TV. Why are you asking?"

"Yesterday, I went to see a client I lent some money. Sometimes, I ask Al to pick up the loan payment on his way home. Al went there last week. The owner was away visiting relatives down south, but she'd left her husband in charge. For some reason, Al went berserk and beat the guy up. I was just wondering why since I never thought Al had such a violent streak."

"I don't understand it, either, Dad. Al doesn't fight."

"He did this time. The guy never even had a chance to pull the first punch before Al had him flat on his back." Silvio hid a smile behind his hand so Georgann wouldn't see it. It was difficult for him to keep a straight face; it was a source of pride to have a son-in-law more in line with his own standards.

"All I can tell you, Daddy, is that he's been really stressed having to work such long hours at Revlon and the stores. He doesn't want to let you down, either even though I asked him to spend more time with me and Nicky. I'll have a talk with him tonight. Maybe I can find out what's bothering him."

"You do that, Georgann," Silvio said patting her hand. "I wouldn't want anything to happen to Al."

At dinner that night she said, "My father came by today."

I didn't look up from my plate. I pretended disinterest. I was hoping Silvio didn't decide to tell about the Ed incident. "Really? What did he have to say?"

"He wanted to know why you beat up this guy, Ed. He told me you were out of line. What's going on with you?"

I just let it all out without taking a breath. "I can't take working with Silvio anymore. We used up all our savings in that stupid property your parents dragged us into. I'm worried about Nicky. Your mother's interference in our lives is driving me nuts. I'm having a nervous breakdown!"

She didn't believe me; she thought I was joking.

Scaramouche Al.

12

Married with In-laws

Marie couldn't leave things alone. With the plans for the house in New Paltz on hold, she began working on Georgann to sell our house next door to the Marinos and move in with them.

"Georgann, why should you shell out money for a mortgage when you could live with us for nothin'? If Al knew what he was doing, our houses in New Paltz would be half done by now. Silvio said he wasn't putting another dime into the property until Al comes up with his share of the dough. He blames Al for the screw up. If you sell this house, you can use the money from the sale to begin building again."

"I don't know, Ma. I don't think Al wants to live with you and Daddy. He likes his privacy."

"Sure he does. In your house there's no one to keep an eye on his comings and goings. You have to think about Nicky, too. It would be better for her if we both lived in the same house. I would be there all the time to help take care of her. Once our houses are built, we can work out some other arrangement."

"I guess you're right, Ma. I'll talk to Al tonight."

"Don't ask him, Georgann; tell him that's what he's going to do. Silvio and me will back you up."

After dinner that night, Georgann told me what she and Marie had decided. "You got to be kidding, Georgann. Your mother practically lives here now. She even knows when I'm going to take a shit, because she's already standing outside the bathroom door ready with the Lysol spray. No way we're moving in with your parents."

"But Al, listen, if we sell this house we can use the money to build my new house. Living with my parents would save even more money, because they wouldn't ask us for rent. I need more help with Nicky now that it's getting nearer the time for her heart surgery. You're hardly ever home to give me a hand."

So, it was already her house, not ours. Heap on the guilt, why don't you, Georgann, saying that I neglect Nicky. I kept saying 'no way', but she kept on nagging me to move in with her parents - she never gave up. Georgann promised that once our house was built, we would live happily ever after. Finally, after two weeks of her persistent harping, I gave in. I had little home life now so what did it matter whose home I was living in to have more of the same.

In late September of 1975, we sold our house, put our furniture into storage and moved in with the Marinos - another really bad destiny decision.

It was evident that Marie had been planning this move for some time, because she already had a duplicate of Nicky's bedroom in her house. The woman never ceased to amaze me with the depth of her scheming or the patience she exhibited to get what she wanted. Now that Georgann and Nicky were under her roof, Marie's world was complete. Silvio and I were expendable.

With a new injection of money from the sale of our house, Silvio agreed to resume building in New Paltz. Before foundations could be laid, the property required serious remedial work to bring it up to the specifications required to obtain the proper building permits. Silvio and I hired some local licensed contractors for the site and foundation work and for the framing. By the time the houses were framed in, all the money I made on the sale of the house in The Bronx was gone.

Once we moved in with the Marinos, the years of fun vacations and sumptuous Friday night dinners at Ann & Tony's Restaurant were over. Marie was the text book personification of the controlling, Italian mother-in-law; not merely taking it to new extremes but writing a whole new chapter. Her need meter was lethal; her psychotic behavior impossible to predict. Often, I'd come home to elaborate dinners she had lovingly prepared for the four of us. Most of the time the dinners were civil, but too often Marie took the opportunity to attack Silvio for any or no apparent reason. Many times the confrontation turned violent and food and fists flew. Leaving Georgann to calm Marie down, the men took their cue to disappear - Silvio into the den, me out the door. This nightmare of living at the Marinos never ceased and was putting me further over the edge. Georgann and I had no home, no money, and no personal life.

Disgusted with everything that was going on in my life; I concentrated on keeping my job with Revlon for the health insurance I knew would be needed to cover Nicky's heart surgery. My very capable salespeople handled the management of the baby store, and I let Frankie take full responsibility for the store I partnered with him. Finding little else to care about, I went home later and later each night taking solace in the women who saw me as Big Al, the man with the big car, money to throw around, and the grease ball attitude. In my in-laws house, I was invisible.

It was during this time that Georgann and I developed a closer relationship with Frankie and Phyllis. To get away from the Marinos, we spent many pleasurable Sunday afternoons at their house on Allerton Avenue in the Bronx. Nicky enjoyed playing with their two daughters.

Our stores in The Bronx were doing well enough for Frankie and me to consider expanding our partnership. We found a store for rent in the town of Katonah. We took out a $10,000 loan from the local bank, had the store renovated and opened a fancy, Bronxy-style boutique we named Desiderata - my favorite poem.

Unfortunately, it wasn't long after opening Desiderata that the baby store in The Bronx began to flounder. The neighborhood was changing, and there was less call for the high priced children's clothes and accessories the store offered. Also, my partnership with Frankie had become tenuous since opening the boutique in Katonah. We erroneously thought that women in Westchester had the same fashion sense as those in The Bronx, but they were more upscale. I made the mistake of letting Frankie do all the buying, but he had no idea how to choose the right merchandise to appeal to their more sophisticated tastes. Frankie ignored any changes I tried to recommend; the store was also heading for bankruptcy.

Mired with the stress of having no control over my living arrangements or my family, I was barely maintaining the accounts I had established at Revlon and incapable of finding the will to create new business strategies to keep the baby and Katonah stores from going belly up. Thank God I was still able to distance myself from Silvio's dealings, but I felt like a speeding train tunneling to wits-end. I was certain of only one thing - Georgann and I had to get away from the Marinos.

One night, after witnessing a particularly gruesome scene between Silvio and Marie, Georgann and I retreated to our bedroom. I pleaded with Georgann, "Forget the new house for now, Georgann. Living with your parents is not doing our marriage any good. Let's rent an apartment and get out of here. You'll get your house, I promise, but right now we need to get our marriage back on track."

"I don't know what you mean, Al," she said. "I don't see living with my parents as a problem in our marriage. Sure, Mom is a little high strung and sometimes she acts out, but she and my father have been really good to us.

"High strung! She's not high strung, Georgann, she's nuts! I don't even want to come home at night if I know Silvio won't be here. Not that it's much better when he is, but at least she focuses her rage on him and leaves me alone. What I wouldn't give to finish a dinner without agita! I'm telling you, Georgann, I don't know how much more I can take of this!"

My pleas fell on deaf ears. "Don't be so melodramatic, Al. It's not that bad. It's just for a little while longer," she insisted. "As soon as we move into our new home, everything will be perfect."

I sighed, no use arguing. I went to bed.

Dysfunction junction at the Marinos continued almost non-stop. For some reason, Georgann didn't see or was immune to her mother's behavior. But, that immunity didn't extend to me. And, the dysfunction included Georgann's other family members, too.

One Saturday night in June, my in-laws went to a wedding in New Jersey. We invited Donna and Dennis over for a barbeque. We were sitting in the back yard having a few glasses of wine waiting for the steaks to grill. After putting Nicky to bed and setting the table in the dining room, Georgann joined us. Donna was drinking heavily and began to babble. Every other word out of her mouth was, "Fuck this…, fuck that…. fuck them." We all tried to ignore her hoping she would sober up after she had dinner.

Once the steaks were done, I put them on a plate, and we went into the house, Dennis holding Donna's arm to steady her. She pulled away from him, "Get your fucking hands off me!" She tripped on the sliding door frame entering the house letting out a loud, "Fuck!"

Georgann couldn't take it anymore, "Donna, could you please lower your voice and stop cursing so much. My ears are starting to hurt. Let's sit and enjoy these great steaks Al made for us."

"Don't tell me what to do, Georgann. I'm not Al."

Dennis, taking his seat at the table mumbled, "Calm down, Donna and let's eat."

Donna snapped back at him, "You shut the fuck up and put your nose in your steak like the fuckin' mutt you are." Dennis lowered his head over his plate and started shoveling food into his mouth.

Georgann tried again, "Donna, please stop. You're drunk. You don't know what you're saying."

Donna turned on her sister, "You shut the fuck up, too. I can say what I want. One thing I do know is that you can't even make a healthy baby!"

Georgann's mouth opened, but no words came out. Her eyes flooded with tears and spilled down her cheeks that were turning white as the blood drained from her face. She ran upstairs.

I could never bear to see Georgann cry. I stood up, no longer trying to hold in my temper. "I've had it! Shut your ignorant mouth."

"Fuck you, too," Donna said spitting saliva in my face.

Without thinking, I grabbed my steak off the plate and slammed it into her face with such force she went flying off her chair. Although an abusive shrew, Donna was still his wife and Dennis had to defend her. He leaped up from his chair and rushed at me. I grabbed him by the front of his shirt and rammed his head into the wall so hard it made a hole the size of a basketball.

"Get out of my house, both of you," I shrieked with my fists in the air. "Don't bring that foul mouthed bitch back here again, Dennis, or you'll get worse than this."

Donna helped Dennis up. Holding onto each other, they ran out of the house and jumped into their car. I heard the tires screech as they sped away.

Georgann had gone into Nicky's bedroom, crying and heartbroken by her sister's hurtful words. She held her sleeping daughter rocking her back and forth. I watched this tender scene for a few moments before going to the kitchen to clean up. As I was heading back to my family the phone rang. It was Marie's brother, Sonny, who was in The Bronx visiting Grandma Vingo.

"Al, this is Sonny," he said, "I'm coming over. Don't go anywhere."

"I'll be waiting for you on the porch." I knew he wasn't coming for a friendly visit. He'd be the first person Donna would call, because he was the only reasonable member of the family she could count on. I went upstairs to tell Georgann that Sonny was on his way.

"I bet Donna couldn't wait to get to a phone to call him. I wonder what lies she told him to get him here. I'll bring him upstairs and you can tell him what happened. He'll believe you. Are you ok?"

"I'm all right," she whispered. She had stopped crying, but her eyes were swollen and her nose red. She hiccupped, "My sister's a bitch." Add idiot to that description, I thought.

I waited for him in a deck chair on the porch. Sonny pulled up four cigarettes later. He strolled onto the porch, lit a cigarette of his own and stared down at me. He smoked half before he spoke never breaking the stare. I knew better than to hurry him.

"I got a call a little while ago from Donna."

"Oh, yeah," I said. "What did she want?"

"She called me from the emergency room at Miseriacordia Hospital. I drove to the hospital to check on her before coming here."

"Really? How is she?" It was no use of me feigning ignorance.

"Actually, both Dennis and Donna checked into emergency. Dennis has a slight concussion and Donna has a black eye. Nothing broken. You wouldn't happen to know how they got hurt, would you? I couldn't get a sane word out of the two of them."

"I have my side of the story, yeah, but I'd rather Georgann tell you what happened. She's upstairs with Nicky."

"Okay, buddy, let's go."

Sonny knew Donna had a trash mouth, and he had little respect for Dennis, because, to Sonny, a husband who couldn't control his wife wasn't much of a man. Given Sonny's opinion of my brother-in-law and sister-in law, I knew whose side of the story he would believe.

I opened the bedroom door and whispered, not wanting to wake Nicky, "Georgann, come on out. Sonny's here."

We stood in the hall outside Nicky's bedroom. Georgann told Sonny the story starting from the beginning. "My parents went to a wedding in New

Jersey. Al and I thought it would be a good time to invite Donna and Dennis over for barbecue so we could catch up on things. Donna was drinking a lot of wine. You know what her mouth is like after she's had a few. I asked her to calm down and stop cursing so much. That set her off even more. When I asked her again to quiet down not to wake Nicky, she turned on me and said….." Georgann started to cry and was unable to repeat her sister's hurtful words.

I continued. "The bitch told Georgann she was responsible for Nicky's heart condition. Georgann broke down and ran upstairs. Donna continued to scream some more incomprehensible garbage even after I asked her to stop. At that point, I picked up my steak and smashed it into her face. I would have rammed it down her throat if that's what it took to shut her filthy mouth. Dennis tried to grab me so I pushed him into the wall. I guess he hit his head a little too hard."

"Okay, that's enough," Sonny said. "I get the picture. I probably would have done the same thing maybe even more. You know my son, Ralphy, was born with some physical problems. I wouldn't let anyone talk to me about him the way Donna did about Nicky, family or not. I'll smooth it over with Donna and Dennis."

Sonny was a big teddy bear; he didn't have the vengeful, violent Vingo DNA like his brother and sister. I felt better. I said, "Let's go downstairs for coffee."

Georgann made a pot of coffee and brought out the cannoli we were going to have for dessert. As we sat at the dining room table drinking coffee and eating cannoli, Sonny noticed the hole in the wall made by Dennis' head.

He laughed, "That hole's so big you won't find a picture large enough to cover it up." Finishing his coffee, he said to me, "You're already number one on Marie's shit list, asshole. I'm leaving you to deal with her all by yourself. That's punishment enough."

We hugged goodbye. Embracing Georgann, Sonny whispered in her ear, "If things get ugly with Marie call me no matter what the time."

We were asleep when Marie and Silvio got home that night. The next morning, Marie was in the kitchen giving Nicky her breakfast when Georgann came down.

"Mom, is Daddy up yet?"

"No, honey, not yet. Why? Nicky, eat you cereal and stop playing with that doll!"

"Nothing, Mom, I just need to ask him something."

Georgann went back upstairs and knocked at Silvio's bedroom door. "Yeah," he answered, "What is it?"

"It's me, Daddy. Can you come downstairs?

"Sure, bella, give me a few minutes to get dressed."

Georgann came into our bedroom. "Al, hurry up downstairs. We have to tell my parents what happened last night before Donna gets a chance. I want them to hear our side of the story first."

I got dressed, went to the kitchen and sat at my place at the table. Marie was putting a cup of coffee in front of me when Silvio walked in. Georgann waited for him to get his coffee before she began. She related what happened in the same words she used with Sonny. At the same point of the story where Donna accused her for Nicky's problems, Georgann began to cry. Marie put her arms around Georgann and started to cry, too. When she recovered enough to talk, Georgann finished telling them how I put Donna and Dennis in the emergency room with a black eye and a concussion.

Silvio sat there without saying a word, his head down, staring into his untouched coffee.

I broke the silence saying, "I'm sorry. I guess I lost it."

Silvio shook his head. Finally, looking up, he said, "Al, you're part of this family, but you ain't blood. I understand Donna was out of line, and you were just protecting Georgann, but don't ever touch my daughter again. If there's a problem, you come to me. Capisce?"

"I understand."

That was the end of it. I patched the wall.

The Donna rotten apple does not fall far from the maternal tree. A few weeks after the barbecue incident, Silvio and Marie went to a union function in Fort Lee, New Jersey. Georgann, Nicky and I were asleep when we got a call from the New Jersey State Police.

After identifying himself, the state trooper said, "Sir, are you Mr. Al Volpe?" I said I was. "Do you know a Mrs. Marie Marino?" I said I did. "Can you please come to the Fort Lee State Police Department to escort Mrs. Marino home?" I said I could.

"What happened?"

"We found Mrs. Marino wandering in the road and took her to the station. Mrs. Marino appeared to be intoxicated. She didn't seem to know where she was and was incapable of speaking coherently. We got your phone number from an address book in her purse."

I dressed quickly and headed to New Jersey to bring Marie back home. She slept in the car the whole way back to The Bronx.

As soon as I pulled to the curb in front of the house, Georgann came running out. We managed to get Marie into the house and upstairs to her room without fully waking her. While Georgann was putting Marie to bed, I checked in on Nicky who was sleeping like an angel

The next morning, Marie told us "Maybe I had a little too much to drink at the union meeting. Silvio was angry at me for some reason. On the way home, we got into an argument in the car. I wanted him to pull over so we could talk, and I grabbed the wheel. I guess he thought I was trying to crash the car. The bastard punched me in the mouth and knocked out my front tooth." She showed us the missing canine. "I don't remember anything else."

Silvio didn't come home for almost a year.

13

Separation

Because Georgann relied a great deal on her mother for help with Nikol, I understood why she was reluctant to alienate Marie by us moving out. Georgann seemed to turn a blind eye and deaf ear where her mother was concerned. I was the one who couldn't deal with Marie's erratic behavior.

Without Silvio around, Marie turned her hostility on me. She took every opportunity to belittle me in front of Georgann. As soon as I came through the door at night, she would start in on me.

"Al, when are you going to start building Georgann's house again?"

"I don't have the money, Ma."

"Al, where do you go when you come home so late?"

"I'm working, Ma."

"Are you still spending your money on those bimbos you hang out with instead of getting Georgann her house?" (Trick question)

"No, Ma."

"You mean you stopped with the bimbos? When are you going to spend more time with your daughter?"

"I will, Ma."

"You hear from Silvio?"

"No, Ma."

"I don't believe you."

A couple of months after Silvio left for parts unknown, I'd finally had it. On a Saturday afternoon when Marie was taking Nicky for a walk, I said, "Georgann, I need to talk to you. Sit down."

We sat close together on the couch in the living room. I took Georgann's hand, "Your mother is making me crazy. At least when Silvio was here, he had some control over her, and she stayed off my back. With him gone, her mouth knows no bounds where I'm concerned. I have to get out of here. I'm begging you, please; we need to find our own place."

"I can't, Al. I have to think about Nicky. I really need my mother's help right now. When Daddy comes back, it'll be better. You'll see."

"Your father isn't coming back any time soon, Georgann, and you know it. He's shacked up with one of his goumare. If I stay here any longer, I'll either kill myself or your mother. What's your answer, can we get our own place, or not?"

"I can't. I need my mother." She dropped my hand, shut her eyes and let her head fall to her chest.

"Okay, then I'm going without you." I went upstairs to pack my bags. I threw some shirts, underwear and toiletries into one suitcase and suits and shoes in another. When I came back down, Georgann hadn't moved from the couch.

After I loaded my bags into the company car, I went back into the house to make one last plea for Georgann to change her mind. She didn't say a word or even look at me. I put on my coat, shook my head in sorrow quietly closing the door on my way out.

Before I could get halfway down the walk, Georgann came running out. "Please, don't go, Al. I'll talk to my mother. I'll make her leave you alone."

It was too late. Sure, Marie would lay off me for a while to appease Georgann, but it wouldn't be long before she would consider me her personal punching bag again. I didn't say anything to Georgann. I kissed her good bye, got into my car and sped away without looking back. I knew that if I saw her crying, I wouldn't have the nerve to leave.

I drove aimlessly north on the Post Road before booking into a cheap motel in Mamaroneck. The sleazy, cinder block room was decorated in mold; everything had a greenish tinge including me when I woke up the next morning. I found a 'men only' rooming house in Elmsford that was clean and affordable and checked out of Mildew Motel. The first few nights I spent in the rooming house, I slept with the pillow over my head so the other boarders wouldn't hear me crying myself to sleep. I wasn't very good at sleeping alone.

The weeks of our separation turned into months. During the day, I worked at Revlon and the clothing stores. To ward off the loneliness I felt at night, I resumed some of my bachelor ways. There was always a friendly lady ready to share a hotel room with a handsome, single guy with money to spend. Ah, it was good to be Big Al again. (Reader, just because I screwed around didn't mean that I didn't love Georgann with my whole heart. She was my soul mate. Really!)

One night, I met a couple of Pan Am stewardesses on layover in New York in the bar of the Lexington Hotel in Manhattan. Their home base was Stockholm. I invited, so I thought, one of them to spend the night with me in a room I had prearranged (just in case) in the hotel. I did not realize that in Sweden women may be more open-minded when it comes to sex. They both decided to join me. Not wanting to spoil the illusion that I was a man of the world, I went along with them to the room, swaggering like a big shot. Actually, I had no idea what I was supposed to do with two women. So, I did what Chicken Al knew how to do best. When one went to take a shower, I screwed the other, got dressed, told her I was going down to get cigarettes and high tailed it back to Elmsford. Big Sport Al hadn't even paid for the room.

Marie acted as though she was the woman scorned, and she wasn't talking about Silvio. She demanded that Georgann divorce me for desertion although she knew I was sending money for her and Nicky. She wasn't aware that during our six month separation, Georgann and I were keeping in close contact. That really would have made her go berserk – or more berserk than was her usual.

For example, one Saturday afternoon, about two months into the separation, I was at the baby store in The Bronx. I needed a break and decided to walk around the corner to get a pack of cigarettes. As I was coming out of Rocco's candy store, Marie, in her best spy mode, just happened to be driving by Rocco's when she saw me before I saw her. She was both outraged and pleased at catching sight of me. She slammed her foot down hard on the gas pedal, jumped the curb onto the sidewalk and tried to run me down. I managed to leap out of her way just in time, and she just managed to miss hitting a woman wheeling a baby a carriage before jamming on the brakes.

Having failed in vehicular homicide, she left the car half on the sidewalk, jumped out screaming and pointing her finger at me, "You're a fuckin' dead man, asshole. I've got a contract out on you."

"Get out of my face, you witch," I yelled back at her. "You can take your contract and shove it up your ass." I can be crude, too.

My come back really pushed her maniac button. She grabbed the curbstone her car had loosened when it jumped the curb, and, with superhuman strength, hurled it at me. It whizzed a couple of inches past my head and into Charlie the jeweler's display window shattering it to pieces and setting off the store alarm. People came rushing out of the surrounding stores, and along with those walking on the sidewalk, stopped to gape at the commotion. Charlie ran out, looked at the damage to his store front and began to wail holding his head with both hands and rocking back and forth; sirens were blaring in the distance. In the chaos, I took the opportunity to disappear into the crowd leaving Charlie and the police to deal with Marie. Somehow, Marie managed to escape arrest probably by pulling a big wad of money out of her old lady purse and paying off all concerned.

Although Marie had done her best to divide and conquer us, even during the separation Georgann and I remained committed to each other. When we could arrange it, we'd sneak away to meet for lunch.

I'd joke with Georgann, "Its déjà vu all over again. (Thanks Yogi) Eleven years of marriage and we're still sneaking around to meet." She would laugh like a teenager and give me 'the look'.

On the weekends we were apart, Georgann brought Nicky to Frankie and Phyllis' house. They and their daughters would leave to allow us to spend family time together. The knowledge that Marie really hated Frankie - that Sicilian weasel - made our clandestine meetings even more delicious.

After six months apart, we were ready to reconcile. Marie was not going to win; we just had to figure out how we could resume our marriage and keep me alive at the same time.

During the past six months, Georgann and Marie were vigilant in monitoring Nicky's health. It was becoming obvious that the need for her heart surgery was becoming imminent. She was beginning to show the slight, bluish tinge around her upper lip that Dr. Yuan warned us to look for as an indication that the banding around her heart was beginning to restrict her heart's functioning. Any problems Georgann and I might have in our marriage were trivial compared to Nicky's health. Putting our daughter's welfare first gave Georgann the strength to face Marie.

"Ma," Georgann said, "Nicky's lips are a little blue. You know what that means."

"Of course I do. What kind of grandmother do you think I am? Nicky needs her operation."

"Yes, Ma, and I want Al to be there with us."

"I'll go with you when Nicky has her surgery. You don't need that 'gavone'. He hasn't even tried to visit or call Nicky these past six months."

"No, Ma, Al is Nicky's father. He wants to be there. He has the right. And, you're wrong, he has seen Nicky. We've spent a lot of time meeting and talking these past few months. We are going to work things out. I love him and he loves me, but he doesn't want to live with you and daddy. We're going to get our own place."

Marie was uncharacteristically quiet after hearing Georgann's news. I don't think she really believed Georgann would actually go against her mother's wishes, but, if Georgann was serious, Marie had to cool her inner rage lest she completely alienate her favorite daughter.

"Ok, Georgann, I guess I can't talk sense into you if you want to go back to that bum, but I'm going to be there, too, when Nicky has her operation."

We found a beautiful apartment on the Shore Road in New Rochelle. Even though she seemed to accept our getting back together, Marie fumed when Georgann finally made the move. "You're ruining your life going back to that miserable excuse for a husband. You're breaking your mother's heart."

From that day on, Marie's resentment toward me festered at an exponential rate. She could bide her time, but in the long run, she knew that she would triumph and win her daughter back.

She was a woman of indomitable will, patience, and totally pazza.

14

Yuan Gone

Two weeks after we moved to New Rochelle, Georgann and I made an appointment with Dr. Yuan to schedule Nicky's surgery. At that time, surgical procedures for children were grouped and performed by Einstein's regular surgical team. We asked Dr. Yuan whether it would be better to have Nicky's operation in a hospital dedicated to pediatric surgery. With his deep voice and slow method of speaking, he adamantly insisted that he and his team were eminently qualified to perform Nicky's surgery, and Einstein's surgical facilities were first-rate. Given the resolute manner in which he assured us, Georgann and I did not question him again.

Because the banding around her heart had also restricted her growth, Nicky was smaller than the other children who were scheduled for heart surgery at Einstein. I was made to understand that body mass is an important factor in the success of this type of surgery. As a precaution, Dr. Yuan deemed it necessary to delay Nicky's surgery a few more months to give her time to gain more weight. He insisted that the delay would not be injurious to Nicky.

On the way home from Dr. Yuan, we stopped by the Marinos to pick up Nicky. Silvio had not yet returned from his time-out from Marie. In the living room, Georgann and I sat together on the couch facing Marie who sat upright on a dining room chair she had pulled into the room. Nicky was still napping. In the simplest terms, we tried to explain what Dr. Yuan had told us. Marie's stupidity was sometimes funny, but not when the welfare of my daughter was concerned. Ignorant people like Marie listen to little of what is said to them and misinterpret the little they hear.

As soon as we finished talking, Marie jumped up, "I'm gonna call Donna and tell her what you just told me." She rushed into the kitchen to use the phone. Between the two, from one brainless ear to the other, the conversation inflated Nicky's medical condition into something horrifying.

I heard some of the conversation and could imagine the rest.

"Donna, Georgann took Nicky to that chink doctor this morning. Nicky needs heart surgery or she's gonna die. She's so sick she might not even make it to the surgery. If she doesn't die before then, the doctor said the surgery might kill her because she's so little! Oh God, Donna, what did I do to deserve all this suffering?" She ran to Nicky's room and grabbed her out of her crib still lamenting her fate.

From then on, believing Nicky was going to die, Marie was at our apartment day and night. She never ceased mumbling that God was cruel to do this to her that she created even more stress for Georgann over Nicky's health.

I would come home from work to find Marie sitting in the rocking chair in Nicky's room holding her tight and crying. "My poor baby; Nana loves you so much. Please don't die!"

What I would have given to put Marie on the operating table with me doing the surgery on her with a butcher knife.

Our apprehension for Nicky's well-being increased with every passing day. Two months after her last visit, we took Nicky back to Einstein for another appointment with Dr. Yuan. In the lobby, we ran into a woman Georgann had met during her prior visits. Her five year old son had the same heart surgery the month before with a group of other children. She was holding her little boy's hand.

Georgann hugged her. Looking down at the boy she asked, "Joanie, how is Tony doing?"

"He's doing fine, Georgann." She picked up the little boy and kissed his cheek. After she put him down, he bent his head and smiled shyly up at us. He looked like a healthy, happy kid. "You remember Nicky, don't you Tony? Tell her how good you're doing since Dr. Yuan fixed your heart."

Tony gave Nicky a wink and with a know-it-all smile. "Piece of cake, Nicky. You wait and see."

"How are the other children who had the surgery doing, Joanie? Do you know?" Georgann asked.

Joanie's face turned ashen. "Oh, Georgann, it was terrible. Six children were scheduled for surgery, my son and two others on the first day and the other three the second day." Leaning in to us, she whispered, "Two of the children in the second group died during their surgeries. The hospital hushed it up. I only know this, because I am in a support group with the other parents."

Georgann and I didn't know what to say; we were too stunned. Georgann gave me the 'we'll talk later look,' before giving Joanie another hug and saying she would keep in touch.

"Let's get a cup of coffee, Georgann. We have time before our appointment with Yuan. Let's talk." No more Doctor Y for me. We went to the hospital cafeteria.

I got our coffees, and after settling Nicky on a booster seat with a hot chocolate, we put our heads together. "Georgann, I'm worried by what Joanie just told us. I'm not sure we should have Nicky's operation here at Einstein. Maybe we should find a hospital that specializes in children's surgeries."

Georgann grabbed my hand, "Al, I'm scared something terrible might happen to Nicky, but Dr. Yuan is so sure he's the best doctor for her. What should we do?"

"He's just too sure of himself for my taste. I don't want him to do the surgery. We'll ask him to make arrangements with a children's hospital and have Nicky's surgery transferred there. Come on; let's go before we're late for Nicky's appointment."

Georgann wiped chocolate from Nicky's face. I picked her up, and we took the elevator to Yuan's office. We only had to wait five minutes before the receptionist directed us to the examining room.

Yuan was waiting already there. After examining Nicky he went into to his office without uttering a word to us. After Georgann dressed Nicky, we joined him. He sat at his desk waiting for us, the model of patience. We barely sat down, Nicky in Georgann's lap, before he began speaking; he was out of patience.

"I've scheduled your daughter's surgery for one week from today. My receptionist can answer any questions you might have when she goes over the forms you need to sign." He put his hands palm side down on the desk and slowly began to rise as a gesture of dismissal.

If he was in any way concerned about performing heart surgery on our daughter in a hospital with a 33% failure rate as far as I was concerned, he sure didn't show it.

Georgann didn't move or speak. She remained seated holding tightly onto Nicky.

I stood up, leaned over the desk and stared into his bespectacled eyes forcing him to sit back down, "Doctor, I have just one question I'd like you to answer."

"Yes, Mr. Volpe, what is it?"

"Is it true two children died last month during the same surgery you want to perform on my daughter? If so, I want to know what happened."

His face turned red with indignation, beads of sweat forming on his brow. His glasses slipped down his nose and he pushed them up with the middle finger of his right hand before speaking, "That information is confi-dential. I will not discuss it with you."

"But, is it true?" I leaned over getting my face closer to his never losing eye contact, an arm's length of desk separating us.

Dr. Yuan recoiled back, "I'm her doctor. I've scheduled her surgery for next week, and that's all I will discuss with you. Please see my receptionist on your way out." He straightened up in his chair, smoothed back his hair and adjusted his glasses again before picking up the phone, "Miss Byron, the Volpes are leaving. Please give them all the necessary forms to fill out for their daughter's surgery." He bent his head over some papers on his desk.

Finito.

That's what he thought. I stood up so fast, my chair flew back. I said, almost in a whisper, "Nicky is not having heart surgery or even a hangnail clipped in this hospital." I held up my fist and shook it at him. "Nor will you lay a finger on her. I want you to contact a children's hospital and get us an appointment with a qualified surgeon!"

"That's impossible. It's not medical protocol. There is no time to waste. Nicky needs surgery as soon as possible." Sitting up straighter, he repeated, "I am a highly qualified heart surgeon and Nikol's surgery will be performed at Einstein."

Georgann began to cry. Nicky started to squirm, because Georgann was holding her tighter. "Mommy, you're squishing me," wailed Nicky.

"Oh, baby, I'm sorry. Mommy's sorry," Georgann managed to whisper through her tears as she buried her face into Nicky's soft, brown curls.

"Let's go, Georgann. Nicky is not having her surgery here." Turning back to Yuan, I said, "You can take your protocol and shove it. Come on, Georgann." I slammed open the office door and held it for Georgann and Nicky.

I was so angry, I envisioned smoke coming out of my ears like Curly, one of the Three Stooges. Yuan's receptionist jumped up waving the release forms she was holding at us. I went up her, grabbed the forms out of her hand, tore them in half and threw them in the air. Turning, I blew out of office without waiting for Georgann to follow.

"Al, slow down. I can't keep up with you."

We got halfway down the hall before I ran out of steam and stopped to catch my breath. Georgann caught up to me. Leaning against the wall, I said. "I'm sorry, honey. He got me so angry with his high and mighty attitude. Give me Nicky, let's go home."

The week before the debacle with Yuan, Georgann's parents had gotten back together. To make amends for punching her out and deserting her for a year, Silvio took Marie to Florida for a reconciliation vacation. As soon as we got home from the hospital, Georgann called her parents at the hotel they were staying at in Miami. Crying the whole time, she told her mother what happened at the hospital with Yuan.

Marie went ballistic, "That fuckin' chink! Who the fuck does he think he is?" Georgann sobbed harder.

I grabbed the phone from Georgann. Marie was screaming so loud I swear I didn't need the phone to hear her all the way from Florida. When she paused to take a breath, I said, "Put Silvio on, Marie." Silvio got on the line; I told him again what had happened with Yuan ending with, "He won't contact another hospital."

Silvio listened in silence. After a few moments, he said, "Al, there's a doctor from Virginia staying here at the hotel. We had dinner with him and his wife last night. I told him I was worried about my granddaughter, be-cause she needed open heart surgery. I didn't tell him who her doctor was or what hospital. I'll talk to him tonight and get his take on this Yuan situation. Don't do anything until I get back to you."

At ten the next morning, Silvio called us back. He put the doctor on the phone. He introduced himself as Dr. James McCall, a surgeon at the University Of Virginia Medical Center. He asked me some questions about Nicky's diagnosis and treatment. He listened as I answered the best I could. Before hanging up, he said, "Al, I'll make some calls today. We'll talk again tomorrow afternoon."

Silvio got back on the phone. "How's Marie taking this?" I asked.

He laughed, "She's off the deep end. I'm afraid to go for Chinese food." I couldn't help but laugh. Silvio for all his vices could read people. If he gave this doctor some credence then I was willing to listen to him. Georgann and I went to bed that night feeling more hopeful than we had since leaving Yuan's office.

The next afternoon, Silvio called, "Get a paper and pen to write down what Jim tells you." He put the doctor on the phone.

"I called Texas Children's Hospital in Houston, Texas. It's rated as one of the best children's hospitals in the United States and is part of Texas Medical Center. I made an appointment for Nicky with Dr. Denton Cooley in three days time. He's a great surgeon and I know personally. Here's the contact information. They're expecting your call, Al."

Just like that.

As soon as I hung up, I called the hospital. I held the phone between us so Georgann could be in on the conversation. We spoke to Dr. Cooley's assistant, Diane Moore, who already knew who we were and was expecting our call. Georgann and I took turns answering all her questions. Before hanging up, I asked, "Should I call Einstein to get them to send Nicky's medical records to you?"

"That won't be necessary, Mr. Volpe. Einstein wouldn't release them anyway. Besides, Dr. Cooley relies on his own pre-op examination. We will be expecting to see you and Nicky in three days. Please, don't worry; we will take care of everything when you get here."

We didn't know anything about Texas Children's Hospital or Dr. Denton Cooley, but, for some reason, Georgann and I trusted Dr. Jim's advice. Georgann called our travel agent and made reservations to Houston. As she was packing, Georgann asked me, "Should I call Dr. Yuan to tell him what we decided?"

I won't repeat my response, but out of my mouth came my mother-in-law's words.

15

Texas Children's Hospital

The Marinos took the first plane back to Westchester. Three days later, on February 20, 1977, Georgann, Nicky, Marie and I were on the plane to Houston. We went directly to Texas Children's Hospital from the airport to make the final arrangements for Nicky's surgery. Dr. Cooley's assistant, Diane, was ready for us with all the necessary forms when we arrived. After we signed the forms she tried to allay our obvious nervousness. Diane gave us a brief - and simple - explanation of what to expect during Nicky's stay at the hospital.

"Dr. Cooley will conduct a very extensive examination on Nicky. Our diagnostic equipment here is state of the art. Once Dr. Cooley evaluates his findings, he and his team will schedule and perform Nicky's surgery after which she will require a short recovery period. I will be here to answer any and all questions you may have, so don't be afraid to ask."

Georgann and I nodded; we were so overwhelmed by everything happening so quickly we couldn't think of any questions to ask. Marie stood mute by our side. Diane escorted us to the children's ward and introduced the ward nurse before returning to her office.

Nurse Lily Wagner was about thirty-five whose short blond hair was tucked neatly under her cap and her trim figure in a starched white uniform. Her pixie face crinkled with delight as she bent down to greet Nicky. "What a lovely young lady you are Nikol Volpe. I am Nurse Lily." Taking Nicky by the hand she said, "Let's go to the nursery and get you settled in. Your mommy, daddy and nana can come, too."

Marie undressed Nicky and put on her pajamas while Nurse Lily smiled and nodded at her new, little patient. Once Nicky was comfortably settled in her hospital bed, we kissed her good-bye promising to return as soon as we checked into our hotel. Marie let out a sob when she hugged Nicky good-bye. Nurse Lily assured us that she would stay with Nicky until we returned.

Georgann booked us into the Holiday Inn across the road from the hospital. She booked Marie into an adjoining room. Mistake. As soon as we dropped off our luggage, Georgann and I went back to the hospital to stay with Nicky as we promised. Marie said she was exhausted from the plane ride and wanted to take a nap.

When we got there, Nicky and three other children were in the nursery watching Sesame Street. After greeting us with a big smile, she turned back to the television. Georgann sat down on the floor with Nicky; I went into the corridor to give them some mother-daughter time. As I stood outside the room, a doctor came bustling through the door of the stairwell followed by two younger doctors. I didn't know who he was at the time, but I was impressed by his brisk stride, white coat open and billowing behind him as he marched down the corridor. When he passed the elevator, the doors opened and an entourage of white coats exited falling into lock-step behind him and the two other doctors.

Who was this guy? I stopped a nurse passing by me in the corridor and asked. Looking at me like was I stupid or something for even asking she said, "Dr. Denton Cooley."

I already told you readers that I never heard of Dr. Cooley. How was I to know that he was reputed to be one of the world's most renowned cardiac surgeons? Along with his mentor and partner, Dr. Michael DeBakey, Dr. Cooley pioneered many techniques used today in cardiovascular surgery. In 1968, he was the first surgeon in the United States to successfully transplant a human heart. In 1969, he performed the groundbreaking implantation of a totally artificial heart in a man. He and his surgical team had successfully performed thousands of open heart surgeries. Wow!

(Note: Dr. Cooley died in November of 2016).

I went back to the nursery. Sesame Street was over. The other children were climbing back into their beds. Georgann helped Nicky into her bed whispering loving words in her ear as she tucked her in. We were going to wait until she fell asleep when, about ten minutes later, Dr. Cooley and his entourage showed up. He introduced himself to Georgann and me holding out his hand. I was afraid to shake it for fear I would break something! This tall Texan had the easy manner of the former high school basketball player he had been rather than that of a famous surgeon.

After greeting us, Dr. Cooley went over to Nicky. He bent over and tenderly ran a forefinger across her forehead. His dimpled smile was so gentle it took all my restraint not to hug him on the spot. In his slow, Texas drawl, he said, "Hello Nicky. My name is Dr. Cooley." He lightly tapped her chest over her heart. "You have a little problem here that I'm going to fix, Okay?" Nicky smiled and nodded at this larger-than-life saint.

He stood up, the smile never leaving his face and stepped to the foot of Nicky's bed to look at her chart. After a few moments, he replaced the chart before turning to Georgann and me. He shook my hand again and patted Georgann on her shoulder. "Mr. and Mrs. Volpe please don't worry. Your little girl is going to get the best care possible. I've performed dozens of similar operations - all successfully. She'll be playing like any healthy six-year old in no time." With that said, Dr. Cooley strode out of the room to continue on his rounds, his entourage following close behind him.

Georgann and I looked at each other and breathed a sigh of relief. Dr. Cooley instilled the confidence we didn't have with Yuan.

Some background: Texas Children's Hospital is a pediatric hospital founded in 1954 and located in the Houston Medical Center. It provides full-service medical care for children, the training of pediatric medical professionals as well as conducting extensive research. The hospital has multiple, dedicated surgical teams who work with one another - exclusively. For heart surgery, no team member is any less important than the surgeon. If a team member is missing, that team shuts down. The hospital's reputation is so great that children are flown in from around the world for the specialized heart surgery provided there.

At the same time Nicky was at the Center, David Vetter, the Boy in the Bubble, was also there. He was born in 1971 with severe combined immune deficiency syndrome which weakened his ability to ward off disease and infection. Immediately after his birth, he was placed in a specially designed, plastic, germ-free environment at Texas Children's Hospital intended to be his home for most of his life where he played, slept, ate and attended school. After receiving a bone marrow transplant from his sister, he became ill with lymphoma - a cancer later determined to have been introduced into his system by the Epstein-Barr virus. He died fifteen days later on February 22, 1984. Though David lived only twelve years, the study of his condition led to significant contributions in the study of immune system disorders.

Two days after Nikol was admitted into the hospital, she had her surgery. Marie, Georgann and I sat in the waiting room - not talking, barely breathing - until Diane came in with the good news; Nicky was out of surgery and doing fine. In addition to the scheduled surgery, Dr. Cooley was able to repair a tear in Nicky's heart that was never diagnosed at Einstein. I didn't want to imagine what might have happened had we allowed Yuan to perform the operation.

That evening, we met with Dr. Cooley. He explained everything to us. "Nicky is doing fine," he assured us. "Children have amazing healing powers so don't be alarmed if you see her up and playing with the other children in a couple of days."

I grabbed his hand and nearly shook it off, "Thank you, Doctor. Thank you." Georgann was leaning against me showing her gratitude by the tears of relief that ran down her cheeks.

Marie rushed over to him and hugged him tightly, "God bless you, Doctor."

We went to the ICU to see Nicky. The atmosphere in the massive, dimly lit, highly technical room was peaceful. It was like nothing we'd ever seen before in a hospital. Nicky was propped up inside an oxygen tent; vapor mist surrounding her face like an angelic halo. I had a moment of terror when I saw a priest praying by her bedside until Nicky smiled and waved to us. She was fine. It was only Father Tonio giving thanks to God for all the children saved by Him and Dr. Cooley.

We stayed with Nicky until she fell asleep. I gave Georgann the keys to the rental car and told her to take Marie back to the hotel without me; I needed some time to be alone. As I walked the deserted streets of Houston, I realized I had for the first time a glimpse of God's divine intervention for surely it must have been He who sent Silvio's doctor friend in Florida and Dr. Cooley to us.

The second day after her surgery, sure enough, Nicky was riding a big wheel up and down the corridor in the children's recovery ward. The hos-pital staff worked hard to make every child's stay at the hospital as pleasant as possible. The hospital provided a gigantic, highly supervised playroom and even had a clown and magician on staff solely for the children's entertainment.

Nicky was scheduled for discharge in four days. Georgann and I were overjoyed. We hoped we could get Nicky to leave, because she was having so much fun.

Of course, there was always a black cloud without a silver lining hovering over us whenever Marie was involved. As it happened, when Georgann and I were visiting Nicky at the hospital without her, Marie was calling Frankie from her hotel room. She wasn't taking a nap that first day; she used it as an excuse to call Frankie. I was surprised, because she hated him more than she hated me. Whatever her motivations, no doubt they couldn't be for any good – they never were. Instead of being delighted by her granddaughter's surgical success, she viewed it as another means to bring Georgann and me closer together which, in her furtive mind, pushed her further and further out of her daughter's life. To make trouble, she invited Frankie to come to Houston. Stunad that he was, he showed up.

I actually thought it touching that he chose to be with us at this time. Frankie was my partner and, until then, my friend. Georgann and I picked him up at the airport and settled him in at our hotel. Marie gave Frankie a cursory nod of welcome before we all went to visit Nicky after which the four of us went to dinner. The meal was cordial probably because Marie and Frankie only had a few glasses of wine. We returned to the hotel and to our respective rooms. Quiet night.

The next day, we all trooped off to visit Nicky again, but this time, Frankie and Marie didn't stay long. They took the car and went back to the hotel; Georgann and I remained to spend more time with Nicky. After grabbing a quick dinner at the diner, it was after nine when we got to the hotel – giving Marie and Frankie just enough time to get shitfaced.

Because Georgann and I were too tired to deal with their alcoholic nonsense, we said good night and went to our adjoining room. We left the door open a crack between our rooms just in case one of them fell or passed out and hit their drunken head on a night table. Unfortunately, leaving the door open also meant we could hear their inebriated conversation.

For reasons known only to Marie, we heard her tell Frankie in an uncharacteristically saccharine voice, "I know you really love Nicky like one your own daughters. I'm sure you love Georgann more than Al does, don't you, Frankie? He's a rotten husband who chases after bimbos every chance he gets. She'd be better off with someone who really cares for her - someone like you."

"Yeah, you're right, Marie. I been friends with Al a long time, and I know exactly what kind of a bum he is. Georgann deserves better."

"Why don't you divorce Phyllis, Frankie? I can make sure Al doesn't stand in your way." Wink, wink, nudge, nudge.

"Okay, Marie. I'll ask Phyllis for a divorce as soon as I get back home." Like I said, Frankie wasn't the smartest frog in the pond.

All of a sudden out of nowhere, Marie jumped to her feet and spewing saliva screamed, "I knew it! You," pointing her boney finger at Frankie, "want to take my daughter from me, too, just like that bastard in the other room," She gestured her thumb at the adjoining bedroom door. "As soon as I get home, I'm going to have you both killed."

Frankie gagged and grabbed his chest as if he was having a heart attack. He tried to get out of his chair but was too drunk to move. Marie stood over him glaring blurry eyed.

Georgann lay in my arms listening to her mother's terrible words. She began to tremble, and I began to seethe. Marie managed to manipulate Frankie into admitting he loved Georgann before turning on him like a viper. What a piece of work was my mother-in-law!

Finally, I'd heard enough. I threw back the covers, jumped out of bed, pushed open the adjoining door and yelled, "Frankie, get out!"

Frankie too stunned and too drunk, didn't move. I went up to him, grabbed him by his throat with my right hand and lifted him to his feet. I opened the door with my left hand and was about to fling him into the hall when suddenly Marie was on me like a wild animal. I kept my hold on Frankie's throat, let go of the door, and pushed Marie back onto the bed. Still in my grasp, Frankie was reviving and beginning to put up a struggle. Without thinking, I picked up an empty vodka bottle that was on the dresser and broke it over Frankie's head. I let go my grasp on this throat, and he flew out the open door. Staggering and holding his bleeding head, he ran down the hall to his room.

From the bed, Marie pushed herself up on her elbow and seized a second empty vodka bottle. While I was making sure Frankie went into his room, out of the corner of my eye I saw Marie get up from the bed and charge at me brandishing the bottle. Instinctively, I raised my arms up to protect my head.

Georgann, hearing all the screaming, came running in. "Stop it! Stop it!" she yelled grabbing her mother before she could bash the bottle over my head. "Have you lost your mind completely?"

Marie began to blubber, "Georgann, they all want to take you away from me. I won't let them."

"Hush, Mama, no one is going to take me away from you. Lie down; I'll stay with you until you fall asleep."

I didn't say a word. Thoroughly disgusted, I went back to our room. Home or away, the scenario never changed. Marie, as usual, blacked out in Georgann's arms.

As I lay on the bed smoking a cigarette, someone knocked on the door. I thought it was Frankie so I said, "Get lost, scumbag."

A deep voice I didn't recognize answered, "Open up."

Stamping out my cigarette in the already full ash tray, I opened the door a crack to stare up at a big man in a big hat with a big badge in the shape of a star pinned to his shirt and six-shooter on his hip. The badge read Ranger Smyth.

He introduced himself before saying, "There's been a complaint about a ruckus coming from your room."

"We were celebrating our daughter's successful heart surgery with some champagne. I guess we got a little loud. We are so happy our little girl is going to be fine."

"I'm glad to hear it," he said, "but you all will have to keep it down."

"Yes, sir," I answered, "We're all done celebrating now. See?" I stood aside to let him in. The ranger looked around the room. Since it was just me in the room wearing only my pajama bottoms, it was obvious all was quiet now.

Before he left, Georgann came back into the room through the ad-joining door. "My mother is sleeping now." Seeing the ranger, she was startled. "Who are you? Why are you here?"

"Sorry, ma'am, if I alarmed you. My name is Ranger Smyth. I'm following up on a report of a disturbance coming from your rooms. I can see that there's no sign of any commotion now so I'll be on my way." He held out his hand to me, "Congratulations on the successful outcome of your daughter's operation, but in the future, take it easy on the celebrating." He tipped his hat and left.

As soon as I closed and locked the door behind him, I went over and locked the adjoining door to Marie's room. I turned to Georgann.

"I've had enough. Get Frankie and your mother out of here. Make sure they take the first plane back to New York in the morning. My fondest wish is that they kill each other on the flight home."

"Okay, Al. You're right. I just want to spend the rest of our time here with Nicky and you. I don't want to worry about what crazy thing my mother might do next."

The next morning, Marie and Frankie took a cab to the airport without saying good bye to me. I was so offended. Marie, of course, had no recollection of what happened the night before.

Three days later, Nicky was released from the hospital. We said our good-byes to the hospital staff, hugging and thanking everyone. Since the weather in New York was freezing, we decided that a trip to Florida, thanks to the American Express card, would do us all good. We spent a week in Ft. Lauderdale. Nicky's recuperation was amazing. Except for the scar on her chest which would fade with time, no one seeing this active, little six year old would ever have imagined the ordeal she'd gone through just the week before.

I began to believe in miracles.

16

Happy New Life – Yeah, Right

Georgann and I did a lot of talking the week we spent in Florida. Now that the anxiety over Nicky's health was behind us, we could concentrate on getting our marriage back on track - time to begin a new chapter in our lives. First, we decided to get rid of the quasi-built house and property in New Paltz and use the proceeds to buy an affordable house. Second, or maybe first, we needed to make a clean break with the Marinos.

Before putting the property on the open market, we offered it to Georgann's parents. This way they couldn't say we were going behind their backs.

"You got to be kidding, Al," Silvio said. "You must be nuts to dump such a choice piece of real estate!"

"We ain't kidding, Silvio. Nicky's operation cost a lot. We can't afford to put any more money into finishing the house. The money we get from the sale of the property will go to paying down Nicky's medical bills and for buying a smaller house."

"You got to live next door," bellowed Marie, "You need me to help with Nicky!"

"We'll manage," I said staring Marie down. End of conversation.

Silvio realized we weren't going to back down on our decision. "Ok, Al, if that's the way you want it, I'll buy you out and finish the house myself."

Financially, we weren't in great shape. More interested in swinging than selling, I had neglected my sales job with Revlon during the months of separation from Georgann. Worse, I was so preoccupied with Nicky's operation and recovery; I hadn't bothered to notify personnel at Revlon that I was leaving for two weeks to go to Houston and then Ft. Lauderdale. Even a top notch salesman like me couldn't talk myself out of this evident dereliction of responsibility - I was canned.

I began my search for a new position in retail sales as soon as we returned from Florida. I was running myself ragged going on interviews and managing Nikol's Tot Boutique. I was still in partnership with Frankie in the stores in The Bronx and Katonah although I avoided any further social contact with him.

It was evident that the clothing store in Katonah had the wrong merchandise from the outset and that Frankie was no entrepreneur. Shortly after returning from Houston, we were forced to close it.

After a particularly disappointing job interview, I came home that night more discouraged than ever. "Georgann," I said, slumping on the bed in our room, "I don't think I'm cut out for this suit and tie life. I'm more of a Hawaiian shirt kind of guy. Besides, I don't want to end up like those sorry men I meet at scalp hunters; beaten down by the system by the time I'm forty. Remember Bob from Reynolds dragging his family all around the country just to keep his job?"

"I remember, Al. You're a good salesman and you have a good head for business. I know the Katonah store didn't work out, but maybe it was the partner you had. Frankie isn't exactly the Mr. Cassini of the Westchester fashion world. Since you hit him in the head with the liquor bottle in Houston, according to my mother, he's been holding a grudge against you. Not the best situation for a partnership."

"You think?" I said choking back a laugh.

In the weeks that followed, Georgann continued to encourage me to take a chance and go out on my own. After much soul searching and with no prospects for a sales job, I agreed with her. I hung up my business suits and reopened the Katonah store as sole proprietor - new name, new image, and new merchandise - no Frankie.

We used the money we got from selling our share of the Westchester property to Silvio to pay down Nicky's medical bills and to buy a small, three-bedroom, raised ranch on a quarter acre lot in Purdys, New York. Purdys is a hamlet of Croton Falls located about fifty miles north of New York City and only ten minutes to the revamped Katonah store.

By July of 1977, we had our new beginning – a new house, a healthy daughter, and a new business. We also had a mortgage, medical and credit card bills, no health insurance, and an outstanding bank note for $10,000 from the original Katonah store. This destiny decision to reopen the store in Katonah was a blend of circumstance, business acumen, common sense, op-timism, balls, and dumb luck.

I began to put my plan for the new store into action. I negotiated a lower rent from the landlord. I told Frankie that I'd pay the monthly installments on the loan note as long as the store stayed open. If the store closed, he'd be responsible for his remaining half of the note. I felt this was fair to Frankie because most of the loan money had been used to fit-out the original store. Behind my back, everyone called me an asshole for letting Frankie off the hook for his half of the loan. Neither of us had five grand to pay off the note, and, as long as I made a profit from the store, I could swing the payments by myself.

I was sure I could make the store work with the right merchandise. I borrowed $8,000 from my parents and restocked the store with new goods I felt would appeal to the Katonah customers. I combed the discount wholesalers on the lower East Side of New York City, checked out every going-out-of business ad from Westchester to Hackensack, New Jersey and followed up on resales to buy the right merchandise at the right price - always cash and carry. I'd leave early in the morning and not return home until I had loaded up my car with goods leaving only enough room for me to see through the windshield. I renamed the store 'Express Yourself.'

We held a grand opening on October 26, 1977. It received a lot of free press in the local newspapers because of the store's unique, eclectic blend of merchandise. In a matter of months, the store caught on with the local residents. I hired two sales women to free up my time so I could acquire accounts for the separate, wholesale silk-screening business I created that specialized in t-shirts for schools, local sports teams, churches and clubs.

Express Yourself was a big success. The t-shirts were almost pure profit costing a buck fifty to make and selling for fifteen a pop. I paid off the bank loan and my parents within a year. The story changed from me being an asshole for letting Frankie off the hook, to me being an asshole for screwing Frankie out of his share of the business.

I knew that the glory days of retail were over in The Bronx where hold-ups were as common as horse flies in the neighborhood where the stores were located. As soon as the Katonah store began to realize a consistent profit, I closed Nikol's Tot Boutique and gave Frankie full ownership of The Bronx store thereby severing all my connections in The Bronx and with him.

It wasn't long before our new beginning was overshadowed by an old reality. Phyllis and Frankie sold their expensive, Bedford home and bought a smaller house on the same street as ours in Purdys. Georgann, Phyllis and our kids remained best of friends, but, since Houston and the dissolution of our partnership, I distanced myself from Frankie. True to his word, Silvio completed both houses in New Paltz and sold what would have been our house to Donna and Dennis. We were one big, dysfunctional family again; only the zip codes had changed.

The years had not mellowed Marie, but they had Silvio. He still had a full head of wavy hair but now it was all white; his face was still unlined but sans mustache. The paunch he had developed was hidden by tailor made suits, but his obsession to become a made-man overshadowed everything else in his life. To everyone's horror, he stopped making any attempt to control Marie's conduct. She was so confrontational that even family and friends avoided her. Ever the dutiful daughter, Georgann was the only one who tried to include her mother in some of her own social life, but, one by one, Georgann's friends begged off if they knew Marie would be tagging along.

Donna's life emulated her mother's. Both she and Marie had huge, museum homes, but neither had any friends. Even Grandma Vingo, Marie's mother, wouldn't stay with her own daughter. She'd stay with us in our little house during her visits from The Bronx.

New Paltz was the town over from Purdys. Given she had nothing else going on in her life; Marie was again a daily fixture in our household. The years had turned her slim figure into the warm, matronly appeal of an Italian grandmother. But, don't let looks fool you. She was both relentless and insidious in plying her wits to usurp our parental authority with Nicky. She nurtured Nicky with the mantras of hatred toward me and disrespect for Georgann.

I imagined the lullaby Marie sang to Nicky when she put her to bed at night. "You don't have to listen to your father, Nicky. He left you when you were sick. Grandma took care of you and your mother. Grandma loves you more than mommy and daddy. Good night, my sweet little princess."

Here's a life lesson I learned from a quote I read somewhere. 'There's nothing so absurd that if you repeat it often enough, people will believe it.' A child's mind is like a savings account; each deposit gets paid back with interest over time. By the time Nicky was nine; her account was earning double digit interest.

Nicky quickly learned to do an end-run to Marie if we didn't give her what she wanted. She would dash to the phone, "I'm calling Grandma. She'll get it for me! She loves me better than you!"

By now you must be asking yourselves, "Why did Al and Georgann allow Marie to create such a wedge between them and their daughter?" 'Easy' is the operative word here. I had the easy excuse of trying to earn enough money to take care of my family even if it meant coming home late at night and working weekends.

I turned over all the responsibility for raising Nicky to Georgann who found it easy to turn over some of that responsibility to her mother. By nine, Nicky was becoming a willful, uncontrollable brat – but not with Nana. After all, who loves you, my little princess?

Easy peasy.

17

Bye-Bye Frankie

By 1979 and two years after moving to Purdys, we were finally on the road to solvency. Nicky's medical bills were all paid; and my businesses were doing great. Georgann worked part-time as an administrative assistant with Fashionetics, a company located in Armonk that sold sewing accessories. It provided us with a welcome group health insurance policy. Being a stay at home mom wasn't enough for Georgann. She liked dressing up, socializing, and having her own money. To her credit, she never let her job interfere with her care of Nicky. She was home each day to meet Nicky's school bus. And, there was always Marie in case she needed back-up

After we parted business ways, Frankie became a partner in a couple of clothing stores in New Rochelle with Sally O, one of Silvio's Mafia buddies. Sally O was savvy enough to know that Frankie was an airhead and only required him to show up at the stores a couple of hours a day and pretend to be the boss. After that, Frankie's time was his own. Not having much of a life, he would stop by my house to smoke pot and bullshit with Georgann before his daughters and Nicky got off the school bus. I was not a jealous man, not Big Al, and certainly not of Frankie, but I didn't like that he was bringing an illegal substance into the house even if it was only weed. I really became suspicious when Georgann knew things about me that only Frankie and I were suppose to know. Frankie had no control over his mouth when he was high.

I confronted her. "Georgann, how did you know I lost a couple hundred bucks at the racetrack last May? Did Frankie tell you?"

"Of course not, Al. Why would he? You were talking in your sleep the other night. 'Georgann,' you said, 'I put two bills on Scheherazade's nose and the nag didn't even show. I lied when I said I had to buy a couple of tires with the money.' That's okay, Al," she said patting me on the head, "I forgive you."

She was so good she almost had me convinced that I talked in my sleep.... almost. That night, pretending to be asleep, I tossed out a few beans on Frankie.

"Frankie," I mumbled, "You better watch your back around Sally O. He's gonna find out how about those gowns."

Georgann opened one eye and moved in closer to me. She whispered in my ear, "What gowns?"

"The designer knock-offs you told Sally were the real deal. You even showed Sally a bogus receipt. You kept the difference, remember? When Sally finds out, Frankie, you're gonna be in deep shit." Georgann gasped.

I couldn't keep it up and burst out laughing. "Are you still going to tell me I talk in my sleep?" Georgann recovered her shock and hit me in the head with a pillow. I threw my pillow at her resulting in a hilarious pillow fight.

Once we caught our breaths and settled back in bed, she said, "Of course, it was Frankie who told me the stuff about you. When he gets a little high, he babbles away."

"Joking aside, Georgann, tell Frankie to smoke pot in his own house. I don't want him coming here anymore especially if Nicky's home. Either you tell him or I will - my way."

Georgann knew that when I was serious; there was no reasoning with me. "Sure, Al. I'll tell him the next time he shows up."

"And make sure that's the last time he comes around when I'm not here." To show I meant what I said, I turned my back to her and went back to sleep. No kiss and make up.

The very next day, Frankie came to our house. Georgann wouldn't let him in. "Frankie, don't come around anymore. Al doesn't like it."

"Why not? We ain't doing anything wrong - just talking."

"I know that and you know that, but I don't want Al to get any other ideas in his head. Save us both some grief, Frankie, stay away."

Thinking himself slick, Frankie started showing up at Georgann's job. He would wait for her in the parking lot when she got off from work. After a couple of weeks, Georgann confronted him again. "Frankie, stop coming to my job. If you don't, I'm going to tell Phyllis that you're bothering me at work."

Frankie was more afraid of his wife than he was of me. "Okay, okay, Georgann. I'll stop, just don't tell Phyllis."

That promise lasted only a week before Georgann again found Frankie waiting for her in the parking lot. Georgann didn't know how to get rid of him. Her only alternative was to give Frankie up.

"Al, remember when you said I had to tell Frankie not to come to the house anymore?"

"Yeah, what of it? Did you?"

"Of course I did. He doesn't come to the house anymore, but he's been showing up at my job. I threatened to tell Phyllis, but the threat only works for a few days."

"Didn't you tell him I would beat the crap out of him if he didn't lay off?"

"I didn't. I thought it would be better to use Phyllis as a threat. Al, I'm afraid of him. He's almost as crazy as my mother." She wasn't really afraid of

Frankie, no one was, but Georgann knew what to say to me to get off the hook.

"Ok, Georgann, I'll take care of Frankie."

"Please don't hurt him, Al. He's just a harmless jerk."

"I won't touch him, Georgann." I had my fingers crossed behind my back.

The following morning, I called a friend of mine who owned the gas station across the road from Georgann's office park. "If you see Frankie's red Corvette around, call me."

I was at the Katonah store that Friday when, at noon, my friend called. "Frankie's 'vette is parked in the lot." That's all he needed to say.

Fortunately, Georgann had taken that day off from work to go to a doctor's appointment. I made a plan. I told Margie, my store manager. "Turn out the lights. Put the closed sign on the door. You're coming with me to Armonk to look for Frankie. I might need a witness."

"For what?" asked Margie.

As we walked to my car, I told her, "Son of a bitch, Margie, Frankie's looking for trouble. He won't stay away from my wife even though she told him to get lost."

Margie sputtered, "I always said Frankie was an asshole. He never knows when to quit." We jumped into my car and sped to Armonk.

Margie was married to Phyllis' brother. She was a good employee who never questioned my reasons for doing anything whether personal or work related. At forty-five; her five foot four body was a little scrawny, but she had big, doe eyes and curly, auburn hair surrounding her narrow face giving it a softer look. And, she was funny as hell - although she didn't think so. She had a medical condition that presented itself whenever she got nervous - her body would begin to twitch and she would start talking like Porky Pig. It wasn't funny; it was hilarious. She also had a truck-driver's mouth over which she had even less control when her nerves kicked in. Frankie was her brother-in-law, but she didn't hold him in any high regard. She knew there was bad blood between us after the Houston incident.

When I got to the gas station, my friend told me Frankie pulled out of the Fashionetics parking lot about ten minutes before. I drove around town looking for him, but, no Frankie. Margie was starting to twitch. I needed to calm her down.

"Margie, as long as we're here, let's get some lunch at Par's Steakhouse. (Closed in 1992) Let's see if the salad bar and burgers are as good as I heard."

I parked my car in the restaurant's parking lot, and we got out. I held the restaurant door open for Margie, and we strolled in. Par's catered to a big lunch crowd and, because it was Friday, the place was jammed. The maitre d' seated us at a table a couple of rows over from the salad bar. We ordered burgers and cokes, and Margie calmed down as we ate. We chatted about the store and tossed about some ideas how to increase business. We didn't mention Frankie.

After finishing our lunch, I was looking around for the waitress to bring me the check when I spotted Frankie standing in the entrance scoping out the dining room behind his Raybans. Margie had her back to the entrance and didn't see him come in. I picked up the discarded menu to hide my face. Peering over it, I waited until he got in front of the salad bar.

"What are you doing, Al? I thought we were leaving. Do you want dessert?"

"Hush, Margie. Frankie just came in. Pretend you don't see him."

With a wide, stupid grin plastered on my face, I put down the menu, got up and headed toward Frankie. He was too stunned at seeing me to move. Measuring him up for sucker punch range, I hauled back with my right and whacked him into the salad bar. His left hand sank wrist deep into the bleu cheese dressing, his head into the lettuce bowl. I pulled him up and got a good headlock on him. We tumbled around the dining room knocking over tables and chairs, spilling food and tableware onto the floor and onto patrons; pretty much turning the room into a shambles. Diners jumped up from their chairs trying to get out of our way brushing food and drinks from their laps.

A well-dressed, young man sporting gold-rimmed glasses came running in from the bar and tried to break us up. He ran right into my fist and went down get-ting trampled in the pushing and shoving melee. I let Frankie loose, and he fell, face down into the salad bar mess on the floor. He didn't get up. I looked for Margie.

I found her leaning against the wall shaking from head to toe. I grabbed her arm, "Let's head toward the door. This place is getting too dangerous." I saw Frankie get up and duck into the kitchen.

Margie and I were walking toward the entrance when the police arrived. They spilled into the restaurant wielding billy clubs. They ran past us into the dining room. Once they regained order, the cops looked around at the mess that was once a high class restaurant. Tables and chairs were over turned, glass, dishes and food were scattered everywhere; men were holding crying women.

The cops pulled aside the grill chef who was standing in the middle of the room, gaping at the mess in stunned silence, "What the hell happened here?"

He looked around, caught sight of me, pointed and said, "He started it."

All eyes turned to stare at Margie and me. Two of the biggest cops, billy clubs slapping their palms, came over to us. The bigger of the two said to me, "Okay, buddy, let's go outside."

All sweetness and light, I said, "Of course, officer." I took Margie's hand, and we were escorted out the door into the parking lot by one cop on each side of us. Cop cars had the entire entrance to the parking lot blocked off.

The big cop asked me, "Let's see some identification."

"It's in my car, officer," I answered. We walked across the parking lot to my car. I practically had to carry Margie, because she was shaking so violently.

The cop opened the passenger side door of my car, "Ma'am, you sit in the car while I talk to your friend here," he told her.

"He's n..n...n...not m…m…m…my f...f...f…fuckin' fr.. fr…fr…friend," she said, "He's m…m…m…my f…f….f…fuckin' b…b…b…b…boss."

I took my wallet out of the glove box and handed it to the cop.

"Please remove your license and hand it to me," he said ignoring the hundred dollar bill I kept folded in the wallet opposite my license. I handed him my license, and also, because it couldn't hurt, my membership card for the Katonah Chamber of Commerce Department as well as my military service card.

"Mr. Volpe, can you explain to me what happened here?"

"I have to give you some background first. You see that guy standing over there with Mr. Par?" I said pointing to the front of the restaurant.

Frankie had obviously latched onto Par for protection. "His name is Frankie. We used to be business partners. He's a little bitter about the breakup of our partnership, but I can handle that. He used to come to my house when I wasn't home to see my wife. I put a stop to that. When he started showing up at Fashionetics where my wife works, I got more concerned. Even though she told him to leave her alone, he kept going back like he was stalking her. She told me she was frightened of him. I took my manager out to lunch today, because it's her birthday. That's her, Margie, in the car. I was just about to ask for my bill when I saw Frankie come into the dining room. I went over to him to ask very politely to please stay away from my wife. He told me to go fuck myself and raised his fist to hit me. I ducked the punch and he sailed past me into the salad bar. I tried to walk away, but he came at me like a raving lunatic. He was throwing wild punches at me and jumped onto my back. I couldn't get him off! We slammed into this poor guy who was just trying to help. I guess we smashed into one or two tables, too. I was just defending myself, officer. It all happened so fast, I really don't remember much. I'll take responsibility for the damage. I just want him to leave me and my wife alone."

The officer was staring at me seeming to deliberate the veracity of my statement. I tried to look as innocent as I could smiling meekly up at him. With sirens blaring, an ambulance showed up and made its way through the crowd of by-standers who had come out of the A&P next door to gawk. Most of the lunch crowd at Par's had run to their cars and disappeared. The ambulance parked in front of Par's; two EMTs got out carrying a stretcher and ran into the restaurant. They came out a few minutes later carrying the young man with the gold rimmed glasses. They put him into the ambulance and sped off toward the hospital.

Margie asked for water to take some tranquilizers she had in her purse.

"I'll get it," said the other cop. "I want to see if anyone in the restaurant wants to make a statement."

The big cop stayed with me. "Do you want to press charges?"

I shook my head.

With a glass of water in his hand, the officer came out of the restaurant, but instead of going to Margie, he saw Frankie rushing across thé parking lot at me. I stiffened readying for more trouble. The cop stopped him before he got to me.

“He attacked me,” said Frankie pointing at me as he neared.

“Keep him away from me, officer. He’s lying. I did not attack him. He's a madman."

The big cop stood between me and Frankie. "Stand back, sir," he said to Frankie. Frankie stopped short, glaring over the cop’s shoulder at me. I glared back.

The cop handed Margie the water. He reported, "No one was seriously hurt. The fellow in the ambulance got trampled, but it looks like he is only shaken up. The owner of the restaurant is assessing the damage now. You come with me, buddy," he said, leading Frankie to the other side of the parking lot holding his right arm in a firm grip.

We waited. The big cop checked in on Margie. She'd taken so many pills; she was stuttering and talking to herself like Porky Pig after he'd had a few margaritas. “F…f…fuckin’ b…b…bullshit. Th…th…th…they’re b…b…both sick b…b…bastards. Lock them up and th….th…th…throw away the k…k…k…keys.”

She was a scream. The cop tried hard not to laugh. “She’s a pisser,” I said. He rolled his eyes.

Mr. Par came over to me. He held out a piece of paper on which he had itemized the damages to his restaurant I said I would pay for. "Here you are, sir," he said handing me the list. "It comes to $385."

I didn’t question his figures. “Does this include our lunch bill?”

"No," he said adding another $19.00 to the sum. "Thank you for telling me."

I pulled out a wad of bills from my pants pocket and counted out $425. “Give our waitress a nice tip. I’m very sorry for disrupting your place of business.”

First he looked down at the money and then at me, “Nothing personal, sir, but please don’t ever come into my restaurant again.”

I smiled, “I understand.” The big cop covered his mouth with his hand to keep from laughing out loud and walked back to his patrol car.

Frankie was still arguing with the cops on the other side of the parking lot. They spread eagled him against the patrol car and did a body search. When they were done, the cops allowed him to straighten up. I watched him walk back to his 'vette, get in and take off. I guess he didn't have any pot on him. Too bad.

The officer who had searched Frankie came over to me, "Your friend has a real wise mouth. Since no charges have been pressed, you're free to go."

I shook his hand thanking him for his courtesy. Holding onto my hand, he winked, "If I see him around town, I'll find a reason to lock him up." He looked inside my car to wish Margie a happy birthday, but she had passed out in the front seat because of all the tranquilizers she had taken. I drove her home to Yorktown and helped her into her house before heading back to reopen the store. I couldn't help laughing aloud each time I thought about the scene at the restaurant. My customers must have thought I was crazy.

Over dinner that evening, Georgann announced she was pregnant. She hadn't said anything to me before then, because she wanted to be sure. Her due date was in June.

All I could say was, "Oh, wow!" I couldn't rustle up the same enthusiasm she felt. Life was pretty good now

Nicky had spent that afternoon at Frankie's playing with his daughters. At dinner, she told us, "Uncle Frankie went right to bed as soon as he got home. Aunt Phyllis had to keep bringing him ice packs for his head."

I almost choked on my dinner. It was obvious that neither Georgann nor Phyllis knew anything about what had happened at Par's or Georgann would have mentioned it to me right away. If Frankie didn't say anything, neither would I. I figured the ice was for the sucker punch that landed him into the salad bar. That punch cost me a $425, but it was well worth it.

On Monday, Georgann went to work. When I came home that night, she said, "Al, I was talking to a young man who works with me. His face is all bruised, and he had duct tape holding his glasses together. I asked him what happened."

"He said, 'I tried to break up a fight at Par's on Friday and wound up in the hospital. This guy in dark glasses came into the restaurant. This other guy who was sitting at a table with a woman got up, went up to dark glasses and punched him into the salad bar.' What do you think that was all about, Al?"

Georgann usually went to Par's for lunch on Friday's with the women from her office, but she hadn't that Friday because of appointment she had with the doctor.

"I'm so disappointed I missed all the fun."

"Gee, I'm really surprised. Armonk is such a quiet town," I said.

I kept a straight face and went back to eating my salad, afraid to look at Georgann for fear of laughing.

Margie didn't come back to work until Wednesday. It was then that Georgann learned the truth. She happened to call the store looking for me, and Margie answered the phone. She told Georgann everything she could remember about the fight. When I got home that evening Georgann confronted me.

"I'm really disappointed in you fighting with Frankie in public, but I'd be even more embarrassed if anyone in my office found out it was you, my husband, who started a riot at Par's."

I laughed, "I'm sorry your friend at work got hurt, but Frankie deserved what he got. I don't think he'll bother you again. You should have seen Margie. She was a pisser!" Georgann gave me 'the look' before we broke into mutual laughter.

Frankie and Phyllis sold their house in Purdys and moved to Florida before Georgann was scheduled to give birth.

Good riddance.

18

Pregnancy Two

(Note: Although the following narrative is true, the names of Georgann's obstetricians have been changed.)

I was getting excited about having a new baby. The businesses were doing great, Frankie was gone, and Marie was behaving herself. At thirty-six, Georgann wore her five month baby bump like a badge of honor. Because of her age, her obstetrician, Dr. Albert Kirsch, scheduled Georgann for amniocentesis. Given what we went through with Nicky, we nervously awaited the two weeks it took to get the results back from the test. You can imagine the joy we felt when we were given the good news - our baby girl was fine.

Georgann was her usual, vibrant, healthy self the next two months enjoying a normal pregnancy – that is until, early in her seventh month, she noticed a slight vaginal discharge. She waited several days before telling me about it. Although my ignorance of pregnancies was on par with that of child rearing, I was more concerned than she. "Call Dr. Kirsch, Georgann, and make an appointment."

"My seventh month check-up is next week. I'll tell the doctor then. The discharge isn't much. It will probably have stopped by then." The only thing Georgann hated more than doctors was dentists.

"Okay," I said, "Gotta run. See you tonight." Because Georgann didn't seem concerned, I didn't give it another thought. To my great relief, Georgann didn't bring it up again. I never went with Georgann to her doctor's appointments because that was women's business. I didn't feel too guilty; she always had her mother for companionship.

On the day of her appointment, Georgann still had the discharge. Dr. Kirsch was delivering a baby that day. Although Georgann preferred seeing her regular doctor, rather than make another appointment, she chose to be seen by his associate, Dr. Bryce Brandman.

That night, Georgann told me everything that happened at the appointment with Brandman. After a cursory examination, he told Georgann, 'Mrs. Volpe, let me assure you that the discharge is nothing to worry about. The baby is fine, if somewhat smaller than average. You probably have a urinary tract infection which is a common occurrence during pregnancy. I'll give you a prescription for an antibiotic.' He filled out the prescription and handed it to Georgann with the admonition, 'Make sure you take the prescription for the full ten days. You can continue working, but don't go jogging.' He laughed at his little joke. What a prankster.

Georgann faithfully took the antibiotic for the full ten days, but the discharge did not let up. If anything, it had gotten heavier. I told her to call the doctor's office. I listened in.

"This is Mrs. Volpe," she told the receptionist, "I'd like to speak to Dr. Kirsch."

"I'm sorry, Mrs. Volpe, but Dr. Kirsch is not in today. I can put you through to Dr. Brandman."

When Dr. Brandman got on the phone, Georgann blurted out, "Dr. Brandman, the pills you gave me didn't do any good. The discharge is worse than ever!"

It took a few moments for him to realize who what Georgann was ranting about. Finally, he answered, "Calm down, Mrs. Volpe. I can assure you there's nothing to worry about. The first antibiotic was probably not strong enough to eliminate the infection. I'll call your pharmacy and have them prepare a prescription for a stronger antibiotic. Take the pills for another ten days to give the medication time to take effect." He rang off before Georgann had a chance to say anything more than thank you.

Six more days went by; the second antibiotic was not having any affect whatsoever. By this time, Georgann was almost in her eighth month. Because the discharge was so heavy, she had to wear two sanitary napkins and change them constantly, and she had to stop going to work. Georgann was beginning to panic. She called the doctor's office and demanded to speak to Dr. Kirsch, not Brandman. Again, Kirsch wasn't in, but the re-ceptionist promised to give the doctor the message as soon as she could reach him.

An hour went by before Kirsch returned Georgann's call. He said, "Keep taking the antibiotics Dr. Brandman prescribed and don't worry, I'm certain there's no problem. I am going on vacation for a week, but I'll be back in plenty of time for your delivery. When I return, I will give you a thorough examination." He hung up. That was Monday.

Don't worry. Don't worry. That litany was getting really old.

Here's the truth. Brandman should have admitted Georgann into the hospital on that first appointment. She had been leaking amniotic fluid because the amniocentesis procedure had ruptured the amniotic sac. As the baby grew in her womb, the sac expanded causing the rupture to tear further which in turn leaked more fluid with each expansion. Brandman had dis-missed the problem as a mere urinary tract infection. What he didn't do but should have done was examine Georgann, take a sample of the fluid, have it tested, and make the correct diagnosis.

Georgann stayed close to home the week Kirsch was on vacation. She was dizzy and nauseated most of the time and had to sleep with a towel between her legs to absorb the constant discharge. Because we didn't want to frighten Nicky, we sent her to stay with Marie. The pills did nothing. I kept trying to get her to go to the hospital, but Georgann would not. She insisted on waiting for Dr. Kirsch; he was her doctor, she trusted him.

By early Friday evening, Georgann looked ashen and was so weak she couldn't even go to the bathroom without me helping her. She lay in bed with the bath towel between her legs trying to sleep. I sat in the chair next to the bed in case she needed me. I must have dozed off, because I awoke with a start when Georgann poked me. It was early in the morning.

"Al, my lower back is killing me. I can't find any comfortable position. Maybe I just need to go to the bathroom. Can you help me up?"

"Sure, but as soon as I get you back in bed, we're calling Kirsch's office. Enough is enough." I helped Georgann into the bathroom and then back into bed. This time, I called the doctor's office. The answering service picked up. "Yes," the operator told us, "Dr. Kirsch is back from vacation. Can I take a message?"

"Have him call Georgann Volpe right away. It's an emergency," I gave the operator our phone number trying to keep the anxiety I was feeling out of my voice. Before hanging up, I repeated, "Tell him it's an emergency."

An hour later, he returned our call.

I put Georgann on the phone. "Dr. Kirsch, I feel so weak I can't stand up without Al's help. I have terrible pains in my back, and they're getting worse. I haven't been able to leave the house for over four days, because the discharge is so heavy I need to use a bath towel to soak it up. Please, Doctor, what should I do?"

I was listening in on the extension and could hear laughter and loud talk in the background. He must have been at his tennis club.

"Georgann, take it easy." The next words were muffled as if he had his hand over the phone. "Sorry," he said, "Someone was talking to me. I'm going to call in a prescription for a different antibiotic. Tell your husband to go over to the pharmacy to pick it up right away. Start the pills. I'll see you in my office tomorrow morning."

Can you believe this, another prescription? Obviously, he hadn't paid any attention to what Georgann had said, but I rushed to the pharmacy anyway to pick up the new prescription. When I returned, I helped Georgann out of bed to wash up, change her undergarments and replace the soaked towel before getting her back into bed. As I was putting the towel in the hamper, I noticed that it was soaked with a clear, pinkish fluid.

I gave her the new antibiotic. "Try to sleep, sweetheart. Don't worry about Nicky. Marie is taking good care of her."

I worked around the house the rest of the day checking in on Georgann every thirty minutes. By early afternoon, I was getting even more concerned. Her color was worse, and she was so weak she could barely put her legs over the side of the bed. Georgann was not a whiner. If she complained about the pain in her back, I knew it was serious. Still, she refused to let me take her to the emergency room insisting she would wait to see Dr. Kirsch in the morning.

Around five o'clock, Georgann looked so bad I really began to panic. I called our neighbor, Rose Carlin, and asked her to come over to check on Georgann. Rose was a nurse at Westchester Hospital, and I valued her opinion.

I threw open the door as soon as I saw Rose on the front step. "I'm so glad you're here, Rose. I'm really worried about Georgann." I dragged her into the house and to the bedroom.

Rose took one look at Georgann and threw me out of the room. "Get out. I need to examine Georgann. You'll only be in my way."

I sat in the living room holding my head in my hands. Ten minutes later, Rose came out of the bedroom. She grabbed my arm and said, "Al, Georgann is in active labor. Call the doctor immediately!"

With shaking hands, I made the call, got his answering service and, again, left an urgent message. We waited. Rose sat by Georgann, holding her hand. I went outside to chain smoke. Twenty minutes later, Dr. Kirsch called. I handed Georgann the phone. In a whisper, she told him the pains in her back pain were worse and she couldn't walk. When he spoke, it was as if she hadn't said anything at all.

In his best bedside manner, he said, "The new antibiotic needs time to take effect, Georgann. You'll be fine. I'll examine you first thing in the morning. In the meantime, get a good night's sleep." He was about to hang up when Rose grabbed the phone.

"Dr. Kirsch, my name is Rose Carlin. I have worked as a registered nurse at Westchester Hospital in the obstetrics ward for over twenty years. My opinion is that Georgann is in active labor. She cannot wait until the morning to see you. I demand you see her now."

Kirsch was struck silent by Rose's aggression. Nurses are not supposed to talk to doctors like that. Putting aside his opinion of himself, he agreed to meet us at his Yorktown office in half an hour. Rose and I got Georgann up and into her robe and slippers. She was so weak; I had to carry her to the car. When we arrived at the office, Kirsch was just pulling into the parking lot. As he got his Lexus, I saw he was in dress clothes obviously on his way to some formal affair. He didn't bother to hide his annoyance; we were evidently interfering with in his social life. He opened the office; Rose and I helped Georgann into the waiting room.

I'd never met either of Georgann's doctors. Marie always went with her for her prenatal checkups. Kirsch grabbed my hand and shook it vigorously, "Al, I feel like we're old friends. I've heard so much about you from mutual acquaintances."

I returned his shake but said nothing; I just looked him in the eye. I didn't realize we had 'mutual acquaintances'. Kirsch was in his late fifties, 5'11", with a wide forehead because of a receding hairline but without a strand of gray in his dark brown hair and eyebrows - which I imagined, came mostly from a bottle. Although barrel-chested, he kept his body trim obviously from all the tennis and racket ball he played with our 'mutual acquaintances.

Letting go of my hand, he turned his attention to Georgann. He spoke to her as if she were a child who had just scraped a knee. "I'm sure there's nothing to worry about. The exam will only take a few minutes. Rose, please assist me by prepping Mrs. Volpe for examination. Let me know when she is ready." He sounded so confident and self assured that I began to doubt Rose's insistence that Georgann was in active labor. He chatted with me a few minutes more about what I have no recollection. He excused himself and went into the exam room.

After he left, I remembered that Kirsch hadn't seen Georgann in over two months. He had accepted Brandman's diagnosis of an UTI without question. He probably assumed we were overreacting. I admit that I didn't know anything about medical stuff or pregnancy, but I did know that that Georgann was neither faking nor overreacting.

I went outside to smoke hoping it would calm me down. For some reason, Dr. Kirsch asked Rose to leave the exam room and to wait in the outer office until he completed his examination of Georgann. Rose called me back in to sit with her and wait - in silence - for Kirsch to finish. Suddenly, the exam room door flew open; the doctor staggered out in obvious panic. His hands were trembling. He was mumbling to himself, "Active labor; baby double breach."

His composure was gone; he stumbled back to his office without bothering to close the door so disoriented; he hadn't noticed Rose and me sitting in the waiting room. Rose went into the exam room to help Georgann dress; I followed Kirsch into his office. I watched him fumble through the files on his desk. His hands shook so violently that papers fluttered out of a file and onto the floor. He located a file which I assumed was Georgann's, because he picked up the phone and pressed a speed dial key.

He said, "Bryce, I've got Georgann Volpe in the office, you know, the pregnant woman you were treating for a UTI. She's in active labor, and the baby is breach."

He used some medical terminology I didn't understand to describe her condition. The gist was he was telling this Bryce guy, 'You fucked up, buddy -

big time.' It took me a second to realize he was talking to Brandman. He still hadn't noticed me standing there.

I backed out of the office. Kirsch was holding the phone in front of him, staring at it - stupefied. Brandman had hung up.

I went over to Rose, "Come on Rose, help me get Georgann into Kirsch's office. The shit is about to hit the fan." Rose looked at me with a bewildered look on her face, but she did as I asked.

Kirsch placed the dead phone back in its cradle and was bending to pick up the files scattered on the floor when we entered his office. He looked up, startled to see the three of us staring down at him. Rose and I, holding Georgann gently by each arm, guided her into a seat in front of Kirsch's desk; Rose took the chair next to her. I stood by Georgann's side, my hand resting lightly on her shoulder. Kirsch finished retrieving the files, sat back up in his chair and slowly placed them neatly on his desk. He straightened his shoulders and folded his hands in front of him on his desk in an attempt to compose himself. Speaking directly to me and avoiding eye contact with Georgann or Rose, he began to rattle off some more medical jargon.

"Whoa," I said, "Take a step back. Talk English."

Kirsch said, "Of course, Mr. Volpe. Mrs. Carlin was right. Georgann is indeed in active labor. The baby is a month early and very small. The facilities at Northern Westchester Hospital are not equipped to deliver such a small, premature baby. Al, we can't do anything for her here. You have to get Georgann to New York-Presbyterian Hospital in Manhattan right away." His manner did not indicate that Georgann's condition necessitated an emergency even if he insisted we leave immediately.

Georgann started to cry. Rose put her arm around her and, talking softly in her ear, helped her back to the waiting room leaving me to deal with Kirsch. I continued to stare at him, my eyes turning to slits as the gravity of his words began to sink in.

Kirsch repeated more urgently, "Mr. Volpe, you must get Georgann to New York-Presbyterian Hospital immediately. You're wasting valuable time. Jump in your car and get going. I'll call the hospital to alert them that you are on your way." Translated - get her the hell out of my office.

My senses were short-circuiting. It began to register with me that Kirsch wanted me to take Georgann to New York-Presbyterian Hospital, not because she would get better care there, but because he believed that Georgann and the baby might not survive. Solution: transfer them some-where else, protect his practice; cover his ass - problem solved.

I couldn't talk; I couldn't move; I stood unblinking, mouth open as I watched him begin to write down directions to New York-Presbyterian Hospital. Once he was done writing, he pushed all the papers back into Georgann's file, placed it neatly in the center of his desk, and relaxed back in his chair, a smug look on his face. As far as he was concerned it was New York-Presbyterian Hospital's problem now. Case closed.

My adrenaline kicked in. I went around his desk and lunged for him. I pulled him up out of his chair by the front of his shirt and planted his ass hard onto the desk. With both hands, I held onto his shoulders shaking him like a maraca. I screamed; spit flying onto his face, "Fuck your directions! You're the one who is going to help Georgann. You're her doctor! She trusts you! You take care of her, not some goddamned New York-Presbyterian Hospital. You hear me! If you let Georgann die, I won't rest until I make you pay!"

With his face three inches from mine, I saw fear. I let go of his shirt, threw him back down into his chair, turned and walked out of his office. I knew if I stayed a minute longer, I would kill him.

I sat down next to Georgann and Rose in the waiting room, my head was spinning. I felt myself moving in and out of consciousness. Having heard every word between me and Kirsch, they stared at me without speaking.

My outburst must have shocked Kirsch out of his apathy because a complete metamorphosis took place in him. He came out of his office and walked straight to Georgann. Taking her hand, he told her he was not going to abandon her.

He came over to me, "Al, take Georgann to the Northern Westchester Hospital Emergency Room. I'll make the call right now so the hospital will be ready for you when you arrive. I'll meet you there."

I carried Georgann to the car and Rose settled her into the back seat before getting in next to her. She barely had time to shut the door before I gunned the motor leaving rubber as I raced out of the parking lot.

As much as Georgann was in pain, she still had concern for me, "Slow down, Al, or I'll give birth right here." Glancing in the rear view mirror, she actually gave me 'the look.' Although we were beyond laughing, Georgann was still trying to raise my spirits.

Our baby was about to be born on April 20, 1980.

When we arrived, two emergency room attendants were waiting outside the hospital with a gurney. The attendants helped Georgann out of the car and onto the gurney, wheeled her into the hospital, into the elevator, through the hospital corridors, and into the delivery room in a matter of minutes. Rose and I ran alongside the gurney, me holding one of Georgann's hands, Rose the other until Georgann was wheeled into the delivery room. I went in with Georgann leaving Rose to find a pay phone to call Marie.

An anesthesiologist was already in the delivery room. After introducing himself to me, he said; "Al, I'm going need your help. Get dressed and scrub-up."

I ran to the dressing room. I was so nervous, my foot got caught in the scrub pants leg, and I fell backward into the canvas laundry bin filled with dirty scrubs. I made it back to the delivery room just in time to watch the doctor begin to administer the anesthesia.

Before she succumbed, Georgann smiled up at me "Al, you look just like a real doctor so watch who you examine." My lovely Georgann, always making sure her last thoughts were for me.

A nurse came into the operating room, then Dr. Brandman. Both assumed I was part of the hospital staff.

Brandman was in his early thirties, 5'6" at most on a sunny day. As with many men, he compensated for his short stature with a loud, cocky attitude. Inappropriately, and talking to no one in particular, he talked about his afternoon tennis match, "My opponent had these great pair of knockers. I could hardly concentrate on my serve."

Har-dee-har-har.

Everyone in the operating room ignored him; they were focused on their jobs. Dr. Kirsch came in. He would be performing the caesarian section on Georgann with Brandman assisting.

At the first cut, a wave of nausea rippled through me. I thought I was going to faint and roll under the table. I managed to slip out of the room and into the hallway before crumbling to the floor. When I regained the use of my legs, I got up and plastered my face against the small window to the operating room door. Fortunately for me, given my sensitivities to blood and gore, both doctors blocked my view of the operation. After about twenty minutes, I saw Dr. Kirsch hand a bundle to a nurse. She took the bundle to the far side of the operating room, placed it in a bassinette, and began pumping what looked like a black bellows bag up over the bassinette. I couldn't see anything else. Kirsch walked out leaving Brandman to stitch up Georgann. When he was done, Brandman walked past the bassinette, peered into it, and shook his head before leaving the operating room.

Another nurse went in and wheeled Georgann through a side door to the recovery room. I remained outside the operating room, my eyes transfixed on the nurse hovering over the bassinette. When she looked over at me and nodded, I got the impression that she knew who I was although I was still wearing the hospital mask.

I must have been standing there more than half an hour watching the nurse continue her labors at the bassinette until I was startled out of my reverie by a voice calling my name. It was Dr. Kirsch, already in his street clothes. If he was surprised to see me still in hospital scrubs, he didn't show it.

Approaching me, he said, "Georgann is recovering well. You can go to her in an hour or two." Kirsch didn't mention the baby. I blocked that out of my mind, more concerned for Georgann. I managed to say thank you to him.

Strange, before leaving he turned to me and said, "No, Al, thank you." I don't know what he meant by those words, I didn't take the time to consider them or care

I watched him walk down the hall for a few moments before turning back to continue my vigil at the nurse hovering over the bassinette. Another hour went by. A doctor wearing a white lab coat, his face hidden by thick, black glasses and a mask entered the operating room. He went over to the nurse and said something to her. She turned her head and nodded toward the door at me. The doctor came out of the room and stood in front of me. I was afraid of what he might tell me.

Removing his mask and extending his right hand, he said, "Mr. Volpe, I am Dr. Harding, the pediatrician on call tonight. Your baby experienced a very distressed, premature birth. At this time, Northern Westchester does not have the life support equipment necessary to sustain babies in her condition but New York-Presbyterian Hospital in Manhattan does. I put in a call to their mobile neonatal unit over two hours ago. Unfortunately, the unit mistakenly went to Westchester Medical Center in Valhalla instead of coming here to Northern Westchester in Mt. Kisco." He hung his head remorsefully. "The neonatal unit was your baby's only hope. I am afraid that too much time has already elapsed to save her. I'm sorry." With that statement, he excused himself. "I'm going back to my office to check on the unit's whereabouts."

My heart sank. He was telling me that my beautiful, new baby was not going to make it. My only consolation was that Georgann was okay. We could have another baby.

A nurse ran past me and into the operating room. She went over to the nurse at the bassinette who turned, nodded, and again pointed to me with her eyes.

The nurse rushed back out to me. "Mr. Volpe, the mobile unit has arrived. Would you like to go in to see your baby before they take her to New York-Presbyterian Hospital?"

My first reaction was to say, "No, I don't want to look at my dead child." I turned my gaze back to watch the nurse at the bassinette. Looking up, she locked eyes with me. I'm sure she could read the fear and pain in mine. She nodded, her eyes slowly closed and opened as if to say, "Come in. It's okay." I pulled my facemask back over my nose and mouth and walked hesitantly into the operating room.

I went up to the bassinette, afraid to look in. The nurse, removed the black bag, and said, "You have a beautiful, little daughter, Mr. Volpe. What's her name?"

I peeked down and saw an angelic, little face staring up at me. Only three pounds, she was so tiny, but she was alive, and I couldn't take my eyes off her. I bent over to touch her hand, thinking I was imagining it all. She grabbed my finger and held on tight. An emotional euphoria enveloped me. This tiny person stole my heart. I mumbled, "Her name is Gabrielle."

The nurse said, "Gabby likes her daddy. You don't mind if I call her Gabby? She isn't letting go of your finger." Her laugh was muffled by her mask, but it was music to my ears.

Gabby, I said to myself. That's a better name for such a tiny baby than Gabrielle. From now on we will call our daughter Gabby, too.

The doors swung open again. This time a nurse, the pediatrician, and the neonatal team came rushing in. The doctor pried my finger loose from Gabby's grasp and pushed me out of the way. Working at a feverish pace, the team began hooking up the life support equipment.

The doctor turned to the nurse, "Take Al to his wife. I'll make sure the unit brings the baby by the recovery room before she's transported to New York-Presbyterian."

A baby as premature as Gabby often has breathing problems, because the lungs are not fully developed to enable the baby to breathe on his or her own. Manual hyperinflation also known as manual ventilation or 'bagging' was the technique the nurse used on Gabby until the neonatal unit could hook her up to their breathing apparatus. Until then, that ER nurse with her bagging was the breath of life for Gabby.

Despite all the chaos, I remembered to look around for the nurse who had kept Gabby alive to thank her for her efforts. She had disappeared. No one could tell me her name. I couldn't describe her, because she wore hospital scrubs and a face mask. I only knew that her eyes were big, brown and filled with compassion. To this day the identity of the guardian angel that probably saved Gabby's life remains a mystery.

Chalk up another miracle.

19

Gabby

Georgann was propped up in bed; Rose sitting at her side when I walked into the recovery room. Her tousled, dark hair curled prettily around her serene face. Georgann looked terrific. I looked like I was the one in need of a hospital bed. My scrubs were saturated with sweat, the facemask hung soaked with tears around my neck like a water balloon, my hair was standing straight up in clumps, and my eyes were bloodshot.

Rose got up. She didn't even look at me "I'll leave you two alone. I'm going to grab a coffee. Would you like me to bring you back one, Al?" She seemed to be in a hurry to get out of the room.

"You're a godsend, Rose, in more ways than one."

Georgann looked me up and down. "Al, you look terrible. Was it you or me who just had a baby? Come here; let me give my big, brave man a hug." I let her fold me in her arms for a well needed embrace. "You just missed Dr. Kirsch, Al. I asked him how our baby was doing but he just mumbled something I didn't understand. I guess I'm still a little groggy from the anesthesia. He patted my hand and ran out the room. Maybe he had to hurry to another delivery."

Rose had heard very clearly what Kirsch said. That's the reason she left the room in such a hurry as soon as I got there. She did not want to face another bearer of such dreadful news. Instead, she took it upon herself to call Marie and her that Georgann was fine, but the baby didn't make it. A few minutes later, Rose returned, drying tears from her face with the back of her hand.

"Rose, where's my coffee?" (Whoa, Al the Jerk) "What's wrong, Rose?" I didn't know what she heard Kirsch tell Georgann.

Georgann looked at Rose, her mouth began to tremble. "Al, is our baby….," she tried to ask me about Gabby, but the words caught in her throat.

Kissing Georgann's cheek, I whispered, "Gabrielle is tiny but the most beautiful, angelic baby I've ever seen. A neonatal team is preparing her for transport to New York-Presbyterian Hospital where they can take better care of her than this hospital. They promised to bring Gabrielle by the recovery room before they take her away." I didn't point out that a nest of scorpions would give better care can than Kirsch and Brandman.

Georgann's face lit up. She whispered, "Gabrielle, my baby, she's all right." Tears of joy, not sorrow, flowed down her pretty face. Rose's jaw dropped.

"After they took you to recovery, I stayed glued to my spot outside the delivery room and watched as this nurse pumped on some black bag over Gabrielle's bassinette. I didn't know what she was doing, but I couldn't move. I watched that nurse pumping non-stop for almost two hours. Another nurse woke me out of my trance when she tapped me on the shoulder to let me know that the neonatal unit had arrived. I gave her a quick nod before turning my attention back to the nurse with our baby. When she saw me, she motioned to me with her head to come into the delivery room. She asked our baby's name but when I told her Gabrielle she said she was going to call her Gabby. Me too, I said. I touched little Gabby's hand, and she grabbed my finger as if she knew it was me. In all my life, I never felt such a thrill. That nurse saved our baby, Georgann, and I didn't even get her name!" I said this all in one breathe.

I would have kept on rambling if the neonatal team hadn't arrived. They wheeled Gabby's incubator over to Georgann's bedside. Rose and I helped Georgann turn to look into the incubator.

"Can I touch her?" she asked. They opened the little porthole in the incubator. Georgann slid her arm through the bedrail and into the hole. Gabby grabbed hold of her mommy's finger as she had with me.

They left with our little angel. After wishing them Godspeed, I yelled, "Do you know your way home?"

The team leader turned to give me a thumbs-up before disappearing into the elevator. Rose went to phone Marie again but this time with good news. I held Georgann's hand until she fell asleep.

I drove Rose home kidding her all the way about her tendency to overreact. "If a neighborhood kid sneezes, Rose, you want to quarantine the whole school for a week." She punched me lightly on the shoulder. Pulling up to her house, I jumped out and opened the passenger door for her. "Seriously, Rose, thank God we listened to you today. You saved Georgann's and Gabby's lives. I'm forever in your debt." I gave her a big hug.

Rose hugged me back. "Thank God you hadn't strangled Kirsch or Georgann and your baby would be visiting you in prison." Without another word, but chuckling to herself over her joke, she turned and went into her house.

As soon as I got to my house, I went straight to my bedroom and collapsed on the bed without undressing. I couldn't get to sleep; I was unable to get my new daughter's sweet face out of my mind. I thanked God again for Rose and for that nurse at the hospital who wouldn't quit. Strange, I thought, how often I was acknowledging God's grace these days.

Waking early the next day, I peeled off my sweaty clothes and jumped into the shower to wash off the hospital smells, my thoughts still absorbed with Gabby. How could something so tiny steal her way into my heart like no one had ever done before? As I sipped my morning coffee, I was over-come with an unbearable thought – what if we lost her?

I put down my coffee and ran to the phone to call New York-Presbyterian Hospital. After some runaround, I was directed to the reception in the neonatal unit. The nurse at the desk forwarded me to Gabby's attending clinician.

A male voice answered the phone. "Nurse Roger O'Brien speaking, may I help you?"

I blurted into the phone, "Is she okay?" There was silence on the other end. I realized he didn't know who the hell I was or what the hell I was talking about! "The baby girl the neonatal unit brought in from Northern Westchester last night." Obviously, I wasn't capable of putting together a complete sentence.

"May I ask who is speaking?"

"Al Volpe. The baby is my daughter."

Nurse Roger said, "The hospital was not given any contact information for the baby. We assumed she was abandoned at birth."

"Oh my God," I moaned. "Everything happened so quickly I didn't think to fill out any paperwork. I thought the doctors took care of that."

"No," said Roger, "We didn't receive any notification or paper work from any doctor. We admitted the baby into New York-Presbyterian as a Jane Doe."

Those bastards, Kirsch and Brandman, walked out leaving the hospital to clean up their mess. Hippocratic Oath, my ass!

I practically shouted into the phone, "Is she okay?"

Nurse Roger began to recite some stuff about vital signs, head size, weight, until I stopped him. "I don't understand anything you're saying. Just tell me, is she alive?"

"Yes, she is. Don't worry, Mr. Volpe, we at Presbyterian are committed to the survival of your baby." 'Okay' was obviously not a medical term used in critical care units, so Nurse Roger didn't understand my question. After he assured me that my baby was alive, I was finally able to breathe.

"What's your daughter's name?" he asked - a simple question in response to the anxiety he heard in my shrill voice.

"Gabrielle Volpe."

"No middle name?"

I hadn't thought about it, but then it struck me, "Her middle name is Irene the same as her mother's. We're going to call her Gabby."

"May I call her Gabby, too?"

"Sure," I said.

"Gabby's condition is delicate," he began. "I don't want to frighten you, but you need to be prepared for the worst. On Gabby's arrival, the hospital staff had little hope she would survive the night. We called in the chaplain to perform last rights for her and put the staff on a round-the-clock alert. We were relieved to discover this morning that her vital signs were slightly improved. Mr. Volpe, the hospital is doing all we possibly can to save your baby."

"Thank you, Roger. I am putting my trust in you and in God. And call me Al."

Before hanging up, I asked Roger to switch me back to reception, so I could give the hospital our information. The receptionist transferred me to patient registration. After I finished giving registration my particulars, she transferred me back to reception. "By the way," I asked, "have any of my wife's doctors called to inquire about the baby?" I would give Georgann the contact information for the hospital when I visited her.

Checking her call log, she said, "No one but you has called."

As I dressed, I rehearsed what I would or wouldn't tell Georgann. I didn't want to frighten her, but I also didn't want to give her false hope about Gabby's condition either. I went over and over the narrative in my mind trying to find the right words.

Georgann gave me a big smile as soon as I walked into her room. She looked great. "Have you seen Gabrielle yet? I can't wait to hold her."

"I haven't been to the hospital yet, but I called New York-Presbyterian Hospital this morning to check on Gabby's condition. I spoke to the clinician in charge. His name is Nurse Roger, imagine."

Georgann stopped me. "Is our baby okay?"

Carefully reciting my well-rehearsed speech, I said, "Gabby's is in very critical condition, but she is receiving the best care possible."

Before she could ask me any more questions, I said, "The hospital didn't have any paperwork on her. Poor Gabby was classified as abandoned, could you believe it? Administration had made a nametag for her incubator with 'Gabrielle' on it, but Nurse Roger changed it to Gabby Volpe - in big pink letters."

Georgann's face lit-up with this simple acknowledgment that Gabby was our baby. "You rest now, sweetheart. Later, we'll both call New York-Presbyterian and talk to Nurse Roger."

I sat by her bedside while she slept. When she awoke a couple hours later, we called the hospital and asked to speak with Nurse Roger. We listened intently as he told us that Gabby's condition had not changed since he and I spoke this morning. "She's a real little fighter, Mrs. Volpe. As soon as you're feeling better, I'll arrange for you and Al to visit. Till then, you can call me anytime."

"Thank you," we both answered before hanging up. We both took encouragement in Roger's words, and Georgann sat back on her pillows looking a little more relieved. "I can't wait to hold my baby," she sighed.

That afternoon, Marie brought Nicky to visit Georgann. Georgann decided that it would be best for Nicky to stay with Marie until she came home. I left them all chatting to get some coffee and a sandwich before going back to spend time with Georgann until visiting hours ended.

. When I got home that night, it was just me and Sundance, our bad-breath miniature schnauzer, sleeping with me at the foot of the bed. The next morning, we were both startled awake by the phone.

I grabbed it without lifting my head off the pillow. Holding it to my ear, I mumbled groggily, "Yeah."

"Mr. Volpe, I am Mrs. Kearns, the head administrator at New York-Presbyterian Hospital."

I sat up fully awake. "What's wrong?"

"Your daughter requires a surgical procedure as soon as possible. We need you to come to the hospital to sign a parental consent form before the doctors' can perform the surgery, or, if you have a fax machine, I can send you the form for you to fill out and return to us."

"Don't bother with a fax," I told her, "I'll be at the hospital in an hour." I didn't wait to ask what procedure was needed. I was dressed and heading for Manhattan in ten minutes. Pulling into the hospital courtyard, I jumped out of the car asking the parking valet for directions to the neonatal unit.

"You go in the front door, take the elevators on the left to the third floor," he told me, "but you don't have a parking pass. You'll have to self-park in the garage on the next block."

I folded a $20 universal pass around my keys, shoved it in his hand and took off into the hospital before he could object. I managed to find the neo-natal unit and sign the consent form at the nurses' station before seeking out Nurse Roger. He was sitting at a desk outside the unit. He looked exactly as I pictured him from his voice. Wearing the protective clothing required to enter the unit, his shock of curly, red hair stuck out from under the hospital cap. He was probably in his late twenties, but it was hard to tell, because his smooth face with its abundance of freckles begged to have its cheeks pinched like that of an adorable child. No mistaking him for a kid, though, once you looked into his bright, baby blues.

He stood up as I approached. "Mr. Volpe, Al, very glad to meet you. Please, sit down." He motioned to the chair next to the desk.

"Mrs. Kearns called me this morning and said Gabby needs an operation. I rushed over as fast as I could. What operation?"

Nurse Roger explained the procedure, "Because of her premature birth, Gabby has not yet developed the ability to suckle and therefore cannot be fed by mouth. It is necessary to implant a feeding tube into her stomach. This is a very common procedure. Don't worry."

"I want to see Gabby before her operation."

"All right," he said leading me to the prep room, "Hurry and put on the scrubs. The operating team is ready now."

He watched me suit up in scrubs to make sure I did it right, before, he led me through glass sliding doors into a space-age unit. Dozens of doctors and clinicians all dressed the same looked like robots functioning within this massive maze of incubators. Arriving at Gabby's station, I was paralyzed with fear. In her bubble, her shriveled, grey body was wired up to a mass of tubes. I put my hand in the porthole to touch Gabby's little hand. Like a magnet, she grabbed and clung tight. I couldn't stop myself; I cried. Who's the baby?

Gabby was still holding my finger when the transport team arrived to take her into the operating room. Legs shaking, I walked alongside Gabby's incubator as they took her down to surgery. I wasn't allowed in the operating room, but a nurse brought me a chair to sit on outside. I barely moved on that chair as the procedure was performed - it seemed like most of the day but was probably only a couple of hours. Finally, a surgical nurse came from the operating room to inform me that Gabby was back in the neonatal unit. Without a word to the nurse, I got up, walked to elevator, rode it up to the neonatal floor, went into the unit, and shuffled over to Gabby's bubble before I realized where I was. I put my hand through the port hole. She again grabbed my finger. I was soaring at this tiny gesture of life.

Still in a semi-stupor, I changed back into my street clothes before going to the nurse's station. I hadn't bothered to wash the sweat and tears off my face. One look at me and the nurse handed me a bunch of tissues before saying, "Your wife called asking for you. I told her you were here, but I didn't say anything about the surgery. I thought it best to leave that to you."

"Thank you," I said. "Thank God, Gabby survived the procedure. I'm going back to Westchester now to my wife. If she calls again, please let her know I'm on my way."

"Call if you need any more information," she said handing me a valet parking pass. With a tender look, she stuffed more tissues into my pocket for the road. I thought about buying some stock in Kleenex.

Before leaving, I thought to ask, "Have any of my wife's doctors called asking about Gabby?"

Checking the logbook, she said "No calls other than from your wife and you."

I lit a cigarette as soon as I was outside. I needed it. My car pulled up in front of me and the valet got out. Brandishing my new parking pass, I held it out to him.

He smiled. "Do you want your twenty back?"

"Nope," I said, "You keep it. Thanks for helping me out."

On the drive to Northern Westchester Hospital, my only thoughts were for my precious daughter. How could I explain Gabby's condition to Georgann to make it sound positive? I parked in the hospital garage, stopping first in the men's washroom to wash my face and compose myself before going to Georgann's room.

As soon as she saw me, her face lit up. "Al, how is Gabby? Why did you have to go to New York-Presbyterian this morning?"

I tried out the lie I had formulated on the way. "The hospital needed our insurance information. I decided it would be better if I drove it there rather than fax it to them. I wanted the chance to look in on Gabby. She was sleeping like an angel."

She was satisfied with my answer and didn't question me any further. I was so drained by the emotion of the morning that I all could do was flop into a chair by the window. I picked up an old Reader's Digest and pretended to thumb through it while Georgann sat up in bed chatting on the phone with her mother. Just as she hung up, the room door opened. Dr. Brandman strolled in. He didn't see me.

He sat down on the corner of Georgann's bed. He took hold of her hand and tried to make small talk. "How are you feeling, beautiful? You look wonderful. You know Dr. Kirsch gave you his special C-section incision. You'll be able to wear your bikini this summer." He just loved his little jokes, but he made me want to puke.

I kept my head down pretending to read. I wanted to hear what kind of fairytale he was about to spin for my wife. I already knew the truth.

His voice turned somber. "At a time like this, Georgann, it's a normal psychological response to feel guilty. I can recommend a support group if you want."

I couldn't believe what I was hearing! This swine thought our baby was dead! He was telling us not to feel guilty!

Georgann looked at him with a confused expression on her face. "What are you talking about?" she asked. "I don't understand. Why should I go to a support group? Has something happened to my baby?"

Brandman began fumbling for words, "Gabriel is in the place God wants him to be."

At these words, Georgann stiffened and pulled her hand away, "My baby's name is Gabrielle. She is not with God!" She began screaming, "Why would you say that? You're a filthy liar. Get out of here! Don't you ever come near me again! Get out!"

He probably thought she was in denial over the loss of her baby. He reached out his hand to pat Georgann's shoulder in a false attempt to comfort her. Georgann flinched back before he could touch her.

I flew out of the chair, pulled him by his necktie and punched him square in his forehead. The impact sent him reeling through the door and into the hall colliding into a meds cart before hitting the wall.

My first reaction was to go after him, but Georgann's hysterical crying brought me back to my senses. She needed me. Brandman was on his own. I kicked the door shut, and went to sit next to her on the bed. I held her close whispering, "Everything is fine. Gabby is doing fine. Forget that jerk."

The hospital intercom began blaring out a rainbow of color-codes. There was a commotion in the hall outside the room. Suddenly, two security guards burst into the room only to see Georgann and me holding hands and smiling lovingly at each other. The guards were confused. They thought they must be in the wrong room. I stood laying Georgann's hand gently on the bed.

"I believe it's me you're looking for. Can you ask somebody to stay with my wife before I go with you?"

One of the guards picked up the phone to call a nurse. As soon as she stepped into the room, I kissed Georgann and gave her a wink before the guards led me out.

Brandman had already been removed on a stretcher. The guards escorted me to the security office where a Mt. Kisco police officer and the hospital administrator were already seated. They motioned for me to take a seat opposite them.

"Mr. Volpe," Mrs. Kearns began, "Why did you attack Dr. Brandman?"

I told them the whole story.

"My wife went into early labor yesterday and Brandman assisted Dr. Kirsch in an emergency caesarian section performed on her. Because the baby was premature and very small, Dr. Kirsch told us that Northern Westchester didn't have the necessary facilities to provide the specialized care required for my daughter and had her transported to New York-Presbyterian Hospital by a neonatal team. My baby is alive and now in the best of hands. Brandman showed up this morning to see Georgann without having even bothered to check if the baby was dead or alive. He didn't even know it was a girl!"

The more I explained the situation, the more pissed off – and more vulgar - I got. "That scumbag almost killed my wife and my baby. Then, to save his bony ass he tried to lay a guilt trip on us by saying we shouldn't think it was our fault the baby died!" I ranted, "I hope you make a big deal out of this, because I want the newspapers to get a hold of this story so all of Westchester will know what pieces of shit Brandman and Kirsch are."

The administrator fidgeted in her chair. I'm sure she was mulling over how to handle this would-be crisis for his hospital. Her silence stretched on. I waited. The cops waited.

Finally, a guard asked Mrs. Kearns "Is the hospital going to press charges against Mr. Volpe?" The administrator shook his head.

"What about Brandman? Is he going to press charges?"

"I don't know," said Mrs. Kearns. She got up and left the office with one of the guards leaving me with the other security guard. Ten minutes later, they returned. The administrator announced, "Mr. Volpe, you're free to go. I just spoke with Dr. Brandman, and he is not pressing charges. I suggest that, in the future, if you feel that strongly about Dr. Brandman, you get a restraining order to keep him away from your wife."

The cop said, "You won't need a restraining order, Mr. Volpe. He's learned the hard way to stay away from you." Everyone laughed. Well, maybe not the administrator.

Neither the hospital nor the obstetricians wanted the story to go public. I got the impression Mrs. Kearns wasn't a big fan of Brandman, either, but she was glad I wasn't taking issue with his hospital.

I headed back to Georgann's room. She was chatting with the nurse but gave me a big smile as soon as I walked in. "If you got arrested, I wouldn't be able to help you. They won't let me out of this bed yet."

"Nobody's getting arrested. Did you miss me?"

The nurse said, "The way you slammed him, we thought she'd be missing you for five to ten for manslaughter."

"That's not funny," I said.

On her way out, she had to add another taunt, "I'll leave you two jailbirds, oops, I mean lovebirds, alone."

Georgann and I talked all day about how wonderful it will be to have Gabby home with us even if we didn't know when that would be.

That evening, Rose and Sally came to visit. Rose asked, "Al, how are you doing?"

"Good." I was becoming a really skillful liar.

Georgann said, "Oh yeah, Al's doing real good. He's lucky he's not sitting in jail."

She was itching to tell the girls the story. It was time for me to make my exit. It had been a long day. I was tired, and I longed for my bed.

When I got home, Marie was helping Nicky pick out more clothes to take back to her house.

"Your friend, Dr. Brandman, had an accident today," I told Marie.

Marie had already heard the story from Donna who heard it from Georgann. She smirked. "He's lucky you only sent him to the emergency room. If I had gotten my hands on him, he would have ended up in the morgue."

Marie can be humorous at times.

Before heading to Northern Westchester Hospital the next morning, I stopped by the store to tell Margie that she was in charge of running the place. My priorities were Georgann and Gabby at this time. She asked about Gabby.

"My baby is very sick, Margie, but New York-Presbyterian Hospital is the best place she can be right now." That became my standard answer to everyone who asked about Gabby.

At Northern Westchester, the incident with Dr. Brandman had gone viral throughout the hospital. A nurse stopped me in the hall, "Thank you, he deserved that."Apparently, I wasn't the only one who thought Brandman was an asshole.

No matter much I tried, I couldn't protect Georgann from learning the harsh truth of our daughter's tenuous condition forever. On the third day of Gabby's life, Georgann got a call from a pediatrician at New York-Presbyterian. He told her that because Gabby was so tiny, the pressure in her respirator had caused the back part of her brain to hemorrhage; Gabby had had a stroke. Having little hope for Gabby's survival, she had again been given last rights.

Georgann was beyond hysterical when I arrived. "My baby's going to die!" she cried. "Al, what are we going to do?"

I wrapped my arms around her, "Hush, Georgann. You're going to make yourself sick. We'll call Nurse Roger right now."

I got Roger on the phone. Gabby had survived the crisis. The respirator was adjusted and she was breathing again.

"Al, I have to go to my baby," she said as soon as we hung up the phone.

"You need to get stronger first, Georgann. I don't want to have to worry about you, too."

"Okay, Al, for Gabby's sake, I'll wait until the doctor says I can go home." Friday afternoon, Georgann was released from the hospital.

On the drive home I said, "If you feel okay tomorrow, I'll take you to visit Gabby." She said nothing, only stared at me. We both knew she was going to the hospital the next day with or without me.

Georgann was up early the next morning, showered, dressed and so anxious to get on the road; she barely let me have a cup of coffee. I knew she was going to be alarmed seeing Gabrielle's limp little body, but I didn't know how to prepare her for the shock. I said nothing to her on the way to the hospital.

20

Survival

Outside the neonatal unit, Roger greeted us warmly. He took Georgann's hand between his, "I've spoken to you so often over the phone, I knew you'd be as lovely as your voice," he said. What a charmer. I started to get jealous but caught myself. "Let's go see your beautiful, baby girl."

Once we suited up, Roger led us into the neonatal unit. Georgann practically pushed him aside so great was her maternal need to see her baby. Entering the unit, Georgann was as overwhelmed as I had been by its size and complexity. I stood behind her at Gabby's station. Thankfully, Gabby's skin wasn't as grey as it had been the last time I saw her. Georgann put her hand though the porthole to rub Gabby's little hand. Gabby stirred, then grabbed tight to Georgann's finger as if she knew her mommy was finally there.

For ten minutes, without speaking, we gazed into the incubator. Gabby never let go of Georgann's finger until Roger told us we had to leave. Georgann twisted her head to keep sight of Gabby's incubator until we were out the door.

Roger took us to the lounge to talk. In the gentlest way possible, he attempted to inform us of the medical issues Gabby was facing. He wasn't trying to scare us, only prepare us for what we might expect in our baby's near medical future.

"Gabby was one month premature and only three pounds. One of the many problems indicative of a premature birth is Hyaline membrane disease also called respiratory distress syndrome. Infants with this syndrome need extra oxygen to aide in their breathing requiring them to be in an incubator. Although Gabby began breathing again on her own after the stroke, we felt it necessary she remains in the incubator for now. Also, she will continue to need constant neurological care. If she survives, we won't know for some time the extent of brain damage caused by the stroke. In addition to Hyaline membrane disease, Gabby has a condition called cerebral palsy which is marked by impaired muscle coordination or spastic paralysis. This condition is typically caused by damage to the brain before or at birth and will require long-term treatment which may include physical therapy, drugs, and sometimes surgery."

Is that all?

We didn't question what Roger had just told us, because we didn't know what to ask. Roger said that we could call him at any time if we needed to talk. He sent us home to wait.

The drive home was quiet. We were both too absorbed in our own thoughts to discuss Roger's grim news. As soon as we got in the door, Nicky ran up to Georgann and hugged her. They went into the living room and sat next to each other on the couch. Marie sat bolt upright in the chair across from them; I stood just outside the room.

Georgann took Nicky's hand, "You have a beautiful baby sister, Nicky. Do you know her name?

"It's Gabrielle. I helped pick it out."

"That's right, but we will call her Gabby for short."

"Gabby," Nicky repeated. "I like that. When is she coming home? I want to hold her."

"Not for a while, sweetheart. Gabby is very sick. The doctors and nurses at the hospital in New York City are wonderful and will take good care of Gabby until we can bring her home. Until then, you can pray that Gabby gets well in a hurry. Big sister's do that, right?"

"I will mommy. I love Gabby."

"Thank you, sweetheart. I'm sure Gabby and God will hear your prayers."

Marie didn't say a word. She heard the sadness in Georgann's voice and knew enough to keep quiet. Slowly, she got up from the chair, went silently over to Georgann and gave her shoulder a squeeze before taking Nicky to the playground. I took Nicky's place on the couch next to Georgann and put my arm around her. She leaned her head on my shoulder. There we sat, unspeaking, gaining whatever solace we could muster in the knowledge that we would share whatever the future might hold for Gabby.

The next morning, we began the daily routine that would last for almost six months: get up after a fitful night's sleep, then shower, grab a quick cup of coffee, get Nicky ready for school and onto the bus, and head into Manhattan to New York-Presbyterian Hospital. We arranged for Marie to pick up Nicky when she got off the bus each day in case we were unable make it back from the hospital in time.

The very first morning at the hospital, the receptionist at the neonatal unit told us that she had tried to reach us at home, but we had already left for the hospital. Her instructions were to direct us immediately to the head neurosurgeon's office as soon as we arrived.

No way was Georgann going anywhere before seeing her daughter.

Roger was waiting to escort us into the unit after we suited up. Only our second day and we had already learned not to look around at the heartbreaking group of little forms in their incubators. We kept our eyes focused on Gabby's station. We took turns rubbing Gabby's little arm and speaking softly to her before leaving for our meeting with the surgeon. We found him sitting behind his massive, mahogany desk shuffling through papers. He was a gaunt man whose pale skin and darkly circled; washed-out, gray eyes reminded me more of a mortician than a doctor.

Without even looking up, he said, "I've scheduled the surgery for 10:00am tomorrow." He held up a release form for me to sign.

Georgann asked, "Surgery? What surgery? What for? No one told us anything. Will Gabby be alright?"

He ignored Georgann. He made no attempt to explain or to soften his medical assessment. "If she survives the surgery and collateral medical damage, she'll never be much more than a vegetable intellectually and probably very handicapped physically."

My heart sank; Georgann burst into tears. I didn't know what to do. I grabbed the release forms out of the doctor's hand and managed to lift Georgann up out of the chair and out his office before I instigated another Brandman incident. What kind of man was this? How could he be so insensitive to the feelings of distraught parents? He might be a great surgeon, but he was a disgrace as a human being.

We rushed to find Roger. "Please, Roger," begged Georgann, "What is wrong with our baby?" We followed him to the staff room and sat at a table. Roger brought us some water before telling us what was involved in the surgery about to be performed on Gabby.

"Because of the stroke, it became obvious that the fluid on Gabby's brain was not draining. When this is the case, a tube called a shunt is surgically implanted into her brain. The shunt valve drains off cerebral fluid buildup from around the skull to alleviate the condition medically called infantile hydrocephaluc or, fluid on the brain. The valve is implanted at the base of the skull and connects to a thin tube under the skin which drains excess fluid build-up within the skull down into the stomach. This is the operation scheduled for Gabby tomorrow morning." Roger continued, "Gabby will need the shunt for the rest of her life. It will require constant monitoring and will have to be replaced to accommodate her growth."

We nodded our heads after Roger's explanation, as if we understood the total import of what he was saying. The only thing we understood was that it sounded horrible.

Again, we made the drive home in total silence. That night, Georgann tried to explain Gabby's impending surgery to Marie. She said, "This is what I understood from Nurse Roger. On May 12, my birthday, Gabby, who will be just three-weeks old, will have a shunt surgically inserted into her brain which will drain the fluid by tube into her stomach. Gabby will have to live the rest of her life with the shunt in her head."

Blunt but true words.

Marie sat down hard in a chair, her hand clutching at her chest. "My poor baby," she moaned. After a few moments, she was able to talk. "I'm going with you when Gabby has the surgery. Arrange for Rose pick up Nicky at the bus stop and take her home with her. Tell Rose to take care of Nicky for as long as we're gone. In the mean time, I'm staying here."

On May 12th, the three of us took Nicky to the bus stop. We gave her hugs before she got on the bus. We waved goodbye to her until the bus turned the corner. After that, we were on our way to Manhattan.

At the hospital, Georgann and I showed Marie how to suit up before going to Gabby's station in the neonatal unit. When she first saw her granddaughter', limp little body, Marie was so overcome with emotion her legs gave out, and I had to catch her to keep her from falling. Held up by Georgann, all Marie could do was moan until the transport team arrived to take Gabby in for surgery. We followed them to the surgical suite. Georgann held on tight to her mother's arm both for support and for comfort. Once Gabby disappeared into the operating room, we went to the waiting room to sit for hours anesthetized in fear not saying a word to each other. Georgann and I held hands; Marie sat alone in her own silent reverie.

Finally, a nurse came into the waiting room to tell us that the operation was over; it was successful. We went to the surgical suite waiting outside until Gabby was wheeled out. Marie almost fainted again. The sight of Gabby enveloped in bloody bandages was too much for her - for me and Georgann, too. But, Gabby had survived the surgery; she would live another day. We left the hospital like dead men walking. Marie cried the whole drive home.

At New York-Presbyterian Hospital, the neonatal unit runs 24-hours a day, seven days a week; there is no day or night in the critical care unit. We had to organize our priorities to be available around the clock should they need us. Marie moved in to care for Nicky. I told Margie and the other sales women at Express Yourself to figure out their own work schedules, buy the merchandise and make sure the store stayed open during its posted hours. I told them not to rely on me showing up or even being available by phone for a long time. They had to run the store without me, and, God bless these ladies, they did a great job.

The shunt valve wasn't working properly. Three days after the operation, Gabby needed to undergo another operation for a shunt revision which put her fragile condition into further physical distress. Again, she survived the operation. From that day on, Gabby clung to life, her every breath tethered to total life-support. There were times when the hospital called us in the middle of the night, because Gabby's condition had worsened. We would run out of the house dressing in the car on the way praying that this would not be our daughter's last moment of life.

One night, we had just got home from the hospital only to have Marie meet us at the door. "Get back to the hospital! Gabby had a turn for the worse as soon as you left." We jumped back into the car and back to the hospital.

Weeks passed. We went to the hospital every day. When Gabby had been in the hospital a couple of months, we got a call at 6:30 a.m. Her heart had stopped; she'd suffered another stroke. The Chaplain ministered last-rights as the doctors worked on resuscitating her in preparation for surgery. Georgann and I flew out of the house.

We sped to Manhattan along the Major Deegan, across the Willis Avenue Bridge, and onto the F.D.R. Drive when all traffic stopped. We were stuck in the bumper-to-bumper morning rush hour. In a panic, I drove over the median and onto the service road only to gain one city block. In complete desperation, I turned into a one-way street heading toward Second Avenue going the wrong way. As I approached the corner of First Avenue, I almost hit a police car. Two cops jumped out, hands on side revolvers ready to draw. They must have thought I was driving a getaway car.

I pulled to the curb. The cops came over to my side of the car and bent to look in at us. They saw Georgann on the passenger side, shaking, and wide eyed too frightened even to cry. I could only stare straight ahead believing we had lost our only chance to see Gabby once more.

"Let me see your license and registration," one of them said.

I handed them to him, "Give me a ticket or whatever you need, officer, but, please, let us go. We need to get to New York-Presbyterian Hospital right away."

I must have looked like a wild man, hair standing straight up from running my fingers through it, face unshaven, and ghostly pale with anxiety.

The cops looked at each, realized our desperation, and gave a nod. "Follow us." They jumped back into their patrol car.

With roof lights spinning and siren blaring on their cruiser, I tailgated them through Manhattan traffic right to the front doors of the hospital. Frantically, Georgann and I leaped out of the car leaving doors open and engine running hoping the valet would take care of it. We ran into the hospital just in time to catch the transport team as they were taking Gabby into surgery. We waited outside the operating room with a priest who never stopped praying for Gabby. Georgann and I held each other up, unable to control our trembling. After an hour, the priest left to continue his hospital ministrations.

The doctors worked furiously on Gabby for three hours. We never left our spot although Roger was kind enough to bring us coffees and chairs to sit on. After it was over, I overheard a doctor say to another as they left the surgery, "It's a miracle she survived."

Crisis to crisis, Gabby clung to life. She survived numerous flat lines, setbacks, and additional surgeries. Our baby was given last rights more times than I could count. The medical term 'stable' was the most positive description we could hope for her condition. Gabby never quit fighting, and we never gave up hope.

The hospital staff was Gabby's rooting section and our support team. Each night on the way home, we'd stop at the all-night deli on 69th street before getting onto the F.D.R. As soon as the owner saw my car pull up, he had our coffee order ready to go by the time I got out of the car. I dubbed the deli owner our pit-stop crew.

When Gabby was able to suckle, Georgann pumped breast milk each day and put it in the cooler we kept in the car to carry to the hospital. Gabby's welfare consumed us emotionally and financially; it took its toll on our family and my businesses, but it was especially difficult for Nicky who hardly ever saw the two of us at home.

Marie was indispensible during this time. She took care of Nicky. She kept our house in spic and span order and she cooked all our meals - she was the force that allowed us to spend long hours with Gabby at the hospital. Without her, we would not have been able to maintain our erratic schedules. Unfortunately, everything Marie did come with a cost. Left alone to care for Nicky, Marie was unfettered. She seized every opportunity to further brain-wash Nicky.

Before Gabby's birth, as a joke, I bought Marie a hat with a revolving light on top calling it her Nicky-rescue hat. Sadly, this was so close to the truth that it ceased to be funny. In the past, if Marie tried to undermine any control or direction Georgann or I had over Nicky's vulnerable, young mind, we were able to curb her efforts. Now, with our focus directed on Gabby's survival, neither Georgann nor I realized how seriously damaging Marie's mentoring was affecting Nicky's character - the nurturing of a future Mafia princess.

After five and a half months of medical miracles, Gabby was taken off life support. She continued to breathe on her own. The day finally arrived we could bring Gabby home. It was October 10th. Both nervous and happy, we said our teary-eyed good-byes to our hospital family. Georgann held Gabby close to her as we entered the elevator and headed for the hospital exit. When we stepped outside, I realized that this was the first breath of fresh air that Gabby had ever taken. My valet friend brought the car up giving me a little gift for Gabby. I thanked him for his help.

He said, "Al, you sure you don't want that twenty back?"

Georgann told him, "Don't ask him twice." She got into the back seat with Gabby.

On the drive home, I sneaked peeks in the rear view mirror. With Gabby snuggled her arms, Georgann had the blissful look of every mother with her newborn baby.

21

1980-1991

Gabby's reduced lung capacity made her highly susceptible to infection. Her vulnerability demanded Georgann's constant care and attention. We all took precautions, but, as always, Marie took the situation to the extreme. She duck taped a mask onto the face of anyone who came into the house; they had to leave their germ-ridden shoes on the front door step; and we all had wash our hands, twice, with Lysol, numerous times a day. No one could touch Gabby except her, Georgann or Nicky - especially not me. Not only did I bring home filthy germs from the store, but also disgusting diseases I caught from the bimbos she said I had on the side. Even the mailman was afraid Marie would make him mask-up if he got too close to the house. After six months of constant anxiety, we all breathed easier when Gabby's immune system had finally gotten strong enough to ward off infection.

Gabby continued to thrive. At one year, she was tiny but healthy although weighing only sixteen pounds and 27-inches long. She had rosy cheeks, a big smile, her mother's enormous, dark eyes, and my thick, black hair which curled like a pixie's around her heart shaped face. She was lovely, but she was slow to develop. Though a year old, she was only just trying to sit up putting her physical development about six months behind that of a normal baby. Gabby also hadn't made any attempt to talk although, according to Georgann, she was a fine yodeler. Georgann wasn't worried about her progress. "If she can handle it, we can handle it."

Gabby's early years were filled with doctor visits, weekly trips to Blythdale Children's Rehab Hospital in Valhalla, NY for physical therapy and almost constant care and supervision. Again, Marie stepped up to the challenge. She tended to the needs of both Nicky and Gabby and, at times, had to force Georgann to take some needed rest which Marie didn't seem to require. She was indefatigable as cook, house-keeper, babysitter, chauffeur, and, above all, doting grandmother. Because I was Redundant Al and Silvio was busy with his own affairs, Marie didn't waste her time on being a good mother-in-law or wife.

In 1982, Georgann and I decided to initiate a malpractice law suit to expose the obstetricians' mishandling of Gabby's birth and delivery. The full account for this venture is narrated in the next chapter.

Despite Gabby's handicaps, Georgann was determined she be treated like any other little girl. At three, Gabby began preschool. I'd drive her to the school three mornings a week on my way to the store. We would sing her nursery school songs on the way; she trying to sing as loudly as she could to drown out my off-key baritone.

As much as we wanted Gabby to believe she was just like as any other little girl, she was too smart to fall for our subterfuge. Although physically handicapped, she was not mentally challenged in any way. One morning, as I watched her go into the preschool, I saw a little boy deliberately push her down. My anger meter kicked in - no little brat was going to touch my daughter! I got out of the car, sneaked up behind him, and secretly gave him a half noogie on his head. He started to cry. Gabby saw me and ratted me out to Georgann when she got home from school.

That night, Georgann scolded me in front of Gabby. "Al, you know better than to make a little boy cry. It was very bad of you to give him a tap on his head. Tell Gabby that you will never do anything like that again."

"Mommy is right, Gabby. I was very wrong, and I promise you will never see me do that again." Damn right, she won't see me.

Gabby never let her physical limitations defeat her. She took every new challenge in stride handling most situations better than Georgann or I ever could. At five, when Gabby attended kindergarten Georgann worked closely with the special resource people at the elementary school to mainstream Gabby into the regular program with the other children as much as she was capable. Gabby asked no quarter and expected none. Her pure heart and sweet nature drew everyone to her like the proverbial bee to honey. She was truly her mother's daughter - fighters with no quit in either of them. Gabby's after school programs consisted of a round-robin of physical therapy, tutoring and a slew of doctors' appointments. Somehow, Georgann and Gabby managed it all and still found time for shopping at the mall.

As soon as Gabby entered first grade, Georgann took a part-time job as a receptionist for the Katonah Medical Group. She loved it! Self-employed, I was paying high premiums for health insurance after Georgann left Fashionetics to stay at home with Gabby. The Medical Group allowed us to pay into their group health insurance plan removing a big financial burden from our expenses. Georgann also managed to land a part-time job as a travel agent providing our family with reduced travel rates and hotel perks – travel was Georgann's passion second only to shopping. At forty-one, the few gray hairs in her wavy, shoulder length hair were taken care of by the beauty salon. Although a couple of inches were added to her waistline, her gorgeous smile and soulful big, brown eyes were the same as the first day I met Georgann.

I still had my thick head of hair although my forehead seemed to have gotten higher. I put on a couple, well, maybe, twenty or so pounds which mostly sat around my middle, but my legs were still beauty pageant material – did I mention that I won the 'best legs' contest at the Mafia country club beating out the other contestants who were all women. Big Al was still Big Al - at least in my book.

In 1984, my parents died within ten months of each other. Uncle Augie soon followed. I wish them God's eternal peace, my dear mamma, papa and favorite zio. Grandma Vingo threw her last rock the same year and shares a resting place with her Colombo family husband in Woodland Cemetery. Pepe, Marie's schnauzer, bit his last ankle about the same time as Grandma Vingo. I never asked what the Marinos did with his wretched remains.

Gabby adored Nicky so much; she wanted to be just like her big sister. At eight, Nicky had begun dance lessons and, by sixteen, was quite talented. She had the slender body of a graceful dancer; her long, dark hair - straight and shiny - swayed like a gentle breeze when she moved; she was a very beautiful teenager – on the outside. When she was six, Gabby asked if she, too, could take dance lessons. We agreed, as always, but we hoped that her physical disabilities would not present too many difficulties. Inherent in Gabby's determined nature, she worked hard at learning all the dance routines. I videotaped her first dance recital just as I had done for all of Nicky's recitals. After watching the video, it was evident to Gabby that she couldn't keep up with the other children. She quit, but not after having given it her all.

By the time Gabby was eight, she was well aware that her handicaps prevented her from participating in most games with the other children. Still, she stood on the sidelines cheering them on. I built her a swing set in our small backyard, but when her friends came over to play, they swung faster and higher than she could. She stayed out of their way but laughed along with them. My heart broke each time I witnessed these moments. Gabby accepted them without a tear or a complaint.

In 1985, at sixty-eight, Silvio had a heart attack. He realized that he wasn't young, strong, or vicious enough to continue being an independent hoodlum. He decided to become a 'made-man.'

"I've been a loyal member of The Family for a long time. They know who I am. I never cheated them out of their cut of everything I made from my operations, at least from the ones they knew about. I got some friends who will vouch for me and put me up for invitation. I just gotta wait until the books are open."

"What books?" I asked.

"The books of who's in The Family. You can't get an invitation until somebody dies and makes an opening."

"Invitation to what, Silvio?"

"The initiation ceremony, you babbo. You sit down at a table with the capo. There's a gun and a knife on the table. Someone uses the knife to prick your finger until it bleeds and you take the oath of omertá. It's a blood rite that says I put nothing above The Family. It's a lifetime commitment."

"What's the gun for?"

"To shoot myself if I don't make it. OK?"

"Sure, Silvio, I get it. But, why make the move now?"

He answered, "I will have the respect and honor of everyone else in the Family. When I die, they'll be three hundred made men at my funeral."

I guess that's philosophical; no one wants to die without a big crowd to mourn him. But, becoming a 'made-man' meant kicking-in to The Family a piece of every score he earned. It's like tithing to the church. When he was younger, Silvio never willingly wanted to give up anything to anybody if he could get away with it. But now that he was older, I guess Silvio needed to feel like he was part of a wider organization. It was worth the price he had to pay for that comradeship. (Part of the price also included 'making your bones'. I never asked.)

During the two weeks he was in the hospital recuperating from his heart attack, he trusted me to make collections for him. From his hospital bed he said, "Don't let anyone know I'm sick, not Mongo, not nobody. Someone might try take over my territory."

Any suggestion of weakness was a sure signal for a thug to take advantage. I felt I couldn't let him down. Fortunately, there were no Clara's Diner incidents those two weeks.

Although I had distanced myself from Silvio's world, he still knew me as a stand-up guy. Except for doing Silvio's collections the time he was in the hospital, I was able to steer clear of his other Mafiosi businesses. Silvio was aware that Marie hated me, but he wasn't going to lift a finger to interfere. It was Marie's beef with me, not his. As long as Marie didn't try to pull him into her grievances, he didn't take them too seriously. And, as long as I treated Georgann right, he didn't see a need to interfere in my life, either.

Although in her sixties, Marie had not slowed down a bit. Her modus operandi didn't change much over those years either. Besides considering herself indispensable in our household, making trouble for me and having confrontations with everyone else (except her daughter and granddaughters) continued to be Marie's favorite hobbies. I wasn't bothered as much by Marie as I had been before Gabby's birth; I was busy elsewhere.

Georgann gave Marie full rein in Nicky's life in order to devote her time to Gabby, her jobs, and her social life. The more attention Georgann gave to Gabby, the more attention Marie showered on Nicky often encouraging sibling rivalry. Still, Georgann remained a dutiful, respectful daughter and preferred to overlook Marie's failings rather than face up to them especially where Nicky was concerned. She took her mother shopping, out to lunch, and often accompanied Marie on country club weekends with other Mafia wives. If

Marie continued to mentor Georgann on the art of hiding money from me, I never knew about it, because I never asked. I immersed myself in expanding my businesses while using my free time for social occasions that didn't always involve my family. Georgann and might have been aware of Marie's complicity with Nikol, but we turned a blind eye to it out of convenience.

Marie constantly urged me to become involved in her brother Jimmy's schemes. I digress here to give you, reader, a little Jimmy history:

Rumors were circulating that government agents were looking for him because of such 'incident' which involved gunshots fired into a 1970 Cadillac parked in front of Colombo's house in Brooklyn. Sitting in the car were Colombo's two sons and two bodyguards - one who just happened to be Vinnie (Jimmy) Vingo. When questioned by the police, no one knew anything - of course. The 'incident' may have also sparked a vendetta with other Mafia families which gave Jimmy more cause to become invisible. He still continued to live high in Las Vegas, Florida and who knew where else keeping one step ahead of the mob and the feds. Georgann and I decided it best to keep very loose contact with him. Do you wonder why?

On the other hand, we saw Georgann's Uncle Sonny and his family frequently. (Remember, he was the only member of Georgann's family who liked me.) He did well on Long Island owning three hair salons by 1990 and staying clear of The Family business.

Because I chose to remain aloof from Silvio's and Jimmy's corrupt tug, Marie labeled me ungrateful - which was the nicest name she called me. Tyrants will use any excuse to get pissed off.

In 1976, a few years before Gabby's birth, my family and the Marinos began renting a beach house in Puerto Rico during Nicky's winter break from school. Silvio always paid and, admittedly, his wheeler dealer schemes appealed to me. I voluntarily participated in a traveler's check scam with a friend of Silvio's named Kiko who worked as a pit boss in one of the casinos. Silvio or I would cash a couple of grand in traveler's checks at Kiko's table in return for chips: the checks never made it to the cashier. Next morning, Kiko would join us for coffee at the beach house, give us back the checks, and we'd rack up the money from the cashed in chips minus Kiko's cut.

Unfortunately, way too many times during these vacations a violent fight would break out between Marie and Silvio for one reason or another - mostly after Marie had too much to drink. By 1984, Silvio had enough of Marie's nonsense and stopped going with us. Silvio was my pal on these trips. He managed to maintain a margin of control over his wife's behavior. Without him, the vacations stopped being much fun, because Marie turned to using me as her personal punching bag. In time, these vacations became pure agony for me, and I began to bow out on some of the trips, too. I used my businesses as an excuse to stay home.

My last vacation with Marie and family in Puerto Rico was in 1987. As always, we stayed at the El San Juan Hotel, because it had a casino. Without Silvio as back-up muscle, I didn't want to pull any scams. We spent the first couple of days touring San Juan, swimming in the pool, or basking in the sun on the beach. On the third night, Georgann, Marie and I went to the casino leaving Nicky with Gabby. Marie, as usual, had a lot to drink. She started shooting off her big mouth about how we used to bilk the casino out of thousands. She was overheard by a security guy. He came over to us and requested that we step outside – request being the polite word for 'move it buddy'. I had to do some fancy talking along going deep into my chino pockets to keep the three of us from getting arrested. After securing my money safely away into his own pocket, the guard asked us to leave and never come back.

Not able to leave well enough alone, Marie was about to mouth off at the guard. Oh no, I thought, another arrest for Marie. Fortunately, Georgann was able to pull her mother away and get her up to her room and into bed so fast that she barely had time to get out one 'fuck you' at the guard who, fortunately, hadn't heard her.

I was so pissed off at Marie for ruining another vacation that I threw my clothes into a suitcase, said adios to Georgann, and left the hotel in the middle of the night. Waiting for the morning flight back to New York in the San Juan airport, I found playing cards with the janitor preferable to spending another minute with Marie. That night, I called it quits on taking any more vacations with Marie. Georgann could keep the winter vacation tradition going, because she knew that Marie would be very hurt if she canceled, but count me out. Georgann warned Marie that if she ever did anything to embarrass or upset her or her daughters in the future, the vacations would end. Marie was in her glory - no Silvio or me - only her and 'chicklets'. No one missed me or Silvio

When Silvio's union disbanded in 1987, he tried staying home to enjoy the castle he built in Westchester, but Marie made his life unbearable. All the years he worked, she bitched at him for not spending enough time with her. Now that he was home, she bitched at him for being under foot all the time. To escape from Marie, he took another time out for almost a year. Marie hired a private investigator who reported that Silvio was staying with a 'friend' in Yonkers named Pat, gender unknown. The PI knew enough about Silvio's connections to give Marie no more info than that. During his absence, Silvio never tried to contact me, although I know he was secretly in touch with Georgann. (After all, she was his princess.)

Marie was like a lost puppy that year. Alone in that big house with no Silvio to fight with, she took an overdose of pills. Fortunately, Georgann found her in time to get her to the hospital to have her stomach pumped. Georgann finally realized what I had known for a long time: Marie was chronically depressed and suicidal. Her niece, Sandy, took Marie to Bible study classes hoping they might comfort her. I had a lot of respect for Sandy. She was a steadfast Christian who raised her three children on her own after her husband, Vincent, died of cancer at a young age.

Before Marie found God, she used to make fun of Sandy's Christian beliefs. Marie would say, 'Tithing to a church is like paying vigorish to hoodlums for protection – giving up something to get nothing.' But, after attending a few classes of Bible study with Sandy, Marie began carrying a Bible and misquoting scripture.

Without Silvio around, Marie again turned her loaded guns on me. She would take every opportunity to criticize, demean, and try to dethrone me as a father, husband, and businessman. She and I had some go-arounds, but, like Georgann, I felt sorry for her most of the time and refrained from reacting to most of her barbs. If I did battle with her, she went toe-to-toe with me. If I walked away from an argument, she got even more fired up. I couldn't win for losing.

During one confrontation, Marie waved her Bible at me screaming, "Vengeance is mine."

I seriously asked, "What's your ministry, Marie, The Church of Latter Day Morons?" She didn't get my sarcasm.

Marie's behavior was its own cause and effect. Finally, after years of her troublemaking, I had my fill. I didn't move out this time; after all, this was my house. I took the easy way out; I just didn't go home at all if I knew Marie would be there. Sometimes, I went to Paul's house and waited for Georgann's call to let me know that Marie had gone home. Other times, I went to the Holiday Inn in Mt. Kisco. It had a great bar and there was always the chance I would meet a woman who would be delighted to spend a few hours with 'Big Al.' I made friends with the hotel manager who always had a room on reserve for me.(I know, Al the Creep.)

My businesses continued to prosper. I had a good staff of saleswomen who not only knew current fashion but were able to anticipate the needs of my customers. I did the buying based on their advice. Running the t-shirt silk screening business I was able to service accounts from all the local schools and sports teams. I even landed an IBM account for their softball team's t-shirts. Because of my great sales and manufacturing staff, I had the luxury of being able to take afternoons and weekends off to spend with my family or others. I took up oil painting - mostly landscapes copied from snapshots taken on our weekend trips - and lighthouses, because I liked them. Although I never had a lesson, the paintings were good enough for me to have a showing at the Katonah Arts Center in 1988.

During the winter breaks from 1988 to '91, my family enjoyed the sun and sand in Puerto Rico. Marie stayed on her best behavior. I stayed home and devised my own form of entertainment.

In 1991, I got a call from my friend Vinnie the Nose. We had been friends since we were fifteen and kept in touch over the years. I wouldn't have called his nose aquiline, it was more like a zucchini someone had carved to look like a nose and slapped it on his face. It didn't help that he had a beetle forehead and kinky, black hair he combed straight back to resemble rippling waves on a moonless night. He had just bought a 1985 Carver Yachts 45' Cabin Cruiser that he moored in a marina on City Island in The Bronx. He wanted me and Joey Mangione to travel with him along the east coast to Norfolk to test it out.

Joey was another pal from the old neighborhood but we hadn't kept in touch. I remembered him as a scrawny kid with a wise mouth. He still had a wise mouth, but had put on about seventy-five pounds which sat mostly in his gut. The three of us arranged to have our goumare come along with us to make the trip more enjoyable. Vinnie hired a guy from the marina to captain the yacht during the trip as well as give him lessons on boating. He wasn't allowed to bring a girlfriend; someone had to steer the boat.

I drove to City Island the following week having prearranged with Shirley, my current lady friend, to meet me on the dock at noon. As I walked along the dock, I heard Vinnie yelling, "Hey, Al, over here!"

I knew his boat was big, but the boat I saw Vinnie standing at the prow of would have knocked my socks off had I been wearing any. The yacht had berths for nine with an aft cabin suite, a forward stateroom, a dining table/double berth conversion, a salon living area, and an enclosed fly bridge where the captain would be spending most of his time. There were two steering stations, an aft stern deck with a barbecue (no shitting), and a generator, just in case.

I jumped on board, grabbed Vinnie's hand, and pumped it up and down saying, "This is some tub you got here, Vin. Thanks for the invite."

"You are very welcome, Al" he said with a sweeping bow. "The three of us are going to have a great time."

"What do you mean, 'the three of us'? What about our girl friends?"

"Tina and Joey's girl couldn't make it so we get to howl solo."

I was about to tell him about Shirley, when he whistled, "Oh boy, do you see what I see walking along the dock?"

I turned around to see a stunning blond heading toward us. She was wearing tight jeans, stiletto heels, and a black leather jacket cinched tight around her waist which emphasized generous breasts and a great ass. Her heart-shaped face with its cute, upturned nose and bright blue eyes was surrounded by long, flowing hair in the style that Farrah Fawcett made popular at that time and went perfectly with her kick-ass body.

She stopped in front of the yacht. Raising her hand to her forehead in a sailor's salute, she said, "Hi ya, Al, permission to come aboard."

"Sure, Shirley, permission granted."

Shirley daintily stepped on board and gave me a kiss on the cheek. She held out her hand to Vinnie. "You must be Vinnie," she said.

I had to nudge Vinnie to stop him from drooling. He closed his mouth before taking her hand and muttering, "Nice ta meet 'cha."

"Since me and Shirley are the only twosome on this trip, I am commandeering the captain's suite. Got any objections, Vinnie?"

Still not taking his eyes off Shirley, he stuttered, "Sure, Al. Whatever you say."

I grabbed Shirley's bag and my own and led the way down to the cabin. I opened the cabin door and looked inside. I said, "What do you think, Shirley, isn't this something?"

"All I got to say, Al, is you sure know how to pick your friends."

Once we had settled in, we went back on deck. The captain and Joey had arrived, and the yacht was pulling out of the marina starting the three day trip to Norfolk.

To make this story short, Shirley and I had a ball on Vinnie's yacht. After breakfast, (it turned out that Joey was a gourmet cook - hence the weight gain) we would sit on deck sunbathing. After lunch, Shirley and I would take a nap to be refreshed for dinner. Our first layover was Atlantic City. Shirley and I dressed to the nines and had dinner at Harrods before doing some gambling. Joey and Vinnie stayed on board.

Our next layover was in Baltimore where a boar can go to the very heart of the city by its canals. Shirley and I took in the beautiful, city lights of Baltimore before returning to the yacht. Joey and Vinnie stayed on board. By the time we reached Norfolk, Shirley and I were both fed up with the sour grape vibes Vinnie and Joey were emitting.

After another breakfast staring at Vinnie's and Joey's sullen faces, I said to Shirley, "The trip has been great so far, but what do you think we get off here? I can rent a car and we can head back north."

"Suits me," she said, "I'm tired of looking at their grumpy pusses."

After packing our bags, I went on deck to tell Vinnie of our plans. I held out my hand to thank him again for inviting me, but he didn't make a move to shake it. I started to get angry, but Vinnie was an old friend so I let the insult pass.

With a curt, "Have a good trip back," he turned his back on me and went to the aft deck to talk to the captain.

He sold the yacht that spring.

My brother-in-law, Dennis, got nailed in an airport sting in 1990. He spent a year in the Allenwood, PA penitentiary for his sticky fingers. That whole year, every time we saw her, Donna whined that he was framed. Everyone in prison was either framed or completely innocent. Ask them.

It was during these years that Georgann and I met the best friends we would ever have - Paul and Josephine Abruzzi. They were also displaced Bronxites and lived two houses from us in Purdys. The four of us spent many happy hours over glasses of wine reminiscing about the old neighborhood. Paul was the older brother I never had. At fifty-two, the sight of his homely face, balding head and lopsided grin never failed to give me comfort. Josephine was a year younger than Paul and, despite her warm, motherly nature and looks was someone I could always count on to be straight with me even if it hurt. This wonderful couple would play a major role in my life in the years to come.

As Nicky matured into a teenager, her tantrums morphed into outright insolence and rebellion. If Georgann or I said no to any of Nicky's demands, she would whine to Marie that we loved Gabby more than her. Nicky's tears and screaming fits were defended by Marie who insisted that her bad behavior was a cry for attention and love - she needed our understanding, not our rebuke. Maria was groundlessly convinced that if Nicky's parents didn't give her the affection she craved, her grandmother was eager to step up to the job to make up for our indifference.

I didn't know how to respond to a rebellious, teenage daughter. It was easier for me to let Georgann deal with her. Nonetheless, baseless as it was, I still resented Georgann and blamed her for allowing her mother to have so much influence over Nicky. Georgann didn't see it that way. Marie was her mother and Nicky's grandmother who loved both of them unconditionally. As far as she was concerned, I was just being jealous and spiteful. According to Georgann, Nicky was only trying to find herself at a time when being a teenager was very difficult.

By the time I realized the consequences of my unawareness to what was happening and the extent of Marie's interference, it was too late for us to counter Nicky's behavior and too late for the four of us to be a loving family. What could we do? We were guilty. We gave in. Whatever Nicky wanted whether it was a nose job at sixteen or a new car, we gave it to her as substitutes for our attention. Although Nicky was very pretty the saying 'pretty is a pretty does' definitely made Nicky the cruel, ugly sister in our too-real fairy tale.

When Gabby was seven and Nicky seventeen, I bought a used 20' Chris Craft we kept at a marina on Candlewood Lake in Danbury, Connecticut. Georgann, Gabby and I spent many happy hours that summer cruising on the lake. Nicky never even saw the boat.

In 1987, I bought a Ford Econoline van and had it customized with a television, VCR, bench beds, table, and reclining captain's chairs. Gabby loved it. On Sundays, the three of us, and sometimes Paul and Josephine, would pile into the van and take day trips throughout New England. Nicky never came even once. She preferred staying home with Nana or hanging out with her hooligan friends.

When Nicky turned eighteen, Georgann and I both thought sending Nicky to an out of state college would be a good experience for her. We agreed on an expensive, little private college in Maine. The four years Nicky was there were the most peaceful our family experienced. Georgann and I could devote our time to Gabby, and, best of all, Marie had fewer excuses to be at our house.

Sometimes, when Nicky was at college, I'd say to Georgann, "I'm almost beginning to miss Nicky."

Then she'd come home for a few days, and I'd choke on those words.

22

Malpractice Suit

Once Gabby's health stabilized, Georgann and I had begun the search for a law firm who would prepare a malpractice suit – a highly technical segment of civil law - against the obstetricians. We were so incensed by the cavalier, irresponsible manner in which Kirsch and Brandman treated Georgann that we wanted them to pay for the pain and suffering we both experienced notwithstanding the physical handicaps our daughter will have for the rest of her life because of their negligence. We consulted several firms before deciding on Kramer, Dillof, and Livingston, a major New York law firm located in the Woolworth Building in the Wall Street area of lower Manhattan. Attorney Tom Moore was assigned to our case.

I wanted to make sure Moore was good a lawyer so I did some research. Here's a short bio: As a senior partner with Kramer, Dillof, and Livingston, Tom earned a reputation as the most successful trial attorney in the United States, having won more cases with settlements for his clients in excess of one million dollars than any other lawyer. He twice received the National Law Journal's Lawyer of the Year. He was our man!

Our first meeting with Mr. Moore was in May of 1982. A few minutes after the receptionist announced us, he came out of his office for a personal greeting. He shook our hands before escorting us into his office. He made sure were comfortably seated in the two leather chairs in front of his desk before taking his own seat. His bright green eyes shadowed by bushy brows and a dimpled chin warmed us to him immediately.

"Mr. and Mrs. Volpe, may I call you Al and Georgann?" he asked with only a slight accent belying his Irish heritage. We nodded. "I went over all the medical records for your daughter, Gabrielle, and decided to take your case but with one stipulation." We continued to look at him without speaking but with obvious anticipation written all over our faces. "I realize that you rightfully blame the obstetricians for your daughter's problems, but I will only proceed if New York-Presbyterian Hospital is included in the suit."

"But, it was the hospital that saved our little girl," I blurted out.

"I understand your feelings, Al, but I must insist on including them."

I looked at Georgann who gave me the 'it's up to you, Al' look.

"If you think that's the right thing to do, Mr. Moore, then we say go for it." With that said the crusade for justice for Gabby began.

I had no idea how many man-hours were required to prepare a malpractice suit for trial. It seemed like the process would go on forever given the numerous trips Georgann and I made to Manhattan to confer with the attorneys. The legal process is nothing like the slip-and-fall ambulance chasers you see on TV, feeding off a sue'em culture in order to make a quick insurance score. Malpractice suits require extensive research; the poring over of volumes of written medical reports; interviewing potential witnesses; and tedious toil by junior attorneys to determine the likelihood of a positive outcome for all the effort expended. Believe it or not, this effort went on for almost ten years. Finally, Mr. Moore informed us that he was ready for the pretrial hearing. It was scheduled for Wednesday, March 4, 1992 at the courthouse for the Southern District of New York located in lower Manhattan.

A week before the hearing, Georgann and I met with Tom to go over the pretrial process. Succinctly, he explained that the agents for all parties involved in the suit were required to appear before the judge whose job it was to define the legal parameters involved for the upcoming trial. Once all parties acknowledged that they understood the requisites, the civil suit would be put on the medical malpractice docket.

The morning of the hearing, Tom introduced us to his legal assistant, Sam Kaminski. Sam had been Tom's assistant for over ten years. He was in his mid thirties, light brown hair neatly trimmed, and a serious expression on his clean shaven face - that is until he smiled. Then his hazel eyes accompanied by a charming wink said there was a mischievous side to him. Rather than walk across City Hall Park, Tom asked Sam to drive us to the Courthouse in Foley Square for the pretrial. He left us in front of the Thurgood Marshall United States Courthouse and went to park. We stood gaping like tourists at the beautiful, columned building whose massive front steps led to New York Southern District halls of justice.

Once in the courtroom, Tom showed us where to sit before leaving to speak with the other attorneys who were already there - two young lawyers from the insurance company representing the obstetricians, and Attorney James Gargan, representing New York-Presbyterian Hospital. We were surprised not to see Kirsch and Brandman until we later learned that their presence was not required.

Judge Ira Gammerman, primarily responsible for presiding over all the medical malpractice cases in the Southern District of New York at the time, came in and took his seat at the bench before beckoning the four attorneys to approach. Georgann and I strained to hear what was being said, but they were speaking in hushed tones. We did see the insurance lawyers hand papers to the judge who, in turn, gave them to Tom and Gargan. Judge Gammerman dismissed the insurance lawyers. We watched them walk past us, smiling and high fiving each other on the way out of the courtroom - very professional.

Gargan, Tom, and Judge Gammerman continued in conversation. Ten long minutes later, Judge Gammerman rose and left.

Tom shook Gargan's hand before coming over to us. He saw the confusion of our faces. "Let's go back to my office," he said. It's going to take some time for me to explain what was just decided." We left the courthouse, but this time we walked across City Hall Park; Georgann and I could barely keep up with Tom's speed demon pace.

Once we were seated at the table in the conference room with cups of coffee in front of us, Tom began. "The insurance lawyers for the Westchester obstetricians came to court today ready to settle. Kirsch's and Brandman's medical malpractice insurance carries a two million dollar liability policy cap with their insurance company. The papers you saw them give to the judge were settlement and release forms for the two million. As you are aware, my firm originally filed a fourteen million dollar suit against both the Westchester obstetricians and New York-Presbyterian Hospital. The two million dollar settlement released the obstetricians from any further involvement in the upcoming trial. The negligence liability must now be borne solely by the lone defendant - New York-Presbyterian Hospital. I am not legally allowed to even mention the obstetricians or their settlement during the trial."

I now understood why Tom's law firm wouldn't take Gabby's case unless they could implicate New York-Presbyterian Hospital in the suit. Their fee on a settlement of the $2 million liability policy held by Kirsch and Brandman, LLC was not nearly enough for a high-powered, malpractice law firm like Kramer, Dillof, and Livingston to waste their time. New York-Presbyterian Hospital had the big insurance dollars which substantially raised the potential award. It also allowed for a venue change to the fertile money fields of Manhattan. With the case against the obstetricians expunged from the upcoming trial, Tom's challenge was now to convince a jury that New York-Presbyterian Hospital was solely responsible for Gabby's medical condition. The trial would start the following Monday morning with the choosing of the jury.

"How how long will the trial last?" I asked Tom.

"About a week, after that, it will be up to the jury. I want to instruct you both on how to behave in court. You will be sitting with me at the table. Keep your chins lowered as an indication of how serious and concerned you are about your daughter's welfare. Don't smile; don't talk much to each other nor, under any circumstance, make eye contact with the jury. You can look at the Judge and the witnesses but only with expressions of understanding or of trying to understand what they are saying. Got it?"

Sure, we got it.

Before we left his office, he added, looking pointedly at Georgann, "One more thing. It is very important that you both dress conservatively during the trial. No expensive jewelry or flashy clothing. The jury's first impressions of you will color their future decisions. You need to connect with them as if they were trading places with you in the courtroom." He shook our hands. "See you two on the ninth."

On the way home, I reflected on the morning's events. We had waited over ten years to face the obstetricians in court, but the pretrial settlement barely took five minutes, and their presence was not even required! They were off the hook with merely a slight monetary slap on their wrists; their reputations intact. I wanted Brandman's and Kirsch's heads on a platter, but we didn't even get the satisfaction of telling them off. Two million dollars! Ordinary people might carry that amount of insurance in their home and car liability policies. As a limited liability corporation, Brandman's and Kirsch's personal assets were protected. Settlement or trial, two million was all we were going to get, and not even from them. Their insurance company probably earned two million in investment income by stalling the case for the past ten years. Brandman's negligent pre-natal care and Kirsch's medical indifference almost killed Georgann and destroyed Gabby's chance for a normal life. Yet, they would never spend a minute in court nor miss a single tennis match for all the heartache and harm they had caused. I later learned that their practice had numerous malpractice suits filed against them, but, like our daughter's, were settled in pretrial and never reached the public eye.

Insurance premiums are actuarially calculated by medical specialty so good doctors pay the same as bad doctors. There is validity in curtailing the preponderance of frivolous lawsuits, but it is irresponsible for the medical community to allow inept doctors to continue to practice. The bartering of money as compensation for justice is a lesson I had to personally learn the hard way.

Just my opinion

Georgann and I had a lot of planning to do before Monday. Because we didn't want to disrupt Gabby's daily routines, Georgann reluctantly arranged for her mother to stay at our house during the trial. Fortunately, Nicky was away in college working on a master's degree in education. We didn't have to worry about Marie causing sibling rivalry trouble.

On Saturday, Paul went with me to the Tarrytown Thrift Shop where I bought ten conservative ties at 50 cents each and a navy blazer for $5.00 - all perfect courtroom attire. I also bought a brand-new Jones of NY suit for Georgann. What was I thinking!

"Take it back," she said, "I won't wear clothes from a thrift store even if it is new."

I gave the outfit to Rose Carlin when I went to her house to let her know that settling with the doctors eliminated any need for her to be called as a witness. Months earlier, Tom had asked me to provide him with potential witnesses to testify on behalf of our case. I'd taken both Rose and Marie to Tom to interview. Tom chose Rose telling me in private, "Mrs. Marino is rather unstable, isn't she. I don't think she would be an asset in Gabby's case."

Laughing, I said, "No fooling, but I'll leave it to you to tell Mrs. Marino that her testimony won't be needed." I knew from past experience that the messenger as well as the message pays the price with Marie. From that day on Marie held an irrational grudge against Tom and Rose solely because Tom chose Rose over her.

Monday morning on the 16th, Georgann and I left the house at 7:00 am. Marie was already up and had coffee and toast ready for us. Gabby was still asleep. Of course, Georgann ignored Tom's instructions and wore her full length Blackgama mink coat and her two-carat diamond engagement ring.

"I don't think you should dress so ritzy," I said to Georgann. "Tom told us to dress conservative."

As usual, Marie had to put in her two cents. She said to me, "You want to dress like a buffone, go right ahead. My daughter wears what she wants. She's got her pride which is more than I can say about you." She gave me the Italian salute.

I didn't want to start an argument with Georgann; we were both nervous enough. I figured it would be all right for her to wear what she wanted the first day since it was only for jury selection.

We got a spot for the car in an all-day parking lot and walked the couple of blocks to the courthouse. We took the stairs to the second floor. As we approached the courtroom, we found Tom pacing the corridor, obviously in deep thought.

"Good morning, Tom."

Tom stopped pacing to stare long and hard at Georgann. Grabbing hold of my arm, he dragged me down the hall out of Georgann's earshot.

"Why the hell is she wearing a fur coat and that diamond ring? I told you two to dress conservatively; to dress like you needed money, not to look like you were slumming."

"I tried, Tom, but she wouldn't listen to me. You tell her. Maybe she'll listen to you."

Tom walked back to Georgann. Glaring down at her, he whispered loudly through clenched teeth, "Ditch the fur coat and the diamond ring. I don't want to take the chance that any of the jurors might see you."

Georgann started to say something, but Tom cut her short. "Look," he said, "I told you that the jury's first impression of you is very important. Don't dress like that again. Do you understand?"

Although Georgann gave an imperceptive nod, her face remained defiant. She took off the coat, turned it inside out so only the satin lining showed and twisted the ring to her palm.

Before he went into the courtroom for the jury selection, Tom told us to wait on the bench outside. About ten minutes later, we watched six lawyers march double file down the corridor and enter the courtroom across the hall from ours. A couple of minutes later, a Latino man and woman in their mid-forties entered the same courtroom. The Latino man was wearing neck and back braces and struggling to walk with two canes. The woman was holding his arm and helping him along They were accompanied by a short, balding man in an ill fitting three piece suit and carrying a briefcase.

We exchanged 'good mornings' as they walked past us..I couldn't help feeling sorry for the man; he looked like he was a lot of pain.

Georgann was still fussing about Tom's dressing down. "Who does he think he is telling me what to wear? If my mother were here, he wouldn't be so quick with the orders."

"Right, Georgann. As soon as Marie opened her big mouth, Tom would probably quit and you wouldn't have to worry about him telling you what to wear. Forget about having your fashion sense offended. Just do what Tom tells you. He's our lawyer, not Marie. Remember, this is about Gabby's future, not about winning a beauty contest."

Sam showed up with coffee and buttered rolls. I told him what Tom told Georgann about her outfit.

Still offended, Georgann asked, "Why was Tom so short with me? You would think I was the criminal instead of the victim."

"Let me get something straight with you two," he said. "When Tom is in trial mode, he is totally focused like a pro athlete putting on his game face ready to do battle. The jury's impression of you is as important to the outcome of Gabrielle's future as is the testimony of expert witnesses. You want to do what's right for your daughter, don't you?" he finished. Giving me a wink, Sam turned and went into the courtroom.

Georgann watched him walk away obviously mulling over what he just said to her. Sam knew just the right words to mollify Georgann. He was great at straddling the line between diplomacy and sincerity by appealing to her motherly nature. From then on, Georgann never failed to ask for Sam's approval about what she was wearing before she went into the courtroom.

We were still glued to the bench when Tom came out of the courtroom and over to us. The selection of the jury was complete. He said, "The trial will begin at 9:30 tomorrow morning. Remember what I told you about how to look and behave." He turned and left; we went home to prep ourselves.

23

Court

We arrived at Foley Square with just enough time to grab a bagel and coffee from a vendor across the street from the courthouse. We were sitting on a bench near the vendor eating our bagels when TV camera crews pulled up and congregated on the steps of the courthouse.

"What's going on?" I asked the vendor.

"It's the Leona Helmsley trial. You know, the 'Queen of Mean' woman charged with tax evasion."

We had heard about it. A few minutes later, a black limousine pulled up in front of the courthouse. Sure enough, out stepped Leona. Surrounded by her troupe of lawyers, she waved and smiled with her big, red lips to the news teams as they followed her up the steps. She certainly preempted our piddly trial. (Note: After an eight-week trial, Leona was convicted of evading $1.2 million in federal taxes by billing Helmsley's businesses for personal expenses ranging from her underwear to $3 million worth of renovations to the her estate in Connecticut. She was wrong when she said 'only the little people pay taxes'.)

The pre-trial settlement from the obstetricians' insurance company left a sour taste in my mouth, but I needed to remind myself that Gabby's lawsuit was not about revenge but about recompense. I tossed our garbage, took Georgann's hand and, with heads held high and shoulders back; we climbed the steps into the courthouse.

Tom was already pacing in front of the courtroom when we got there, but he took the time to scrutinize Georgann as we approached. She had made an attempt to dress down - not the thrift store outfit – but a plain, dark pantsuit, white blouse and low heels. The only jewelry she wore was her wedding ring. Tom nodded his approval. Sam winked (I was beginning to think he had a tic) before ushering us into the courtroom to our seats at the table.

Ten minutes later, court was called into session. The clerk asked us to rise as Judge Gammerman entered the room and took his seat before we were allowed to sit again. Tom and Attorney Gargan approached the bench, and. after a brief conversation with them, the judge ordered the bailiff to bring in the jury.

I now realized what Tom meant by first impressions. As the jurors took their seats, each examined us as if we were specimens on a glass slide. We kept our heads lowered to avoid eye contact but sneaked peeks at them when we thought they weren't looking. Because this was a civil suit, there were six jurors; three men and three women - all middle-aged and white.

The attorneys began their opening statements. Gargan's defense would be based on the supposition that Gabby was already in critical condition when she arrived at New York-Presbyterian Hospital. Her medical issues were pre-existing due to birth trauma and inept prenatal care. The issues were so severe that the medical staff did not expect her to survive. Gargan would prove to the jury that, despite her frail condition, New York-Presbyterian Hospital saved Gabrielle's life.

Tom's turn.

Tom was (and probably still is) a master of circumlocution. By using more words than necessary, his intention was to weave a tapestry of doubt in the jurors' minds by indirectly questioning the medical procedures and protocol carried out at New York-Presbyterian Hospital resulting in Gabby's current condition. He spoke for forty minutes using highly technical medical terminology designed to impress the jury. He never once referred to his notes and made eye contact with each juror as if he were speaking only to him or her. No one understood most of what he was talking about, but it sure sounded credible, plausible and factual to me. If you throw enough dung on a pile of shit, you'll eventually create a mountain. The jurors listened intently to his dynamic presentation.

Tom ended his statement with, "Gabrielle's pre-existing conditions were exacerbated by the bad care she received at New York-Presbyterian Hospital thereby incurring permanent physical damage. And, despite New York-Presbyterian Hospital's negligent care, Gabby survived." Tom was Academy Award material.

The jury was dismissed for the day at 4:00.

The following morning, Mr. Gargan began his presentation. Without mentioning the obstetricians by name, he skillfully emphasized that the cause of Gabby's congenital damage as well as pre-existing birth defects were due to inept prenatal care and birth trauma - all of which were present prior to her admittance into New York-Presbyterian Hospital's neonatal unit. He painted a vivid picture of that night, almost twelve years ago, when Gabby arrived at the hospital in such critical condition that the staff held little hope of her surviving the night. The final diagnosis was that Gabby's cerebral palsy, hydrocephalous, and hyaline membrane were congenital defects and not due to any negligence on the part of New York-Presbyterian Hospital. Gargan related all the medical concerns the hospital staff dealt with during Gabby's six month stay there - acidosis, stroke, low oxygen level absorptions and multiple shunt revisions - again, all as a result of pre-existing conditions. New York-Presbyterian Hospital was Gabby's savior without whom she would not be alive today. He championed Gabby's courage even to the extent of displaying the newspaper article written on Gabby's first year birthday which dubbed her the miracle baby. Gargan continued to impress upon the jury that it was New York-Presbyterian Hospital's excellent care that saved Gabby from certain death.

Well done, Mr. Gargan.

That day, I left the courtroom with the ominous feeling that the jurors were perplexed. If Gargan's argument was more convincing than Tom's, we were sunk.

On our way out, Georgann and I met the Latino couple we saw on the first day at court and stopped to chat with them. Their two-week trial had ended on Monday afternoon. They were sitting on the same bench Georgann and I sat on when we waited for our jury selection to be over. We sat next to them. They told us their story.

They were Roberto and Emilia Rivera. Roberto was forty-seven years old. His broad face with its thick, black mustache and vivid, dark eyes would be handsome if it wasn't for the frown lines etched around his eyes and mouth caused by constant pain. Emilia, in her early forties, plump and pretty, sat quietly next to Roberto holding his hand, her sorrowful, brown eyes never leaving his face. If a spasm of pain crossed his face, she winced as if his pain were her own.

Roberto had worked as an elevator operator for twenty five years in an old, eight-story hotel building in Manhattan. Five years earlier, while alone in his elevator, the cable broke and the safety mechanisms failed. Free-falling six stories, he shattered just about every bone in his body. The five lawyers we saw marching in lock step the first day each represented a defendant litigant: the elevator manufacturer, cable manufacturer, safety mechanism maker, the hotel maintenance company, and the elevator inspector of City of New York. It was the job of each defense attorney to shift blame away from his client. By the time each attorney finished making his statement, the jury was so confused they didn't know who to hold liable. Who was responsible for Mr. Rivera's accident? The Scales of Justice statue is blindfolded, because she can't bear to see what's going on in today's legal system. Earplugs would be an appropriate addition to her form.

Georgann and I listened silently to their ordeal. Already dazed by Gargan's presentation, we couldn't help feeling compassion for the Riveras. When we got home, Georgann explained to her mother what had happened in today's proceedings. When she tried to share the heartbreak of the Riveras' story, Marie, as usual, dismissed our concerns about the Riveras.

Marie was all about the money and not much about heart. "Who cares about those spics," she said, waving her hand as if she were chasing away a fly. "Gabby's going to be a millionaire."

She believed the trial was just a formality, a mere show before the judge ordered the hospital to hand over the $14 million. Her delusional mind expected that Georgann would be bringing home the money in shopping bags any day now. She boasted, "I'm going down there and set the judge and jury straight if they don't hurry up."

Popinjay Donna chimed in, "Why did Al buy Gabby a bicycle? She doesn't need to learn to ride a bike; she'll be riding in a chauffeured Porsche!"

They even made up songs they would sing as they carried Gabby around the house. "When you're a millionaire, Gabby, don't forget Nana and Auntie Donna." Tra-la-la.

Their obsession with money was loathsome to me. I had no patience for their insensitive ignorance. No amount of money could give Gabby the ability to live as healthy, normal little girl.

Next day, Gargan called witnesses for New York-Presbyterian Hospital. Two doctors on staff at the hospital gave testimony in consensus with Gargan's statement: Gabby was admitted to the hospital in a very distressed state. They related the procedures used to save Gabby's life.

Tom's cross-examination relied on closed-end questions where any answer given sounded incriminating. He asked, "Is it possible that accepted medical protocol be compromised in a moment of imminent peril to save a life?"Of course the doctors' could only answer yes.

Tom continued to cross examine the doctors in this manner. Medical terminology alone can lend itself to semantic ping-pong; fertile ground for jury fodder. Dazzle the jury with unpronounceable medical terms and then baffle them with bullshit. Tom's ready, aim, fire oratorical approach was staccato. The hospital doctors' prior, long-winded medical explanations and legal unwariness made them easy prey for this sharp trial lawyer. Tom skillfully neutralized their testimonies by giving the impression that the hospital might be hiding something. Gargan rested his case. After the day of examination and cross-examination, the jury's understanding, as well as mine, could be summed up in one word – Duh?

We stopped to chat with the Riveras on the way out. No decision yet.

I was a nervous wreck by the time we got home. I was positive that the jury wouldn't attribute all of Gabby's medical problems to the hospital. Mr. Gargan skillfully made them aware of pieces missing in this puzzle i.e. the prenatal care Gabby had received. At home, I sucked down a bunch of aspirin and headed to bed, leaving Georgann to explain to her mother why she hadn't brought home the money.

On Friday, Tom began his presentation by calling our expert witnesses to the stand. Expert witnesses are like hired guns. They receive upwards of $300 an hour in exchange for their specialized expertise and sometimes biased testimony. Our first witness was Dr. John Robertson, a retired hospital administrator whose credentials would give weight to some of the fathomless medical issues Tom had twisted to create suspicion on the hospital. I won't go into Dr. Robertson's testimony, but it was apparent, at least to me, that Mr. Gargan's cross-examination neutralized any negative impressions the jury might have had concerning the hospital's guilt. Back to square one.

We broke for lunch. The Riveras were still on the bench. Georgann and I asked them if they'd like to join us. They said they were too nervous to eat but thanked us for the invitation. We walked the few blocks to our favorite restaurant in Chinatown - #28. My head was throbbing with apprehension, and when I get nervous, I eat. My anxieties didn't seem to rub off on Georgann who quickly finished her small portion of lunch and left to do some shopping. No matter what the situation, Georgann could always find the time to shop. It was her stress reducing activity.

She said, "Take your time, Al. I'll meet you at the shoe store on the corner."

"Okay," I mumbled stuffing my face with her leftover Mu Goo Gai Pan. I went over the last two days in my mind. Maybe my analysis that the jury was confused was overblown, but I didn't think so. I asked for the check and tried to reassure myself by repeating the mantra, "Tom is the best. Tom is the best. I don't need to worry. Tom is the best" I took extra hand wipes to clean the duck sauce off my tie.

Back at the courthouse, we met Tom in the corridor. He was in conference with our second expert witness. Months before the trial, we met with Dr. Leon Charash, a semi-retired doctor whose medical expertise was in pediatric neurology and who had more initials in his credentials than alphabet soup. He was a staple on the Jerry Lewis marathons for muscular dystrophy as well as renowned for starting a clinic in Brazil for children with cerebral palsy. This highly respected champion for children with life threatening illness had examined Gabby and evaluated all her medical, psychological and therapeutic needs.

After swearing in Dr. Charash, Tom led him through his roster of credentials before having him paint a vivid, realistic picture of Gabby's past, present and future challenges. He brought to focus the harsh realities that Gabby's limitations would place on her physical, emotional and financial needs. Dr. Charash explained the neurological concerns of Gabby's cerebral palsy which affected her small muscle motor movements and brain sequencing.

"Gabrielle will never be able to perform many of life's simplest tasks which most of us take for granted like buttoning her blouse, zipping a zipper, hooking her bra, or tying a shoelace. Gabby will never be able to drive a car or live independently without the help of a caregiver. In addition, the shunt that drains the excess fluid from her brain into her stomach will be necessary for her existence for the rest of her life and will require constant revisions."

Dr. Charash's compassionate evaluation of these unforgiving realities was based on his medical experience with cases like Gabby's and it left the jurors with a better sense of Gabby's plight. The looks on their faces registered sympathy for the challenges she would confront every day. Dr. Charash neither accused nor condemned anyone for Gabby's disabilities; he merely related the limitations that would be in her future.

Mr. Gargan did not cross-examine Dr. Charash. There was nothing to refute in his testimony. A somber, melancholic atmosphere pervaded the courtroom as Judge Gammerman adjourned for the weekend. The jurors left the room, heads bent and glassy eyed, overloaded with the conflicting medical jargon they'd been subjected to all week. I hoped that foremost in their minds was Gabby's needs and how they might help my child.

Although Dr. Charash's account was clear to anyone listening, and Tom had done a great job of pitching, my count was behind in juror's court. To me, none of Tom's expert testimonies connected any proof of liability to the hospital. My sickening fear stemmed from the jury gaining any knowledge of Georgann's and Gabby's inept prenatal care. Fortunately, this evidence was inadmissible due to the settlement made by the obstetricians' liability insurance. I hoped that void would not obscure the jurors' determination that the hospital's negligence was solely responsible, especially when Gargan made it clear from the onset that Gabby's congenital birth defects were present prior to her arriving at New York-Presbyterian Hospital.

Before we left the courthouse, Tom told us, "Have Gabby here at eleven on Monday. I'm putting Melissa Connors from Blythdale on the stand first. I'm putting Gabby on to close."

In the corridor, the Riveras were sitting on our bench, both crying. We went to them handing each a wad of tissues. Georgann sat down next to Mrs. Rivera and took her hand. I sat next to Mr. Rivera and patted his shoulder. As soon as he regained some control, Mr. Rivera told us that his trial had ended in a deadlocked jury which forced the judge to call a mistrial. The jury had deliberated all week but couldn't come to an agreement on how to apportion the liability for Mr. Rivera's accident. Apparently, each of the defendants' lawyers was successful at shifting blame away from his represented client. No one disputed that Mr. Rivera had sustained horrible injuries, but each attorney claimed his client was not the party mostly if any at fault.

The confusion by the jury how to apportion a settlement for Mr. Rivera's injuries turned the trial into a legal piss fest; the jurors and Riveras used as urinals. No matter what you want to call it, the defense attorneys had succeeded in round one - Mr. Rivera was thrown out with the dirty bath water. If he wanted any recompense for his injuries, the only option Mr. Rivera had was to start over. That meant another year or two for a new trial with a new jury.

All Georgann and I could do was say we were very sorry and wished them well as we said our final good-byes. Georgann and I talked about how sad we were for the Riveras to avoid any discussion about our trial.

Our trial was almost over. I had a pressing, unsettled feeling in my gut that the jury was not convinced of the hospital's negligence. All weekend, my thoughts kept slipping back to the Rivera trial. That confusion of blame ploy perplexed their jury and could do the same to ours. Burden of proof must show that New York-Presbyterian Hospital as the only defendant was 100% negligent and liable for Gabby's medical problems. If they were not responsible, then no one was. Needless to say, I got little sleep the whole weekend.

Georgann and I arranged for Paul to bring Gabby. Marie refused to allow Gabby to go alone to the courthouse Monday morning. Marie was excited. She was ready to set the judge and the jurors straight. Let them explain to her, personally, what was holding up the 'juice'.

Georgann and I took our seats in the courtroom. Paul, Marie and Gabby sat on 'our' bench to wait until Gabby was called in by the bailiff. Paul was in charge of making sure Marie did not barge into courtroom. I never asked Paul how he managed to curtail Marie's enthusiasm.

As soon as the Judge Gammerman called the court to order, Tom called Melissa Connors to the stand. Melissa was Gabby's physical therapist at Blythdale Rehabilitation Hospital. As with Dr. Charash, Tom led Melissa through her professional credentials before asking her to put in plain words her relationship with Gabby. As her therapist, Melissa had thorough knowledge of Gabby's physical limitations and was able to confirm her life-long need for therapy to keep her muscles from atrophying. Melissa also expressed accolades for Gabby's determined spirit and courage. I snuck looks at the faces of the judge and jurors. I could tell they were impressed by Melissa's heart-warming testimony. Tom said he no further questions for Melissa. He thanked her for her testimony and looked to Mr. Gargan who stood, thanked Melissa and said he had no questions.

After dismissing Melissa, Tom walked to the jury box, paused for a moment, placed his hands on the rail, leaned forward, looked straight into the eyes of each juror before saying, "Now, ladies and gentlemen, I'd like you to meet the young lady this has all been about, Gabrielle Volpe." He held up his arm and swept his hand around, pausing, palm up in welcome, toward the courtroom entrance.

Sam held open the door to allow a petite, dark haired young girl to enter. I watched with everyone else in the courtroom, as, on her own, Gabby walked down the aisle toward the witness stand, a little off-balance, slightly dragging her left leg, but carrying herself with poise and dignity. I was on the edge of my seat ready to jump up to catch her if she stumbled.

The courtroom remained silent. Everyone was holding their breath as she slowly negotiated each step to take her place in the witness box. A sigh of relief was heard throughout the room once she was safely seated. I sat back, pride overflowing from every pore. I grabbed Georgann's hand and squeezed it sensing in her the same pride I felt for our daughter.

Judge Gammerman asked her name for the record. Shyly, peering up at him through her dark lashes, and answered, almost inaudibly to all but the judge, "My name is Gabrielle Irene Volpe, but everyone calls me Gabby."

"Thank you, Gabby. You may precede Mr. Moore".

Smiles broke out on the faces of everyone in the courtroom. I had a grin so wide on my face it hurt.

Tom questioned Gabby about her family. With a soft voice and a sweet smile that never left her face, she spoke lovingly about her mommy, daddy, big sister, and nana. She enchanted the jurors.

Tom asked her to talk more about Georgann.

"My mommy has to help me dress in the morning, but she lets me pick out what I want to wear. She takes me everywhere with her, but the most fun is shopping at the mall. I love to dress up."

"Daddy takes mommy and me for trips on the weekend in our big van and sometimes we go boating on Candlewood Lake. I love it. He used to drive me to school in the morning when I was little. I take the bus now with the other children. Don't tell him, but the songs we used to sing were corny. He has a terrible voice. I never told him that, because I didn't want to hurt his feelings."

"Nicky is my big sister and really beautiful. She's away at college now studying to be a teacher,. but she is also a wonderful dancer. I wish I could dance like her."

"I love to visit with my Nana on weekends. She makes the best lasagna and lets me stay up late to watch television. Don't tell mommy and daddy."

"Do you like to go to school, Gabby?" Tom asked.

"Oh yes. I love to read and make up stories. At recess, I can't play all the games with the other children, but I like to watch them, because they have so much fun. I pretend we're making a movie, and I'm the director."

"How does it make you feel when you can't play with other children?"

"Sometimes it makes me sad, but that's okay. No one can be happy all the time. I'm walking real good now and learning to ride a horse!" Her big eyes shone bright as she said, "Daddy's going to buy me a pony for my next birthday!" Gabby paused for a second before continuing. Lowering her voice to a whisper, she said, "Sometimes my head hurts because of the shunt. I tell mommy right away and she takes me to the doctor and he fixes it."

Georgann held my hand, tears unabashedly streaming down both our faces. I doubted there was a dry eye in the room.

Tom had no further questions, and Gargan would have been out of his mind to cross examine - unless he had a death wish.

"Thank you, Gabby; for your excellent testimony," said Judge Gammerman. "You may go now."

"Thank you, your honor," she politely said.

Gabby negotiated her way down the steps and, walking with the same dignity she had when she first came though the courtroom doors, paused as she passed us at the table to blow us a kiss. Tom, or should I say Gabby, had unknowingly created the purest emotional mind theater.

Tom had instructed Sam and Paul to keep Marie out of the courtroom when Gabby was on the stand. Tom's brief encounter with Marie several years before was experience enough for him to be wary of what foolishness she might try and usurp Gabby's moment. As soon as Gabby left the courtroom, Paul ushered her and Marie out of the courthouse so fast that Marie wasn't able to run her mouth by asking anyone and everyone when Gabby was getting her money or, worse still, by making threats on the judge and jurors' lives for not being quick about it. Paul did his job well. Before lunch recess was over, he was already in Westchester with Marie and Gabby. If Marie made a fuss, I never heard about it.

That afternoon, the attorneys made their final summations to the jury. Again, Tom portrayed New York-Presbyterian Hospital as the culprit completely liable for Gabby's physical damages. Great as Tom was, emotions aside, I hoped I was reading it wrong. In my mind, the burden of proof hadn't connected liability to the hospital. In his summation, Mr. Gargan championed Gabby's plight, but insisted New York-Presbyterian Hospital was not negligent nor were they the cause of her medical damages. In closing, he again reinforced his defense insisting, "New York-Presbyterian Hospital saved Gabby's life."

The jurors had listened attentively to both attorneys. What it came down to was that they had to decide in the following days whether New York-Presbyterian Hospital was totally liable or the hospital wasn't liable at all. I could tell that a vapor of confusion hung heavy over that jury. When the jurors filed out of the jury box, I was unable to read whether their expressions were for or against Tom's interpretation.

On the drive home, I remained silent, absorbed in my worrisome doubts. I was in no mood to listen to Marie's tirade about being dragged away from court before she could set everyone straight, so I headed to bed. Tomorrow, Judge Gammerman would give his instructions to the jury before releasing them to begin deliberation. I had a fitful night, plagued by the nagging conviction that the jury was not convinced the hospital was to blame.

Judge Gammerman began his lengthy explanation to the jury on the law in malpractice cases. He started by saying, "Malpractice law consists of two components, negligence and resulting damages. Burden of proof must be met in both elements to award a liability claim. Negligence not resulting in damage or damage not resulting from negligence does not warrant any liability."

Judge Gammerman spoke for over an hour on the application of burden of proof liability. He explained each juror's responsibility. "Burden of proof must prevail as do negligence and resulting damage to render New York-Presbyterian Hospital liable."

When the Judge finally shut-up, the jurors - and me - were left more confused than ever. I had an empty feeling that Gammerman's burden of proof application sounded more like 'All or nothing at all'; award Gabby millions, or, if the burden of proof is not there, award Gabby zero.

Judge Gammerman released the jury for deliberation. Georgann and I took the Riveras place on the bench to await the decision. Tom paced the corridor like a caged tiger. I sat numb, lost in apprehension. Georgann spent the afternoon alternately reading magazines or talking in the lobby phone booth with her mother. We remained this way until five o'clock until we were told that the jury had not reached a decision and was dismissed for the evening. We drove home without a word.

As soon as we got home, Georgann, worried because I was so quiet, asked, "Al, are you feeling all right?

I mumbled, "My allergies are bothering me. I don't want any dinner. I'm going to bed. After the kind of day we just had, the last thing I want to hear is your mother and sister talking about money." My head was throbbing so much, all I was able to do was swallow a bunch of aspirin, puke, and drop into bed.

The next morning, Georgann and I took our places again on the bench, holding hands but not looking at each other. Now that the trial was over, Tom and Gargan were chatting like old golf buddies. After a couple hours, Judge Gammerman summoned the attorneys into his chambers.

Squeezing Georgann's hand, I said, "This could be it."

Tom returned thirty minutes later. Standing in front of us, he turned his face to me. "The jurors sent a note to the judge requesting more information about 'burden of proof' liability. The judge replied by note that he couldn't give any further explanation to their questions by rule of law. A jury in deliberation can only request to see the trial transcripts or physical evidence; they can't ask the judge for anything else."

What Tom was saying confirmed my worst fear - the jury was confused or, at worst, undecided. I couldn't keep my mind from racing back to the Riveras' deadlocked jury and mistrial. Were we going to experience the same disaster in Gabby's case?

I was panicking. Ten years of waiting had taken serious financial and emotional toll on our marriage. A mistrial would be devastating. What if Tom's law firm decided not to pursue the expense of a retrial? How could we afford to take care of Gabby in the way she needed for the rest of her life? Who would take care of her if something happened to me or Georgann or to the both of us? Where is the justice? I couldn't stop these horrible thoughts from racing through my mind.

Again, the jury had not reached a decision and was dismissed for the day.

By the time we got home that night, I was a basket case. All I could think about was all the 'what ifs' and nothing else. I went up to my bedroom to gnaw down more aspirin before going to bed. I left Georgann to explain to her mother what had happened in court today. From the bedroom, I could hear them.

"The jury wanted the judge to explain more about 'burden of proof.' I think the jury is confused about who is to blame for Gabby's condition," said Georgann.

"Are those fuckin' jurors all stupid or what? It's simple. If the hospital is the one who's going to give us the money then they're to blame. Finito. It's Gabby's money, and she should get it - now."

Marie expected New York-Presbyterian Hospital to hand us over $14 million – in cash. After thirty years of her arrogant ignorance, she still never ceased to amaze me. To her, someone had to pay, and she did not care who that someone was. Her piercing voice added to my inner chaos. All I could do was put the pillow over my head to try to muffle out her shrill voice out. It didn't help much.

We spent all day Thursday on our bench without hearing a word about the jury's deliberation. Tom and Gargan attempted to posture coolness, but the tension in the air became more palpable with every passing hour. Georgann and I sat lifeless on that bench like two mannequins propped up against each other. The sunlight waxed and waned through the high windows casting long shadows across the marble floor.

Stress can test your sanity. I began making up little scenarios to pass the time. My favorite was Marie doing a number on Dr. Brandman which led Judge Gammerman to commit her to an asylum for the criminally insane. On Sundays, Georgann and I would visit Marie and bring her flowers and cannoli. She'd tell us, "There's nothing wrong with none of us in here. It's everybody outside who's fucked up."

For the fourth time, we said goodnight to the attorneys and left the courthouse drained beyond belief. Now what? At this point, I knew the jury was deadlocked. Tomorrow was Friday. The jurors had already sacri- ficed two weeks of their personal lives to this case: nobody's coming back Monday. Even more ominous than the Judge calling a mistrial was the fear of a run-away jury decision - peer pressure to end it one way or the other - all or nothing - let's go home.

Again, I was so distraught by the time we got home, I went straight to bed. Closing our bedroom door, I could hear Marie ranting, "Those jurors are all be morons and that fuckin' judge has his head up his ass." The pillow over my head didn't work this time, either.

With the covers over my head, I said, "Good night, Irene," to both Georgann and Gabby.

Next day.

I was an emotional corpse. Georgann was no better. As soon as we got off the elevator at the courthouse, we saw Tom and Gargan face to face in deep conversation. Their intensity signaled something was up. We took our seats on the bench, never taking our eyes off of them. When they realized our presence, they stopped talking. Mr. Gargan walked past us, and with an uncharacteristic big smile, said, "Good Morning," before disappearing into the rotunda.

Tom waited until he was gone before approaching us in his usual hyper mode. I stood to face him, and, without even a hello, he said, "Al, the hospital offered three and a half million dollars to settle Gabrielle's case. You must decide to accept or reject the offer right now."

My knees got wobbly. Georgann spoke up, "I don't understand. Why does he have to decide right now? What about me?"

Tom cut her short, "I apologize for my abruptness, Georgann, but as Gabrielle's legal guardian in this case; only Al can accept or reject the hospital's settlement offer." Tom turned back to me, "Come on Al, Gargan is waiting. I need your answer - now."

Stumbling for support, I grabbed at the arm of the bench before answering, "Tom, this is Gabby's future. I don't want to make a mistake. What do you think I should do?"

He stared at me for a moment before saying, "I'm prohibited by law to give you any legal advice on this. The decision must come solely from you. There isn't even any time for you to talk this over with Georgann. What's it going to be?"

My mind raced back through the trial, the confused looks on the faces of the jurors, their asking for more clarification, my own misgivings. What if the judge was forced to call a mistrial, because they couldn't reach a decision today? Ten years of waiting and Gabby's future now hung on a moment's decision. I couldn't gamble Gabby's financial security on a mistrial or on a roll of the dice-runaway jury decision. The jury was very aware of Gabby's distressed condition prior to arriving at New York-Presbyterian Hospital, because Mr. Gargan emphasized it from the outset. Was Tom's refutation enough to sway them? Would they show compassion and award Gabby the settlement because of her needs despite who was actually to blame? Were we going to be the next Riveras?

I asked Tom; “Is that figure negotiable or is that it?”

Tom responded, “It may be negotiable. I can try. What settlement are you thinking of?”

“Okay, Tom, get the hospital to go for four million, and we’ve got a deal.” As if this was a garage sale transaction.

With a steely, unblinking stare, he looked into my eyes, “I’ll try.”

I caught my breath. Georgann stared at me with her ‘I don’t understand’ look. Throwing that four million dollar figure at Tom was just a stall to get him out of my face. If the hospital says no, then we’ll take their offer of three and a half million. I would rather lose the half million than take a chance on losing it all.

Tom reappeared and headed toward us at full tilt. Hugging Georgann, he blurted out, “It’s over. We got Gabby four million!"

I lifted Tom off his feet and swung him around, "Thank you. Thank you, Tom."

When I put him down he apologized, “Sorry, Al, for putting so much pressure on you, but the decision was yours to make. I can say it now, you did good!"

“Only you could have pulled off getting that extra half a mil for Gabby. I’ve been shaking in my socks all week, repeating to myself, ‘Tom is the best; Tom will handle it; Tom’s the man.’ I even started to believe it myself. Almost.”

He broke into a big smile. "We all did our best, Al - even Mr. Gargan."

"Thank him for me and for Gabby,"

"I will," he said. "Come to my office next week to sign the release forms. Mathew Gaier from our office will help you set up Gabby’s trust agreement for court approval."

Tom hugged Georgann again and gave my arm a squeeze. "It’s over. Go home and raise your precious daughter. Give Gabby a kiss for me. She won the jury over. Until I put her on the stand, I didn't think there was a chance in hell of getting a dime from the hospital." With that said, he disappeared into the judge’s chambers.

Between the years of waiting and this past week's high stakes drama, closure seemed somewhat anticlimactic - so many unresolved issues. The real guilty parties got off with barely a slap on their wrists. The jury would never hear how despicable Brandman and Kirsch were as doctors or why they were abruptly dismissed by the judge today. We’d never know what really went on behind the closed doors of the jury room as they deliberated or what would have happened if I hadn’t decided to take the settlement. Would the jury have awarded Gabby anything?

As I continued to sit on the bench warmed by the Riveras, I thought to myself, four million dollars from the hospital combined with the doctors’ two million made a solid settlement. I could not have asked for a more positive ending. It might have turned into a far worse scenario if the doctors had stood trial with New York-Presbyterian Hospital. Gargan would have led the jurors, step by step, through the obstetricians' inept prenatal care, Gabby's premature delivery and their final release of Georgann and Gabby to the care of New York-Presbyterian Hospital. I have no doubt the conclusion the jurors would have come to - the obstetricians, not New York-Presbyterian were responsible for Gabby's birth defects.

Following the Judge's definitions regarding 'apportion of blame' and 'burden of proof,' the jurors would have felt compelled to award a settlement to Gabby with the liability assigned solely to the doctors. And, the jurors would have been righteous in their decision. If the money followed that scenario the outcome would have been financially devastating for us. I went over the calculations in my mind: as a limited liability, the obstetricians' practice carried a maximum liability policy of two million dollars - that's all Gabby would get regardless of how much the jury decided to award her; the attorney fees, based on a two million award, would have been about seven hundred thousand; Gabby's final settlement would then be $1,300,000. Not chump change to be sure but not six million. You can lose for winning but, always remember, a cow pie rolled in powdered sugar doesn't make it a jelly donut.

Georgann went to call her mother to tell her that the trial was over. Sitting alone on that bench, waves of joy, sorrow and relief washed over me. I had no regrets; we'd all done our best for Gabby. The final settlement left Gabby almost four million after the attorney's fees. It would provide Gabby with the expert care she would need in life we financially could not.

To celebrate, I bought us two hot pretzels from a street vendor. Georgann spent the drive home on the car phone alternating laughing and crying as she talked with her girlfriends.

I still smoldering with the disappointment of not having Brandman and Kirsch pilloried. I also knew I was in for some trouble at home. I wasn't looking forward to facing Marie. Of course, Georgann's first call was to her mother to tell her the trial was over and the amount of the settlement. If Marie was expecting us to have a cashier's check for $14 million in our hands when we walked in the door she was going to be bitterly disappointed. I swear I heard her screaming how she was going to have the judge, Tom - and me - killed. My imagination, I know, but justifiably founded given past experience with Marie.

As soon as I pulled up to the front door, Georgann rushed out of the car and into the house longing to hug and kiss Gabby.

I called after her, "I'll be there in a minute. I want to clean out the car." I needed a few moments to wind down and to prepare myself for Marie's onslaught. I took my time filling a garbage bag with the accumulation of a week's gum wrappers, cigarette butts and coffee containers before heading into the house.

Marie was in the living room yelling. I couldn't make out the words, but I could guess the content. Obviously, Georgann told her about the final settlement.

I went into the kitchen to phone Margie and tell her the good news; I would be at the store the following day. I was just hanging up when Marie burst into the kitchen slamming the door open hard enough to take it off its hinges.

Barking in my face like a pit bull fighting over a T-bone, she raised her fist as if to hit me, mouth foaming, "Who the fuck do you think you are to make the decision about how much money Gabby should get? You're nothing but the chauffeur in this family. You don't okay nothin', you hear? My name belongs on those court papers, not yours. I'm Gabby's real guardian. You're just the mutt my daughter brought home. I would have got her the whole fourteen million," she said poking her thumb at her chest for emphasis.

I stood dumbfounded as this raging psychopath spat at me and spewed vile insults in my face. What a pathetic excuse for a grandmother! No, what a pathetic excuse for a human being!

Georgann came running into the kitchen. She grabbed her mother and pushed her into the dining room. "What's wrong with you? Have you lost your mind completely? Why are you yelling at Al? Stop this now!"

Marie snarled, "He's nothing in this family, Georgann. You know that my name belongs on those papers, not his."

"Shut up and get out. I'll talk to you later after you've calmed down," Georgann said pushing her mother toward the front door. I'd never seen Georgann behave so confrontationally to her mother.

Marie in her fury, threw open the front door. She turned, pointed an accusing finger at me and, between clenched teeth, said, "You're a fuckin' dead man, mutt." She walked out leaving the door wide open.

I closed the door and locked it. You'd think that I would be used to her threats after all these years, but this time I was more repulsed by her outburst than angry. My only real regret was that Gabby had come downstairs and had witnessed Marie's hostile demonstration.

When I went back into the kitchen, Georgann was holding Gabby on her lap, talking quietly to her. To me, she said, "I'm sorry, Al. I never expected my mother to behave like that."

I threw my arms around Georgann and Gabby, "You're mother's way past having any effect on me. She'll get over it." I didn't believe it.

Gabby looked frightened. She burrowed her head into Georgann's shoulder, saying softly, "I love Nana. I hope she's going to be okay."

I said, "Sure, honey. Don't worry. She'll be fine tomorrow. You'll see." More words I didn't believe.

Today should have been a happy, family time, but Marie ruined it. Again. I lied when I told Gabby it was all right. It wasn't all right now, but what I didn't realize was it would never be. (Spoilers)

Georgann, Gabby, and I went out to dinner at Pizza and Brew to celebrate our good fortune. We stopped for ice cream on the way home, double vanilla-chocolate swirl for me and a single swirl of vanilla for Georgann and Gabby. After putting Gabby to bed, we turned off the phone and collapsed into bed.

The next morning, the phone rang off the hook. I let Georgann take all the calls. Everyone had different versions of the stories Donna and Marie were spreading. Of course, Marie was telling everyone I screwed Gabby out of millions and that she was going to make sure that the judge, the jurors and especially me were going to pay. With Donna, it was as if Georgann had won the lottery instead of a settlement. She was making plans on how to spend Gabby's cash. Money was everything to these ignorant bitches! My blood began to boil. I wanted to snatch the phone out of Georgann's hand and slam it down hard enough to break Donna's eardrum. Instead, I left for the store. I hadn't heard a word from Silvio.

It was a relief to get back to work after being gone for almost a month. I needed something else to occupy my thinking rather than dwell on the stupidity of my in-laws. Getting back to the daily routine of running the store fit the bill.

Margie had already heard Donna's account of what had transpired in court. After working for me for fifteen years, Margie knew me well. She also knew Donna. When she finished telling me Donna's version, she leaned back in her chair and said, "Now, tell me the real story." We both laughed although it wasn't really funny.

That night, Georgann cooked Gabby and me a fabulous meal - filet mignon, baked potatoes, romaine salad with arugula and tomatoes, home-made apple pie - ala mode, of course.

"Why did you go through all this trouble? You must be exhausted," I said.

"I just needed to get out of the house and away from the phone. I went to the super market to buy groceries. It's amazing the stories those two came up with. That's my mother and sister for you," Georgann sighed. She discarded their calumny like yesterday's cold lasagna.

Non fa niente.

24

The Trust

The Wednesday following the trial, we went to Tom's office to discuss Gabby's trust agreement and to sign all the necessary legal forms. Still angry with her mother, Georgann made arrangements with Sue Mondale for Gabby go to her house after school that day. Sue and Georgann had become fast friends after we met Sue and her husband, Fred, at our first neighborhood block party in Purdys. Fred worked as an auditor for an insurance company in White Plains and Sue was a stay at home mom caring for their three daughters, Ashley, Denise, and Patricia. Ashley was only two years older than Gabby, but she took Gabby under her wing like a big sister. Gabby adored her. Denise and Patricia were Ashley's younger sisters. They all rode the bus together every day and spent most afternoons at either my house or theirs.

Georgann and I arrived at Tom's office at ten. The receptionist escorted to the conference room where Tom and Mathew Gaier were already seated. Mathew began his association as an attorney with Kramer, Dillof, and Livingston in 1987. He would manage the preparations required for drawing up Gabby's trust agreement. As soon as we entered the room Mathew greeted us firmly by shaking my hand before holding out a chair for Georgann to sit. He offered to bring us coffee before resuming his seat. He faced us with steady, dark blue eyes and a tight lipped smile that only slightly bared his teeth. The one disarming feature in his narrow face was the big dimples in his cheeks.

Although Mathew would oversee the trust agreement, we also needed to hire an independent attorney to represent Gabby's interests. We asked Mathew to recommend an attorney closer to home, because we were tired of traveling back and forth to Manhattan. He recommended Lois Gruen, an attorney with experience in structuring trusts for minors and whose office was in Mt. Kisco. Georgann would be more comfortable having a woman attorney represent Gabby and even more so once she learned that Mrs. Gruen was a mother with two teen-age daughters. We gave Mathew our okay and he called Mrs. Gruen directly to arrange a meeting at our house on Friday, the following week.

Today, we had other business that needed our attention.

Mathew began, "I took the liberty to invite Keith Hollender, a vice president at Morgan Stanley Smith Barney, who is adept at structuring investment trust fund portfolios for minors. I also ordered lunch for us. I hope you like pastrami on rye and cream sodas."

Mathew continued, "Mr. Hollender will outline the basic structure required to establish a trust fund for Gabby. I put yellow pads and pencils in front of each of you to jot down any questions or thoughts you might have from this meeting. Mrs. Gruen and I will address your questions when we meet at your house on Friday."

As we waited for lunch to be delivered, Mathew led us through our personal and financial information. I did the talking leaving Georgann to do the listening and jotting.

Lunch and Keith Hollender arrived at the same time. Just forty, Keith's six foot frame was wire-thin from running marathons. He sat at the table and knocked back his pastrami sandwich, coleslaw, fries and a diet coke before explaining the ramifications and limitations involved in structuring an investment portfolio for minors that would pass court approval. He showed us some examples of portfolios - all very conservative; no speculative stock, only triple-A rated bond acquisitions and the like. Since Gabby was a minor, it would be necessary to open a joint brokerage account in which to place Gabby's settlement with both Georgann and me as her legal guardians. Hollender instilled so much confidence in us with his professional presentation that we hired him on the spot feeling he wo0uld do his best to protect Gabby's financial future.

Georgann and I also received a check for $150,000 for the pain and suffering we experienced - a separate settlement from Gabby's. After all she had endured with Gabby's birth and the sacrifices she made lovingly caring for Gabby these past twelve years Georgann certainly deserved the money, but I was amazed that she could still joke as she reached for the check, "I'll do a little shopping after lunch."

Besides Gabby's trust account, we also commissioned Keith to set up a separate brokerage account for us. Georgann reluctantly handed back the check.

After signing numerous forms in triplicate, as co-trustees, Georgann and I began to appreciate the intricacies and legalities of the stewardship required to protect Gabby's trust investments. Having been schooled on Marie's investment strategies of collecting Hummel statues or heading to Bloomingdale's to corner the gold market at the jewelry counter; Georgann realized Marie's system would not fly where Gabby was concerned. Georgann and I had a lot to think about.

We spent the next few days sitting at the kitchen table going over the notes Georgann had taken at the meeting. Our talking and thinking had us going in circles about what to expect at Friday's meeting. Our heads were spinning; we were out of our element.

On Friday, Georgann had coffee and pastries ready for our meeting with the attorneys. Lois Gruen and Mathew Gaier arrived within minutes of each other. We took seats around the kitchen table ready to begin the pro-cess of preparing Gabby's trust agreement.

We liked Lois immediately. Although dressed in a conservative, navy blue suit, we knew she was our kind of person because her red high heels matched the headband holding back her short, black hair. Mathew was a nuts and bolts attorney, but we hoped Lois, who had experience dealing with parents, would be more sensitive to our concerns. We were right. Taking her time, Lois carefully explained what the four of us were about to accomplish.

"A trust is a defining, irrevocable instrument formulated to protect the minor. The process begins with chain of authority. You will both be named co-trustees. If either of you dies, the survivor will remain as sole-trustee. In the event you both die before Gabby reaches full age to administer her own trust independently, Nicole will be appointed as interim co-trustee along with a trustee from the Bank of New York." (Spoiler – Remember this info for later.)

Georgann and I nodded in understanding, but I had a question. "You said that Gabby will someday be in charge of her trust. How does that work?" Gabby was only twelve; we couldn't envision her either as an adult or ever making financial decisions for herself.

The task of formulating at what age Gabby could eventually assume control over her trust was not an easy one - the reasoning required both insight and foresight. The focus of the trust was to address everything relating to Gabby's future - emotional, physical and psychological, as well as financial concerns. As parents, these were powerful problems that we didn't want to think about. What would happen if Gabby married, had children, or became incapable of handling her own trust? Until then, as co-trustees, Georgann and I would be legally bound and accountable for all investments and expenditures distributed from the trust until Gabby reached her age of maturity.

This is what we decided: Gabrielle would assume 25% control of her trust at age eighteen, another 25% by twenty-one, 25% more by twenty-five, and total control of her trust by age thirty. If, at any time, it was established that Gabby could not administer her trust, the chain of trusteeship would prevail, and if both Georgann and I were no longer capable of maintaining trusteeship, Nicole Volpe would assume those duties. (Spoiler)

At the end of our work session, we agreed to meet again the following Friday to develop the personalized portion of the trust. At that time, we would evaluate Gabby's future physical, medical, educational, and special needs for incorporation into the trust.

Lois told us, "For the meeting, I want you two to write down everything and anything you can think of Gabby might require or want in the future. Take into consideration physical therapy, medical expenses, special needs, educational resources ... let your imaginations run wild. And, next week, I'll bring the bagels."

Mathew chimed in, "I'll bring the coffee."

Georgann spent the weekend imagining a big expansion to our 1,100 square foot ranch which sat on a quarter of an acre. We had one of the nicer homes in the neighborhood, because I had done a lot of remodeling over the years, but the property was too small for an in-ground pool, and the neighborhood didn't warrant a McMansion. That didn't stop Georgann. Sunday morning, I spied her in the back yard with a tape measure trying to figure out how to fit a thirty-foot in-ground pool into a twenty-foot back yard.

Our little, three-bedroom ranch was cozy and paid off, but it did not have a formal dining room, family room, extra bedrooms, or a pool. Still, the size was not as important to me as putting a stop to the open door policy Marie and Donna felt they were entitled to have. They never bothered to knock; they just used their keys.

Monday morning, I called Lois to ask if it were possible to buy a larger home with the trust money. Lois told me that she would discuss the issue with Mathew and have the answer at our upcoming meeting. True to their word, the attorneys showed up Friday with bagels and coffee. We began the meeting by discussing the possibility of purchasing a larger home that would include such amenities as a pool and an exercise room Gabby could use to improve her physical strength.

As if he had read our minds, Mathew had already gotten court approval for funds from Gabby's trust to be used toward the purchase of such a home. At the time, a house that would suit Gabby's needs would cost upwards of $500,000 in Westchester or Connecticut. Both attorneys agreed that a co-mingling of our funds with that of Gabby's for such a purchase was allowable. Mathew was prepared to write us a check for $300,000 from the trust.

Georgann was ecstatic. She and Gabby would get their dream house. Further discussion of the trust was set aside until after coffee and bagels. Mathew and Lois, caught up in Georgann's excitement about a new home, chatted with her about neighborhoods to check out.

I remained quiet playing devil's advocate to this concept in my mind. What does 'co-mingled funds' legally mean? Who owns what? Would joint ownership expose Gabby's trust to liabilities Georgann and I might personally encounter? What if we sold the new house; how would the equity be divided? The more I thought the more questions I had further adding to my misgivings. I excused myself and took my coffee out on the porch to smoke and think.

When I came back in, I interrupted their house party with my concerns. Both attorneys stared at me blank-faced. They had assumed that co-mingling our money with Gabby's to buy a bigger house was a realistic resolution. The frown on Georgann's face told me I was raining on her parade.

As legal fiduciaries, we would be accountable for all investment and expenditures from Gabrielle's trust. Mingling our funds with Gabby's left loose ends alerted me to the possibility of a range of legal interpretations. Money makes people do crazy things. Because of Georgann's family, over the years I'd become litigation and in-law phobic. Could Marie's envy of me as guardian of Gabby's money and Silvio's greed somehow attach that stench to Gabby's trust? (Spoilers) Georgann and Gabby deserved their dream house, but we all deserved a break from this dysfunctional group called family.

"Maybe I shouldn't have said anything," I said.

"Let's have another cup of coffee," said Lois "We'll take a break to think through Al's concerns."

Georgann sat sulking. I went out on the porch again to smoke. My gut misgivings over this co-mingled funds concept needed legal assurances, not exploitable what-ifs.

As I smoked, I got an idea. Would it be possible for Gabby's trust to purchase the new house outright? Through the trust Gabby would own the house as an investment asset removing Georgann and me from any financial claim to the property. As Gabby's caregivers, we would live in the house as long as Gabby required our care but would need to make some other arrangements should that scenario change. We still had our house in Purdys.

Putting out my cigarette, I thought, "This idea sounds too simple." I was reluctant to mention it to everyone when I went back inside.

During the break, the attorneys had not come up with any definitive legal alternative regarding co-mingling of funds. Georgann was still sulking.

I threw caution to the wind, "This may be a stupid idea, impossible or not even legal," I said. Everyone got quiet. "Could Gabrielle's trust purchase a home outright as an asset?"

Mathew looked at Lois, Lois stared back at Mathew. Their clamor of silence got me ready to apologize for my dumb proposition.

After a few seconds, Mathew exclaimed, "I think Al has something there!" Getting up, he said "Let me call my office and go over this idea with my associates. Give me a few minutes."

Ignoring me, Lois and Georgann continued to chat about houses, and I stepped outside to grab yet another cigarette and mull over Mathew's surprising response.

He had just finished his phone call when I returned to the table. Sitting down, he folded his hands in front of him before announcing, "Full trust ownership is a court approvable solution to purchasing a home. It eliminates the liability concerns you have of co-mingling funds."

Georgann looked at me as if amazed by my incisiveness. I just shrugged, similarly amazed. If my suggestion offered the way to get what Gabby and Georgann wanted, I was in.

We spent the next few hours hammering out the details. A buy figure up to $500,000 for the purchase of a trust owned property was incorporated into the agreement. In addition to the money set aside for a house and for expenses for Gabby's care, Georgann and I would receive $50,000 a year from the trust as Gabby's caregivers. By day's end, the rough draft was complete. We would receive the final draft in the mail the following week. We were instructed to read it over very carefully before signing, after which, our attorneys would present it to the court for approval sometime in July.

Before they left, we called Gabby, who had been watching television in her bedroom, to come out and meet Mathew and Lois.

"Pleased to meet you," she said shaking their hands.

"It is my pleasure, Gabby," said Lois. "We have some exciting news for you. Can I tell her, Georgann? I don't want to spoil the surprise." Georgann gave her a smiling okay. "Soon, you will be moving into a big house with a swimming pool. Your mommy told me that you will be the one to choose where you want to live."

Gabby's eyes lit up. "Is that true, mommy?"

"It sure is, sweetheart. Daddy is going to take us shopping for our new home starting this weekend. Right, Al?" Georgann's piercing look and Gabby's evident joy made it impossible for me to refuse.

On her way out, Lois hugged Georgann and Gabby, "You girls get busy house hunting." She turned to me saying, "You know, Al, you'd make a good lawyer."

That's me, Perry Mason Al.

25

Moving

Georgann picked up some real estate brochures at the supermarket that Saturday morning and scrutinized the classifieds - the race to find the perfect house had left the starting gate. She and Gabby went into high gear in their search. Each weekend for the next three months and armed with a list of addresses of houses for sale, Georgann marshaled Gabby, Paul, and Josephine into the van to look at properties. I was the designated driver. Top on my list of requirements was safety and location. Top of Georgian's and Gabby's long list was 'I'll know it when I see it.'

We concentrated on houses within a twenty-mile radius of our present home, because we didn't want to change Gabby's school or disrupt her after-school activities. Georgann zeroed in on the Ridgefield and Danbury neighborhoods in Connecticut. If we couldn't put much distance between us the Marinos and Weigarts at least we could move to a different state.

In early August, we went before Judge Gammerman to receive the court seal of approval for Gabby's trust agreement. The Judge surprised us by saying that it was the most thoroughly thought-out and explicitly detailed trust agreement he could ever remember approving in his twenty plus years on the bench. He wished us all the best.

Needless to say Marie was panicking. She lived vicariously through Georgann and reserved her love solely for her daughter and granddaughters. Her need meter could not handle Georgann's financial independence and, worse, her emotional independence from her beloved mother. Marie went to such odds that she tried to entice Georgann into buying their house in Bedford.

Wearing the appropriate sorrowful face, Marie approached Georgann. "The house is too big for me and your father. You guys can move in here. We can build a smaller house on the corner of the property. It'll be just like old times."

Over my dead body!

Georgann didn't want to hurt her mother's feelings by telling her she also didn't want to live next door to them. I took great pleasure in taking the bullet for nixing Marie's buy-back house offer.

"We're moving to Connecticut for good reasons," I said to Marie. "For one, Connecticut doesn't have a state income tax. With our new investments,

Georgann and I need to consider every possible tax loop hole. Gabby is really excited about moving. You don't want to disappoint your granddaughter, do you?" I figured that cheating the government out of money was something Silvio would agree was a plus; making Gabby happy couldn't hurt either.

I was wrong.

To Marie, I was taking Georgann away from her again in the same way I did after we reconciled twenty years before instead of divorcing. Although almost fifty, Georgann would always be the princess whom Marie loved more than anyone else had a right to, especially me. After all, wasn't it Marie who took care of Georgann when I was in army basic training in South Carolina? Wasn't it Marie who held her hand when we separated? When she needed help taking care of Nicky and Gabby, wasn't it Marie who stepped up to the plate? Wasn't she the one person who was always there for Georgann, not me? After all her sacrifices how could Georgann desert her mother now?

Maybe Marie had some justification in her resentment, but when she attacked me in my own kitchen after the trial, she crossed the line with me for the last time. I was done overlooking her vile, intrusive, derisive, un-dermining, insane behavior. She slashed my tires, tried to run me down, threatened my life with Mafia contract killers, did her damndest to turn Nicky against me, and done anything and everything she could to break up my marriage. I opened my home, my marriage, and my children to her self-serving ignorance, because she was Georgann's mother. Georgann was the only one in the family who cared enough to turn a blind eye to some of Marie's outrageous behavior. I did my best not to antagonize Marie for Georgann's benefit, but envy has a way of destroying what it admires most. Although she did not realize it, Marie was alienating Georgann further with each new assault on me.

While Nicky was away at college, she was temporarily out of Marie's sphere of control. We feared Marie would use the same manipulative tactics on Gabby, but would increase her efforts now that there was four million to sweeten the pot. Neither Georgann nor I wanted to lose another daughter to Marie's authority. We agreed that it was vital to put some distance between us and the Marinos.

By mid-September, Georgann and Gabby found their dream house in the Aunt Hack section of Danbury. It was perfectly located – five minutes from I-684 and less than a twenty minute drive to Gabby's school and after school programs. It was almost thirty miles from the Marinos and Weigarts - just far enough to keep them from dropping by unannounced whenever they felt like - I hoped (foolishly).

The house was five years old, built on two acres of interior lot with a long, winding driveway that sloped gracefully down to the front door. The property backed up to a wetlands preserve providing a quiet, bucolic setting. It sported an in-ground pool, a large family room in the basement, a great room off the kitchen, four bedrooms, three baths, and even a solarium with a hot tub. Georgann and Gabby loved the house at first sight. Some of the workmanship was shoddy, obviously to cut corners on the cost of building, but nothing major. This upper, middle class, residential section of Danbury justified any capital improvements we made to the property.

We negotiated a selling price of $370,000, well below the allowable $500,000 trust approved figure. We would put the rest of the allowable funds into the renovations required to upgrade the building and for the additions we believed would suit Gabby's special needs and Georgann's desires.

We moved in on October 12, 1992. During the first month of occupancy, there was a steady stream of workers in and out of the place. We had the house painted inside and out and installed a sophisticated air conditioning filtration system in the bedrooms to help with Gabby's breathing. For privacy, we had a high, wooden fence constructed at the back of the property that abutted the wetlands. Big Wally, the carpenter, Clipboard Bill, the electrician, and Ike the Pipe, the plumber, were kept busy repairing, replacing and upgrading anything and everything that needed it. I had Wally build Georgann a big pantry in the kitchen equipped with automatic lights and revolving shelves. She was ecstatic.

Georgann cooked for the workmen every day. She made meatballs and spaghetti, sausage and peppers, eggplant or chicken Parmigiana. Sometimes she served the workers big bowls of pasta e fagioli with hunks of garlic bread dripping with extra virgin olive oil. There was always dessert of canolli, Italian cheese cake and other pastries. The workmen devoured the food saying, "You don't have to pay us; just keep feeding us."

Georgann and Gabby were so happy. Their joy gave me more pleasure than I can put into words. I knew this was going to be the turning point in our lives. I made a solemn vow that nothing bad was ever going to happen to either of them again. As I already said, I was not only none too bright, but I was also a lousy fortune-teller. (Spoilers)

We made friends with our neighbors and especially with Bob who lived next door. One day, when I was building a raised vegetable garden in the backyard, Bob came over to chat.

He asked, "What are you going to plant in the garden?"

I said proudly, "Heirloom tomatoes and dente de leone."

"What's dente de leone, Al?"

"Dandelions."

Bob laughed, "Al, this is New England. People in Connecticut spend hundreds each year trying to kill dandelions."

"These are special, Bob."

Seeing I was serious, Bob did his best not to guffaw, "Ok, Al, I'll be over for my share of the weeds when they're ready."

True to my word, when the tomatoes were ripe, I brought him a big bowl of dandelions and tomatoes drenched in extra virgin olive oil and balsamic vinegar. He took one bite and swooned.

"These are the best weeds I ever ate," he said. "Do you know how to make gourmet food from compost or what?" I beamed and thanked my Nonno for his guidance.

I knew she was a chip off the old Marie noggin, but I never fully realized what a major cause of division Nikol had become in our household until the move to Connecticut. Georgann appeared to be desensitized to Nicky's misbehavior, but I saw it as a sign that Nicky cared little for her family - grandmother excepted. I never understood how sweet, little Nicky had become vicious, animal Nicky. Before Gabby's birth, Nicky was daddy's little girl; I felt really close to her. I taught her how to ride a bike; I took her skiing and snowmobiling; I was official photographer at all her dance recitals. I was close to Nicky in a way I could never be with Gabby because of Gabby's physical limitations.

Georgann and I lost the final battle for any control over Nicky's behavior when we allowed Marie to become her major caregiver after Gabby was born. We might have been victorious in some of the skirmishes with Marie during Nicky's first ten years, but, after Gabby's birth, Marie won the war.

Marie fueled Nicky's sibling rivalry as the dethroned little princess. Unlike Georgann, who gave up her throne willingly to marry Al the Frog, Nicky fought kicking and screaming, refusing to give up her crown to the 'retard' - her affectionate name for Gabby.

Over the years, as Marie's resentment festered toward me, she gained the momentum needed to further persuade Nicky to hate me while encouraging her to have little respect for her mother and sister, because they did not hate me. This kind of twisted manipulation was hard for me to get my head around, but somehow Marie managed to make it work with Nicky. Nicky had turned into Marie's clone.

Although Georgann and I understood that Nicky was not to blame for her rebellious behavior, it didn't mean we were immune to her. Nicky was not only sapping the joy from our family life, she was draining us dry.

If we couldn't do anything about Marie, we tried to stem Nicky's bad behavior. When she was a teenager, Georgann urged her to go for counseling to resolve her sibling issues, but she refused. Nicky told Marie that we were trying to have her committed, because we thought she was crazy. To squash any further of our attempts to get Nicky help, Marie accused us of being coldhearted bastards who were only looking to drug Nicky into submission rather than try to understand her needs. Only Nana was there for Nicky. Because Georgann and I felt a twinge of guilt that Marie's assessment of our parental devotion might be accurate, we relented.

Nicky's resume read like a Who's Who of college graduates. She was respected by her peers and had a master's degree in education that certified her to work with challenged youth. Go figure. She was also a licensed fitness instructor and an accomplished dancer. Paper resumes are for the world to see, but they don't reveal true character.

When Nicky finished college, she moved back with us when we were still living in Purdys. She obtained a position in a local school. After she had been working for a few months, Georgann and I hoped Nicky would find an apartment and move out. Nope. When she was dating Jerry, the plumber, we hoped Nicky would get married and move out. Nope. When a girlfriend of hers asked Nicky to share a condo rental, we hoped she would move out. Nope. After years of disappointment with Nicky we reached the point where our only hope was that she would just go away.

Georgann was desperate that Nicky not live with us in our new home in Danbury. She suggested that we allow Nicky to remain in the house in Purdys and pay us rent.

I laughed, "Nicky pays for nothing. We pay her $200 phone bills. She has free maid service, laundry, room and board. You and Gabby do everything possible to appease her, yet she treats you both like dirt. Nicky answers to no one and does for no one except Nicky. We can help her with the rent, but she has to get her own apartment. She'd turn our old home into a flophouse before we see dollar-one of rent. Besides, our neighbors in Purdys would never forgive us."

Upshot - she came to live with us in Danbury. It didn't take long for Nikol to have our new neighbors up in arms. She sped through this quiet, upscale enclave neighborhood in her red Camaro; her current boyfriend Chuck's loud motorcycle following behind. One day, a neighbor flagged Nicky down to request that she please slow down because of the small children living in the nearby houses. Nicky flipped him the bird and told him to go fuck himself.

I was right on the money. Nicky was an animal and the beast wasn't going anywhere.

On another front, we thought that the move to Connecticut would be a chance to put some geography between the Marinos and our family. More wishful thinking - we had only dragged the barnacles of dysfunction to another harbor. Marie had keys to our new home almost before I did. I would come home from the store to find her and Donna rearranging our furniture while Georgann was out with Gabby. I was so beaten down; I didn't even try to stop them. I just dragged myself up to my bedroom and shut the door.

Al proposes; Marie disposes.

26

Jail

By the time Nicky was twenty four, her drinking and driving had increased and deteriorated respectively. More than ever, Georgann and I were concerned for her safety, but there was little we could do. Nicky was not going to change her behavior, especially if we asked. The best I could do was to install a car phone in her Camaro in case she broke down or had some other emergency. Georgann demanded that she call us whenever she was heading home from one of her bar hangouts. She was warned her that if she didn't call or wasn't home by a certain time, I was going out to look for her. The last thing she wanted was for me to barge into one of her haunts and embarrass her in front of her drinking buddies.

On a Friday night a few weeks after we moved to Danbury, Nicky called at eleven. Georgann picked up. "Mom, I'm getting ready to leave the bar in Mt. Kisco. I'll be home about midnight."

"Are you okay to drive?" Georgann asked, "You're not drunk, are you?"

"No, mom, I'm not drunk. Quit worrying, okay? I'm fine." She disconnected.

Georgann was disgusted. She had heard that fairytale from Nicky too many times before. "I'm going back to sleep," she told me, "If she doesn't come home by midnight, you do what you want." With that said she rolled over and fell promptly back to sleep.

Like a schmuck, I pulled up a chair in the hall outside our bedroom to wait up for Nicky. I dozed off. At 2:17 am, I was awakened by her car roaring down the driveway. I stood up; roused myself awake and leaned against the wall at the top of the stairs to make sure she was okay. First, she slammed the car door and then slammed the front door so hard the whole house shook. She staggered up the stairs using the banister to pull herself up the stairs hand over hand.

When she had successfully maneuvered to the top of the stairs, I confronted her. She hadn't seen me standing there, but she came close enough for me to smell the alcohol on her.

"You're drunk. You told your mother you would be home by midnight. What took you so long?"

Startled, Nicky staggered back a step before screaming, "None of your fuckin' business. I don't have to answer to you. I'm an adult and you're a jerk."

"Lower your voice. You'll wake your sister," I told her.

"Fuck you! Don't tell me what to do!" She charged at me. Swinging wildly, she managed to give me a hard blow on my shoulder.

Her punch sent us both tumbling head over heels down the stairs landing at the bottom, me face down. Nicky scrambled to her feet, grabbed the lamp off the side table, and, before I could stand up, shattered it across my back. The impact of the blow threw her off balance, dropping the lamp before falling on her butt. I rolled over, grabbed her legs, and turned her face down on the carpet, pinning her arms behind her back. She arched her back flailing her legs like a fish out of water trying to get out of my grip. I held her down, and, for one moment, all the resentment I felt toward her came soaring to the surface. It took every bit of my self-control not to strike her.

Georgann, wakened by the commotion, came running down the stairs. "Oh my God," she yelled, "Al, what are you doing to her?"

"Me?" I gasped, "She's the one who's tried to kill me. She broke that lamp over my back. I'm just trying to keep her from doing more damage to me or herself. She's a drunken maniac!"

Georgann bent down to Nicky. As she stroked her hair, she said, "You can stop struggling now, sweetheart. Mommy's here. Daddy doesn't want to hurt you. He's going to let go of you now. Okay?"

"Please, mommy, get him off of me. He is hurting me." She sounded like a little girl.

"Let her go, Al. You've done enough. I'll take care of my daughter now."

I let go of Nicky's arms, rose and backed up against the wall. Georgann helped Nicky to her feet, put her arm around her and guided her out the front door.

I was shaking with rage and hatred toward Nicky. If she had hit me in the head with that lamp instead of my back she might have killed me. Although I wasn't cut or bleeding, I was in pain - physical and emotional. I felt miserable. My relationship with Nikol had come to brawling like a couple of lowlifes. What intensified my pain even more was the realization that Georgann had taken Nicky's side. Her daughter! Her daughter! Not ours! Until now, I could always count on Georgann to at least see my side.

I checked in on Gabby who had miraculously slept through the whole ruckus. I tiptoed out of her room closing the door quietly behind me. In our bedroom, I went over to the window and watched Georgann and Nicky walk slowly up the driveway, Georgann's arm still wrapped around her daughter's shoulder. Although I couldn't hear them, I knew Nicky was sobbing, because I could see her body convulsing. I assumed that Georgann was trying to calm her down before coming back into the house and putting her to bed. I also assumed that once she had settled Nicky in, Georgann would apologize for even thinking I had it in me to harm out daughter.

Sleep was not going to happen; I got dressed. My back was killing me. While I waited for Georgann to return, I lay down on the bed trying to figure out why Nicky hated me so much. It was evident that the years of Marie's brainwashing finally succeeded instilling in Nicky the same contempt that her grandmother felt for me. But, why wasn't Nicky's resentment directed toward Georgann, too? Hadn't she neglected her older daughter in favor of Gabby? I was truly at a loss to understand such abject disdain only for me. Sure, I was busy making a living and gone a lot, but that was nothing new - I was always doing something, business or personal that kept me out of the house.

I was so lost in my thoughts before I realized that Georgann and Nicky had been gone a long time. Suddenly, I saw headlights dance across the bedroom windows. I got up from the bed to look out - two police cruisers coming down the driveway. I ran downstairs, yanked open the front door only to face two startled uniformed officers. They were young, no more than twenty five, but that was where the similarity ended. One was tall and black, his neatly pressed uniform fit tightly over his muscular frame. The other was white, brown hair cut in a crew, shorter, a couple of pounds extra but solidly packed although not nearly as dapper as his partner.

"Are you Al Volpe?" the white cop asked.

"I am," I answered. "What's this about?"

"I'm Officer Maldonado and this is my partner Officer Reynard. Your wife called us from her car phone. She said you attacked your daughter."

I took a step back inside the house. "That's not what happened, Officer. I did not attack Nicky. I don't understand why my wife called you."

"That's not your wife's story," he said. "Place your hands on your head and step slowly out of the house."

"I'm not going anywhere," I said. When I tried to close the door on them, Officer Reynard drew his gun.

When I still hadn't moved, they shoved the door open and stepped inside. I hit the wall hard staggering to maintain my balance.

"We tried to be nice, Mr. Volpe," Reynard said, "I guess we just have to do it the hard way." They grabbed hold of me, pulled my arms behind my back and handcuffed me. "Now move it," said Maldonado pushing me out the door.

I froze in my tracks, "Hold on, Officers. My younger daughter's asleep upstairs. I can't leave her alone. She's handicapped. Where's my wife?"

Maldonado said, "Your wife will be back as soon as you come with us."

"Where are you taking me? I didn't do anything!"

"You're spending the night on the city, buddy. Now, move it. Don't make me ask again."

They hauled me to the cruiser, opened the back door pushing my head down as they lowered me into the backseat. When the cruiser turned from the driveway into the street, I stared out the window to see Georgann and Nicky sitting in the backseat of the other patrol car. They were both crying, Nicky's head was resting on her mother's shoulder. Georgann looked up, our eyes met, but she only stared back as if she were looking right through me.

At the police station, I was fingerprinted and taken to the basement for cell lockup. The hall lights were dim, the cell dark. I sat on edge of the metal bunk, its thin mattress barely keeping the cold steel from freezing my ass; I was thoroughly miserable. It was about 3:00 am. - forty five minutes was all it took to destroy my life. It seemed like an eternity ago that I believed the move to Connecticut would be a new start for my family. Another delusion:

I felt a tap on my shoulder. Startled, I hadn't realized I wasn't alone in the cell. A black man stood in front of me offering a wad of toilet paper to dry my eyes and blow my nose. His long face and graying, tightly curled hair indicated a weariness that was greater than his years which I assumed to be over fifty. He was actually forty. He was a small man whose stooped shoulders diminished his slight frame even more and bespoke a demeanor of a man totally beaten down by life.

"This your first time, right? Don't be scared. Jail ain't so bad."

"It's all a mistake. I shouldn't be here," I said.

"Me either," he said. "This is the third time I been locked up for domestic violence. My wife beats me up; someone calls the police, and I wind up in jail."

"Why don't you call the police on her?"

"I just can't. I love her. I don't want her to go to prison. My name is Wally. What's yours?"

"Al," I said. "But, Wally, I don't understand how I got into this mess. My wife called the police on me even after I told her it was my daughter who attacked me first. I was just trying to keep her from injuring herself and killing me."

"Looks like they just wanted to get you out of the house. You sure you didn't hit your daughter?"

"No way, Wally! I would never lay a finger on her no matter how angry she got me. She was drunk. When she swung at me, she lost her balance and fell down the stairs taking me with her. We landed at the bottom and she tried to bean me with a lamp. I was just trying to calm her down, that's all. I don't understand why my wife called the cops? She's always had my back before."

"OK. Leave it. That kind of thinking won't help you. Let me explain what's going to happen next," he said, "I'm an expert, practically got a law degree in domestic violence. Here's how it works. When police respond to a domestic dispute, someone's gotta go to jail. Ninety-nine percent of the time it's the man even if he was the one being beat."

From what Wally was saying, I realized that's exactly how I wound up in jail. Cursed, punched, pitched down a flight of stairs, a lamp shattered over my back, manhandled, fingerprinted, and thrown in a cell just for asking my daughter if she was all right.

Wally continued, "You have to spend the night in jail. Tomorrow, you go in front of the judge. If no criminal charges are filed against you, the court handles it as a police complaint. Since it's your first offense, the judge will probably order you to attend anger management counseling. Once that's done, your slate is wiped clean."

Wally and I talked the night away, he telling me his tales of woe, me listening. He was a diversion and prevented me from giving myself a full blown pity party. At 7:00 am, the officer on watch brought Wally coffee and an egg sandwich.

As I looked hungrily at the food, the officer told me, "Sorry, you don't get anything. You booked in too late for the breakfast order."

Like I said, when I'm nervous, I get hungry. I was starving by then.

Wally said, "Here Al, take mine. I don't drink coffee; it's bad for my nerves, and eggs are bad for my cholesterol."

I thanked him as I wolfed down his egg sandwich and coffee. At nine, they transported five of us to the courthouse on White Street in Danbury.

A public defender met with each of us for a few minutes. When he saw how nervous I was, he said, "Relax, it's your first offense. The judge will just order you to attend anger management counseling." Just like Wally told me.

After the public defender read through the statements in the police report, he asked me, "Who is Marie Marino?"

How did her name get into my police report? I wanted to say, "She's the miserable bitch who's the cause of all my troubles and who wants me dead." What I said was, "She's my mother-in-law."

He closed the file and looked at me for a few moments before saying, "Al, I've seen hundreds of scumbags pass through the system. You don't look like one to me. No charges have been filed against you. Do your counseling and be careful." Then he moved on to the next defendant.

Three minutes in front of the judge got me signed up for anger management counseling and released.

I used the public phone in the lobby of the courthouse to call Paul and ask him to pick me up at the courthouse. We stopped at the Holiday Diner across the street from the courthouse so I could get another breakfast. I was really nervous so I was really hungry. I ordered eggs over easy, bacon, home fries, pancakes, toast, and coffee; Paul had coffee - decaf.

I related the events of the prior night. Repeating Nicky's words really brought home how deeply-rooted was her hatred for me. Or, should I say, Marie's hatred. Then again, how much could I blame Marie? Nicky was old enough to run her own life. Maybe I should have been home more, taken more of an interest in Nicky's life after Gabby was born. Maybe it wasn't fair of me to let Georgann handle the outrageous behavior of both her mother and Nicky alone. For the first time, I woke up and smelled the stench to which they had subjected Georgann, merely because she loved me. I knew I was none too bright, but I didn't realize I was also insensitive. (You, the reader, may have surmised this by now, but I didn't.)

"Paul, I'm all mixed up. I need to sort out my thoughts. It's a good thing we haven't rented our house in Purdys yet. I think I'll stay there for a few days. Please drive me to my house first so I can pick up some clothes and get my car. I really appreciate you being here for me."

"I'll always be here for you, Al," said Paul picking up my breakfast tab. He drove me home. "I'll wait outside while you get your things in case there's a problem."

No one was there. I grabbed some clothes, a pillow and blankets. I left Georgann a note letting her know I was going to stay in Purdys for a while. The ball was in her court now. Before I closed the front door, I turned for one last glance into the house I had hoped was going be a loving home for me, Georgann and Gabby. Just another pipe dream gone bust.

Paul was leaning against his car; his arms folded over his chest. He stood up as soon as he saw me. I threw my arms around him hugging him hard. "Paul, you are my best friend; more like a brother. Thank you. Thank you."

"You don't have to keep thanking me, Al. That's what friends do for each other." He got in his car and drove off.

I threw my sparse belongings into my car and drove to the old house. I dumped the stuff on the floor before going to Paul's for dinner. Josephine was already up to date on this particular disaster in my life so I was spared the agony of reliving it. Dinner was pretty quiet. My friends could not think of anything to say to cheer me up.

Josephine had invited Sally Quinn to come by after dinner for coffee. Sally was Georgann's oldest friend both having attended the Villa Maria Academy together when they were girls. They lost touch for some years but reestablished their friendship when we moved to Danbury. Sally also lived in Danbury with her husband, Matt, and their two sons. I knew she would be the second person Georgann called after I got arrested - Marie being the first, of course.

I waited until we had our coffee in front of us before I grilled Sally. "What did Georgann tell you? Don't say nothing, because I know she called you."

"You're right Al. Georgann needed to talk to someone. She felt so guilty not believing you. After the police took you away, she and Nicky went back into the house accompanied by a cop. Georgann wanted to make sure Nicky wasn't hurt tumbling down the stairs so she called Marie to have her and Dennis drive to your house and take Nicky to the emergency room at Danbury Hospital. Georgann had to stay at home with Gabby. The cop followed Marie and Dennis to the hospital to take an account of Nicky's injuries for his report. The hospital took x-rays of Nicky's head checking for a concussion."

"What?" I stopped her, "If she had a concussion is was when she hit her head falling down the stairs. I never laid a finger on her."

"Let me finish," said Sally, "They found a glitch on the x-ray of Nicky's nose. Marie wanted Nicky to lie to the police and tell them that you broke her nose after you tried to rape her when she was a teen-ager. To her credit, Nicky wouldn't lie. Hard to believe, she actually told her grandmother to shut up."

"You know damn well where that so called glitch came from," I said. "It's a remnant of scar tissue from the nose job I paid for when she was sixteen. I always knew Marie was skilled at using any contemptible means to get at me, but to accuse me of rape is even lower than I thought she was even capable of being."

"I know," said Sally. "The cop warned Marie about the consequences of making false accusations. He still wrote down what she said in his police report. The hospital didn't find anything wrong with Nicky and released her. After Dennis and Marie left, Nicky told Georgann what had happened between you two. She also told Georgann what Marie tried to pull at the hospital."

Now I understood why the public defender asked me who Marie was and also why he told me to be careful.

Later that night after Sally left, Georgann called me.

"Are you okay? You're not hurt are you?" she asked.

"Just my feelings," I said trying to make light of this sick situation. "Sally told me about the bullshit your mother tried to pull at the hospital."

"I know. My mother's a not a well woman," said Georgann, "but I'm the one who called the police. When I saw the two of you at the bottom of the stairs, I didn't know what to think. Sitting on top of Nicky, the look of hatred on your face frightened me to death. I thought you were going to kill her. I was afraid for both of you. The only thing I could think of was to get you out of there. I called the police from my car phone to report the fight and ask them to remove you from the house before Nicky and I could go back in. When Nicky sobered up, she told me what really happened. I'm so sorry, Al, that I ever for a moment believed you would hurt Nicky."

"I know, Georgann. I understand. You didn't file any charges so the court just ordered me to attend anger management counseling. Ask your mother and Nicky if they'll help me with my homework."

"Only, if you want to fail."

I imagined she gave me 'the look.' We were all right again. "How's Gabby and Nicky?"

"They're fine. Gabby didn't even wake up until the morning, and Nicky was just sore from falling down the stairs. She doesn't remember much else probably because of the huge hangover she's got. Serves her right. Are you sure you're okay? Paul told me you want to spend some time alone. Put him on the phone. I want to talk to him."

Georgann didn't believe me when I said I was okay. I handed the phone back to Paul. A few minutes later, I heard him say, "Don't worry, he's fine. He just needs some time to think."

Paul rounded up a sleeping bag and the some camping gear for me to take to Purdys. He drove me there, because I was in no condition to drive myself. The next morning, Georgann and Sally brought me some food, clothes and a coffee machine.

Georgann asked me, "How long are you running away from home? Me and Gabby want to run away, too."

"Oh no, I'm running away by myself," I laughed

A week later, I returned to Danbury with little to show for my solitude.

27

Furniture

The incident with Nicky blew over. I went to my anger management classes and passed with an A+. Nicky and I weren't real friendly, but we behaved ourselves in front of Georgann and Gabby.

Our house in Purdys was much smaller than our new Connecticut home. Once all the renovations were completed, it was evident that we needed a lot more furniture. Even though the purchase of new furniture was covered by Gabby's trust, Georgann knew she was married to Cheapskate Al and contacted several furniture wholesalers in High Point, NC, the furniture capitol of the world. I banked on saving thousands by buying the furniture in North Carolina and having it shipped to Connecticut.

We decided to make the trip to High Point a mini-vacation. We invited Melissa Corsaro who was home from college on holiday break to keep Gabby company. Melissa was the daughter of John Corsaro, a doctor in the Katonah Medical Group where Georgann had worked. Melissa often babysat for Gabby when we lived in Purdys. We rarely asked Marie to babysit Gabby if we could help it. The day after Christmas, we loaded up the van and the four of us headed south. Nikol, home on winter break from teaching, was not invited.

Asking Melissa to join us was a great idea. During the trip, she and Gabby spent many happy hours playing board games, watching videos, chitchatting or just looking out the windows at the scenery going by. I chauffeured and Georgann navigated. We stayed one night in Richmond, Virginia, and, after eating a leisurely breakfast at a Cracker Barrel, were back on the road. By late afternoon, we arrived at the fancy hotel Georgann had pre-booked for us in the center of town in High Point

Although Georgann's part time job as a travel agent gave her a lot of perks and freebies they did not include the hotel robes and towels she packed for home when we stayed at the Floridian in Disney World a few years before. The hotel added $300.00 to my bill to cover the 'oversight.' I made sure I told Georgann not to make the same assumption on this trip.

Georgann and I spent the next three days frantically running from show room to show room hitting most of the wholesale furniture dealers in the area. We bought a truckload of furniture. Gabby and Melissa had a ball swimming in the hotel pool, watching TV, and ordering room service.

Finally, we were done. Georgann and I were exhausted from the hectic pace we had kept. To wind down and do a little sight-seeing, we decided to spend New Year's Eve in historic Williamsburg, Virginia, the halfway point on the journey home.

As I drove, Georgann sorted through the furniture orders asking me if I remembered this couch or that lamp. I stopped answering 'no' each time she asked me and just nodded my head making the girls giggle. I was furnitured-out; I didn't remember nothing.

We booked adjoining rooms for us and the girls at the Inn in Williamsburg. After driving around Williamsburg still lit up with Christmas lights, and after great dinner in the hotel dining room, the girls headed back to their room to watch television. Georgann and I sat by the wood burning fire in the lobby enjoying our coffee and letting the warmth of the blaze soothe our overtaxed nerves. Georgann had eaten little, but I attributed that to furniture burn-out. I had no idea she was biding her time waiting for the opportunity to get away from me.

Around eleven, Georgann suggested, "Why don't you check out the souvenir shop. It's still open. I want to spend some time with the girls. I'll meet you back at the room in time to watch the ball drop. I'm going to call my parents and wish them a happy new year." She knew I couldn't resist the hokey knick knacks in the hotel shop.

Georgann appeared unusually edgy when I went to room. The girls were still up; we brought them into our room to watch the ball drop in Times Square. After that, I scooted them off to their room with instructions to go right to bed, because we were leaving early in the morning. I chalked up Georgann's restless night to the excitement of getting all new furniture. But, the next morning, Georgann still appeared uneasy.

"Al, can you take the girls down for breakfast? I didn't sleep well last night. I need a little more time to make myself beautiful."

"Sure, Georgann, I want to go back to the gift store anyway. I saw some cute dolls dressed like pilgrims I know Gabby and Melissa would love to have as souvenirs of our trip." She didn't tell me this time, but as soon as I left the room, she called her mother again.

The drive home was eerie. I thought everyone was just tired. Georgann pretended to doze in the seat next to me while the girls slept in the back.

It had snowed in Connecticut while we were away; the roads were dirty and slushy. We got home just after five. As I drove down our long driveway, the van's headlights picked up tire tracks in the snow and beer cans littering the sides of the driveway. The house was dark. I opened the garage door with the remote and pulled in. We entered the house from inside the garage. Brandy, our white bichon poodle and Bianca, our white Persian came running, happy to see us. That was the only greeting we got.

Georgann told Melissa and Gabby, "I'll order pizza. We're all really tired so let's just go to bed after we eat. Melissa, you can sleep in the extra bed in Gabby's room. I'll take you home in the morning after breakfast. Leave the bags until tomorrow."

After we finished the pizza the girls went up to Gabby's room, and I asked Georgann, "Where's Nicky?"

"She didn't want to stay in this big house alone so she went to Donna's."

Dead on my feet from all the driving, I didn't ask anything further about Nicky and trudged up to our room. Georgann undressed and got quickly into bed with just a murmur of a good night before turning on her side. I brushed my teeth, flopped into bed and was asleep in two minutes.

A week later, I was talking with my neighbor Bob who told me he had called the police on New Year's Eve. "I was keeping a watch on your house, Al, while you were gone. There was a party going on in full swing. This is a quiet neighborhood, Al. I didn't want you or your family to get a bad reputation so I called the police. Soon after the cops got most of the kids out of your house, I saw a woman and a man pull up in separate cars. They went into the house. The kids who were still partying ran to their cars and sped away leaving their mess behind. The man came out with Nikol, put her into his car and drove away. I watched the lights go on and off in all the rooms and saw the woman drag lots of black garbage bags out to her car. Then, she left, too."

I told Bob the man and the woman were my mother-in-law and brother-in-law.

From his story, I was able to piece together what had probably happened. After all, I had become an expert on the Marie-Georgann conspiracies whenever Nicky was concerned.

Nicky had asked Georgann if she could have a New Year's Eve party at our house during our absence. Although Georgann told her no, Nicky wasn't above ignoring her mother's orders. Georgann had a foreboding that she would go ahead with the party anyway and needed to know if she had been right. She called Nicky from our room. Sure as shit, there was a big party going on at our house. The neighbors had already called the police who managed to usher some of the more raucous party goers out of the house, but the party was still in high gear when Georgann called. She told Nicky to get everyone out of the house immediately. Knowing her threats were falling on deaf ears, as soon as Nicky hung up on her, Georgann called the only person on whom she could rely - her mother.

I realized Georgann that was the real reason for calling her mother on New Year's Eve. As always, I hadn't a clue what had transpired in my absence since Marie and Georgann always kept any incident involving Nicky hush-hush from me.

This is how I imagined Georgann's morning phone call went.

"Mom, how did it go last night?"

"Your daughter must have had over a hundred kids at the house. Dennis and me threw them out threatening to call the police again if they didn't go quietly. Nicky was drunk. She didn't understand why her friends had to leave, because you said it was okay for her to have a party."

"I absolutely told her she could do no such a thing."

"I know you did, sweetheart. Dennis and I came in separate cars. After we got everybody out, Dennis took Nicky to his house. I stayed to clean up the mess."

"Did they destroy anything in the house? I don't want any surprises when we get home. Al doesn't need another run-in with Nicky."

"Forget about telling Al. We'll make sure he doesn't know a thing."

"Thanks, Mom. I love you. We'll be back tonight."

The house was just as we had left it. Marie was a hell of a house cleaner!

Nothing was ever said to me about the party although, when I asked about the beer cans on the lawn, I was only given a shrug by Georgann.

I never mentioned to Georgann that I knew what had happened. Even though I was used to being lied to by Marie and Georgann, I was surprised by how apathetic I had become where Nicky was concerned.

Happy New Year!

28

St. Thomas

At the beginning of the New Year, we rented our house in Purdys to Dr. Jonah Winig and his family. He was on temporary assignment at the Katonah Medical Group, and as soon as his assignment ended he intended to return to his former practice in upstate New York. Because of this, he preferred to rent rather than buy a house. He would be the perfect tenant until Georgann and I decided what to do with the house.

By the end of January, all the furniture we ordered in High Point began to arrive. Georgann spent the next few weeks happily decorating (and redecorating) while I broke my back moving furniture around. In no time, (seemed like eons to me) she had the house looking the way she wanted. I was really pleased to see that she even hung some of my oil paintings on the wall of the staircase leading to the second floor. Gabby and Georgann's 'dream' house was now a reality.

Winter break 1993: Georgann begged me to go with them on vacation, but I refused. I could think of a lot of things I wanted to do with (to) Marie rather than spend vacation time with her. This year was going to be their first trip to St. Thomas, and everyone was excited they were going to a new, exotic place.

The snow was piled high on the sides of the driveway as Danny's stretch limo weaved its way down. Our driver for many years, he was taking Georgann, Gabby and Nicky to LaGuardia Airport. Marie was already in the back seat of the limo peering out at me with a grin on her face as wide as a runway - happy I wasn't going with them. I kissed my wife and daughters bon-voyage (yes, Nicky, too), helped them into the back seat of the limo and waved good-bye.

I was already engrossed in thoughts about my own plans for this winter break. But, that's for another book.

Georgann called me as soon as they landed in St. Thomas.. At the luggage roundabout, she looked around for Willis, the local cab driver. Georgann hired Willis to take them around St. Thomas during their stay. She spotted him holding up a sign printed with the name '

Marino'. Of course.

Marie dubbed Willis their 'Leroy Brown' because he looked so bad. She was proud to inform everyone that nobody in St. Thomas messed with her 'chicklets' when Willis was around.

Willis immediately took my girls under his wing. Besides being their appointed chauffeur, he became 'the chicklets' unofficial travel guide, bodyguard, and friend. Willis was a mountain of a man at 6'5" and three hundred and twenty pounds of sentimental mush. f Gabby got too tired to walk when they went sightseeing,, Willis carried her on his shoulders, the wide grin spread on his broad, black face read Gabby was no burden; she was a treasure. They had a wonderful, uneventful time and came back tanned, relaxed, and happy.

As soon as the ground thawed, we hired Don Barshak of Estate Pools, Inc. to design and landscape the property around the pool. Don resurfaced and heated the existing pool adding an incredible waterfall feature. He surrounded the pool with a large cedar deck which he included a hot tub and built a cabana with a shower. Don landscaped the property around the deck with native shrubs and perennial flowers. The improvements included widening the driveway and repaving the walkways.

By early spring, the landscaping outside and the inside renovations and decorating were complete creating a uniquely beautiful home for Gabby and Georgann. I did not consider what Nikol might have wanted in the plans.

In April, we celebrated Gabby's thirteenth birthday around the pool. Georgann hired a DJ and invited family and friends from Westchester and our new friends from Danbury to the party. Even though the weather was still a little chilly, the heated pool tempted quite a few of the more hearty guests to enjoy swimming and sitting under the waterfall. Even I went into the hot tub.

That summer, the pool became the center of our social life. Financial worries behind us, Georgann, Gabby and I spent many happy hours with family and friends swimming, barbecuing and having a great time. We hosted a lot of all girl parties for Gabby and her friends. Where was Nicky? If she went into the pool, it was never when I was around.

Georgann, Gabby and I came close to living as a normal suburban family. During the first summer in the new house, I taught Gabby how to drive the lawn tractor. Georgann would laugh hysterically watching me exhaust myself running back and forth alongside the tractor. As promised, I bought Gabby a pony for her birthday and boarded her in the stables at Rogers Park in Danbury. Each Saturday, I took Gabby to the stables for riding lessons.

But, I did say close to normal - not completely normal. The triad of disharmony - Marie, Donna and Nikol - was always lurking in the wings. Nikol remained a sullen, remote member of the family, never a willing participant in any activities. Marie never missed an opportunity to cause trouble, and Donna was her mother's ever willing, brainless side-kick.

For instance, one night I came home from the store to find that Marie and Donna had replaced all my paintings along the staircase wall with framed posters.

"What's this shit on the walls?" I asked Georgann. "Where are my paintings?"

"They're in the basement. My mother said your paintings cheapened the décor of the house. She and Donna replaced them with posters as their house warming gift to us."

"I'm getting my paintings out of the basement and hanging them back on the wall right now. Since when did those two lamebrains become interior decorators? Why didn't you stop them?"

"I didn't want to hurt my mother's feelings. She spent a lot of money on the posters. Don't you like them?"

"Yeah, I like them well enough to use as kindling in the fireplace."

"I'll take them down, Al. I'll tell my mother that you thank her for her thoughtful gift, but that it was me who didn't like the way the posters looked in the stairway."

"Never mind, Georgann; just tell Marie thanks. Leave the posters. They don't look so bad."

I knew the real reason Marie and Donna removed my paintings. Marie hoped I'd get angry and take it out on Georgann for letting them have their way. I refused to get caught in any trap Marie set in an attempt to cause dissent between me and Georgann.

In August, the High Point gang took a two week road trip to Lake George, Niagara Falls, and the Thousand Islands. Sure as shit, there was a repeat performance from Nikol. Not even asking Georgann's permission this time, she threw another party at our house. Again, the neighbors called the police who broke up the bash and emptied out the house before they could do any damage. Ever the good grandmother, Marie went to visit Nicky the next day. She found her dead asleep on her bed fully clothed. Instead of waking her, Marie cleaned up the mess before calling Georgann. Of course, they kept that party hush-hush from me, too. A few days after we returned from our road trip, I found out about it again from Bob - my confidential informant.

Over the years, given my experiences with Marie's bizarre behavior, I was amazed I could still be surprised by her lunacy especially whenever she dictated to Georgann where to invest Gabby's trust. No matter how many times Georgann tried to explain it to her, she refused to believe that Gabby's money was completely protected under stringent court approved investment guidelines outlined in the trust agreement. If that wasn't bad enough, she did not accept that the attorneys had gotten two million of the settlement money as their fee. In Marie's warped mind, Gabby's settlement was six million dollars, and she told everyone who would listen that I stole the missing two.

The legality of an investment was of no concern to Marie. It was her exclusive right to advise Georgann on how to spend Gabby's money.

"You should buy my brother Jimmy a present," she told Georgann one day, "to show your appreciation for getting you connected with the right lawyers for Gabby's lawsuit. It's only fair that Jimmy should get a finder's fee. A Rolex would be nice." I didn't recall Jimmy having anything to do with us choosing Kramer, Dillof, and Livingston.

Georgann told me what her mother suggested. I said, "OK, tell your mother I'll discuss buying a watch for Jimmy with Silvio. If Silvio thinks Jimmy should get a Rolex, I'll personally ask the trust for thc money and buy the watch myself."

That ended Marie hounding Georgann about Jimmy real quick. Silvio wouldn't approve of giving Jimmy a Timex let alone a Rolex.

If the Jimmy-watch incident wasn't outlandish enough, a few months later, Marie approached Georgann with another investment opportunity.

"Georgann," she began, "I know a way to get Gabby more money."

"Oh, really," Georgann said, "What is it?"

"For only a $250 thou outlay, you could set up a loan sharking bank. You would be the bank and could keep all the vig for yourself."

"What are you talking about, Mom? I can't do that. The trust wouldn't give me a quarter million dollars unless I told them what it was for. Who would make the collections? What about Al? He would have to approve." Georgann also did not mention to her mother that the scheme was totally illegal – she wouldn't have believed her.

"This is none of Al's business. I'm the person who makes the decisions about what to do with Gabby's trust, not Al."

"We can't do anything about that now, Mom." Georgann was very tolerant. I would have told Marie to go fuck herself. Of course, the scheme never went beyond their conversation.

From then on, whenever Marie came up with some hare-brained or corrupt scheme for Gabby's money, Georgann would tell her that she would ask Mark Hollender if it was ok, leaving me out of the decision making process completely. The next day, Georgann would tell Marie that Mark said the trust agreement wouldn't allow it. Of course, Georgann never made call one to Mark.

With Marie, ignorance and greed outweighed any moral consideration as determinants in choosing a high rate of return investment. As far as she was concerned, I was the reason Georgann ignored her sound financial advice. All Marie's problems would be solved if I weren't in the picture. She continued to pressure Georgann to divorce me and to pressure Silvio to get rid of me using prescribed Mafia methods. Silvio ignored Marie's demands – not his fight - but advised Georgann to make sure Al didn't walk down any dark alleys.

Nikol was our in-house troublemaker. She taunted her little sister with 'Daddy only loves you because you have the money.' It hurt me deeply to hear her call Gabby a retard – this from a woman who taught challenged children!

Georgann did her best to buffer and protect Gabby - and me - from her mother's ceaseless interference and from Nikol's unkindness. These two cretins unmercifully stressed both Georgann and Gabby. I was out of patience with their wretched behavior and ignored both my eldest daughter and mother-in-law as often as I could. I stayed even further away from Silvio out of fear he would try to draw me back into The Family business.

My emotional withdrawal from my in-laws and daughter was an effort to protect my comfort zone, but it was Marie mistook it as arrogant indifference adding unnecessary logs to the bonfire of her hatred for me. Oblivious, as usual, I did not see that Marie's constant badgering Georgann was having a detrimental effect on Georgann's emotional and physical health. (Spoilers)

We kept Gabby in the same school in Westchester, because she was comfortable there and had many friends. Georgann quit her job at the Katonah Medical Group in order to drive Gabby to Sue's house each day so that Gabby and Ashley could take the school bus together. No matter what else Georgann did with her free time, she never missed being at Sue's when Gabby got off the bus in the afternoon. And, she always made time for her mother.

I decided to sell my retail operations after a long, successful run. I had no regrets. I believed that the days of the independent retailer were num- bered because of malls and discount stores. (This was before Amazon and the Internet). I kept the wholesale silk screening business, because it remained lucrative and took up very little of my time. For almost thirty years, I had dabbled in the corporate world, underworld, and fashion world; it was time for a career change.

Georgann thought it was funny to tell anyone who asked what I was doing with myself these days, "Al hasn't decided yet what he wants to be when he grows up."

As the second Christmas in Connecticut approached, Georgann wanted to give a big Christmas Eve party to show off her beautiful new home. With all the new furniture in place (I refused to move even a lamp again) we decorated the house inside and out with Christmas stuff and put my paintings back on the wall. We sent invitations to old friends and new, business associates, and Dr. Corsaro and the girls from the Medical Group - over sixty people showed up.

Marie and Donna showed up, too, ostensibly to help with setting up and refreshments. Silvio was busy elsewhere. Nicky, of course, was not there either. It was more important for her to spend time with her friends than to celebrate Christmas Eve with her family.

Georgann was the perfect hostess; she radiated with house pride and the glow of the Christmas spirit, obviously not inherited from her mother. Both Marie and Donna huddled together in the background, barely speaking to any of the guests.

Georgann proudly showed off my paintings and press clippings from the art exhibit I had in 1986. When someone commented, “I didn’t know Al was an artist?” Georgann would give me 'the look' before saying, “Oh, yes, he’s an artist all right.”

Gabby stayed close to her mother not wanting to miss anything. She got the biggest kick hearing people compliment my paintings laughing each time Georgann made the joke about me being an 'artist.' Seeing Gabby and Georgann so happy with me really scalded Marie.

The party was a great success. Everyone admired Georgann's tasteful decorating and even went to the extent of complementing me on the Christmas light display surrounding the house (which I nearly killed myself putting up). A good time was had by one and all – except, of course, Marie and Donna.

I had a big surprise waiting for Georgann the following morning. We had fun sitting around the huge Christmas tree we all (except Nicky) helped to decorate opening our presents. When Georgann didn’t see anything with her name on it from me, her face registered disappointment, but she blustered good-naturedly through it.

She got up from her kneeling position by the tree and, looking at Gabby and Nicky, said, "I guess we opened all our presents. I’m going into the beautiful, new kitchen your father built for me and make us a big Christmas breakfast."

"I'm glad you appreciate it, Georgann. While you're up, could you get me the newspaper on the doorstep? I want to check the foreclosures." I was knocking around an idea of going into the mortgage rehab business when I grew up.

When she opened the front door, Georgann gasped. There, in the driveway, sat a car wrapped in a giant, green ribbon. It was a 1993 Jeep Cherokee, red with black interior - just the car she wanted.

"Hey, Georgann," I shouted, "These go with the Jeep." I jingled the set of keys to the Jeep. She ran over to me, gave me a big, sloppy kiss, grabbed the keys out of my hand and flew out the door to start up her new car. Breakfast had to wait.

Although Georgann’s Honda Accord was only a year old, I considered the Jeep a far safer vehicle for her and Gabby given the road conditions in Connecticut. I intended to sell the Honda after Christmas, but Georgann begged me to keep it for Nicky, because it handled better on the winter roads than her old Camaro. I might not like Nicky, but she was my daughter, and I was concerned for her safety. I agreed to keep the Honda for Nicky's use knowing full well that cars and trouble somehow always wound up in the same sentence where Nicky was concerned. I was battle worn with Nicky's road encounters.

I started out with the best of intentions concerning Nicky's safety. When she turned sixteen, I said, "Nicky, before you take the test for your driver's license, I want to sign you up for Driver's Ed to teach you how to drive the right way."

Marie had just brought over dinner and was setting the table when she heard me make the proposal to Nicky. Before Nicky could say anything, Grandma Marie, not looking up from setting the table, piped in, "I already taught Nicky how to drive - the right way."

"You did, did you?" I said staring at her, anger already starting to make my blood boil. "When is she going to take her driver's test?" With Marie as teacher, I knew there was no way Nicky could pass a road test.

"I took her two weeks ago. She passed the first time. She didn't need no fuckin' driver's ed." Marie glowered with smugness.

I turned to Georgann, "How come you didn't tell me?"

"I didn't think you wanted to be bothered. Beside, you're hardly ever home at night, and when you are, it isn't long enough for us to have any real conversations, let alone one about Nicky's driving." She was helping Gabby eat and took her time wiping her little face to avoid making any eye contact with me as she dropped this bombshell.

Once again, I had no comeback.

Marie with a smile like the alley cat that just swallowed a rat plastered on her sneering face prodded, "Now that Nicky has a license, why don't you buy her that new, red Camaro she wants for her birthday? If you can't afford it, me and Silvio will get it for her."

Oh, brother, I thought, a red Camaro would go well with Nicky's twenty-eight hundred dollar sweet-sixteen nose job she just got. Nicky looked at me and stuck out her tongue because she was sure she would get the car with or without my money or my consent. This time I didn't cave in to Marie's demands.

"I'll get Nicky a car, Marie. The one I think she should have."

"Probably some heap," she mumbled.

I got Nicky a sharp looking, two-year-old Chevy Cavalier with 8,000 miles on it. Within three months, she had systematically destroyed the car. It was always in Robby's body shop. Somehow, the damage was never Nicky's fault; cars just kept hitting the Camaro when she was parked at the mall.

Marie and Georgann always covered for Nicky, and I never confronted her for the truth. What for? Three against one are not good odds. Then came the fateful day when the Chevy could no longer be fixed by Robby. We called the wrecker and had Nicky's bumper car towed from the front lawn. The upshot of it all, I caved in - again. Nicky got her brand new, arrest-me-red Camaro.

Mentored at an early age in Marie's finishing school, Nicky was taught to drive with the same 'fuck you' attitude her grandmother had toward everything. Marie was infamous in The Bronx for spitting at other drivers, giving them the finger, and using curses that would make a Hell's Angel blush. Once, when I was riding with her, she thought the cab in front of her was driving too slow; she beeped at him and gave him the finger. When the cab and Marie stopped at the same red light, she jumped out of the car and punched the cabbie in the face for having the audacity to give her the finger back.

By twenty-three, Nikol had amassed her own history of driving inetiquette. What Georgann had failed to tell me when she asked me to give her Honda to Nikol was that her license had been revoked, and she couldn't renew the registration for the Camaro in her name. Now, Nicky was to drive a car registered to me without a valid driver's license. That was ok because, according to Marie, who needed a license anyway?

Che cozzo*!*

29

St. Thomas Again

February 1994: Winter vacation approaching again. Because they had so much fun the year before, Marie and her 'chicklets' decided to return to St. Thomas. Georgann expressed some reluctance about going, because she was tired of Marie's constant badgering on how to spend Gabby's trust money and by Nicky's escalating insolent behavior, but she couldn't say no to her mother - this vacation was the highlight of Marie's life.

As much as I understood Georgann's disinclination to take another vacation with her mother, we both knew that, if she refused, I'd get the blame. Somehow, Marie would find a way to get back at me for depriving her of private time with her 'chicklets'. (God, I hate that word.) I was willing to let Georgann take the hit if it saved me some grief.

A few weeks before the trip, as I was having my morning coffee and reading the paper, Georgann said, "My mother keeps giving me a hard time about Gabby's trust. I was thinking that maybe we could pacify her by using Gabby's trust to pay for this year's trip. It would make my mother feel like she had some importance in Gabby's life other than just her grandmother. I already called Mark and he okayed the idea. The trust would put down the trip's cost as a caregiver travel expense. Mark actually agreed that it would be a nice way to thank my mother for all she's done for us."

Coffee flew out of my mouth as I choked. I couldn't believe what Georgann was saying! I let out a harsh laugh. "Thank her for all she's done for us! Let me count the ways." I held up one finger. "Thanks, Marie for brainwashing my older daughter into hating my guts." Second finger. "Thanks Marie for trying to destroy my marriage by demanding my wife divorce me every minute of every day and, oh yeah, how could I forget." Finger number three went up. "My personal thanks, Marie, for not having me whacked - yet! I could keep on going, but I don't have enough fingers. Are you losing it, too, Georgann?"

Since Georgann didn't say anything, I continued. "I'm telling you this, Georgann, using Gabby's money, despite what Mark says, is out of the question. This is the same vacation you've taken for years, mostly on the Marino tab. Now, all of a sudden, it's become a payback! No one got any payback the first thirteen years of Gabby's life. Everything was done out of love for her. This vacation will be paid for with our money. That'll be her pay back from us. You tell your mother whatever you want, but we pay. Okay?"

Georgann nodded in acceptance to my demand. She booked the trip to St. Thomas and hired Willis again. Nicky's friend, Beverly, was also going on the trip. As I insisted, we paid for the plane fares, the hotel, Willis' car service – everything. Georgann didn't tell her mother we had. She let Marie believe that the cost of the trip came out of Gabby's trust. If that lie made life easier for Georgann and shut Marie's mouth, I was fine with it.

Over the past year, Willis and I spoke several times. We had established a pretty good telephone friendship.

"Cum on, Al, take da trip with your ladies. We goin' ta have fun! I show you everyting. Some tings we don't tell your wife or mother-in-law. Ha! Ha! Ha!"

"Not this year, Willis," I said, "Maybe next year." (Spoilers: There would be no next year.)

It was snowing lightly, the sky overcast and gloomy on the February morning my family was departing for the second St. Thomas vacation. I waited on the porch watching Danny slowly maneuver the limo down the driveway as I drank my morning coffee. He stopped in front of me. Marie was sitting in the front passenger seat staring straight ahead. Invisible Al, that's me.

Danny popped the trunk before getting out and strolling over to me on the porch. "Al, why don't you go, too? You look like you could use some sun. This lousy weather will still be here when you get back."

The Caribbean sounded real good to me, too, as I slipped and slid in the slush helping Danny load the luggage into the limo. But, flashbacks of past vacations with Marie sprang to mind and erased any thoughts of St. Thomas if Marie was included.

I said the same to Danny as I had to Willis, "Not this year, Danny, maybe next year. I've got to stay home with Brandy and Bianca. They don't like being left alone."

As soon as my girls and Beverly were seated safely in the backseat, Marie riding shot gun, I watched until I couldn't see the limo anymore before going inside to phone Willis.

"Willis. They're on their way." I gave him their flight number and time of arrival. The animals and I had the house to ourselves for the next ten days.

I poured myself another cup of coffee before going to sit in my armchair in the den to enjoy the quiet. I noticed that Georgann had left an old photo album on the coffee table. I picked it up and began flipping through the family photos. Somehow, Marie had missed erasing me from this album. There was my Nonno in his brown fedora, a cheroot dangling from the corner of his mouth. I stroked a loving finger over the last photo my parents took together. I turned the pages quickly on any photos of the Marinos.

I came to a picture of Nicky when she was six. Georgann, Nicky and I (without Marie, thank God) had taken a trip to California. In the photo, Nicky was sitting on my shoulders holding up her arm and wearing a white glove on her hand in emulation of Michael Jackson whose house we were standing in front of. There were lots of photos of Nicky at Disneyland, Malibu Beach and in Hollywood. She was always smiling or blowing kisses to me and Georgann. What had happened to that sweet, little girl, I wondered?

On that trip to California, we met up with Marie's brother, Jimmy, and his wife, Theresa. They happened to be staying at some fancy hotel in Beverly Hills at the same time. We were staying in a cheaper hotel, because I was paying for this vacation, not Silvio.

As I sat in the den musing over the photos, I thought about the first time I met Jimmy who was unable to come to our wedding, because he was in jail at the time. In 1970, Georgann and I were married almost four years and still living next door to the Marinos. Jimmy was visiting Marie and stopped by to introduce himself. He had just been released from prison and was still in good with the Colombo family, because he did the time rather than rat on a Family member. In those days, Colombo was organizing the Italian-American Anti-Defamation League in protest to the derogatory stereotypes of Italian-Americans generated by the media. To show his allegiance to the family, Jimmy decorated the fenders and bumpers of his new Lincoln Continental with Italian flags and stickers for the IAADL. They made the car look like a parade float promoting the organization rather than a private vehicle. The public display on the Lincoln didn't sit well with the other New York Families.

To impress his new nephew-in-law Jimmy brought the car over to my house to show it off. While admiring it, I noticed some holes in the right fender."The car looks great. You should drive it in the next Columbus Day parade. What are these holes in the door?" I asked peering down at the holes for a better look.

"That's nothing, Al," he dismissed it with a wave of his hand. "I was in Bensenhurst last week meeting with some guys at the Italian-American Club on Pennsylvania Avenue. I left my car parked on the street. While doing some business, I heard what sounded like gun shots, but didn't pay them no mind, because, you know, the streets of Brooklyn ain't the safest in the world. When I got back to my car, I saw the door was riddled with bullet holes. I'm considering taking the flags and stickers off the Lincoln so it won't be so conspicuous."

"Sounds like a good idea to me," I said before changing the subject.

This was before personal computers, but the 'You've got mail' message spelled out in bullets was obvious to Jimmy but not clear enough for Colombo, though. During the second rally held for the IAADL at Columbus Circle in 1971, Joseph Colombo was shot three times in the head and spent the next seven years of his life in a coma without ever recovering. But, that message was received loud and clear by the rest of The Family. A year after Colombo's hit, the IAADL had completely disappeared.

Left over from his prize fighting days, Jimmy retained a showman's flair and liked living large. Now in his late forties, he draped his bantam body in flashy suits - shark skin still being the material of choice by the better dressed Mafia male - sported a diamond pinky ring, and, oh yes, a gold Rolex watch. Theresa, his wife of twenty years, still looked like an Italian showgirl from The Bronx - long, wavy auburn hair piled high on her head, dancer's gams, big boobs, lots of mascara, as well as the ever present wad of Juicy Fruit in her mouth.

I was aware but had no actual knowledge of the particulars of some of Jimmy's shady deals endorsed by the Colombo family. I already told the reader that a few years back, he had rattled somebody's chains and became a fugitive from both the FBI and the underworld. To rehash, Jimmy's low profile probably had something to do with the 1972 ambush attempt aimed at Colombo's sons as they sat in the back seat of a Cadillac outside Colombo's Bay Ridge, Brooklyn home. Jimmy just happened to be one of the two bodyguards in the car who were sought for questioning by the FBI – and the Gallo Family. Georgann and I never knew or wanted to know the details of that particular incident, but we assumed that was why Jimmy lived in condo rentals and hotels all around the world – he was staying one step ahead of the good and the bad guys.

On the third night we were in California, we arranged a babysitter for Nikol with the hotel concierge. Jimmy sent his hotel's chauffeured Rolls Royce to pick us up and take us to a fancy restaurant on Rodeo Drive. We had a great time talking old times and feasting on filet mignon and Chianti. Of course, Jimmy picked up the tab. After dinner, we all piled back into the Rolls; Jimmy, Terry and Georgann sitting in the back seat and me in the fold down seat facing Jimmy.

As we headed to our hotel, Jimmy leaned forward in his seat checking first to make sure that Georgann and Theresa were deep in conversation before whispering, "Al, I need you to do me a favor."

Here it comes, I thought, never something for nothing with Jimmy, but Jimmy had always been generous to Georgann and Nicky, so I felt I had to at least listen to what he had to say. I hoped I could turn him down without getting put on his shit list.

"Sure, Jimmy, what do you need?"

"I want you to go to my house in Las Vegas tomorrow. I got money stashed in a floor safe. I'll give you the combination. You get the money, take it back to New York with you and hold it for me. Marie will pick it up. It's all arranged."

"Why don't you or Theresa get it?" I asked even though I knew I wasn't going to like the answer.

"The FBI is watching me. They have all my places under surveillance. I can't take a crap without one of them handing me the toilet paper. I figure you're clean so you could get into the house, grab the money and get out before they get wind of it."

"What if they catch me?"

"Here's what you tell them if that happens. I already worked this out with Marie, and she's a hundred percent behind me. You tell them I called Marie a couple of weeks ago to let her know I was going out of the country for a month, but I was worried about my house in Las Vegas, because I forgot to set the security alarm. She told me you were taking a trip to California, and would be happy to go to my house in Vegas and set the alarm as thanks for all I done for you. I mailed her the keys and the alarm code to give you before you left for the coast. Got it? Simple."

Wow! As long as Marie had his back, who was I to question the plan. He wasn't completely right about the FBI, though. If I got caught in one of Jimmy's houses, it would be the second time the FBI associated me with a known felon. The year before, Jimmy graciously lent us his beautiful home in Florida for a week. I found out from Silvio - no love lost between him and Jimmy – his place was under FBI surveillance the whole time. Thank goodness Jimmy didn't show up. It wasn't like I could refuse Jimmy's request. With his 'plausible' story ready - just in case - I made the four hour drive to Vegas leaving Georgann and Nicky to hang out with Jimmy and Theresa.

All the way there, I kept looking in the rear view mirror to make sure I wasn't being followed. When I got to the house, I pulled into the driveway, got out and looked left and right checking for some sign of the FBI - as if I would know - before opening the front door with Jimmy's key. I peeked in before stepping over the threshold. No one inside, either. Okay. So far, so good.

Once in the house, I tried about twenty times to open the safe using the combination Jimmy gave me. No luck. I didn't care I was leaving empty-handed; I just wanted to get out of there as fast as possible. Locking the door behind me, I made haste to my rental, but my getaway was stopped by a black sedan blocking the driveway. It was the FBI.

A tall guy with the obligatory deadpan expression frozen on his face, cropped fair hair, and wearing a nondescript gray suit, got out on the passenger's side. His chiseled jaw which suggested an over abundance of testosterone was dimpled just like Dick Tracey's. The fed on the driver's side stayed in the car staring out the front.

Flashing his badge, Dick said, "May I see some identification, sir?"

"Have I done something wrong, officer?" I asked. Thank God, I wasn't able to open the safe!

"Special Agent Paulley. No, Sir. We're just checking."

I showed him my driver's license.

"What is your business here, Mr. Volpe? We were informed the house was vacant."

I gave my rehearsed story but got a sickening feeling that the free dinner on Rodeo Drive was going to end up on my tab. To my amazement, Dick believed me or at least appeared to believe me, because he let me go advising me not to return. The G-man got back into the sedan and they drove off. I stood in the driveway for five minutes holding my license and sweating bullets.

When I got back to my hotel in California, I called Marie to let her know that my trip to Vegas was a bust. I handed Georgann the phone as soon as I heard her scream the first 'asshole.' As usual, I left Georgann to deal with her mother and looked in on Nikol. Jimmy and Theresa had departed for one of their other abodes before I returned. We enjoyed the rest of our trip without a problem.

Unfortunately, we hadn't heard the last of the FBI. My neighbor, George Carlin, Rose's husband, noticed a strange car parked outside our house in Purdys a few days before we got home. We didn't know it, but the FBI had put a tap on Marie's phone. They intercepted the call from Jimmy telling her that he was coming to New York for a visit the week we were back from California. Jimmy liked to talk in code, and, somehow, the message was misinterpreted by the FBI or Marie, who used her own ID10T code. The FBI thought that Jimmy was coming to my house.

The day after we got home, Georgann went to the A&P to get some groceries. George happened to be in his yard with his dog, Andy, when Georgann pulled away. He stood behind his hedge spying on the unmarked FBI car. He heard the car radio crackle, 'A woman in a brown Honda is leaving the house.' Minutes later the radio crackled, 'We lost her.'

Obviously, there was a stakeout in place at our house in case Jimmy showed up and to follow me or Georgann whenever we left the house. George laughed to himself. He knew how Georgann drove. There was no way a tail could keep up with her. Thirty minutes later, Georgann returned home with the groceries. She drove right past the stakeout without noticing them. She beeped and waved hello to George and Andy who were still standing in their yard waiting for something exciting to happen. George and Andy were very disappointed. Two days later, the stakeout was gone and George filled me in about his own stakeout. Thank goodness Marie got Jimmy's message all screwed up. Otherwise the FBI would have staked out the Marinos instead of us probably grabbing Jimmy.

A happy ending for all - except the FBI.

30

Stress

The first week my girls (and Marie) spent in St. Thomas was great. Georgann called me every night to rub in what a wonderful time they were having without me. Willis was again the most super of guides taking them shopping, to local restaurants, and to off-the-beaten path places. They picnicked in beach spots known only to the natives and on lunches of local food made by Willis' wife. They went to dinner at Willis' house and took his family out to dinner. Everyone, including Marie and Nicky, was having so much fun; I almost wished I was with them. Almost.

When Georgann called the second Sunday, it was from the hotel lobby instead of her room. By the uneasy tone in her voice, I sensed something was wrong.

"Are you okay, Georgann? You don't sound good. Are you sick?"

"No, Al. I'm fine. Nicky and my mother had one of their arguments at dinner tonight. Same old, same old. They gave me a headache." She changed the subject by telling me what they had done that day. Before hanging up, she said, "I can't wait to get home."

Bells should have gone off with me when Georgann uttered that last offhand remark. It was the clue – something had happened – something bad. I knew she wasn't going to tell me what it was then, or ever, so I dropped it and let her continue to chat on about their day.

I couldn't sleep that night worrying about what Georgann hadn't said. She was always so upbeat and positive whenever she called me. But, not this last time. She couldn't wait to come home. She never wanted to come home when she was on vacation even if Marie was with them.

Three days later, they returned from St. Thomas looking, as before, tanned and healthy. Gabby resumed her school and activities, Nicky went back to work, and Georgann hardly ever wanted to talk about St. Thomas. I should have picked up on that, too. Whenever I brought up St. Thomas she would mutter a few words and change the subject. She seemed fretful and anxious but did her best to hide it from me. Whatever Georgann was going through, she kept it to herself, and I didn't ask. She would tell me when she was ready. (Spoilers: she never did.)

One morning, about two weeks after her return from St. Thomas, out of the blue, Georgann said, "It's not right that we had a wonderful vacation, and you had to stay home. You could use a vacation, too, to get away from this cold weather. Why don't you go to Florida and spend some time with Frankie?"

"Why would I want to visit Frankie? And, by myself? It's not as if Frankie and I were still best buddies anymore. If you think I could use a vacation then we can go with Gabby over the Easter break, but not to Florida. What's eating you, anyway?"

"Nothing, Al. I just thought it might be nice for you to go someplace warm for a couple of weeks."

"I'm fine where I am, Georgann, here with my family. Drop it."

Georgann didn't bring up Florida again, but she continued to act jumpy. Whenever I left the house, she questioned me about where I was going and how long I would be gone. If I wasn't going to visit Paul or going to the store, she always wanted to come with me.

I attributed some of her uneasiness to concern for her father's health and didn't associate it with anything that had to do with me. Big Al could take care of himself. Silvio was now in his early seventies and having some issues with his heart again. His doctors in Westchester gave him a complete checkup and found nothing more seriously wrong with him. Marie didn't trust the expertise of the local doctors and made an appointment for him with a heart specialist in Washington, D.C.

On Sunday morning, March 6, 1994, Georgann, Gabby, and I picked up Silvio and Marie and drove them to Westchester Airport in Armonk. I parked the car, carried their luggage into the airport, and paid their breakfast tab at the airport restaurant without even a 'thanks shithead' from either of them. I bit my tongue. Since my respect for them had died long ago, I didn't much care how they treated me. I was their son-in-law, but after almost thirty years, I was still only the chauffeur and errand boy.

I said goodbye to the Marinos – Silvio grunted and Marie gave me an icy stare. Georgann and Gabby hugged and kissed them goodbye. I couldn't help hearing what Marie said as she whispered into Georgann's ear, "Don't worry about Al, bella, your uncle Jimmy and I will take care of him." Georgann's face registered alarm.

What did Marie mean saying Jimmy and she would 'take care of him'? I didn't realize there was something wrong with me that required Jimmy's attention. Again, I was Big Al. Given Marie's bizarre nature, I didn't give it another thought, but I should have. (Spoilers)

After dropping off the Marinos at the airport, we stopped in Purdys to have lunch with Paul and Josephine. During lunch, Georgann grabbed her napkin, and spit into it.

"Don't you like the sandwich, Georgann? Can I get you something else?" asked Josephine.

"The sandwich is fine," said Georgann, looking into the napkin. "I just broke off a piece of tooth."

"What did I tell you about that?" I said. "Your teeth are a mess. Why don't you go to the dentist before all your teeth fall out of your head?"

"I hate the dentist, Al."

"Everybody hates the dentist, Georgann. Suck it up and go. I don't want to be married to a toothless hag."

"Thanks, Al, for all your lovely encouragement. I promise, I'll make an appointment."

After lunch, the three girls stayed in the kitchen chatting. Paul and I took our coffees to the rec room in his basement to smoke and enjoy some guy talk.

We sat in recliners, and as soon as we lit up, Paul asked, "How is Georgann? Josephine and me were worried about her after she called us from St. Thomas."

I sat up. "What? When was that?"

"Let me think," he said, "It was the Sunday before they came home. I remember, because I was watching Sunday Night Basketball."

That was the same night she told me she couldn't wait to come home. "What did she want?"

"It was weird, Al. She asked me to keep an eye on you until she got back from St. Thomas. What do you think she meant by that?"

"I haven't a clue."

End of Part One

Part Two

1

Scared to Death

We got home about 6:30 first stopping at Pino's - Gabby's favorite restaurant - for pizza. Georgann helped Gabby to bed and joined Nicky - home only because it was a school night - and me in the family room to watch the 10:00 o'clock news. Shortly after ten, Nicky mumbled good night and went to her room; Georgann sat in my recliner reading a magazine; I was spread out on the couch.

When I began to nod, I got up from the couch. "I'm going up to bed, too. It's been a long day and being around your parents even for a few hours is exhausting."

"I'll be up in a few minutes," said Georgann, "I just want to watch tomorrow's weather report."

I had just finished brushing my teeth when I heard a faint, choking sound, but I couldn't identify from where it was coming. My first thought was Gabby. I listened outside her bedroom door before opening it a crack; she was sleeping soundly. I checked in on Nicky who was also fast asleep. I heard the sound again, but this time, I was sure it was coming from downstairs.

I leaned over the banister and called out, "Georgann, are you OK?" No answer.

I rushed down the stairs realizing that the sound got louder as I neared the kitchen. I halted in the doorway to the kitchen too stunned to move by what I saw. Georgann was bent over the sink choking and gasping for air as she spewed out long, purple clots of blood. I ran over to her; put my hands lightly on her shaking shoulders and watched in horror as she continued to spit up blood. There was so much blood in the sink; I didn't know what to do. Should I call 911 or take her straight to the hospital? I was near passing out with fright.

Finally, able to catch her breath, she straightened up. She rinsed out her mouth with some water and washed her face. I handed her a paper towel to dry her face before helping her to a chair at the kitchen table.

"I'm all right," she said breathlessly.

"What do you mean you're all right? You were spitting up blood! That's not all right! You were okay twenty minutes ago. What happened?"

"I don't know. I got up from the chair, turned off the TV but only got as far as the bottom of the stairs. All of a sudden, I started to choke and couldn't breathe. I felt like I had to throw up so I ran to the kitchen sink."

I peered into the sink; I saw nothing that looked remotely like vomit, but I did see an enormous amount of clotting blood. I sat back down facing Georgann, a little relieved to see her color returning and breathing easier.

"Look, Georgann, I see a lot of blood in the sink but no vomit. Maybe there's something really wrong with you. Sit there. Don't move. I'll be right back."

I flew up the stairs, two at a time, threw on some clothes and grabbed a sweater for Georgann. Before running back down to the kitchen, I opened Nicky's door and shouted in, "Get up, Nicky. Your mother's sick. I'm taking her to the hospital. Watch your sister. Don't forget to lock up and set the house alarm after we leave."

Nicky sat up in bed, seemingly awake. She must have heard the desperation in my voice and nodded her okay. I looked in on Gabby once more before going back to the kitchen. She was still sleeping.

Georgann was still spitting out small drops of blood into the paper towel but otherwise seemed fine. I wrapped the sweater around her shoulders before asking, "Do you want me to carry you to the car?"

She started to push me away. "I'm ok now, stop fussing. I don't need to go to the hospital, and you know I don't like leaving Gabby alone with Nicky. I'll stop by Dr. Corsaro in the morning after I take Gabby to school. Just help me up to bed. All I need is a good night's sleep."

One more look at the blood in the sink was enough for me. "We're going to the emergency room - now. I already woke Nicky and told her we were on our way. She'll set the house alarm and watch over Gabby. Let's go. No more arguing."

Despite what she said, I had to help Georgann to the car, because the exertion after spewing up so much blood left her weak. She slumped in the passenger seat pulling the sweater tightly across her chest. I sped to the hospital going through a few red lights. Georgann kept trying to get me to turn around and go back home – she feared doctors, dentists, hospitals, anything medical. I couldn't blame her given what she had gone through with Gabby and Nicky. But, the blood, so much blood, scared the hell out of me.

It was after twelve when we arrived at the emergency room in Danbury Hospital. I helped Georgann to a seat in the empty waiting room before leaving to park the car in the garage.

When I returned, I ran to the admission desk in frantic mode, "My wife needs to see a doctor right away. Please hurry."

The receptionist looked over at Georgann who smiled giving her a little finger wave. The woman at the desk saw no medical emergency. Turning back to me, she handed me a form, "You need to fill this out. May I see your insurance card?"

Her coolness infuriated me; I demanded even louder, "Screw the form, my wife needs to see a doctor now!"

The receptionist startled and opened her eyes wide. Obviously a raving lunatic was standing in front of her, and he was out of control. She picked up the phone. I hoped it was to call a doctor and not security, because she turned away from me so I couldn't hear what she was saying.

She listened intently, then said, "Yes, doctor." She carefully replaced the receiver in its cradle before turning back to me. "Take your wife through the emergency room doors on the right. I'll open them remotely. Doctor Epstein will there to meet you."

I helped Georgann up from the chair, put my arm around her waist, and guided her through the doors. Dr. Epstein was already waiting for us. I was in such a frazzled state; the doctor could have been Dr. Kildare for all I noticed. He took Georgann by her left arm and slowly led us to an examination room. Georgann kept repeating that she felt fine; she didn't need any emergency care. All I could do was babble about the amount of blood I saw in the sink.

I watched as Dr. Epstein gave Georgann a cursory examination. He was on the verge of sending her home but apparently had second thoughts. Addressing Georgann, he said, "I didn't find anything seriously wrong with you in my brief examination. Your blood pressure, temperature and pulse are normal. Your lungs appear to be clear, but, to be on the safe side, I'm going to admit you and schedule some tests for the morning. It's possible you have a touch of bronchitis or pneumonia."

I'm sure he thought I had exaggerated the amount of blood but, at least, he was acting on the side of precaution.

The doctor's reassuring words did not dispel Georgann's apprehension about having to stay in the hospital. I wanted to stay with her, but she insisted I go home out of concern for Gabby. I acquiesced and kissed her good night, "Don't worry about Gabby. Nicky is taking care of her. I'll be back in the morning after I take Gabby to school."

Outside the exam room, I stopped Dr. Epstein who was talking to an attendant, "Doc, I'm not exaggerating about the blood. I saw what I saw."

He reassured me, "I don't believe there is anything seriously wrong with your wife. We'll know more after we get back the results from the tests I've scheduled. I'll talk to you then. Good night." He finished his conversation with the attendant before going back into the examining room. Although somewhat mollified believing that the hospital was the best place for her right now, I reluctantly headed home.

When I pulled up to the house I saw that the front door was wide open. Frantically, I dashed upstairs to find both Nicky and Gabby sound asleep in their rooms. In my haste to get Georgann to the hospital, I must not have pulled the front door closed hard enough for the lock to catch; the wind had blown it open. Before going to my room and collapsing on the bed, I locked the front door and reset the alarm. Of course, Nicky hadn't gotten out of bed to set the alarm, close and lock the front door, and probably not checked to make sure her sister was all right.

Ten minutes later, the phone rang. It was Georgann calling to give me her room number. She asked, "Is everything all right at the house?"

I half-truth, lied, when I answered. "All quiet here. Nicky and Gabby are fast asleep which I will be five seconds after we hang up. You sleep well, sweetheart. See you in the morning. I'll tell Gabby you had a stomach ache from all the pizza you ate. Don't worry about her. Good night." We blew each other good night kisses into the phone. I slept fitfully dreaming about drowning in a pool of blood.

Monday, March 7, 1994

Georgann woke me 7:00 a.m. She gave me instructions: what Gabby should wear to school; what to make for her breakfast and lunch snacks; and make sure I helped her pack her schoolbooks.

"Don't come this morning, Al," Georgann added after giving me my Gabby orders, "Dr. Epstein scheduled several tests, and I'll be out of the room for most of the morning. Come this afternoon with Gabby."

"Gotcha, Georgann. I'll see you later."

I took a quick shower and got dressed. I heard Nicky slamming things around in the kitchen as I was getting ready, but by the time I got downstairs, she had left for work. She ignored or didn't see the blood in the sink; neither had she waited to ask me about her mother. It also hadn't occurred to her that I might need some help with Gabby. Although Gabby was thirteen, she had difficulty dressing. I cleaned up the blood before going upstairs to Gabby's room; she didn't need to see it. It was bad enough I had.

"Mommy wasn't feeling good last night so I took her to the hospital. She probably caught that bug that's been going around. We'll go see her after school today. Let's see what mommy wants you to wear. I'll help you dress."

"Mommy and I chose these clothes," she said showing me the clothes on the extra bed in her room. Raising her head and sticking out her chin in a show of independence, Gabby said, "I can dress myself."

"OK, big girl. I'll go down and get us some breakfast. Yell if you need anything."

"I won't need anything, Daddy."

When she came down her clothes were in disarray - bra strap twisted, buttons and button holes not matched up, shoelaces undone. I knew how hard she had tried, and I wept inside. Awkwardly, we both managed to get her straightened out. Nicky's uncaring, selfish attitude toward her mother and sister were evident and blistered me.

I helped Gabby get her books together, gave her lunch money, and drove her to school instead of to Sue's. I walked her to her classroom, but she wouldn't hold my hand - it wasn't cool. Before leaving, I stopped by the administration office to inform them that I would be picking Gabby up after school.

Next, I went to Sue's to tell her I had taken Gabby to school and would be picking her up there. I needn't have bothered, because Sue answered the door with the phone on her ear; she was talking to Georgann. She handed me the phone.

"Did Gabby get off to school okay?" she asked. I decided not to mention Nicky's lack of help with Gabby. After I told her Gabby was fine, she gave me a list of clothes to bring to the hospital fully believing she was coming home that afternoon. (Spoilers)

Sue made coffee. As we sat at the kitchen table drinking it, I told her what really happened last night, because I knew Georgann probably made light of it. I described Georgann's coughing, not able to catch her breath and, especially, all the blood. Like the doctor, Sue thought I was ex- aggerating, too.

"Georgann sounded perfectly fine to me when she called," she said.

"I imagine she did. After her coughing fit was over, she seemed fine to me, too. But, once I saw all the clots of blood in the sink, I knew she wasn't fine. And you wouldn't have, either. What do you think about Nicky? She didn't get up to lock the front door or set the alarm. She didn't bother to hang around this morning long enough to help out with Gabby or even to ask about her mother."

Sue moaned, "Georgann is really disgusted with Nicky." She proceeded to tell me about a recent incident involving Nikol.

"My daughter, Ashley, was having a problem with a girl in the neighborhood who is a bully. At the bus stop last week, the girl began picking on Ashley. Gabby, who is such a sweetheart, asked the girl to leave Ashley alone. The girl threw Gabby's book bag in the mud and told her to mind her own business. When she got home from school, Ashley told me what had happened. That same afternoon, Georgann and I went with Ashley and Gabby to the girl's house to speak with her parents. The girl apologized to Gabby and Ashley and said she would never do that again. They all hugged, and it was over. Unfortunately, Gabby made the mistake of telling Nicky. Nicky went to the bus stop the next afternoon. When the girl got off the bus, Nicky attacked her with curses and threats to leave her little sister alone or else. The girl's parents were so upset they called Georgann and said they were going to have Nicky arrested for threatening their daughter. Georgann apologized profusely for Nicky's behavior and begged them not to press charges. They agreed under the condition that Nicky never go near their daughter again. Georgann told me that when Nicky was a little girl, she had seen Marie threaten children in the same way and assumed it was okay for her to do the same. Georgann makes too many excuses for Nicky as far as I'm concerned."

I had never heard a word about this incident - of course. Georgann and Sue were the closest of friends; they confided everything to each other. There was more Sue had to tell me. Although I was aware that Nikol and Marie put a lot of stress on Georgann, it was Sue who knew the full extent that stress was having on her friend's emotional health.

By the third cup of coffee, Sue told me the whole story of what happened during the St. Thomas vacation. No wonder Georgann has been a nervous wreck since returning.

This was Sue's narrative: "They'd all gone out to dinner at a nearby restaurant. Willis had a family affair to go to so they were on their own. Marie and Nicky had a few too many drinks which loosened their tongues more than usual. During dinner, Nicky began picking on Gabby using her pet name for her - retard. Gabby started to cry. Marie went to Gabby's defense swapping words with Nicky. Nicky called Marie a drunk and told her to shut up. Marie called Nicky a tramp and a user. Nicky's friend, Beverly, was able to quiet Nicky down enough to get her out of the restaurant before they were thrown out. Nicky and Beverly waited outside while Marie paid the bill before going back to hotel together. At the hotel, Beverly took a stumbling, drunk Nicky to their room. Marie, grumbling, took the elevator to her own room not waiting for Georgann and Gabby. Gabby was shaking from the fight, but Georgann managed to calm her down enough to get her to sleep before going into Marie's room to make sure her mother was all right."

Sue continued. "Marie was ranting to herself, 'I could have slapped Nicky for talking to Gabby like that. After all, it was Gabby's trust money that paid for the trip so that she and her sloppy, Jew friend could sun their fat asses.' Georgann, still upset from the ruckus at the restaurant, and before she could think blurted out, 'Gabby's trust did not pay for this trip. Al had me pay for it with our money.'

Marie sprang up, 'What?'

'I did ask Al if the St. Thomas trip could be taken out of Gabby's trust money, because Mark Hollander said it would be okay, but Al insisted that we pay for the trip ourselves.'

Sue said, "It was out of her mouth before Georgann could take back her words. When she realized that Georgann had lied to her, Marie went off like a fire cracker."

Sue went on, 'Who the fuck is he to tell you what to do with Gabby's money? And, who the fuck is he to pay for anything for me? Get his name off that trust, or I'm putting a contract out on him as soon as we get back. He's as good as dead already. If Silvio had done what I asked years ago, he would have been long gone, but, no, Silvio told me to mind my own business. Your business is my business, Georgann. Fuck Silvio, too. You better divorce Al. If you don't, I'll have my brother Jimmy get rid of him - permanently.'"

Sue ended her narrative with, "Al, Georgann's been a nervous wreck since returning from St. Thomas. She thinks this time her mother is really serious and will go behind Silvio's back to have you hurt - or worse."

No wonder Georgann couldn't wait to get home from St. Thomas! The pieces began to fit together. Her anxious behavior now made sense; asking Paul to keep an eye on me, urging me to visit Frankie in Florida, and her constant need to know my whereabouts every second of the day. How much could one person bear without having it take its toll? Georgann's worry and concern for my safety was making her an emotional basket case. Unfortunately, I had no idea how much this fear for my life was also affecting her physically. (Spoilers)

"Thanks, Sue, for telling me this. Don't think you betrayed any confidences. Georgann's been protecting me our whole marriage. It's time I do the same for her." I gave Sue a big hug before leaving.

I stopped by the Katonah Medical Group to tell Sally that Georgann was in the hospital and give her phone numbers. "When you call, tell her after I run some errands, I'm going to Paul's until it's time for me to pick up Gabby and bring her with me to the hospital. I need some brotherly comfort."

At Paul's, I retold him and Josephine about the prior night's incident. Josephine said, "Georgann was perfectly fine when you guys were here yesterday except for breaking her tooth."

"I know, Josephine. You would have been as shocked as me if you found her coughing up all that blood."

"You look absolutely exhausted, Al," said Paul, "Why don't you take a nap on the couch? I'll wake you in time to get Gabby."

I had barely closed my eyes when the phone rang. It was Sally. After talking to her a couple of minutes, Paul handed me the phone. Sally was so agitated, she could barely speak.

"I was on the phone with Georgann ten minutes ago when she began to cough so hard she couldn't talk. Next thing I knew, a nurse was on the phone. She told me that Georgann was having some kind of episode and coughing up blood. She was being rushed to the ICU. The nurse asked me to call you. You have to get to the hospital right away, Al!"

As soon as Sally hung up, I called Gabby's school and told them I was picking her up in ten minutes.

2

ICU

Once we got to Danbury Hospital, Gabby and I rushed to the ICU but were told that we couldn't go into Georgann's room because of hospital policy. The nurse at the nurse's station called Georgann to tell her that her husband and daughter were here and asked if it were all right they watch her on the monitor. After getting Georgann's enthusiastic okay, the nurse turned the monitor to allow us to view Georgann. Georgann waved and blew kisses to Gabby who returned her kisses with tears in her eyes. She was obliviously very upset she wasn't being allowed to go to her mother.

The nurse at the station saw how distressed Gabby was and tried to comfort her. "You are just as pretty as your mother. I bet you would be even more beautiful if you smiled."

Gabby gave her a tiny smile before whispering, "Thank you. Can I go to my mommy now?"

"It's really against hospital rules, but I think we can break this one silly rule just this once. Come with me. Your daddy will have to wait here. Girls only." She gave Gabby a big wink before taking her hand and leading her to Georgann's room.

The moment they entered Georgann's room and Gabby saw her mother, she wrenched her hand free from the nurse and threw herself into her Georgann's arms. Although that was also against hospital policy, the nurse didn't stop Gabby. I watched them on the monitor for just a few moments but had to force myself to turn away before I ran into the ICU and threw myself into Georgann's arms, too. Instead, I sought out the doctor for some answers.

"I want to talk to the doctor in charge of my wife's case," I asked the nurse at the front desk. She told me Dr. Ben Patel was Georgann's primary physician and paged him on the intercom.

"The doctor will be with you in a few minutes, Mr. Volpe. You can continue to watch your girls on the ICU monitor until he arrives."

Gabby was on the bed still wrapped in Georgann's arms. I was so entranced by this touching scene I didn't realize the doctor was standing behind me until I felt a tap on my shoulder. Dr. Patel was a slightly built, Asian man whose youthful, friendly face disarmed me. If it weren't for the white coat and the sharp look he gave me with his piercingly, intelligent dark eyes, I wouldn't have believed he was old enough to be a doctor.

He barely had time to introduce himself and shake my hand before I blurted out, "What's wrong with Georgann? Why is she in the ICU?"

"Let's go into the waiting room, Mr. Volpe, where we can speak in private."

In the waiting room I sat on the couch; he pulled up a chair to face me. "Mrs. Volpe had just returned from X-ray and was alone in her room talking on the phone. Because she did not appear to be in any discomfort, the nurse at the station who was monitoring Mrs. Volpe turned away from the screen to respond to a phone call. When the nurse looked back at the monitor, she saw that Georgann was no longer in her bed. The nurse went immediately to her room and found Mrs. Volpe on the floor next to the bed choking up blood and gasping for air. Acting quickly, the nurse got your wife back into bed and suctioned her airway allowing Mrs. Volpe to breathe. Apparently, your wife had an attack while talking on the phone. She dropped the phone and tried to reach the bathroom but collapsed as soon as she stood up. After the nurse ministered to your wife, she noticed the phone dangling off the hook and heard someone yelling on the line. She picked up the receiver hoping it was you. The woman on the line identified herself as Mrs. Volpe's friend whereby the nurse asked her to get in touch with you and request you come to the hospital as soon as possible."

"I rushed here as soon as I picked up my daughter from school. What you just described is exactly what happened to Georgann last night at home."

"Mr. Volpe, I need your permission to conduct more extensive tests on your wife. At this point, we do not know what is causing her episodes."

"Of course, doctor, I'll give you permission to do anything that will help my wife get better."

I went back to the nurse's station with Dr. Patel. "Nurse, please give Mr. Volpe all the permission forms required for laboratory work on Mrs. Volpe." He handed the nurse a list he pulled out of his pocket. Turning back to me, "Don't worry, Mr. Volpe, we'll fix your wife as good as new," he said shaking my hand again before leaving.

Reluctantly, Gabby allowed the nurse to escort her back to me but not before she told Georgann, "I love you, Mommy. Get better." Soup and crackers was all I could get Gabby to eat before she went to bed. I ate cigarette smoke.

Tuesday, March 8, 1994

A shitload of X-rays, scans, blood tests and every other test imaginable was performed on Georgann but proved to be useless in detecting the cause of her blood spewing episodes. In his office, Dr. Patel informed me of the lack of findings by pathology. He pulled out a Cross pen from his lab coat pocket and, poising it over a legal pad on his desk, began to question me about Georgann's general health - had she complained about feeling tired; had I seen her exhibit any coughing lately, etc., etc. I told him all I knew, which wasn't much.

"Georgann stopped smoking thirteen years ago when she got pregnant with Gabby; she had gall bladder surgery eighteen years ago; she never used recreational drugs; she hardly drinks; and takes no prescription medications." I recounted the medical issues of both our daughters. I ended my recollections with, "Georgann is never sick, not even a cold."

"Mr. Volpe, I couldn't help but notice your wife's tan. Had she been going to a tanning salon or used any chemical tanning agents?"

"My family recently returned from a vacation in St. Thomas."

It was as if bells went off! He narrowed his questions to the trip to the Caribbean. As soon as I gave him the particulars of their trip, he capped his pen and returned it to his pocked.

"It is possible your wife may have contracted a blood disorder while on vacation in St. Thomas. I must get back to the lab to prepare Georgann's blood samples for analysis by an out-of-state lab that specializes in detecting rare blood disorders. These tests take time so please let your wife know that she will be staying in the hospital for the rest of the week." With an abrupt goodbye, he rushed out of his office.

Dr. Patel, even though his medical specialty was not hematology, seemed convinced that the cause of Georgann's bleeding had something to do with her trip to the Caribbean. If he had conferred with any pulmonary, vascular or other medical specialists, he didn't tell me, but he was so confident that his diagnosis of some sort of blood disorder was accurate; he dismissed any other possible cause of Georgann's complaint including internal injury. My family appears to have more than its fair share of arrogant doctors

Georgann was allowed regular ICU visits – two a visitors at a time. When I told her that Dr. Patel wanted her to stay in the hospital a few more days to run more tests she said, "I hate it here, Al. I want to go home. Gabby needs me."

"Please don't argue with the doctor, Georgann. It's for your own good."

"All right, Al. I'll arrange with Sue to take Gabby to her house until I get home. That will make it easier for you especially since I expect you to be here 24/7," she said giving me 'the look'. Georgann had learned the hard way not to trust Gabby's care to Nikol. She also wanted to limit the amount of time Gabby spent with Marie. I kissed her good-bye reassuring her I would bring Gabby back that afternoon.

On the drive home from the hospital, I thought about Dr. Patel's diagnosis that Georgann might have a blood disorder. This brought to mind an article I had recently read in the local paper. It was about the daughter of a Danbury physician who had to be airlifted home from the Caribbean, because she had contracted a rare blood disorder while on vacation in the Bahamas during winter break from college. First admitted into Danbury Hospital, her condition rapidly deteriorated, and she was transferred to a special hematology unit at Yale New Haven Hospital. I now understood why Dr. Patel latched onto a blood disorder as a diagnosis.

That afternoon, I told Georgann about the article. "I wonder if it had something to do with Dr. Patel's questioning me about your trip to St. Thomas?

"I don't know, Al. Can you get a copy of the newspaper article?"

Dr. Patel came into Georgann's room while Gabby and I were still there. I thought about the newspaper article but did not mention it to him. Instead, I asked if he thought Georgann should be transferred to Yale Hospital where they had a special unit that dealt with blood disorders.

Stiffening, he said, "Mr. Volpe, as her doctor, I will decide the best care for my patient. At this time, we do not have a positive diagnosis of Mrs. Volpe's problem, but I am sure that Danbury Hospital has all the resources necessary to care for your wife." Shades of Yuan!

Gabby and I had dinner in the hospital cafeteria before going back to Georgann. Georgann told me she had mentioned the newspaper article to Donna when she talked to her on the phone. Donna told her she would make several copies of it to give to Georgann when she came for a visit.

Sue, Fred, and Sally were also waiting to visit Georgann. Gabby and I left to let the others take their turn. We stopped at Pizza Hut to get a slice. Over pizza and cokes, I asked Gabby if she would like to stay at Sue's for a few days until Georgann came home. Gabby enthusiastically agreed; Ashley was her best friend. Always considerate, before leaving Pizza Hut Gabby asked me to bring home a pizza for Nicky.

Making a face, I asked, "With meatballs or pepperoni?"

Gabby laughed, "Meatballs."

I ordered a large meatball to go. To myself I said, "I'd like to give Nicky something, and it wasn't a meatball pizza." Nicky, of course, had not visited or called Georgann.

Beverly's car was in our driveway when we arrived. She and Nicky were in the family room drinking wine coolers. Gabby ran in and sat next to Beverly to watch TV. I went into the kitchen to dish out the pizza and bring it to them. Al Jeeves, the butler.

Beverly asked, "How is Georgann?"

"She's doing well, Bev. The doctor just wants to conduct a few more tests before she can come home. Thanks for asking," I said looking pointedly at Nicky. She ignored me.

Gabby said, "I want to write a letter to mommy. Can you help me, Nicky?'

Beverly, not Nicky, jumped in, "Sure, sugar, I'll help you with the typing. Then we can get started on your homework?"

Nicky ignored them.

I left Nicky staring at the TV taking a sip of her wine cooler before grabbing another slice of pizza. I was too disgusted to even admonish her for not helping with her sister or asking about her mother.

I went back to the kitchen to call Paul. I told him the doctor's lack of findings and read him the newspaper article. "What do you think, Paul? Can this be Georgann's problem?"

"I don't know, Al. All we can do is put our faith in God."

"I guess you're right. I'll keep in touch." I hung up.

I went upstairs to check on Gabby. Beverly had helped her type a letter to Georgann before starting on her homework. Nicky was still in the den fighting on the phone with her boyfriend, Chuck.

"Bev, I want to go back to the hospital. Do you think you could stay here tonight and give me a hand with Gabby in the morning? She's going to stay with Sue for a few days, and I could use some help with the packing."

"No problem, Mr. V," she answered.

"Could you take my letter to mommy tonight?" Gabby asked.

"Of course, sweetheart. It will make her very happy."

As Gabby started to hand me her letter, she pulled it back, "Daddy, this letter is for mommy. You have to promise not to read it."

"I won't," I said crossing my heart.

Georgann gave me a big smile as soon as I entered her room. I sat down next to her on the bed and took her hand. She said, "I talked to my mother a little while ago." I had forgotten all about Marie and Silvio. "The doctors in the D.C. hospital couldn't find anything more seriously wrong with my father's heart than had his own doctors. They'll be back tomorrow night. How is Gabby? Is she looking forward to going to Sue's?"

"She couldn't be happier! She will be spending time with her bestie, Ashley. Beverly's staying over at our house tonight. She offered to help Gabby with her homework and pack for Sue's. She promised to give me a hand in the morning with Gabby before she goes to work."

Georgann, although she said nothing, looked relieved that Beverly was staying over. We both knew that Nicky could never be relied upon to help with Gabby. I handed her Gabby's letter; she read it aloud. In part, it said, "I wish I could be sick for you, Mommy. Please come home soon. I love you. Gabby."

We both cried.

Georgann drifted off to sleep clutching Gabby's letter to her breast. I took it from her hand and taped it to the wall behind her bed before heading home.

Everyone was asleep when I got there. I found a note from Beverly, 'Gabby finished her homework, showered and is all packed.' Sounds just like a big sister.

I locked up, tore off my clothes and threw myself onto the bed. Sleep didn't come right away although I was dead tired. I ruminated over Dr. Patel's blood disorder diagnosis again. In my opinion, he seemed somewhat defensive when I asked about transferring Georgann to Yale New Haven Hospital. Given that both our daughters might not be alive today because of Dr. Yuan and Dr. Bronfman, I was already doctor phobic. I didn't want to think that the ego of another doctor might be overriding Georgann's welfare.

Before I went to sleep, I reread the newspaper article about the girl who was airlifted from the Bahamas. The article reported that while in Danbury Hospital, her respiratory system began to shut down, but the article said nothing about her having any coughing up blood episodes. I also wondered why no one else who went to St. Thomas experienced any unusual symptoms. Georgann, her mother, my daughters, and Beverly all went sightseeing together, ate and drank the same food, and slept in the same hotel yet only Georgann became sick. As far as I was concerned, if Dr Patel was right about this Caribbean blood disorder thing, wouldn't that be even more reason to transfer Georgann to Yale where they were treating that young woman? Even with all these thoughts hammering in my head, I actually fell into a dreamless sleep.

Wednesday, March 9, 1994

Both Nicky and Beverly helped Gabby dress for school before they left for work. I hoped Nicky was finally smartening up, but I knew that expecting Nicky to have any human feeling would be too much to ask. It was more likely that Beverly guilted her into behaving something like a big sister.

After giving Gabby breakfast, I drove her to Sue's. As I turned into Sue's cul-de-sac, I saw Ashley and her sisters standing at the curb holding up a big poster they'd made; 'Welcome Gabby. We love you.'

Sue and I stood waving to the girls as they sped off on the school bus before going into her house for coffee and for me to use the phone. I needed to cancel Gabby's after school appointments for the rest of the week. Before leaving, I put two hundred dollars on the table for Gabby needs.

After a futile argument with me, Sue took the money and put it in an envelope marked 'Georgann.' She grinned, "You're not getting it back. When Georgann comes home, we'll do a little shopping." I rolled my eyes and we both laughed. Sue asked, "Do you think a blood disorder is what's wrong with Georgann?"

"I don't know, but the doctor seems to think so."

Sue confided to me, "Last night, Georgann made me and Sally promise to watch over Gabby and you until she gets home. Georgann's more worried about the safety of the two of you than her own health."

I thought about what Sue just told me for a moment before replying, "Yeah, she thinks I can't make a cup of instant coffee without burning myself." But, I really knew Georgann worried about what damage her mother and Nicky might be capable of doing to me and Gabby if she weren't there to run interference. I thanked Sue again before leaving for the hospital.

I stopped at the nurse's station in the ICU to ask how Georgann spent the night. The nurse told me that she had had another episode where she spewed up blood and was unable to catch her breath. The ICU staff responded quickly and suctioned out the blood from her airways allowing her to breathe, but the incident unnerved even them. One moment, Georgann was perfectly fine, the next, without warning, helplessly choking on her own blood. It was a frightening sight to see even for these specially trained medical personnel. I asked the nurse to page Dr. Patel. Five minutes later, he showed up. As soon as we were seated in the waiting room, he expressed his concerns over the lab findings.

"I am somewhat perplexed at what the lab discovered after examining the blood samples taken from Georgann's regurgitated blood. There were trace fragments of bone matter in the blood samples. I want to run more tests using more advanced methods."

He mentioned some of the procedures which included bronchoscopy, but I blocked out most of what he was saying, because it just sounded like a lot of gibberish to me. "Don't worry, Mr. Volpe," patting my hand as if I were a child, "We'll find out what is causing Georgann's little problem." He stood, gave me his idea of a sympathetic smile and departed leaving me to sit in the chair with my mouth hanging open.

I was a nervous wreck. That made three choking episodes in two days - two of them in the hospital. Throwing some incomprehensible medical jargon at me didn't cut it. All I knew was that he didn't know what, why or how to cure Georgann's 'little problem'.

Before going to visit with Georgann, I went outside for a cigarette hoping it would me calm down. The last thing she needed was to see how upset I was. As I smoked, I thought over Patel's comment about finding trace fragments of bone in Georgann's blood samples. Because she hated going to the dentist, Georgann had put off long needed dental work on her deteriorating rear teeth. Didn't she spit out a piece of tooth after biting into her sandwich at Paul's the other day? Maybe she didn't spit out all of the broken tooth? Maybe she swallowed some of it with her sandwich? Maybe the nurses ramming suctioning tubes down her throat broke off even more of her deteriorated teeth. Maybe I was clutching at straws.

Maybe.

At the nurse's station, I asked the nurse to page Dr. Patel again. I wanted to give him my thoughts. He was too busy to meet with me in person but called the station and spoke with me over the phone. I related my thoughts about Georgann's teeth. I asked the doctor, "Could it be tooth fragments you detected in Georgann's blood?"

After several moments of silence, he said, "You might have something there, Mr. Volpe, although it's almost impossible to distinguish the type of bone fragments in such trace amounts. I will definitely keep what you have just told me in mind when I run more tests. In the mean time, while I have you on the phone, I will tell you I am going to intubate a static suctioning tube into Georgann's windpipe this afternoon to give us better control should it be necessary to remove more blood clots. I'm sure the bronchoscope is an unnecessary precaution, but I do not want to take chances." He hung up.

Patel was less than honest with me. In fact, in just a few hours, Georgann's physical state had become acutely worse. The lower lobes of her right lung were filling with blood and once the lung became saturated with blood, it flowed up into her windpipe, clotted, and obstructed her air supply. As the blood continued to flow, it spilled into her functioning left lung which was beginning to atrophy. Since her last episode, the ICU staff was suctioning Georgann's blood hourly in an attempt to prevent any further episodes. It was the nurse at the station who told me about the hourly schedule, not Patel.

An hour before her next scheduled suctioning, I was sitting with Georgann in the ICU. Exhausted from coughing, blood loss, and the suctioning, she drifted in and out of sleep. When the hospital staff came in to perform the suctioning, they asked me to step outside. As I waited in the corridor, Patel showed up to supervise the suctioning. He suggested that I take the time to have lunch. What a considerate guy!

When I returned from lunch, two doctors were talking outside of Georgann's room. From the few words I caught, I gathered they were discussing blood transfusions.

One said, "Patel wants to wait. He is reluctant to proceed, because a transfusion might contaminate her blood samples." I didn't know what they were talking about at the time.

That afternoon, I walked alongside the gurney as the attendants pushed Georgann to the operating room. The insertion of a suction tube was considered simply surgery. As we waited for the elevator, the doors of the adjacent elevator opened and Marie and her niece, Sandy, stepped out. Catching sight of Georgann, deathly pale from blood lose, Marie screamed and tried to throw herself onto the gurney. The attendants grabbed her in time before she fell upon Georgann. Sandy gripped Marie to keep her from fainting and rolling under the gurney.

Georgann smiled weakly up at her mother. "How's daddy?" she asked. After seeing her daughter so helpless, Marie was too shocked to answer. "Tell daddy I love him. I love you, too Mom." Georgann motioned for me to step closer. I bent my head for her to whisper, "I love you best, Al. Kiss Gabby for me."

(Spoilers - None of us could know that these words would be that last we'd ever hear Georgann utter.)

Sandy held Marie aside to allow the attendants to wheel Georgann into the elevator. She blew us a kiss goodbye as the elevator doors closed.

Dr. Patel told me the procedure would take about thirty minutes. Marie, Sandy and I headed for the small room outside the ICU to wait. To give me something to do, I went to the cafeteria for coffee leaving Sandy to console Marie. They were sitting together holding hands and praying for Georgann when I returned with the coffee.

Marie was sobbing, "If anything happens to Georgann, I'll kill myself. Oh God, please, don't take my Georgann!"

Georgann was Marie's life. I felt sorry for her. She asked me, through her sobs, to tell her exactly what had happened to Georgann Sunday night. (Was it only three days ago?). I told her about the coughing, the blood, how she couldn't catch her breath, and about taking Georgann to the emergency room at Danbury Hospital where they admitted her for tests.

Somehow, Marie's characteristic resentment toward me resurrected itself out of her grief. Narrowing her eyes at me, she said, "Georgann was fine when Silvio and I left Sunday morning for Washington. Look at her now! What did you do to her?"

It was just like Marie to put the blame on me. "I didn't do anything to her," I nearly yelled before I remembered where I was. "After Georgann helped Gabby to bed, we watched the news. I went up to our room and Georgann stayed in the den to catch the weather report. Just as I was getting ready for bed, I heard her coughing. I went down to the kitchen and saw her coughing up blood. I took her to the hospital. That's it! I don't know why she's sick! Patel thinks it might be some kind of blood disorder she caught in the Caribbean."

"Blood disorder! Bullshit! Is he crazy? None of the rest of us is sick. That doctor wouldn't know his ass from a hole in the ground if it bit him." Marie and her mixed metaphors.

Sandy, who had read the newspaper article about the young woman who was transferred to Yale asked, "Shouldn't they transfer Georgann to Yale or Westchester Medical Center, because the facilities are better?"

"I already pressed Dr. Patel twice about moving Georgann to Yale. He told me that Danbury Hospital was good enough. He made me feel like I was some kind of idiot for even suggesting he move Georgann. Why don't you to ask him when you see him?"

Marie turned on me again, "Why did you bring Georgann to this shithole hospital?"

I snapped back, "What did you want me to do, Marie; drive her to the Mayo Clinic?"

In order to stem what surely was about to become a full blown argument, Sandy grabbed Marie's arm and led her back to a seat. "Come on, Marie, Georgann needs our prayers right now, not angry words."

I slouched down in a chair, fuming.

Forty minutes later, Dr. Patel came into the waiting room accompanied by Dr. Wentworth, the anesthesiologist. Patel told us that the procedure was successful. With more assurance than I thought was warranted, he said, "The flexible bronchoscope will facilitate the suctioning of blood. At this stage, I am even more convinced that Georgann's bleeding is related to a rare blood disorder. I am confident that the test results from the outside lab will confirm my diagnosis."

"Doctor," Sandy spoke up, "Do you think that Georgann should be moved to Yale New Haven Hospital?"

At the same time, Marie whipped out her copy of the newspaper article Donna had given her and waved it in the doctor's face. Patel reeled back from Marie's attack and, brisling, answered, "Danbury Hospital is quite well equipped to treat Mrs. Volpe. If I questioned the facilities here, I would have transferred her immediately."

Marie turned ugly. Pointing her bent arthritic forefinger and glaring at both doctors through lizard-slit eyes, she slowly and quietly said, "For your sakes, doctors, (pronouncing 'doctors' the same way she says assholes) you better know what you're talking about. If anything happens to my daughter, they'll find you both in the gutter and no 'doctors' will be able to fix you."

Wentworth made a mad dash for the door, never to be seen again. Patel was so taken aback by Marie's threat that he gagged and clutched his throat as if it had just been slit open with a sharp scalpel. Finally, when he could breathe again, he stammered, "I must get back to the lab," and flew out the door in Wentworth's wake. At that time, no one knew who Marie Marino was other than a venomous crackpot.

Marie and I went to see Georgann in the ICU. She smiled up at us and gestured for us to sit. She was on a respirator and unable to speak because of the suction tube down her throat. I sat next to her, held her hand and kissed her on the cheek so many times; she finally had to push me away.

Marie sat holding Georgann's other hand and looking as if her heart had been wrenched out. Sandy sat in a chair by the door reading her Bible. We remained that way for a half an hour without speaking. We put on brave faces for Georgann, but as soon as were outside the room, we all broke down. Before leaving, Sandy asked us to join hands in prayer for Georgann's speedy recovery. I escorted Sandy and Marie to the hospital's entrance, and, after giving them both a hug, headed back to Georgann.

3

Surgery

I was sitting with Georgann when Patel sauntered into the ICU, but not before he checked to make sure Marie wasn't lurking in the shadows. He needed my signature on yet another surgical release form.

"Mr. Volpe, I'm glad you're here," he began. "It will be necessary to insert a rigid bronchoscope or metal tube into Georgann's trachea to facilitate my ability to pinpoint the source of bleeding. The flexible bronchoscope we have been using allows only small catheters to suction Georgann's blood. The rigid bronchoscope will be more effective in evacuating the blood and clots and give us better control in stemming the blood flooding into her windpipe and spilling into the left lung. During the procedure, once the bronchoscope is in place, we will suction out the blood and then thread a small camera into the bronchoscope to view the lower lobes of her right lung. As you may know, a lung is made up of three sections, the two lower lobes are spongy air sacs lined with capillaries and the top stem which attaches to the bronchia and pulmonary artery. Blood flows from the heart via the pulmonary arteries in the lung stem and into the capillary lined walls of the lung sacs to reinfuse the bloodstream with inhaled oxygen and expels carbon dioxide in the exchange process. Both of Georgann's lower lobes of her right lung are saturated reservoirs filled with blood. I believe that the source of the bleeding is within one of those lower lobes. The procedure is scheduled for 11:00 tomorrow morning and should take about an hour."

The more he talked the more horrified I became. I hardly understood what he was saying, but it sounded dreadful. I may not have understood his medical jargon, but I wasn't so dense not to realize that he still hadn't a clue to why or from where Georgann was bleeding. I signed the form and went back to Georgann. I was past asking questions. What I did not realize at the time was that I was also signing a medical release of liability waiver which protected the doctors and hospital from any litigation that might result from the medical procedure. (Spoilers)

Later that same evening, Patel reappeared in the ICU looking for me. He asked me to accompany him to the small office by the nurses' station. He had a new diagnosis for the cause of Georgann's bleeding and was excited to tell me about it. And, golly gee, if it wasn't based on my tooth sliver theory!

Patel said, "Over time, probably in her sleep, Georgann aspirated deteriorated tooth fragments into her right lung. Like shards of glass, they imbedded into an interior lobe wall of her right lung and sliced into the capillaries which caused blood to seep back into her lung sacs."

I was confused. First, he believed that Georgann had a rare blood disorder. Now, it was tooth shards. Huh? Of course, he failed to tell me (what's new) that he had received the final results from the outside lab that had examined Georgann's blood samples. The results determined that no rare or any other type of blood disorder was in evidence. Patel manifested a new diagnosis about tooth slivers with the same overconfidence he had with his last misdiagnosis.

At this point, my faith in him and Danbury Hospital to cure Georgann was stretched to the breaking point. I again pleaded with him to transfer her to Yale. But, because of his overzealous assurance that his new diagnosis was the shit, he refused to honor my request.

Thursday, March 10, 1994

At 11:00 am, Marie and I found ourselves again walking alongside the gurney taking Georgann to surgery. Again, we waited in the small room outside the ICU. One hour turned into three. Donna arrived, then Sandy with Joe Tomei, a close friend of the Marinos who was also an attorney; last were Josephine and Paul. Four hours went by - no news - we continued to wait. After five hours, Patel finally showed up still wearing his hospital scrubs. He was visibly unsettled seeing the room full of people. He ushered us all to a meeting room across the hall to explain the results of Georgann's surgery and the reason it took so long. As soon as we were seated around the conference table, Marie whipped out a mini-recorder and slammed it on the table in front of Patel before turning it on.

"Mrs. Marino, there is no need to record our conversation," Patel said.

Joe answered for Marie who was glaring menacingly at the doctor. "Let me explain, Dr. Patel. It is obvious that Mrs. Marino is very upset and concerned about her daughter. Mr. Silvio Marino, who was unable to be here, wishes to know exactly what transpired during their daughter's surgery. Mrs. Marino is not sure she would be able to convey your explanation correctly, therefore, the recorder. Please state your name." Throwing in Silvio's name was on purpose.

Patel, beginning to shake a bit, pushed the recorder a few inches away from in front of him before speaking. "First, I want to say that I am firmly opposed to this recording. It is highly irregular."

"State your name, please," repeated Joe. Who did Joe think he was - Joe Friday?

"I am Dr. Ben Patel, pulmonary surgeon at Danbury Hospital." He stopped speaking.

"Please continue with your statement, Dr. Patel," Friday Joe said.

"After Dr. LaPanz administered a general anesthesia, I inserted a rigid bronchoscope into Georgann's airway as a conduit for the insertion of a tiny camera to allow us to view the lower lobes of her right lung. Although we suctioned a large volume of blood from Georgann's lower lobes, the suctioning was not adequate to enable us to scope the source of the bleed via the camera. I had a sample of the blood from the suctioning taken to my lab for immediate analysis from which more traces of bone material was discovered. Based on these findings, Dr. LaPanz and I agreed that the only surgical course of action to stop the bleeding was to remove both lower lobes of Georgann's right lung."

As if he considered his explanation satisfactory, he placed his hands on the table ready to stand up. No 'do you have any questions?' No 'Georgann will be fine.' No nothing.

For a few moments, time and eternity stopped for all of us. We sat frozen incapable of processing what we just heard.

Marie thawed out first and lunged across the table at Patel screaming, "You cut out my daughter's lung? You butcher! I'm going to cut out your fuckin' heart!"

Joe and I grabbed Marie before she could get her hands around Patel's throat. Patel screeched like a girl, slid back his chair to avoid Marie's sharp claws and jumped up with such force that his chair flew across the room and bounced off the wall. He was a green flash out the door.

Sandy tried to calm Marie down, but she was out of control. She broke away from Sandy's hold and ran down the hall chasing after Patel. She continued to scream her threat. "You better run, you bastard. When I get my hands on you, I'm gonna cut your heart out!"

The hospital administrator called the security police. Fortunately, they were able to subdue Marie before she could catch up with Patel, but not before she made more threats to no one in particular. "If anything happens to my daughter, they'll find your corpses rotting on the streets of Danbury."

The security guards escorted Marie to Sandy's car; the others left in silent misery. I sat alone in the empty room for hours, too traumatized to move. At eight, an ICU nurse on her break noticed me in the room.

"Mr. Volpe, the hospital has been trying to reach you at home for the past two hours. We had no idea you were still here. Georgann is awake. Dr. Patel informed the hospital staff that you and only you are allowed to visit her. Hurry, Mr. Volpe, let's not keep Georgann waiting."

Because I was in such a hurry to be with Georgann, I followed the nurse so closely I stepped on her heels. "Sorry," I stammered.

Pulling her shoe back on, the nurse stepped aside as soon as we entered the room but stayed at the door to ensure Georgann was still alert and comfortable.

I ran up to Georgann's' bed. Slightly elevated, Georgann was hooked up to an IV. Her dark curls framed a face so pale I feared what little blood she had left in her would never be enough to put the roses back into her cheeks. In spite of what she'd been through, Georgann managed a smile for me; my spirit renewed. I spent the night at her bedside.

Friday, March 11, 1994

Marie's tirade and threats the day before had put the hospital on notice. I didn't know how they found out, but the staff began calling Georgann a 'Mafia Princess'. Doctors were afraid to treat her; the nurses checked in on her every ten minutes to make sure she was comfortable or needed anything; the cleaning staff tiptoed in and out of the ICU wearing surgical booties to muffle any noise their shoes might make. Patel finally gave orders to allow Georgann other visitors than myself but examined her only when visiting hours were not in effect.

I spent the morning with Georgann who could only smile lovingly at me. At one, I said, "This place is going to be a zoo this afternoon when everyone comes to visit. I'm going to Paul's for a while. I'll grab some lunch and take a nap at his house before coming back to spend the night with you. Have fun with your friends. Just don't talk too much. Just kidding." She gave me a pouty face and a little punch for the tease. I kissed her cheek and waved goodbye at the door before leaving.

I was dozing on the couch when Paul shook me awake. He handed me the phone. It was Donna; she was in hysterics. During her visit, Georgann had another episode. Marie was with Donna while Georgann's other visitors waited their turn in the hall. Both were shooed out of the ICU, but, before anyone could stop her, Marie barged back into the ICU and physically attacked the doctors who were ministering to Georgann.

"Butchers! Murderers!" Marie screamed. "Get away from my daughter."

Hospital security, who were already on Marie alert, arrived fast enough to get Marie out of the ICU before she could inflict any severe damage on the hospital staff or Georgann. She was again escorted out of the hospital, but more gently this time given that she was the mother of a Mafia Princess.

I sped back to the hospital. Everyone was gone by the time I got there. Georgann was sleeping, a peaceful look on her pretty face. She sensed that I had entered the room and awoke giving me that beatific smile of hers. I smiled back, but we both knew we were hiding our fears behind a mask of optimism. Patel was nowhere to be found.

I hadn't slept in days. Late that night nurse came in to the ICU. She said, "Go home, Mr. Volpe. Georgann has been given a sedative and won't wake until morning. You look like you could use a good night's sleep."

"If she does wake up, promise you'll call me. I'll rush right back. I don't want her to be alone." The nurse assured me she would call.

Chuck's car was parked in the driveway when I got home. The house stank of beer and animal piss. I banged on Nicky's bedroom door, "Chuck, time to go."

The door flew open. He tripped pulling a sneaker onto one foot and holding the other in his hand as he ran down the stairs mumbling, "Good night, Mr. Volpe."

He was halfway out the door when Nicky yelled out, "You don't have to go, Chuck. Don't listen to him. Nobody cares what he says." Chuck kept on moving, slamming the door on his way out.

I was in no mood for Nicky's insolence. I didn't even bother to tell her to shut up. I locked up the house, shut my bedroom door and went to bed. Nicky hadn't even asked how her mother was doing.

Saturday, March 12, 1994

Before I left for the hospital that morning, big mouth Donna called me. She told me that everyone at the hospital was walking on eggshells around Georgann, and it wasn't because they were afraid of Marie's threats. Marie played the Patel tape to Silvio. When Silvio learned that the doctors had removed part of Georgann's lung, he decided that it was time he threw a little Mafia weight around. He phoned Danbury Hospital and demanded to speak to the administrator after identifying himself as Silvio Marino, Georgann's father. Speaking in a polite but concerned manner which put the administrator off his guard, he asked how Georgann was doing. During his conversation, he let slip that some of his very important 'friends' in 'The Family' business cared a great deal about Georgann and were very concerned about her treatment in Danbury Hospital.

"It would be very upsetting to me and 'my friends' if anything should happen to my beloved daughter," he said in his most honeyed tone. "I hope you will do whatever you can to bring her safely home to her 'Family'. I truly hope you understand what I am saying."

Oh, the administrator understood all right and communicated his understanding to Patel. Patel was waiting for me outside the ICU when I arrived. He asked to speak to me in private. When I first met Patel, I was wary - as I always am - of someone that arrogantly self-assured. Now, gone was that confident aloofness. His current meekness was so pathetic it alarmed me even more than his egotism. I could smell the same stink of fear on him as if he was one of Silvio's marks late with his vig payment. And, to think, I had put my faith and Georgann's life into this man's hands that now shook so much he had to clasp them behind his back to keep me from seeing them.

In the past twenty-four hours, Patel had locked himself in his lab dissecting and reanalyzing all of Georgann's lung tissue samples. He couldn't find a scintilla of embedded bone matter or sliced capillaries to validate his tooth sliver diagnosis. All the trace bone material had come from breaking off of some of Georgann's rotted teeth when, in their haste to minister to her, the nurses rammed the suctioning catheters and bronchoscope into her mouth and down her trachea. Having this knowledge was of no consolation: Georgann was dying before our eyes, drowning in her own blood. By taking out the lower lobes of her right lung, all Patel and company accomplished was to ring Georgann's death knell.

He didn't tell me any of this, of course. What he said was, "Our more extensive analysis of Georgann's blood samples ruled out the possibility of bone shards cutting into her capillaries."

Did I hear right? - no bone shards, no rare blood disorder.

"Then what is wrong with Georgann?"

He stammered back, "It must be coming from the remaining lung stem."

Although I was fuming inside, I controlled my temper long enough to say, quietly and though clenched teeth, "That's it, doctor. You had your chance. Transfer... Georgann ... to ...Yale ...NOW!"

He hung his head, "I can't. Her condition is too critical. A move might prove fatal."

It took every ounce of control I had left in me not to drag his ass into surgery and cut out his lung with my pen knife, but I needed to keep a cool head for Georgann's sake. I walked away from him.

The surgical release form I had signed for the insertion of the rigid bronchoscope legally covered the doctors' asses; it allowed for emergency surgery if the presiding surgeon deemed it necessary to save the patient's life. However, legality be damned, at this point that was the least of Patel's worries. He knew that if Georgann died; he died. Like I said, Silvio might speak softly, but his threats were never idle nor should they be ignored.

I thought it best not to bring Gabby to visit her mother at this time. But, I couldn't stop Marie, Donna, and Dennis who came to the hospital that afternoon. Now that Silvio had her back, Marie was out for blood. I couldn't stomach being in the same room as this collection of misfits. I went outside for a cigarette.

I was getting out of the elevator on my return when I saw Marie arguing with someone in the hall. I didn't know or care what havoc Marie was instigating. I about-faced and headed for the waiting room at the end of the hall to sit - sorrowful and alone.

I grabbed a magazine and held it up to shield my face so no one could see that my eyes were brimming with tears. A few minutes later, Donna and Dennis came in. They sat next to each other on the couch across from me. They didn't realize I was in the room.

Donna was babbling to no one in particular, "Fuck security, that's my sister in there. I have a right to see her."

Dennis tried to quiet her down, "Honey, they wouldn't let you go into the ICU, because Georgann already had two visitors. That's hospital policy."

Just as Donna started to open her mouth to tell Dennis to shut up, Marie blew into the waiting room. "Come on, let's go, Donna. I've had enough of this fuckin' place. I can't stand to see what those butchers have done to my poor baby." At first, she didn't see me hiding behind a magazine but when she did, she went wild.

She stood in front of me blocking my escape. Glaring down at me with a malevolent stare, she said, "This is all your fault, shithead. You gave those stronzi permission to cut up my Georgann. If anything happens to her, you're number two on the same kill list. You hear me? They'll find you in the gutter along with those other assholes. I knew it would come to this. I told Silvio to get rid of you years ago. First, you steal two-million dollars from Gabby, now you want to murder my daughter to keep all the money for yourself. You're going to pay with your miserable life." She spit in my face. I was about to grab Marie by her scrawny neck and choke the life out of her when Nicky stuck her head into the room. She had obviously heard what Marie had said to me, because she was smiling when she said ever so sweetly, "Let's go, Nana."

Marie spun around to leave but not before hitting me in the head with the big purse she had slung over her arm. We heard her tell Nicky, "Change the locks on the doors. It's not his house. It belongs to Gabby and my daughter. Throw that mutt out."

The three of us sat incredulous at what we had just witnessed. Donna finally said to me, "I told you a long time ago that my mother is fuckin' crazy. She's more bat-shit loony than ever since Gabby got the money. She just doesn't want you gone anymore, she wants you dead. She's the reason my sister got sick. Georgann knew she couldn't protect you anymore." Dennis poked her to shut up. Donna turned on him, "Don't poke me! Al already knows!"

I did.

I spent the night at Georgann's bedside holding her hand and stroking her cheek until she fell to sleep. I had a miserable night sleeping in the chair. In the morning, the night shift nurse came in. "I watched you two on the monitor all night. It was like watching a love story on TV. Where did you find this guy, Georgann? He's a keeper."

"Could you tell that to my mother in-law?" I said.

Georgann rolled her big, brown eyes and gave me 'the look' but couldn't flash me her big smile because of the tubes. I knew it was there.

Sunday, March 13, 1994

No one visited Georgann today. I spent the whole day with her and didn't even go home to shower or change. In the afternoon, I phoned Sue to speak with Gabby. I said to Gabby, "Mommy is right here. She can hear everything you say to her, but she can't talk right now, because she has a terrible sore throat. How are you, sweetheart?"

"I'm fine, Daddy. Aunt Sue is real nice to me, and I'm having a lot of fun with Ashley and her sisters, but I want to go home. I want to be with mommy. When is she coming home?"

"Soon, sweetheart, soon. Say goodbye to mommy. Can you hear her giving you kisses over the phone?"

"Yes, Daddy, I'm giving her kisses right back. I love you, Mommy. Come home soon." I put the phone slowly back in the cradle.

Georgann had silent tears flowing down her cheeks. I used my cigarette addiction to go to the car to do my crying. I didn't want Georgann to see how frightened I was.

As I paced in front of the hospital, I heard a voice call out my name from the darkness. It was Sonny; he had driven in from Long Island to visit Georgann.

"How is she?" he asked.

"You'll see," was all I said.

We rode up in the elevator in silence. When Georgann saw Sonny, her face lit up. I could tell his smile was forced for Georgann's sake, but he couldn't hide the sadness in his eyes. We both stayed by her bedside until she drifted off in a sedated sleep.

Sonny saw I was exhausted. He insisted, "Go home and get some sleep, I'll stay with Georgann. I'll see you in the morning."

"Thanks, Sonny. You're Georgann's guardian angel. I can rest easy knowing you're watching over her."

He walked me to the elevator. He grabbed me in a tight hug - two big chooches holding onto each other for comfort.

Monday, March 14, 1994

I really needed that night's rest. On the way back to the hospital, I stopped at Dunkin' Donuts to grab breakfast for me and Sonny. I found him stretched out on the couch in the waiting room. When I held the coffee under his nose, he popped one eye open, sat up and grabbed the coffee.

After one big sip, he said, "Georgann slept all night. I spent a lot of time talking with ICU nurses. Man, Al, what did Marie do to make everyone so jumpy? They're calling Georgann a Mafia Princess. I haven't heard that term since I was a kid."

"Marie did her usual threatening everyone with 'blood will flow in the streets of Danbury' rant if anything happened to Georgann. But, it was not until Silvio called the administrator of the hospital that set everyone into a panic. Through the usual mob innuendo which the administrator was able to decode, Silvio let them know that he had some Mafia muscle behind his threats. The doctors treating Georgann are afraid that if she dies, their lives aren't worth a plug nickel."

"Marie may be a lot of hot air, but if I know my brother-in-law, there's no bullshit in Silvio. If he says it, he means it. I hear you're on the kill list, too."

"I've been on Marie's list since I married Georgann. I'm just hoping Silvio hasn't put me on his."

"For your sake, me too. I'm going downstairs to call Marie. I'll stay with Georgann again tonight, but then I have to head back to the Island."

We polished off the box of donuts and coffee I brought before Sonny went to make his call. Fifteen minutes later, Patel appeared. After making sure that all the paraphernalia attached to Georgann was working correctly, he asked me to step into the hall.

"My analysis has not produced a clear diagnosis for Georgann's condition. I can only conclude that the problem must lie in the remaining lung stem."

Before I could respond, Sonny came out of the elevator. Patel stared, color draining from his face when he realized that this 280-pound Soprano poster child was heading toward us. He turned and rushed down the corridor leaving a moisture trail. Sonny asked me who he was. When I told him he was Georgann's doctor, he said, "That doctor sure is awful jumpy. Maybe he should prescribe himself some sedatives."

"Your sister's already written his prescription," He laughed giving me a friendly push on the shoulder that knocked me into the wall.

We spent the rest of the day with Georgann trying to give her the impression that we weren't scared shitless for her. At three, I said to Sonny, "Go to my house and grab a shower and a couple of hours sleep. Here are the keys if Nicky isn't home." At the elevator, I hugged him again thanking him for being such a good uncle. This time the loving tap he gave me on my chin almost dislocated my jaw.

Sonny came back to the hospital at ten that evening. "I made a big pot of pasta e fagioli for you."

"You managed to find the Ditilini #40 in that big pantry?"

Sonny laughed, "That pantry is bigger than my first apartment on the Grand Concourse. By the way, your house stinks of dog shit, and the refrigerator is loaded with beer. Nicky and her boyfriend rolled in about eight. I surprised them. She seemed a tad annoyed to see me. I guess she couldn't flop down wherever she wanted with me there. I jumped on her case about not taking care of the animals, and I really lit into to her about her lack of concern for her mother and sister. I know she doesn't give a fart about you. She didn't say anything, just stared daggers at me. The weasel of a boyfriend said 'nice to meet you,' and beat feet out of there. Who is he, anyway?"

"That's Nikol's latest Ditalini," I said.

"Your got that right," Sonny chuckled. I said goodnight and went home to a reeking but empty house.

4

Life-Star

Tuesday, March 15, 1994

I was jolted out of a deep, dreamless sleep by the phone. It was Sonny. "Georgann's lost vital signs. They're going to air-lift her to Yale on a Life-Star. Get here quick!"

"I'm on my way," I yelled into the phone. Throwing on some clothes, I ran out of the house and straight into a blinding blizzard. The Blazer barely made it up the driveway; conditions were total white out. When I finally got to the hospital, I was met with flashing lights in the parking area. The police were rerouting traffic to give the Life Star helicopter a clear landing pad.

I jumped out of the Blazer leaving it in the middle of the street, ran into the hospital lobby and right past Sonny without seeing him. I grabbed the elevator to the ICU; it was in total chaos.

Patel was on the phone at the nurse's station. I stood behind him as he said, "It's a matter of life or death. They must try again." He was talking to the Life Star dispatcher. The pilot was trying his best but was unable to land, because visibility was zero. The dispatcher wanted to abort the mission, but Patel emphasized the severity of his patient's condition. The pilot made another attempt and managed to land the chopper. Hanging up, Patel audibly sighed and took in a lungful of air. He must have felt my hot breath on his neck, because he shuddered before turning to face me.

"Mr. Volpe, I'm glad you are here. I'm transferring Georgann to Yale New Haven Hospital via the Life Star helicopter. Their diagnostic equipment is more specialized than Danbury's. Your wife will get excellent care there."

Wait a minute! Wait a minute! Wasn't it Patel who told me just yesterday that moving Georgann could prove fatal? Now, he's risking her life as well as the lives of the Life Star team to get her out of Danbury through a blizzard! All of a sudden, he was Dr. Compassionate! What I saw was an egocentric blowhard who butchered my wife and now wanted to make sure she didn't spoil his track record by dying on his watch. Thanks to Silvio, the possibility of winding up a dead man might also have had something to do with his hasty decision. I wanted to spit in his face – no, I wanted to smash in his face. Instead, I pushed past him to Georgann's bedside. She was fading in and out of consciousness. I bent over her and whispered in her ear, "I'm here, sweetheart. I won't leave you. Please hold on. I love you."

Sonny barged in, grabbed me by the shoulders and pushed me out of the room, "Life Star's here. You need to get out of their way."

A blur of navy jumpsuits surrounded Georgann. The flight nurse and respiratory therapist from the Life Star crew along with two Danbury nurses worked quickly to get Georgann hooked up to life support and ready for transport. They carefully lifted her onto a gurney and rushed her out of the ICU toward the elevator. I ran alongside the gurney pleading with Georgann to stay with me. When the elevator door opened, the flight nurse pushed me back. "I'm sorry, sir, but you won't be able to come with us."

I didn't argue. They needed to do their jobs without me being in their way. I stood in front of the elevator and stared up catatonically at the descending lights. The ping of an elevator brought me out of my trance. It was Sonny with Marie and Silvio.

Marie ran up to me, "Where's Georgann? Where's my daughter?" she screamed.

Without speaking, I grabbed her arm and pulled her back into the elevator; Silvio and Sonny jumping in just before the doors closed. Years went by before the elevator hit the ground floor. In a rush to get to the parking lot, we almost trampled a stunned Paul who was coming into the lobby carrying a tray from Dunkin Donuts. We ignored the look of 'what's happening' on his face.

With Marie in tow, I ran up the ramp to the parking lot and into the blinding snow, the flashing red lights of the police cars as my only guide. Silvio, Sonny and Paul scrambled behind us. A police officer stopped us at the top of the ramp preventing us from getting any nearer. Georgann and the transport team were already in the helicopter. Standing in a row, the five of us stared at the blur of helicopter lights barely visible through the snow. We heard the chopper's engine rev and the whir of the blades as they began to slowly turn. The engine got louder; the blades spun faster wildly whipping the falling snow like egg whites. A final thunderous roar took the chopper airborne. We watched, barely able to discern its dark shape, until it disappeared into the milky white sky.

I held onto Marie, her inconsolable crying bearing witness to what I felt in my heart. With tears frozen on our faces, she and I continued to stare into the nothingness in which Georgann, the love of both our lives, had disappeared. Paul gently took hold of my arm and guided us down the slippery ramp and into the hospital, me practically carrying Marie. Inside the lobby, soaked and freezing, Paul handed us the coffee he had put down on a table before following us out to the parking lot. Its warmth was comforting to our bodies but could not take away the numbing pain we felt in our souls.

In the meantime, Sonny had gotten directions to Yale-New Haven Hospital from the hospital concierge. He also spoke with Patel who gave him the name and phone number of the contact at Yale. Thank God someone was still able to keep his wits about him. Sonny drove Marie; Paul and I followed behind in Paul's car. Silvio headed back to Westchester.

Because of the blizzard, the thirty mile drive to Yale took over two hours. I would never have made it without Paul; I was so distraught I could barely see straight. Paul dropped me at the hospital entrance before going to park. Sonny and Marie were already waiting in the lobby. As soon as I walked in, Sonny grabbed my arm with one hand and, still keeping a tight grip around Marie's shoulders, ran us over to the reception desk. Because he was the only one of us capable of getting out a coherent sentence, Sonny spoke to the woman sitting behind the desk. After identifying who I was, he told the receptionist that my wife had been airlifted to Yale from Danbury Hospital and that Dr. Patel said I should speak with Mrs. Jones, the surgical administrator, as soon as we arrived. The receptionist called Mrs. Jones who informed her that Georgann had been rushed to surgery and was still in the operating room. In the meantime, Mrs. Jones gave us permission to wait in her office. Paul showed up, and we dragged him to the elevator without saying a word, filling him in during the ride to the third floor.

Mrs. Jones' door was open when we arrived; we walked right in. I stood in front of her desk while Paul and Sonny, still supporting Marie, lined up behind me. In her mid-forties, the neat appearance of Mrs. Jones bespoke efficiency and competence.

She said, "Have a seat," indicating the chair in front of her desk for me and the couch against the wall for the others. Without preamble she said, "Mrs. Volpe was airlifted to Yale in critical condition. Dr. Baldwin, one of our pulmonary surgeons, met the Life Star helicopter as soon as it landed and had Mrs. Volpe transported to the ICU where, after a cursory examination, Dr. Baldwin deemed surgery imperative. He and his surgical team are still in the OR. He will meet with you after the surgery and give you all the specific details. In the meantime, try not to worry."

Mrs. Jones stood, walked around the desk, gently took hold of my arm to help me stand, and led me out of her office nodding for the others to follow. She escorted us to a private waiting room and made sure we were sitting comfortably before returning to her office. There, we sat for hours. I was beginning to believe that half my life was spent in the waiting rooms of hospitals.

As time went by, Marie slowly did her morphing thing. The first two hours she recited the same prayer over and over, "My poor Georgann, please, Lord, take me, not her." Then, more to her style, the recitation became, "I'm going to use those Danbury quacks fuckin' heads for bowling balls."

After a millennium, a portly man in his late fifties whose gray hair was partially hidden under the cap of his scrubs came into the waiting room. We all stared up at him. He looked around at each of us before asking "Mr. Volpe?"

"That's me, doctor," I said starting to get up.

"Please stay seated, Mr. Volpe," he said pulling up a chair to face me. "I'm Dr. Baldwin. I just performed emergency surgery on your wife. To my limited knowledge, Dr. Patel surgically removed the lower lobes of your wife's right lung two days ago in accordance with his diagnosis that the source of recurrent expressive bleeding was located in that area. We quickly conducted our own diagnostic tests prior to Mrs. Volpe's surgery - we have more specialized equipment than Danbury Hospital - and detected a ruptured aneurysm in Mrs. Volpe's right pulmonary artery. The diagnostics indicated that the aneurysm was the source of the bleeding which had nothing to do with the lower lobes of her lung. Our surgical team managed to patch the ruptured artery and stem the bleeding, but Mrs. Volpe's arteries are very weak due to the trauma her body has experienced in the past few days. We can only hope the patch holds and the artery doesn't disintegrate." Dr. Baldwin got up, gave me a small smile and was about to leave before turning to add, "It's a miracle she survived the airlift and an even greater miracle that she survived the surgery. Your wife is a very lucky lady."

I was left speechless by what Dr. Baldwin just told me. As usual with all medical speak, I didn't understand everything he said, but the one thing I did know was that Georgann's survival had nothing to with luck. I wanted to tell him that my wife has more strength and will to live than the all of us put together.

A social worker joined us in the waiting room to obtain my contact and insurance information. After she left, I mulled over Dr. Baldwin's information; not Patel's misdiagnoses – that was evident given the unnecessary surgery he had performed – but of what Dr. Baldwin had not said. The underlying implication of his words was that Georgann's condition was so critical she might not survive. It didn't help to continue to hear Marie moan, "If Georgann dies; I'm going to kill myself -- after I kill the doctors."

I shook myself clear of these thoughts long enough to say to the others, "Why don't you all go home. I'll let you know when Georgann will be allowed to have visitors. I'm going to stay in case she wakes up and asks for me." Reluctantly, Marie, continuing to mumbling the threats against the doctors, allowed Sonny to help her out.

Paul rode back to Danbury with Sonny and Marie leaving his car with me in case I needed it. After they had gone, I paced the hall outside the ICU for hours leaving my post only for cigarette breaks and coffee. After midnight, overcome with exhaustion, I turned off the light in the waiting room and crashed on the couch.

Wednesday, March 16, 1994

Around 4:00 am, a security guard startled me awake by flipping on the light. It took me a few seconds to realize where I was. When I did, I ran to the intercom in the waiting room and called the ICU for an update on Georgann.

Andrea, Georgann's attending nurse, came to the phone. She said, "Mr. Volpe, meet me outside the ICU in five minutes. I don't want to leave your wife unattended for long."

A minute later, I was waiting outside the ICU. The doors opened just wide enough to allow a petite woman in her late twenties to exit. Although she was wearing a surgical cap, I could see that her hair was dark and curly given the tiny wisp that had gotten loose. Her face, free of make-up, was smooth as amber honey and radiated compassion. She approached me and held out her hand for me to shake.

"Thank you, Mr. Volpe, for meeting me. I just wanted to tell you that your wife regained consciousness a few times but only for moments. Each time, she struggled to speak before lapsing back into unconsciousness. I think she was mouthing 'Al' and 'baby.' Do you have a baby?"

"She must have been trying to say Gabby, our youngest daughter. When she wakes again, please tell her that Gabby and I are both fine. How is Georgann?"

"I can't comment on Georgann's condition at this time. I'm sure Dr. Baldwin will update you later this morning. You won't be allowed into the ICU until Dr. Baldwin gives the okay, but I will tell Georgann what you said and let her know that you are here." She squeezed my arm and returned to the ICU. I went back to the waiting room.

To wait.

5

God, Al – What?

A soft voice with a pronounced Jamaican accent woke me 7:00 a.m. "Good morning, Mister. I didn't mean to wake you. Did you spend the night on that lumpy, ol' couch?" she asked.

I sat up. When my bleary eyes focused I saw a five-foot nothing black woman in her late fifties. Her tan uniform was starched and spotless; her cleaning cart neat and orderly.

"My name is Mrs. Evelyn Thomas. I am a member of the senior custodial staff at this hospital. Why you here at this early hour? Don't tell me you didn't go home last night!"

"No, I didn't. My wife was air-lifted here from Danbury Hospital yesterday. She had an operation and is in serious condition. She hasn't come around yet, and I wanted to be here when she does. My name is Al."

Mrs. Thomas sat down next to me on the couch but not before she carefully propped the push broom she was holding against her cart. We began to chat like long lost friends catching up on the news. I told her about Georgann and Gabby and Nicky, and she told me about her five children and ten grandchildren. Her dear husband, Mr. Thomas, had departed this earthly plane (her words) seven years before.

"It was sure nice talking to you, Al, but I got my housekeeping chores to do. Before I go, I want to give you something that might give you some comfort." She pulled a copy of the Daily Word out of the basket on her cart and handed it to me.

As Mrs. Thomas went about tidying up the waiting room, I thumbed through the small booklet she gave me. Its daily messages were supposed to give some kind of spiritual comfort. I was disbelieving.

Before leaving, Mrs. Thomas sat down again next to me. She took my hands in her work roughened ones. Bowing her head, she said, "Please, Dear Lord, watch over Georgann, restore her to health so that she can be with her loving husband and babies. Amen."

"Your mouth to God's ear, Mrs. Thomas," I said.

"God always hears our prayers, Al. I will place you and your family within the prayer circle at my church."

I didn't know what a prayer circle was, but I thanked her anyway. Pushing her cart slowly before her, I was left alone again in the waiting room.

An hour later, I was still reading the pamphlet when the intercom blared, "Mr. Volpe, please pick up. Mr. Volpe, please pick up." I bolted to the intercom, "Yes, yes, I'm here." The voice said, "Dr. Baldwin would like to meet with you outside the ICU."

"I'll be right there," I said. I folded the pamphlet and put it in my back pocket before racing to the ICU. Dr Baldwin met me half way down the corridor.

Dr. Baldwin said, "I am sorry to tell you my news is not good, Mr. Volpe. The seal we placed on the ruptured aneurysm failed. Because of Georgann's significant blood loss this past week, her vital signs, specifically her blood pressure and respiration rate, are critically low. The ICU staff was able to stabilize her, but she requires additional surgery. A surgical team has been brought in to prep and rush her to the OR. I reread the medical report Danbury Hospital faxed to me. I was surprised to see that no blood transfusions were scheduled despite the volume of blood loss Georgann experienced. Do you know why this standard medical protocol was not followed?"

"I think it had something to do with the transfusions corrupting the blood samples Dr. Patel was analyzing. But, I'm not really sure."

"I'll call Dr. Patel when I get a chance. Is there anyone you want to call to be here with you?"

"Her parents, the Marinos," I answered. Not to be with me, of course, but they had a right to be here as much as I. "Also, her sister and some of her friends, if that is okay. I'll give them a call.

Dr. Baldwin nodded, "I'll make sure they are on the visitation list. I must get to the surgery. I will meet with you and the Marinos later."

Trembling, I staggered to a bench in the corridor. Sobbing loudly, I sat holding my head as if it were about to separate from my body. I felt a light hand on my shoulder. Directly in front of me were two large, black ladies holding out tissues. They were both in their sixties, dressed in ankle length skirts and high collared white blouses. Each one had a flowery hat perched on top of an obvious wig. They were so alike; I thought they must be sisters.

"Take these, sir. Whatever are you crying so mournfully about?" said one. They sat down on either side of me and patiently waited until I was calm enough to speak.

I dried my eyes with the tissues and managed to get out, "My wife is very sick. She's having surgery right now. I'm Al and Georgann, that's my wife, needs to get better to come home to me and our daughters." I was babbling like an idiot, but I wasn't able to express myself better.

"Oh you poor man! My name is Sofia and this is my sister, Janice," she said nodding to the woman on my other side. "We are here visiting a member of our church. We walked past you when you were speaking with the doctor, but you didn't see us. We know Dr. Baldwin, don't we, Janice? He's a very fine surgeon. Your wife could not be in better hands."

I appreciated her encouraging words. I needed all I could get.

Sofia bent down and picked up the copy of the Daily Word that had fallen out of my pocket. Handing it to me, she said, "My sister and I could not help feeling some of your pain. When we saw you reading the Daily Word, we felt it was our Christian duty to pray with you to ask for God's healing grace for you and your family."

(You readers are probably aware by now that I am not a religious man, but these ladies were so sincere, and I was so desperate I couldn't refuse their offer.)

"I would appreciate that, ladies."

They actually knelt in front of me each taking hold of one of my hands and joining theirs together. Janice, whose voice was low and rich, boldly began to pray, "Father God, we stand on Your Word to heal Georgann and be a comfort to Al and his daughters in their time of crisis. Give them Your strength and inner peace. We claim this through the precious blood of Your only begotten son, Jesus. Amen and Amen." She and Sofia bent their heads in silent prayer. They remained kneeling for several minutes never go of my hands.

(You, readers, I know, will have to stretch your imaginations to believe what I am now about to tell you.)

I felt bolts of heat pass through me as if struck by lightning. I was overwhelmed with a sense of peace that filled my body and calmed my raging thoughts. I began to tremble and sweat as I rocked back and forth. Sofia stood giving my hand to Janice before going to get me some water. Janice remained kneeling in front of me, holding both my hands in hers until I stopped shaking. Withdrawing one hand, she opened her purse and pulled out a business card. Hers and Sofia's phone numbers were on the back; she tucked it into my shirt pocket. "Call us anytime, Al, and we will pray with you. God does not keep banker's hours."

Sofia came back with the water and handed it to me. Janice rose. "Al, if you need a place to stay, food, or just fellowship, please do not hesitate to call. Our church will be keeping you and your family in our prayers." That makes two prayer lists in the same day.

I pulled the card out of my pocket. The front of the card read 'The Church on the Rock, New Haven, CT'. After they left, I sat thinking about the spiritual epiphany I believed I just experienced. I didn't know much if anything about God, but all of a sudden, I had a burning desire to know more– know in the sense of feeling, not understanding. Mrs. Thomas, Sofia and Janice – was God sending these ladies, saints in polyester - to reach out to me, because He knew I was about to face an ordeal I couldn't bear alone?

I continued to be lost in thought and awe until I was roused by someone calling my name. “Mr. Volpe?” I raised my eyes to see a stout, middle aged woman whose shoulder length gray hair was fashionably styled as was her navy blue business suit.

“Yes, I’m Al Volpe.”

“I am Irene Scanlon, Mr. Volpe. It is my job at Yale to coordinate meetings of patients and the doctors who are attending them with their family members.” She held out her business card to me. I turned it over thinking I might see the name of her church on the back. Nothing.

"I spoke with the Marinos this morning. They will be arriving shortly. We can meet privately in the next room.” She unlocked the door to a small room to the right of the waiting room. She asked, “I know that this is a difficult time for you. Would you like me to arrange for you to speak to a chaplain or a priest?”

I thought a higher power has already spoken to me. "No thank you."

I went into the room and sat, still in wonder over what I was calling ‘my religious experience’ when I heard a commotion in the hall. A minute later, Mrs. Scanlon opened the door for Marie, Nikol, and Donna followed by Sue, Fred, and Gabby.

I went over to Sue and whispered, “Why did you bring Gabby?”

Sue whispered back, “Gabby insisted on coming after Marie told her that this might be her last chance to see her mother alive.”

“I don’t believe it! That’s it! When Georgann comes home, I’m going to ban that woman from ever setting foot in my house again. Let’s drop it for now.” I went over to Gabby and hugged her. “Mommy is going to be just fine, sweetheart. Your Nana is wrong. Let’s sit down. I want to hear about everything you’ve been doing.” Gabby clung to me as I led her to a couch at the far end of the room.

Marie latched onto the social worker - a new ear to listen to her usual tirade. “They butchered my daughter in Danbury. They’re going to pay.” She ranted on and on about suing the hospital and getting revenge on the doctors. Mrs. Scanlon did not know how to respond to Marie so she said nothing. Finally, when she was able to get a word in, she told us she would return shortly with Dr. Baldwin, excused herself and dashed out the door.

I left Gabby with Sue to get coffee for everyone from the cafeteria – a good excuse as any for me to get away from my mother-in-law. When I returned, I handed the coffee around before joining Gabby and Sue in a corner of the waiting room. I gave Gabby a hot chocolate and sat with my arm around her. About twenty minutes later, Mrs. Scanlon returned with Dr. Baldwin.

He barely got into the room when Marie blurted out, “Is my daughter alive?"

"Mrs. Marino, please calm down. Your daughter is resting comfortably. Hold your questions until I explain the situation most of which I already related to Mr. Volpe this morning. Yesterday, we performed surgery on Georgann to repair an aneurysm or rupture in one of her pulmonary arteries. At 10:24 this morning, the artery ruptured again and Mrs. Volpe lost vital signs. The ICU staff was able to resuscitate her after which the sur-gical team prepared Mrs. Volpe for a second emergency surgery. My team tied off the deteriorated artery and rerouted the blood to more viable arteries. Unfortunately, due to blood loss and weakening of her other arteries, Mrs. Volpe remains in critical condition. My associate, Dr. Matthay, will be in charge of her care from now on. As soon as he completes his examination of Mrs. Volpe, he will come here to speak with all of you."

Dopey Donna yelled out, "What about a lung transplant?"

Dr. Baldwin responded, more patiently than I would have given him credit. "Right now, we are doing all that is medically possible for Mrs. Volpe. A lung transplant is not in consideration at this time. I'm sure that Dr. Matthay will be able to answer all your questions." He excused himself and left the waiting room.

Marie and Donna had their heads together whispering and gesturing excitedly. What stupid questions they were dreaming up I didn't want to conjecture. My immediate concern was for Gabby.

Thirty minutes later, Mrs. Scanlon returned with a tall, handsome, silver haired gentleman in his fifties. She introduced Dr. Richard Matthay who was in charge of the Pulmonary and Critical Care Medicine program at Yale.

He smiled around the room, his blue eyes crinkling in the corners and lighting up his face as he nodded to each of us. He reminded me of Dr. Cooley with his easy manner. He went around to each of in the room asking our names and shaking our hands. He stopped by Gabby, knelt before her, took her hand and asked her name

"Gabriel but everybody calls me Gabby," she whispered.

"Gabby, I give you my promise that we are going to take very good care of your mother." He gave Gabby's cheek a gentle stroke before standing up.

Donna and Marie began to badger him with questions. "Hold onto your questions until I explain what procedures we will be undertaking. Mr. Volpe, are you sure you want Gabby to remain? What I am about to say may be difficult for her to hear."

Marie spoke up for me, "My granddaughter has a right to know what's happening to her mother. She stays." Marie grabbed Gabby and held her close. I was overruled again.

Dr. Matthay began, "I won't repeat what Dr. Baldwin has already told you about the aneurysm, but you might understand it better if I could use an analogy. An artery is something like the inner tube of a bicycle tire. When an artery wall weakens, it forms a bubble or aneurysm which can rupture, just like a blowout on a tire. We put a patch on the bubble the same way we would patch the tire. This morning, the patch we put on Mrs. Volpe's artery failed, because the artery was too weak to sustain it. Dr. Baldwin's team tied off the deteriorated artery and diverted Mrs. Volpe's blood to other arteries. We are hoping that those arteries are strong enough to handle the redirection of the blood."

Marie asked, "What caused her artery to rupture in the first place?"

"We are not sure. At this stage, the medical term we are using for the diagnosis is idiopathic pulmonary hemorrhaging - idiopathic meaning 'unknown cause'."

Marie lashed back, "Whadya' mean 'unknown'? Could she have been punched or choked?"

"Absolutely not! The weakening of a person's arterial system can only be caused by one or more of these factors - heredity, bad diet, high blood pressure, stress, and smoking. I can you assure that our team is doing everything medically possible for Georgann. The next seventy two hours will be critical. Quite frankly, it is a miracle that Mrs. Volpe is alive at all. A pulmonary aneurism usually results in instant death."

Marie collapsed. I grabbed Gabby before Marie took her down with her.

"If you have no further questions at this time, I must return to Mrs. Volpe,"

Before he could get out the door, ignoramus Donna yelled out, "Doctor, I don't want my sister to suffer in any way. Should we pull the plug and end it now?"

Gabby began to cry.

Dr. Matthay turned abruptly to face Donna, visibly angry. "That kind of talk, especially in front of Mrs. Volpe's daughter, is not called for nor are you the person with whom I would discuss such an option." He left.

Marie came around, sat up and began to bellow, "I knew it! Those Danbury butchers tried to kill my Georgann. They took out her lung for nothing. I want you," pointing to the social worker, "to get me all her medical records, because I'm going straight to my lawyers to start a suit against those schifosi. By the time I get through with those bums, they'll be so marked even pigs won't let them touch 'em."

In vain, Mrs. Scanlon tried to calm Marie down. Fortunately, before Marie came out of her semi coma to begin her rant, Sue had taken Gabby out of the room. I went to join them. Gabby clung to Sue, her eyes wide with fright. I knelt down by her. She stared into my eyes, "Is Mommy going to die?"

"Of course not, sweetheart. You go with Sue now and show her what a strong, young lady you are. I will stay here with Mommy and give her kisses for you."

"I'll try to be strong, Daddy – for Mommy." She gave me a hug and walked to the elevator holding Sue's hand. Sue turned to give me a tearful nod as the elevator doors opened. They got in; the doors closed and were swept away.

I walked to the end of the corridor and waited for everyone to leave before going to the lobby to call Paul on the pay phone. I asked him to spend the night with me at the hospital; I didn't want to be alone. We met at my house in Danbury to exchange cars, but, I didn't bother to go in. I didn't want to see Nicky. We got into my car and returned to Yale. During the ride, I told him what Dr. Matthay had said.

"Oh, my God, Al. What are you talking about? Are you saying that we might find out if Georgann is going to live or die in the next seventy-two hours?"

My voice cracked, "Yeah, that's what the doctor said. But, what I say is Georgann is going to live. If there's one thing I am absolutely certain it is that doctors don't know shit."

We grabbed some sandwiches and coffee at the deli across the street from Yale before heading to the ICU. In the waiting room I called the ICU via the intercom to let them know I was spending the night at the hospital. I made whomever I spoke to in the unit promise to call me if Georgann woke. Paul and I ate our sandwiches and drank the coffee from the deli before settling in for the night. We didn't exchange more than ten words. He took a seat by the intercom; I stretched out on the couch. I was sure, exhausted as I was; I wasn't going to get a wink of sleep.

Thursday, March 17, 1994

I awoke with a start. Rubbing my eyes I said, "I must have dozed off for a moment." Paul was exactly where I'd left him before going to sleep.

"You were snoring so loud, I was afraid I wouldn't hear the intercom so I stayed right under it all night. No one called."

The morning passed with no word from anyone. I went downstairs to grab a smoke and bring back coffee for Paul. On my way out of the cafeteria, I saw a sign over a door – Chapel. I went in. There were holy books from all kinds of religious denominations - the Torah, the Koran, and the King James Bible amongst them. Even though I was raised Catholic, I'd never opened a Bible in my life nor had I given much thought to religion. Besides being married in a catholic church, I only went to church on Christmas Eve, because Gabby liked to see the lights around the church and to sing Christmas hymns. I wondered if all these books were about the same God.

I sat in a pew facing the altar. I felt a strong desire to kneel and say a prayer for Georgann. I pulled down the kneeler, got down on my knees and tried to remember my childhood prayers, but I couldn't get much past, 'Hail Mary, full of grace' and 'Our Father who art in heaven'. In frustration, I bowed my head and said the only words that came to me, "God, please help Georgann, please watch over Gabby."

I returned to the waiting room with Paul's cold coffee. I asked his thoughts about religion leaving out the epiphany I had experienced with the church ladies. Paul was already worried about my sanity, no need to increase his anxiety for me.

The more we talked, the more astounded I became by his depth of religious knowledge and the Bible. I knew he had been an altar boy, but I had no idea that he once considered entering the priesthood. Once he met Josephine though, the thought of becoming a celibate priest no longer interested him. We talked for hours without any interruption, not even for lunch. No one came into the waiting room or paged me.

Toward evening, Paul called Josephine to check-in and let her know that he would be spending another night with me at the hospital. We decided to get some air, a bite to eat, and find a pharmacy to buy some aspirin for the raging headache I had from drinking too much coffee.

The fresh air felt good. We found a pharmacy, ate at a Subway across from the hospital and bought some fruit, cheese and bread at an open market to bring back to the hospital.

In the waiting room, I said, "Tonight, we take turns on watch."

Paul smiled, "Ok, I'll take the first watch by the intercom."

I rested my head on the back of the couch and fell into a sound sleep waking about six in the morning. Paul never woke me to take my turn.

I love this man.

Friday, March 18, 1994

No one else visited nor were we given any further news about Georgann's condition other than that she was stable. Paul needed to leave. He felt bad about going, but he hadn't realized he would be staying the second night with me in the hospital and did not bring his medications. I called the ICU team to let them know that I would be back in two hours – just enough time to drive Paul to my house to pick up his car, grab a quick shower and search the house for the Gideon Bible I'd stolen from a hotel - for no reason except it was there for the taking - over twenty years before. I found a spiral notebook and figured I could pass the time in the waiting room catching up on Bible verse and jotting down my thoughts.

(This notebook was the first of hundreds I would eventually fill with my ruminations on the Bible and God.)

Saturday, March 19, 1994

It was sunup when I awoke in the waiting room with the Bible lying open across my chest. It was my forty-ninth birthday. I immediately called the ICU. The nurse told me that Georgann had a stable night. Fourteen years earlier when Gabby was fighting for her life in New York-Presbyterian Hospital, stable, then as now, was the only word that offered hope.

I spent the rest of the morning reading the Bible and making notes in the journal. As the waiting room began to fill with the day's visitors, a priest came in and sat down next to me. I hid the Bible under a newspaper. He introduced himself as Father Nicholas, a Greek Orthodox priest whose parish was in Danbury. He was at Yale Hospital offering comfort to the parents of the young woman whose blood disorder was reported in that Danbury newspaper article. He told me she was holding on, but the doctors had no definitive prognosis for her survival.

That afternoon, before going out to get some fresh air, I wrapped the Gideon Bible inside a magazine and tucked it under my arm. Idly strolling through the streets of New Haven, I passed a bookstore and decided to browse the section on religion. The shelves held all kinds of translations of the Bible – The Good News, The English Standard, The American Standard, The Revised American Standard, etc, etc. I decided to purchase a King James Study Bible, only because, for some incomprehensible reason, after twenty years, it seemed sacrilegious to read God's Word using a stolen bible. I left the purloined Gideon Bible on the altar in the hospital chapel.

6

The Search for a Nanny

I read my new bible until 8:00 pm without understanding much of God's word. After calling the ICU and learning that Georgann's condition was still stable, I decided to go home for the night.

Nikol and Chuck were watching TV in the family room when I arrived. They didn't bother to acknowledge me; I did the same. I called Sue to check on Gabby. She said Gabby and her girls were having a ball. I hoped Sue's girls were keeping Gabby occupied so she didn't have time to about Georgann.

After giving Sue the update on Georgann, I said, "Sue, I have no idea how long Georgann will be in the hospital. I can't keep imposing on you to take care of Gabby."

"Don't be silly, Al. We love having Gabby here."

"Maybe so, but I think it might be better if I hire a live-in caregiver for Gabby until Georgann is better. Can you help me find one?"

"Of course I can. I shouldn't tell you this, but when I was at Yale the other day hoping I could visit Georgann I overheard Mrs. Scanlon, the social-worker, ask Donna if she was helping care for Gabby in her sister's absence. You know what Donna said?"

"I can guess although there's nothing you can tell me that would surprise me where Donna is concerned."

"Donna's reply, I am not kidding, was, 'I don't know anything about taking care of a cripple.' Imagine! Her niece! Thank God Georgann and Gabby are nothing like the rest of the Marinos. I'll see what I can do about finding someone for Gabby and let you know."

"Thanks, Sue. I really appreciate this." I went to bed feeling that some of the worry for Gabby's care might be lifted from me.

Again, Nicky hadn't even bothered to ask me how her mother was doing. It's pretty evident what side of the family she took after.

Sunday, March 20, 1994

Before leaving for Yale, I called Mrs. Scanlon's office to make an appointment. I wanted to discuss Gabby's care and get her advice about hiring a nanny. Mrs. Scanlon was aware that I might require help caring for Gabby given her physical handicaps. She had witnessed the lack of concern by both Donna and Nicky.

Georgann and I did not want to disrupt Gabby's school and regime of therapy any more than necessary. Although her grandmother, we both knew that Marie was the last person we wanted to be responsible for Gabby's care. It was enough that we had lost one daughter to Marie. Fortunately, Mrs. Scanlon was working that day and made an appointment to see me at ten.

During our meeting, I told Mrs. Scanlon that Gabby was currently staying with Sue, Georgann's friend, but that I did not want to intrude any further on her kindness especially since I did not know how long Georgann would be in the hospital. "I don't who else to ask, Mrs. Scanlon, and since you are familiar with my circumstance, I was hoping you could help me find a caregiver for Gabby.

Mrs. Scanlon said, "I know of two reputable agencies in the Danbury area that specialize in live-in nanny placements." Right then and there she called the agencies and set up four interviews for the following Wednesday.

I thanked her and started to get up, but she held up a hand to stop me, Mrs. Scanlon looked at me for a few moments before saying, "Mr. Volpe, I realize that this is a very difficult time for you. Are you sure you wouldn't like to speak with a minister or priest?"

I must have looked pretty ragged, I certainly felt that way. I was ready to talk to someone. "OK."

"Good," she said, "I'll call our chaplain and see if he is available. Have a seat in the waiting room."

I was engrossed in Bible reading when someone called my name. I knew he was the chaplain by his short sleeved black shirt with a turned around white collar. He also had the kindliest face I have ever seen.

"Mr. Volpe," he said in a soft voice, "I'm Chaplain Valentine. Mrs. Scanlon told me you might be in need of some spiritual comfort."

He barely sat down next to me before I let loose a torrent of despair, fears, and worry for Georgann and Gabby. He listened for ten minutes without speaking or taking his eyes from mine until I exhausted myself.

Quoting Proverbs 9:10, he said, "The fear of the Lord is the beginning of wisdom and knowledge of the Holy One is understanding."

I got confused, "I'm already full of human fears, now I have to fear God, too? And, I don't understand nothing!"

"Al, all God asks is that you love Him as He loves you. Ask for His support and guidance and you will receive it. Understanding will come with time." We continued to talk quietly for the next half hour. Before leaving he said, "If you wish, I will visit with Georgann every day."

"Thank you, Father Valentine., Georgann and I could use all the help we can get."

Believe it or not, that conversation was probably the most heartening one I've ever had with another human being. If people say that religion is a crutch then it was for me in a good way. I was the cripple, not Gabby.

Monday, March 21, 1994

Update: Georgann still stable but not able to have visitors. After spending the day at the hospital, I went home early to make some needed business calls and to prepare for the interviews with the nannies.

On a call with Henry, my silk screener, I told him about hiring a nanny. He suggested that I call Betty Warner, the mother of his office manager who was a licensed caregiver with great references and who lived in Danbury. I called Betty and we hit it off right away, but the problem was her age – she was fifty five. I felt that Gabby needed someone younger. Instead, Betty and I decided that she would work for me as a housekeeper and cook starting the day before the nanny.

I called Marie to ask if she would like to be present for the interviews – no harm in giving her the impression that I wanted her involved in her granddaughter's welfare. Keep your enemies close.

While I had her on the phone, I had a thought. "Marie, can you ask Sandy if she knows of someone in her church that might be qualified for the job?"

Marie's response was, "Whadya, stupid, Al. They're either filthy rich or dumb niggers. That's all they got in that Church."

This from the woman who misquoted Bible verse to me.

Saint Maria.

7

Not Stable

Tuesday, March 22, 1994

Hospital all day; no visitors; Georgann stable; spent the time reading the Bible. I went home late that night to try and get some rest. I figured I would need it, not because of the interviews but because I never knew how Marie would behave. I needed to be prepared for anything.

Wednesday, March 23, 1994

Marie showed up an hour before the first interview with the prospective nannies. She opened the front door with her own key (yep), walked past me without even a nod and sat down at the dining room table, stony faced, hands folded in front of her on the yellow pad and pen she had pulled out from her old lady purse.

"Would you like a cup of coffee?" I offered. "I just made a fresh pot."

"Thanks, but, don't offer anything to them. We're here on business, not to socialize."

Each of the four candidates showed up at their appointed time. I won't go into what transpired during the interviews. Suffice to say it was grueling because Marie interrogated each of these ladies like they were hardened criminals. I imagined a naked light bulb swinging over their heads. A couple of them did their best to hold back tears

As soon as the last woman left, Marie put her pad and pen back into her purse, stood up and announced, "I wouldn't let one of those women touch my granddaughter. Keep looking." She turned and left. No goodbye, of course.

Thursday, March 24, 1994

I arrived at Yale by 9:30 that morning, but before going to the waiting room, I dropped by Mrs. Scanlon's office to ask if it were possible to find a few more suitable nannies for Gabby's care. She looked at me questionably but didn't ask why any of the nannies we already interviewed were not acceptable. Mrs. Scanlon must have read the anxiety in my face, because she said she would try. This day was a replica of Tuesday's; no visitors; me engrossed in Bible reading. I left at nine to spend the night in my own bed.

Friday, March 25, 1994

Another 7:00 am wakeup call! Georgann was on her way to emergency surgery again - she lost vital signs - again. I threw on some clothes, called the Marinos and rushed to the hospital – again.

Georgann was still in surgery when I arrived. I took my usual seat in the waiting room. Silvio and Marie came in around noon, Donna and Dennis showed up at one; Georgann was still in surgery. They hadn't bothered to acknowledge my presence. At two, Mrs. Scanlon informed us that Dr. Matthay would join us in the waiting room in the next few minutes to tell us the results of the surgery. All we could do was nod; Marie didn't even attempt to grill Mrs. Scanlon.

Dr. Matthay arrived. Head bowed, he stood silent for a moment before beginning. He looked at each of us briefly and began. "I will try to explain what is happening to Georgann as simply as I can. When we attempted to supply enough oxygen to her heart and brain, Georgann's functioning left lung became stressed to point that she lost vital signs this morning. The nursing staff was able to revive her before rushing her to surgery. Our surgical team went beyond all medical bounds to save Georgann."

At this point, Marie began to weep, and I was glad I was sitting down. I gripped myself for the bad news.

Dr. Matthay continued, "We connected a new type of high volume ventilator directly into her left lung which is now pumping 100% pure oxygen at high pressure directly into that lung in an attempt to sustain the oxygen levels in her blood. Pumping this high a concentration of oxygen is a double-edged sword. Although it is keeping Georgann alive, it is also destroying healthy lung tissue. Lung tissue is like a moist sponge of microscopic capillaries that absorb oxygen. High oxygen levels dry and stiffen the tissues which, in turn, cause the capillaries to strain in the process of oxygenating the blood stream. This is a condition known as ARDS, Adult Respiratory Distress Syndrome, which further stresses the heart and arterial system. It was the surgical team's decision to place Georgann in a medically induced coma to reduce the stress on her body. An induced coma shuts down the central nervous system and suspends organ functions."

"She's in a coma?" yelled Marie, "What's going to happen to her? Is she going to die?"

It was evident, at least to me, by the somber way Dr. Matthay spoke with us is that he had little hope for Georgann's survival - the doctors had done all that was medically possible, even more than was possible. His departing words were, "I cannot tell you for certain, Mrs. Marino, whether your daughter will live or die. Georgann's fate is now in the hands of a higher power."

Marie could not refrain from voicing her litany. "They butchered my daughter in Danbury. I'm going to get those motherfuckers. My husband will make sure of it. Right, Silvio?"

Man of a few words, he said, "Right."

I fled the waiting room in Dr. Matthay's wake leaving Mrs. Scanlon to deal with the Marinos. I rushed to the chapel and dropped down on my knees to plead with God for Georgann's life.

When I returned a half hour later, Marie and Silvio were sitting at the table with vengeance in their eyes.

Marie said, "Sit down, you." I sat. She pushed some papers across the table in front of me. "Sign these. I need the medical forms from Danbury Hospital to start a law suit on those butchers. For now, since I am only her mother, you have to sign the release forms as next of kin."

I glanced at the forms before saying, "I'm not signing anything," and shoved the papers back at her.

Marie pushed the papers back to me, "You sign these fuckin' forms now or else!"

"Or else what?

"Silvio, tell him what."

Silvio didn't say a word; he just drew his finger across his neck.

I signed the forms.

Marie couldn't let it go. "If Georgann dies, there's no place you can hide. You stole two million dollars from Gabby, and you let those animals in Danbury carve up my daughter. You're gonna pay."

Silvio, out of the blue, said, "Georgann borrowed fifty thousand from me, and I want it back from you. Got it? Come on, Marie, we're finished here." He banged his cane on the floor to emphasize his point. He stood up, pulled Marie's chair back, held out his arm for her to take, and they walked arm in arm ceremoniously out of the waiting room, Marie waving the papers over her head in triumph.

I was dumbfounded. For what reason would Georgann borrow fifty thousand dollars from Silvio? And, not tell me. Was he trying to take advantage of Georgann's condition to extort the fifty grand from me? Or was it just another ploy on Silvio's part to unnerve me? Wasn't scheming to bring a suit against Danbury Hospital enough for these scum? I roused myself enough to yell at the closed door. "You two are pathetic excuses for parents and human beings. Do the world a favor and drop dead!"

I needed some non-hospital air. I met Mrs. Scanlon in front of the elevator. "Mr. Volpe, is it true that you and Mrs. Volpe filed for divorce before her illness?"

"What? Who told you that?"

"Mrs. Marino after she asked for the medical release forms. When I told her only you had the authority to sign for them she said her daughter was in the process of divorcing you because of abuse."

"Georgann and I are not nor have we ever considered getting a divorce. I have never laid a finger on my wife. Don't listen to my mother-in-law. She's a liar."

So that was what Marie had meant by 'not yet' – divorce not widow-hood. If the divorce didn't work, Marie would have no compunction to get rid of me permanently.

After the confrontation with my in-laws and Mrs. Scanlon's distressing information, I wandered aimlessly through the streets of New Haven for hours. I ruminated on ways in which I could kill my in-laws without getting caught. By eight, I returned to the hospital physically exhausted. Before going to the waiting room, I stopped by the chapel to ask God's forgiveness for allowing those jackals to bring me down to their level.

The waiting room was empty. I called the ICU to ask about Georgann. The nurse said, "Mr. Volpe, finally. We've been trying to contact you for hours."

My heart stopped and my knees went weak anticipating the worst. "Dr. Matthay left instruction that you be allowed to stay with Georgann in the ICU."

When the feeling returned to my legs, I raced to the ICU. Darlene, one of the nurses I had been speaking with via the intercom, showed me where to suit up. I could barely get into the gown, because my hands were shaking so much. I hadn't seen Georgann since Life-Star took her from Danbury Hospital ten days before. Jonah, a young clinician whose smooth face and wide grin radiated sympathy, was waiting for me when I came out of the dressing room.

He held out his hand, "Nice to put a face to your voice, Mr. Volpe." I followed him into the dimly lit room. Amidst the aura of flickering monitors and swishing air sounds, Georgann lay peacefully; her body propped up in the hospital bed and hooked to life support tubes. Her adorable face created an ethereal silhouette that reminded me of Sleeping Beauty.

I couldn't bear to see her this way. I ran out of the room pulling off the facemask unable to hold back the tears.

Jonah came after me, "Are you all right, Mr. Volpe? I know it's always a shock to see a loved one so helpless."

"I'm ok. Thanks for the TLC and understanding." I composed myself as best I could. Jonah got me a new facemask. I went back to Georgann's bedside leaning over to whisper, "I love you, Georgann. I'm right here, and I won't ever leave you again." I knew she heard me. I spent the night holding her hand.

Saturday March 26, 1994

I had fallen asleep in the chair by Georgann's bed. I was still holding her hand when Dr. Matthay came in. He tapped me gently on the shoulder.

I awakened with a start, shaking my head to rouse myself. "Thank you so much, Doctor, for allowing me to stay with Georgann."

"Of course, Al, there is no need to thank me. A sizable amount of research indicates that people in comas can hear and feel the presence of those around them. I am going to give permission for others to visit. Protective clothing won't be necessary since Georgann is out of danger of contamination. I will leave it to you to decide who can visit. In the meantime, you need to get some proper rest. You can return at any time to stay with Georgann."

I shook his hand thanking him again before he left to finish his rounds. When I got home, the first thing I did was call Sue. She was relieved to hear my voice. Yenta Donna had already called to tell her about the confrontation I had with the Marinos that almost came to blows - an exaggeration, of course, but what you could expect from Donna.

"I called Paul and Sally, but no one knew where you had disappeared. We were worried sick that something happened to you. We all know what the Marinos are capable of doing."

"I went for a long walk to calm down. When I got back to the hospital, Dr. Matthay gave me permission to stay with Georgann as long as I wanted. I stayed with her all night and just got home."

"I'm just glad you're safe. Gabby is fine, but she really misses her mother."

"No more than I do. Dr. Matthay said it was up to me to decide who would be allowed to visit Georgann, but I am reluctant to take Gabby. Seeing Georgann hooked up to a lot of tubes may frighten her, but she and Georgann both need each other now. I'll try to prepare her as best I can so she won't be too shocked."

"I agree with you, Al.. If you don't allow her to go to the hospital, she may think something terrible has happened to her mother and blame you. (Spoilers) What are you going to do about the Marinos?"

"I have to allow them to visit Georgann, too. No matter what I think, they are her parents and love her. Besides, if Marie found out I could visit and took Gabby, she would go postal - probably break down the doors of the hospital demanding they let her in to see her beloved daughter. That's the last thing I need to worry about right now."

"Aren't you afraid of the Marinos?"

"Not really. I've been living with Marie putting a smoking gun to my head for over almost thirty years. What troubles me more now is Silvio. He appears to have joined forces with Marie against me. He's more than just talk."

"I guess you know what you're doing, Al, but please, be careful."

"That's my middle name."

I called Marie as soon as I hung up with Sue to let her know that she could visit with Georgann even though she was in a coma. Given Marie's schizophrenic personality, it was no surprise that she talked to me like I was her favorite son-in-law. That's not saying much since she referred to Dennis as a boombotz. I told her, "Dr. Matthay is giving you, Silvio, and Nicky permission to visit Georgann. I'm picking Gabby up at Sue's tomorrow to take her to see her mother."

I wondered why Marie didn't protest about Gabby until she said, "I want to take Gabby home with me for a few days. Sonny's daughter, Gina, is spending the weekend and it would be good for Gabby to be with her family at this time instead of a bunch of strangers."

"Sue and her daughters are hardly strangers, but I think Gabby would like to see Gina. I'll ask Sue to pack a bag for Gabby to bring with her to the hospital."

"Good. I want to be there for Gabby in case she is gets upset seeing her mother in a coma." Almost as an afterthought, Marie asked, "How does my daughter look?"

"Georgann looks like she's sleeping peacefully."

"Thanks for calling, Al. I'll see you at the hospital tomorrow." Bang! She hung up. Wow! She even said 'thanks.' Schizoid.

I took a shower, tended to the animals because Nicky hadn't bothered and went back to the hospital to spend the night with Georgann.

Sunday, March 27, 1994

I called Gabby from the hospital, "Your mommy has to stay in the hospital for a little while longer, sweetheart. The doctors want her to get better as fast as possible so they put her into a coma. Do you know what that is?"

"Yes, daddy, it's when a person doesn't wake up from sleeping."

"Yes, that's right. But, she can hear you and will know you are there. When she is all better, the doctors will wake her up and she will come home to us."

"I can't wait, Daddy. I miss mommy so much."

"Me, too, sweetheart, me, too. Nana will be at the hospital today, too. Did Aunt Sue tell you Nana wants you to go home with her for the week-end? Your cousin Gina will be there. Would you like that?"

"Aunt Sue told me last night and helped me pack a bag. If I can't stay at the hospital with mommy, then I want to go to Nana's. I like Gina, she's fun."

The ICU staff prepared Georgann for our visit – she looked radiantly beautiful - no tubes or scary medical devices showing. We got to Yale at one, and as soon as we entered the room, Gabby ran over to her mother, and, resting her head on her shoulder, remained there for the next hour whispering softly in Georgann's ear. After kissing Georgann hello, I retreated to a seat to watch this touching scene between mother and daughter.

The Marinos and Nicky showed up about two. Silvio, one hand resting on his cane, stroked Gabby's hair as he gazed down at his daughter, vainly trying to hold back tears. The tough man did have a soul – at least when it came to his cherished princess.

Uncharacteristically, Marie said nothing as she approached Georgann. She stood ramrod straight at the foot of her bed, a grim mask of cold anger fixed on her face - eyes narrowed, lips pulled tightly over her teeth betraying the thoughts of the vengeance she would wreak on the doctors who did this to her daughter. Nicky made no attempt to go near Georgann. She stood near the door (in case she needed to make a quick retreat) staring down at her feet.

Twenty minutes later, Marie gently detached Gabby from Georgann. "Kiss your mama goodbye, bella, and let's go." Silvio, who never left his spot at Georgann's bedside, turned, gave me a curt nod and strode stiffly out the door followed by Nicky carrying Gabby's suitcase. Nicky had not even bothered to acknowledge my presence.

Marie, her arm tightly around Gabby who was leaning into her side crying silently, said without looking at me, "Al, call Donna later. She found a nanny for Gabby." She didn't wait for me to respond; it was a command, after all.

Heil to you, too, Marie.

8

Lessons Unlearned

I called Donna from home. "Donna, Marie told me you found a nanny for Gabby. Tell me about her."

"Her name is Kim Day. She's twenty-six and a professional nanny with great credentials. She can start next Monday but only if you pay her an eight hundred dollar start-up bonus."

"Why do I have to give her eight hundred bucks up front? What is she, a Manhattan apartment?"

"No, smart ass, but she's in big demand. You have to sweeten the pot if you want her to take care of Gabby."

"Ok, if that's what I have to do. Does she really come with good recommendations? Are you sure she can start Monday?"

"She's the best, trust me. I met her and she's just what Gabby needs. Marie thinks so, too. She'll be at your house at eight am. By the way, while I have you on the phone, you need to get in touch with Robby." Robby was our car mechanic.

"Not Nicky, again?" I groaned. I sat down.

"Yep, I'm surprised you didn't already know."

"I've had a few things on my mind lately, Donna, if you haven't noticed. What happened?"

"It was on March eighth; the second day Georgann was in Danbury Hospital. Nicky was driving Georgann's Honda on her way home from work when she lost control and hit a guard rail. Her friend Beverly picked her up. Nicky called AAA and had the car towed to Robby's. It's been sitting there since."

"Had she been drinking?"

"She might have stopped for a few. So what? She's a grownup."

Typical of Donna to defend stupidity. Donna knew Nicky's license was suspended because of speeding tickets. She was driving Georgann's old Honda that I never got around to selling, because she couldn't get her Camaro registered. With all I had on my plate, I didn't bother to stop her. I never bothered to look in the driveway for the Honda.

"Why hasn't Robby fixed it?"

"Because your daughter hasn't given Robby the insurance information yet, that's why. Robby tried to reach you but when he couldn't, he called me. Beverly has been picking Nicky up each morning and driving her to work."

"Great. She's lucky to have a friend like Beverly."

"Wait," said Donna, "there's more." Groan. I stayed seated. "Beverly had a fight with Nicky. She told her she didn't want to be Gabby's babysitter when Gabby came home while Georgann was in the hospital - that was her big sister's job. Nicky told Beverly to go fuck herself, and that was the end of her ride. My mother stepped in and registered Nicky's old Camaro in her name to get insurance. Nicky's driving the Camaro now with no license."

Remember what I already said, who needs a license when one has a Nana?

Monday, March 28, 1994

I spent the day at Yale, but before going to Paul's for dinner, I dropped off the Honda's insurance information at Robby's garage. During dinner, I updated Paul and Josephine on the family news; they sat in awe mouths hanging open. Really, who could make all this shit up? After dinner, Sally dropped by.

"I spoke to Dr. Corsaro this morning. His daughter Melissa will be home from college for the summer on May fifteenth. She would love to take care of Gabby then."

"Great, Gabby loves her. The nanny can fill in until then. I haven't yet met or talked to this Kim Day. Donna recommended her, although a recommendation from Donna doesn't actually instill confidence. Still, it's only for six or so weeks. The housekeeper I hired is really nice. Hopefully, Gabby will be well-taken care of when I am at the hospital."

"You know you can call on me any time if you need help, Al," said Sally. Josephine volunteered, too. I certainly am a friend in need. Indeed.

The important business taken care, Sally had something she needed to unload. In the same conversation with Dr. Corsaro, he let drop that Donna called him a couple of times on the pretext of keeping him informed of Georgann's progress. I hadn't even thought about calling him, and I wondered why Donna had. Corsaro, although a pretty good doctor, I knew had a fascination with the Mafia. He used to ask me a lot of questions about the Marinos. What little he knew about my in-laws Mafia connections both thrilled and frightened him. Go figure! Donna was only too happy to feed his addiction. He hung on every malicious word Donna told him about Silvio's threats to the Danbury doctors and to me. Donna knew it would get back to me. I pictured the conversation going something like this:

"My parents are suing Danbury Hospital because those doctors screwed up and almost killed Georgann. They're going to pay, my father said, with their money or their lives or maybe both." Corsaro pressed his ear tighter to the phone to make sure he caught every word. "My mother says Al stole two million dollars of Gabby's trust money and has it hidden in a foreign bank account. She's going to make sure he goes to jail - or worse - too. After Al goes to prison, my mother will have him removed as Gabby's trustee and make her and Nikol trustees."

Is that all? Feeding his movie based notions of how the Mafia worked, Corsaro believed or wanted to believe that the Marinos were going to get rid of me one way or the other. To relieve his conscience, he told Sally everything Donna told him so she could warn me. Donna knew Corsaro would blab every word to Sally. Did I say Donna was dumb?

Pathetic as it sounded, Georgann's illness had become Marie's casus belli or pretext to grab control of Gabby's trust money – now with Silvio's blessing. Without Georgann to run interference, I was the patsy, the low hanging fruit ripe and ready for the picking on their way to Gabby's trust.

Tuesday March 29th to Friday April 1st, 1994.

I stayed at the hospital round the clock the next few days - no one came to visit, no one called. I headed home only to shower and care for the animals since Gabby was still with Marie. When I finally got around to checking my answering machine, I found several messages from Mark Hollander urgently requesting I call him as soon as possible no matter what the time.

I immediately dialed the home phone number he gave me on the message. He recognized my voice immediately and, without preamble, shouted, "Al, who in hell are the Marinos?"

He didn't know who they were, because there had never been any occasion to discuss Georgann's family with Mark. The provisions of Gabby's trust had been so thoroughly established it didn't require his firm's further intervention, and we had very little contact with Mark this past year. Also, Hollander was also unaware of Georgann's illness and hospitalization. Consequently, when out of the blue he received a phone call from Marie demanding information about Gabby's trust account, he refused to comply. Marie put Silvio on the phone to Mark. He made veiled threats and allusions using the same intimidation tactics that always worked for him in the past with the hackneyed 'offer he couldn't refuse' ploy. Mark hung up on him and filed an incident report with Smith Barney's legal department.

"Mark," I said, "Marie and Silvio Marino are Georgann's parents. Silvio's a penny ante thug in the Gambino family. You heard of them, right?" He did. "Since March 6th, Georgann has been in the hospital first in Danbury and now in Yale because of lung problems. It's very complicated. I'll fill you in when we have more time, but the short story is the doctors at Yale put her into an induced coma hoping to strengthen her weakened system. I live in fear that she won't survive. If Georgann dies, I am the only obstacle standing in the way to Gabby's trust. To get me off it, the Marinos, along with my older daughter, Nikol, are trying to prove that I stole two million dollars from the trust and are hiding it in an offshore account. They want me hauled off to prison or worse. If they can't do it legally, they aren't opposed to using more drastic measures to eliminate me from the picture. You know what I mean?"

"Are you talking about having you murdered? That kind of stuff only happens in gangster movies. These people sound both corrupt and crazy. Stupid, too. Don't they realize that the attorneys who took Gabby's case had to be paid? Two million dollars was their fair share of the award granted to Gabby. Besides Smith Barney manages the trust very conservatively and oversees every single expense. You are the most prudent of trustees with Gabby's money."

"Yes, Mark, they are all three – corrupt, crazy and stupid. I told Marie more times than I can count that lawyers don't work for nothing, but she refuses to believe me. I gave up wasting my breath. As far as she is concerned, I sit around on my ass all day doing nothing, running around with bimbos, and living the life of a prince off Gabby's money."

"I'm sorry to hear about Georgann's illness, Al. She is a very lovely lady. Don't worry about the Marinos. I will notify my legal department about their attempts to seize control of Gabby's trust. If they continue in their fraudulent claims, they will invite the possibility of arrest. It's your job right now to stay focused on Georgann's recovery."

"Thank you, Mark. I appreciate your confidence in me." Before we disconnected, I gave him Paul's number as a backup in case he needed to reach me.

As soon as I hung up with Mark the phone rang. It was my niece, Gina. "Hi, Uncle Al, how are you?"

"Hanging in there, Gina. Ho is Gabby doing?"

"She's great, Uncle Al. We're having a wonderful time. Gabby is such a great kid. I'm taking her for her horseback riding lesson tomorrow. After her lesson, we're going to the mall. Nana wanted to go with us, but Gabby insisted just the two of us. Can I borrow Georgann's Jeep? It's more comfortable for Gabby than my Toyota. Donna said she would drop us off at your house to get the Jeep and then pick us up after I bring it back. We're going to her house for dinner."

"Sure, Gina, I'll leave the keys and some money on the kitchen table. Give me a call at the hospital tomorrow and tell me how your day went."

"Thanks, Uncle Al. Gabby wants you to give her mother a big kiss for her. Give Georgann a kiss for me, too."

Saturday, April 2, 1994

Around four in the afternoon Gina called me at the ICU. "How did Gabby's riding lesson go today?"

"Great, Uncle Al. Gabby is really good. Something terrible happened this morning that I was hoping wouldn't spoil the rest of Gabby's day. When Donna dropped us off at your house, we figured Nicky was just getting up, because we heard her stomping around and slamming doors upstairs. The keys to the Jeep were not on the table where you said they would be. There was some money – thanks, Uncle Al – but no keys. We didn't hear Nicky come into the kitchen. She watched us crawl around on the floor looking for the keys without saying a word. Gabby asked her if she had seen them. Nicky reached into her robe pocket, pulled out the keys, dangled them in front of Gabby and threw them on the floor screaming, 'Here, you little fuckin' retard. Now get lost.' I started to say something, but Gabby put her finger up to her lips for me to hush. She grabbed my hand and pulled me out of the house. I thought she would be really upset by Nicky's meanness, but you know what she said? 'I'm used to Nicky. I don't let her bother me anymore like I did when I was little.' I can't imagine how Gabby could ever get used to such a bitch."

"You just got a taste of what Gabby and I have been going through for years with my Nicky and the Marinos. Spend some more time with them and you'll get more than a taste."

I got home at eight that night to an empty house. At nine, Gina and Gabby came in. "What are you two here? I thought you were staying at your grandmother's."

"Gabby wanted to come home and I couldn't blame her. Is it okay if I stay the night?"

"Gina, you can stay as long as you like. Did something happen?"

"I'll tell you as soon as I get Gabby to bed. Come on, Gabby; let me help you get ready for bed. You are so tired you can barely stand up."

Gabby said dreamily, "Thanks Gina. Night, Daddy," and allowed Gina to help her up the stairs.

As soon as Gina settled Gabby into bed she came back to the kitchen. The first words she said to me were, "They're all crazy in that house. Nana is a psychopath; Nikol's a disgrace; Donna's a moron, and Dennis is a big mommalucco. I feel sorry for Georgann and you but especially for Gabby."

"You just found that out? What happened to elucidate you about your family?

"They sat eating this wonderful meal Nana prepared and talked as if Georgann was already dead – in front of Gabby. Marie actually told Gabby that you, Uncle Al, are the reason Georgann is dying. They called you a piece of shit, and I can't even say the other vile names they called you, because I'm too ashamed to repeat them. Nana's delicious food stuck in my throat like sawdust." Gina started to cry, "They're all horrible. They don't care a thing about Gabby or Georgann. All they talk about is getting control of Gabby's money. They make me want to puke."

Gina was crying so hard she began to shake. I put my arm around her. "Go to bed, Gina. You don't have to go back there again if you don't want to. Don't worry about me and Gabby. I can take care of the two of us." I sincerely hoped I wasn't blowing smoke up my own ass.

Sunday, April 3, 1994.

Before going to visit Georgann at the hospital, Gina, Gabby and I went to mass at St. Peter's Roman Catholic Church in Danbury - praying for God's intervention was becoming my constant mantra. Although not religious, I couldn't completely reject my Italian roots. Georgann and I baptized, communed, and confirmed our daughters into the Catholic faith. Somehow, I began to believe that God was building his temple in me stone by stone.

It was a fast drive to Yale that quiet Sunday morning. As before, Gabby ran to Georgann's side and rested her head on her mother's breast. She stayed glued to that spot until it was time to leave. I told Gina to speak to Georgann as if she were awake, because she could hear her. Speaking through tears, Gina stood by Georgann's bedside and told her how much fun she and Gabby had Saturday and what a great horseback rider Gabby had become. Before leaving, she took Georgann's hand, "We all love you very much. God bless you."

Gabby said, "Amen. Mommy, please get well soon. I love you."

At home, Gabby helped Gina pack. Nikol was already locked in her room when we got there. Ten minutes later, Gina came downstairs with her suitcase, "I can't wait to get back to Long Island. I thought my family was screwed-up. I hate to leave Gabby here with those vultures."

I drove Gina to the Marinos. I put her bags in her car and she drove off without going into the house to say good bye to Marie and Silvio. Although that was rude, I understood where she was coming from. I only wished it could be that easy for me.

You think I would have learned by now, but I again made the mistake of leaving Gabby alone with her sister even if it was only for a half an hour. As soon I got home and before I could even close the front door, I heard shouting from upstairs.

I stood at the bottom of the stairs and bellowed, "What's going on?"

I saw Nikol stomp out of Gabby's room and heard her screech, "Nothing," before she went into her own bedroom slamming the door. I went up to Gabby. She was sitting on her bed, head bent, and hands folded in her lap.

I knelt in front of her. Putting my finger gently under her chin, I tipped her head back to look into her eyes before taking both of her hands in mine. "What happened, sweetheart?"

Gabby pulled her hands out of mine and stood up. "Nothing happened, Daddy. I did something Nicky didn't like, and she yelled at me; that's all. I'm ok. I need to get lie down. I'm very tired." She got under the covers and turned away from me.

Whatever Gabby did, I would never learn, but it was obvious that she wasn't going to rat on Nicky. Oh, Georgann, I entreated, how we all need you to come home to us.

Monday, April 4, 1994.

Gabby was up all night coughing. I made her tea with lots of honey and lemon. After drinking the tea, she quieted down enough to get back to sleep. In the morning, I woke to find myself sleeping on the floor next to her bed. I was worried about Gabby. She was so frail and these past weeks had put a great strain on her. I called Sally to ask if Dr. Corsaro would be able to see her this morning.

Sally said, "No problem."

I managed to help Gabby dress, gave her some tea and toast for breakfast and carried her to the car for her appointment with Dr. Corsaro. Nicky – we didn't see her. We picked up Sally on the way to Corsaro's.

Dr. Corsaro examined Gabby before speaking to me. "There is no reason for you to be overly concerned, Al. Gabby has an ongoing bronchial problem which I have been treating over the years. I'll give you some sample inhalers to use if she starts coughing again."

In the past, I had left all of Gabby's medical decisions to Georgann. I didn't know anything about a chronic bronchial problem. What's new?

Sally came back to Danbury with us. She would spend the day with Gabby to give me time to catch up on necessary phone calls and bill paying. Sally and Gabby enjoyed the beautiful early spring morning rocking in the swing on the front porch and chatting happily. I made them tea and grape jelly crackers - Gabby's favorite.

I gave Betty a call to tell her it was time she got busy cleaning the house before the new nanny started the following Monday. Betty's big, old Lincoln rumbled down the driveway about a half hour later. Although Betty was only fifty-five, her persona screamed grandmother ready to offer you home-made oatmeal cookies and a big hug. I introduced her to Sally and Gabby before giving her key to the house and the alarm code, money for groceries and cleaning supplies, and instructions, "Do whatever it takes to make this pig sty livable."

Betty bent down to pet Brandy, and her nose crinkled up; his scruffy, matted fur stunk. She looked up at me "Would you like me to give the dog a bath?"

Sally and Gabby giggled as I pinched my nose, "Pew. Please do."

I sat down with a stack of bills that were long overdue for my attention, but, before paying them, I called the hospital to check on Georgann's condition. It had not changed – still stable. By five, Betty had finished for the day. She had done a spectacular job. Everything looked and smelled clean and shiny - even Brandy.

"You did an amazing job," I said. "I'll see you at eight on Monday morning.

I called the local Chinese take-out and gave them an order for dinner – wonton soup, egg rolls, beef with broccoli, and almond cookies. When I returned from picking up the order, Gabby, Sally, and I sat down at the kitchen table to eat. Just as we were nibbling on the last cookie, Nicky came home, ignored the three of us and headed to her room. Gabby went upstairs to let her know that we (just Gabby) had set aside some Chinese food for her. I put the plate of food in the little basket Gabby used to carry things up the stairs with one hand so she could hold on to the banister with her other hand. Sally and I remained in the kitchen drinking tea and talking about how well Gabby was managing. My curiosity got the better of me, and, with the pretense of needing some papers from the desk in my bedroom, I went upstairs to check on Gabby and Nicky. I was shocked to find Nicky actually helping Gabby with her homework. Had Gabby's sweet offer of food or Beverly's condemnation of her lack of sisterly behavior sparked some tiny flame of guilt in Nicky? I hoped so.

Oh boy was I wrong.

I popped my head into Gabby's room, "Sally wants me to take her to visit your mother. Are you guys okay if we leave for a couple of hours?"

Gabby said, "Yes, daddy." Nicky just shrugged.

On Route 34 to Yale, Sally hesitantly said, "I don't know if I should tell you this, but I can't keep it to myself another minute. Gabby made me promise not to, but you need to know this about your older daughter."

I shut the car radio off to give Sally my complete attention. I had made this trip so often; I could drive it with my eyes shut.

"Go ahead; I'm listening though I doubt you could tell my anything about Nicky that would surprise me."

"I think what I am about to say might shock even you. When you drove Gina back to her grandmother's the other night, Nicky threatened Gabby, because she took Gina's side over hers. Her words went like this, 'That fat, whore Gina fucks niggers and is married to a drug-addict spic. I'll get you if you ever go against me again, you little retard'"

Sally was right. I was shocked. "I don't know what to do about Nicky. When I tried to control her, I spent a night in jail and had to sit through some gruesome anger management classes. For some reason, Gabby really loves Nicky and won't say a word against her. Without Georgann, I'm lost. I hope that when the nanny shows up on Monday, she'll be able to run interference between Gabby and Nicky."

"I hope you're right. You know you can count on me, Al. If there's anything I can do to help, just call."

"Thanks Sally. Your support means a lot to me."

At Yale I introduced Sally as Georgann's closest friend to the ICU staff. Sally slowly entered Georgann's dimly lit room; I had warned her that seeing Georgann hooked up to support was a distressing sight. I left Sally to spend time alone with Georgann and went to the waiting room.

The receptionist saw me and waved me over, "Al, you have a phone call. She said her name is Donna Weigart." She handed me the phone.

"What do you want, Donna? I just got here."

"You better get home right away. Gabby called my mother crying hysterically. Mamma sent Daddy and Dennis to your house. They'll be there when you get there."

"What happened? Is Gabby all right?"

"Don't ask me. Just get home."

I called my house and Silvio answered. Before I could get a word out he said, "Why did you leave Nicky alone with Gabby?"

"What do you mean? Nicky was helping Gabby with her homework. They both said it was okay for me to leave."

"And you believed them, asshole? As soon as you left, they began to argue. Neither is talking, but Gabby says she needs to go to the hospital. Get back here now."

I signaled to Sally from the door at the ICU that we had to go. On the drive home, I told her what little I knew. When we pulled into my driveway, I thanked her for helping with Gabby and visiting Georgann.

Her parting words to me as she got into her car were, "I don't know how you do it, Al. May God give you the strength to carry on." She sped off.

Silvio opened the door before I could get my key out. "It's about time. Don't even take off your coat. My granddaughter needs to go to the hospital. She says her shunt is hurting."

I told Silvio and Dennis to leave before running upstairs to Gabby's room. "Please Daddy, take me to the hospital where Mommy is. My head hurts. I feel sick."

I knew the cerebral shunt which drained the excess cerebrospinal fluid from Gabby's brain could malfunction or shut down at any time. Gabby already had four shunt revisions, and I was petrified she might need a fifth.

I called Dr. Winig. He guided me through an examination of Gabby. I took her temperature, examined the shunt area at the base of her skull, and checked her eyes. He told me my findings sounded normal. He asked to speak with Gabby. I handed her the phone. I didn't know what he was asking Gabby only that her responses were just 'yes' or 'no'. She handed the phone back to me.

"Al, Gabby doesn't seem to be having a problem with her shunt. From what she just told me, I don't think that taking her to Yale's emergency room is necessary. With Georgann in the hospital, Gabby is dealing with a great deal of stress for which she may not be emotionally mature enough to handle. My advice to you is to put cool compresses on her neck area, try to keep her calm, and monitor her through the night. Unless she takes a turn for the worse, bring Gabby to my office in the morning."

I thanked Dr. Winig, hung up and called the Marinos. Marie answered on the first ring. I told her that Winig said not worry, but that I should to keep a close watch on her throughout the night.

Marie said, "Why don't you bring her here for the night?" Marie may be many contemptible things, but she was a good grandmother.

"Ok, Marie. I'll do that. I guess Silvio told you about the argument she had with Nicky. I'm sensing that Gabby probably wants out of here. I'll bring her right over."

Gabby was already in her pajamas; I carried her out to the Blazer. By the time we got to Marie's, she had fallen asleep in the back seat. I carried her into the house, tucked her into bed, thanked Marie for her help and drove back home wondering what Nicky had done this time? I let the sleeping bitch lie for the night.

Tuesday, April 5, 1994

Nicky was already gone when I got up. I drove to the Marinos to pick up Gabby for her doctor's appointment. Marie answered the door and told me Gabby had slept peacefully through the night.

In the kitchen, Gabby greeted me. "Daddy, I'm glad you're here! Grandma made me pancakes and sausage. Do you want some?"

She looked and sounded perfectly fine.

"No, sweetheart, I had breakfast already." That was a lie unless you call five cups of black coffee and six cigarettes breakfast.

"Are you ready to go to Dr. Winig's?"

"I will be in just a minute, Daddy. I just have to put on my shoes. I want Nana to come with us."

"Sure, Gabs. Nana can come along." Marie was standing in the kitchen with her purse already dangling from her arm.

At the medical group, a nurse led Marie and Gabby into an examining room. I stayed in the reception area. About twenty minutes later, Dr. Winig came out and asked me to come into his office.

"Gabby is fine. I'm pretty sure the cause of her headache and nausea was stress-related. Given her neurological issues, I'm not going to take chances. I set up an appointment at ten tomorrow for her to have a CAT-scan at Westchester Medical Center where she had her last shunt revision in 1991.

Marie offered to take care of Gabby for the rest of the week. I had no choice but to acquiesce even though I had my misgivings. What could I do? I wanted to spend time with Georgann, and I certainly couldn't trust leaving her with Nicky. We stopped by Gabby's school to pick up her homework assignments for the week and to inform them that she would be out of class for an indefinite time. I felt secure and somewhat at ease knowing that Gabby would at least be well cared for with Marie.

After dropping Marie and Gabby at the Marinos house, I went to Yale. I had not slept well for days and fell asleep almost at once in the chair alongside Georgann's bed.

Wednesday, April 6, 1994

I woke at eight with only enough time to go home and grab a quick shower before picking Gabby up for her CAT scan. Marie and Silvio decided to come with us.

Gabby wanted Marie to go in with her for the scan. While Silvio and I sat in the waiting room, I took the opportunity to ask him what happened between Gabby and Nicky.

Gruffly, "I told you, they had a little argument. You shouldn't have left Gabby with Nicky. That's all I know." I couldn't tell if he was covering up for Nicky or really didn't know or didn't want to know what had happened between his granddaughters. I dropped it.

About a half hour later, a technician escorted Marie and Gabby into the waiting room. The technician said, "Your daughter was so brave. I wish all my patients were like her."

She had no idea how many procedures Gabby had been through in the past fourteen years. Of course, she was a pro.

"Mr. Volpe," the technician continued, "Dr. Winig made an appointment for Gabby with Dr. Navarro, a neurologist at Westchester Medical. He will go over her CAT scan and compare it to her other scans. Her appointment is this Friday at 3:00." She handed me the information.

We left the office and were heading for the elevator when Silvio made sure that Marie and Gabby were walking far enough ahead of us not to hear him. He took hold of my arm to stop me. "You know that a CAT-Scan machine costs two million. You should buy one for Gabby."

"Maybe I should," was all I said. With his words, I knew I had completely lost Silvio as an ally.

As soon as I dropped Gabby and her grandparents off, I was again on my way back to Yale. Just being around the Marinos this short time so vexed my spirit that I decided to stop at St. Michael's Church in Derby to attend confession. I hadn't been to confession since I got married and only then because it was mandatory before taking the holy vows of matrimony. In the confessional, I fumbled, "Forgive me Father for I have sinned, it's been thirty years since my last confession." Then I spit out everything, leaving no commandment unbroken - nine out of ten. At least I hadn't killed anyone – yet.

The priest asked, "My son, where are you from?" Not knowing what he meant and thinking hell, I answered, "Danbury?" My penance was only one Hail Mary and one Our Father. (I brushed up on those prayers since reading the Bible.) I thought to myself, the priest either felt sorry for me or wanted me out of his church in a hurry before the roof caved in.

I told my neighbor, Rose, who was super religious about my confession and penance.

She said, laughing aloud, "Al, you made that priest's day. He just reeled in a big fish."

9

The Nanny

Thursday, April 7 through Sunday, April 10, 1994

I spent the next few days running back and forth between visiting Georgann at Yale and spending time with Gabby at the Marinos. I loaded the Blazer with bananas, apples and peanut butter crackers. Driving, eating, and sleeping – mostly catching a few hours at the hospital - were a big blur to me. I don't know how I would have made it if it wasn't for the gallons of coffee I consumed. Since March, I had dropped a lot of weight. My hair now had more gray than black in it.

On Friday, I took Gabby and Marie to Westchester Medical Center for Gabby's appointment with Dr. Navarro. After examining Gabby, the doctor reviewed the scans from her last shunt revision and compared them to the new films sent by Dr. Winig. He concluded that the shunt was functioning properly. He agreed with Dr. Winig that Gabby's problem might be emotional.

On the way out, Marie said to me, "You know, Georgann would never have left Gabby alone with Nicky." I kept waiting for the other shoe to drop.

Inwardly I said to myself, 'Lord, give me the strength not to shut her mouth with my fist.' But she never said another word.

The three of us stopped at the Friendly's in Mt. Kisco for dinner. Before dropping Marie and Gabby back at the Marinos. Over coffee, Marie said, "I hear the new nanny has impeccable credentials. She only works for rich people." I guess that was qualification enough for Marie.

I kissed Gabby goodbye, thanked Marie again for taking care of her and returned to Yale where I remained until Sunday night. Because Georgann's oxygen absorption levels were fluctuating, Dr. Matthay was in and out of the ICU the entire night attempting to stabilize them.

During one of the times Dr. Matthay was attending to Georgann I took a break to grab a cup of coffee and a sandwich. In the cafeteria, I overheard the conversation of a couple of doctors sitting at the next table. What caught my attention was they were obviously talking about the young woman from Danbury who was transferred to Yale because of the rare blood disorder she contracted on a Caribbean vacation. She had died. During her autopsy, it was discovered that she had not died from a blood disorder at all. Before going to the Caribbean, she had accidently inhaled insecticide spray while working in her parent's garden. That was what had killed her.

So much for the diagnostic capabilities of Danbury Hospital.

And Yale.

Monday, April 11, 1994

I was ready for Gabby's homecoming. Betty had done a great job cleaning the house, preparing meals, and stocking the freezer and refrigerator with the food I told her Gabby liked. In the oven was a pan of baked ziti – one of Gabby's particular favorites - for tonight's dinner.

I expected Kim Day to show up at 8:00 am, but Donna, Marie, Gabby, and Kim Day all strolled in at five not bothering to call me. Nicky joined us. Betty stayed just long enough to be insulted by Nicky, Marie, and Donna.

Marie said, "The house looks okay for a spot cleaning. I hope you can do better than this."

Nicky said, "Don't clean my room. I don't want you touching my stuff."

Donna said, after looking into the oven, "We don't eat that slop. You can take it with you when you go."

Kim Day didn't say anything; she just waltzed around the kitchen turning over a plate here or looking into a cabinet there. I actually thought I heard her grunt once or twice. I was already picking up bad vibes from this new nanny.

Before she left, Donna said to Kim, "After you drop Gabby off at school tomorrow, come over and we'll go shopping at Weinstein's for that bath oil you like."

Did she say, bath oil or whale oil? Kim Day was twenty-six years old, 5'5", and easily 270 pounds. Her piano legs with cellulite thighs bulged out from too-tight Bermuda shorts reminded me of overstuffed sausage. Her eyes, heavily lined in black, were blue marbles sunk into her pudgy cheeked face. She even had the mandatory satanic looking tattoo on the back of her neck to complete a character description in one of the Stephen King's novels. But, looks aren't everything, right? I needed to give her the benefit of the doubt. After all, she had impeccable credentials.

Attempting a positive attitude, I said, "Gabby, why don't you show Kim to her room? I'll bring up her bags. What would you like for dinner? "I want pizza, Daddy. How about you, Kim?"

"Sure. With extra cheese and pepperoni. Let's go, Gabby." Gabby led her up the stairs. Mind you, she had not said a word to me.

"Kim," I called out to her, "I'll drive you and Gabby to her school in the morning. You can drive back to the house to familiarize yourself with the route and get used to driving the Blazer." I would use Georgann's Jeep.

"Whatever." She said not bothering to turn around.

Tuesday, April 12, 1994

I got up early. I went into the kitchen just in time to see Nicky blow by me without saying a word and slamming the door behind her. Gabby and Kim came down together. They were both wearing shorts and tight t-tops.

I said, "Its forty degrees outside. Won't you be cold wearing just shorts, Gabby?"

With a smirk, Kim said, "Gabby wants to dress like me."

I looked at Gabby. Her skinny legs sticking out from her shorts were a sad sight. I shook my head. Instead I said, "Have some breakfast. I made scrambled eggs and bacon."

They sat down at the table. Kim pushed her plate aside. "I only eat organic food. Give me a hundred dollars. I'll get some healthy food for Gabby and me from the health food store." I guess the pepperoni on last night's pizza was organic.

"Yes, Daddy, I want to eat healthy food."

In that short exchange, I realized this Kim Day was going to be a serious problem adding to the rest of my serious problems. My intuition and experience told me that Marie had gotten to her first with instructions that she didn't have to pay me any mind, because, after all, I was nothing in this family but a user and a crook - it was Gabby's money, not mine, that paid her salary. Every bone in my body screamed that this buffoon calling herself a nanny had been given carte blanche by the Marinos to do everything in her power to undermine me with Gabby. I couldn't even confront her, because Gabby, for some reason, was already very attached to this tub of lard. Plus, I still needed someone to care for Gabby when I was at the hospital with Georgann. My hands were tied.

I managed to get Kim's okay to give Gabby some juice and a little cereal before leaving for Gabby's school. As we were turning out of my driveway, my neighbor Bob was getting his mail. I stopped to introduce Kim as Gabby's new nanny. After a polite hello from Bob and a grunt from Kim, he asked, "How's Georgann doing?"

"She's in stable condition. I'll be heading there as soon as I drop Gabby at school. I'll tell her you were asking for her."

Out of the blue, he said, "Al, I'd like to talk to you – in private – when you get a chance."

"Sure Bob, I'll be back in an hour."

"Come over to my house for coffee as soon as you get back."

On the ride to Gabby's school, I tried to explain the roads and exits to Kim, but she ignored me and fiddled with the radio until she found a heavy metal station. I let her drive back, but her aggressive driving and loud music left me paranoid and with a headache.

As soon as we got to the house, she jumped out of the Blazer and into her Bronco mumbling, "I'm going to Donna's." She sped away.

I walked over to Bob's and rang his doorbell. Bob invited me in. We sat at his kitchen table with our coffees. Before I could take my first sip he said, "I am so sorry to hear about Georgann. But, I am more concerned about what happened at your house the other night. It might have something to do with Georgann." I had no idea what he was talking about.

"Something happened at my house? When?"

"It was Monday night."

"I took Sally, Georgann's friend, to visit her at the hospital. I left Nicky with Gabby." That was the night Silvio called me at the hospital ordering me to get home right away.

Bob continued, "About nine, my wife and I were sitting on our back deck which overlooks your front yard. Suddenly, we heard shouting. We got up to see where the shouting was coming from only to see Gabby on her knees in your driveway. She was crying, and it looked like she was pleading with Nicky. Nicky was screaming. It pains me to repeat them but these were Nicky's exact words. 'You little fuckin' retard, you better be with us on this. Our father's a piece of shit, and he won't be able to protect you. All he cares about is getting your money.' Nicky pulled Gabby to her feet and dragged her into the house. My wife and I were worried she might hurt Gabby. I called your house and asked for you. Nicky picked up. She said, 'He's not here' and hung up. We debated whether to call the police, but about fifteen minutes later, a maroon Cadillac pulled into your driveway, and two men got out and went into your house."

Silvio and Dennis.

"We waited but didn't hear any more commotion. Forty five minutes later, you showed up. Is Gabby all right?"

That was Silvio definition of 'a little argument.' I told Bob about finding Gabby upset and taking her to her doctor Tuesday morning for a checkup. "She's okay, Bob. Thanks for asking and thanks for keeping an eye on my house." And, thank God for my CI Bob.

I promised myself that I would never leave Gabby alone with Nicky again. Feeling despondent and helpless, I didn't know what to do about this horde of psychos called family. Marie's constant badgering Georgann to divorce me or she would be wearing widow's weeds; Nicky threatening Gabby to make sure she was on their side not mine; and Silvio going over to the enemy camp were mounting into problems for which I had no solution. How could I protect my family from my family? And now, I had to throw Kim Day into this pack of degenerates.

When I got home from the hospital that evening I went into Gabby's room and found her sitting on her bed still fully clothed.

"Why aren't you in bed? You don't even have your pajamas on yet. Where's Kim? She's supposed to help you get ready for bed."

"Kim's in her room. She told me that I was old enough to get myself ready for bed. But, Daddy, I can't get the zipper on my shorts down without help."

"I'll help you, sweetheart." I did the best I could to get her into her pajamas and made sure she brushed her teeth before climbing into bed. After we said a prayer for Georgann; I kissed her goodnight, turned off the light.

As I was heading downstairs, I passed by Kim's bedroom. I heard a sound like ice clinking in a glass. I assumed she was drinking something besides soda - alone. And, this was just her first day on the job!

Chuck and Nikol were sprawled out of on the couch in the living room drinking beer. "Why didn't you help Gabby get ready for bed?" I asked Nicky.

Without looking up, she said, "That's Kim's job not mine."

I turned out all the lights in the rest of the house hoping Chuck would take the hint and leave.

"I think your father wants to go to bed. I better go," Chick said.

"Fuck him. You don't have to go. Nobody gives a shit about what he wants."

My blood began to boil. I wanted to slap the pretty right off this insolent bitch's face. This bullshit needed to stop. I went into the kitchen to drink a glass of water to cool down before going back into the living room. As calmly as I could, I said, "Chuck, come outside, I want to talk to you."

"Sure, Mr. V," he said putting on his sneakers.

I lit a cigarette while I waited for him to come out. When he did, I said, "Nothing personal, Chuck, but I think you deserve better than my daughter. I can see you're not a bad kid, but our home is not Nikol's personal flophouse for her friends. Just because I spend a lot of time at Yale with my wife does not mean that Nicky has the run of the place especially with Gabby here." Stomping out my cigarette, I continued, "Let me make this as clear as I can, Chuck." I put my arm around his shoulders and gave them a little squeeze. "If Nicky causes another ounce of trouble or in any way mistreats her sister, I'll personally bury her right here in the front yard. And, that goes for anyone who helps her. You got that?"

Chuck gulped, "Yes, sir, Mr. Volpe. I'm sorry your wife is sick. I'll be leaving now. Good night." He barely buckled on his helmet before getting on his bike and racing up the driveway.

Nicky came running out of the house, yelling, "Chuck, Chuck, you don't have to go."

He didn't slow down as he yelled out, "I'll call you to-morrow."

Nicky ran back into the house, grabbed her keys, jumped into her car and sped after Chuck, cursing me the whole time.

I stared up the driveway for a few moments before going back into the house and to the solace of my bedroom.

Wednesday, April 13, 1994

I got up early and removed all the beer from the refrigerator. I saw that Kim had stocked up on diet energy shakes. Just what Gabby needs, I thought, diet food.

Gabby and Kim came down to the kitchen in shorts again. Kim gave Gabby one of her diet drinks for breakfast. If the situation wasn't so pitiable, it would be laughable - Twiggy Gabby and Fatso Kim. I told myself that I only needed to put up with Kim until Melissa Corsaro came home from college the following month. Kim hit me up for another fifty bucks for more 'health food' before leaving to take Gabby to school in the Blazer.

I went upstairs to get ready for the hospital but decided to look into Kim's room first. She had decorated the walls and dresser with demonic looking posters and knickknacks. I noticed that the window screen was raised. I went to shut it and found wine and beer bottles lined up on the windowsill. I discovered empties under her bed.

As I was dressing, the phone rang. It was Marie. "Nicky just got off the phone with me. She was really upset. Did you tell Chuck that you would kill her? If you lay a finger on my granddaughter, you're going to jail for the rest of your life, that is, if they don't find you with a bullet in the back of your head. Silvio will make sure of that."

"Do whatever you want," I said slamming down the phone.

Marie's threats no longer carried any weight with me, but I didn't like the idea that Silvio might make the odd choice of hiring some thug to eliminate me. With these distressing thoughts rolling around in my head, I left for Yale.

Thursday, April 14 and Friday, April 15, 1994

I stayed at the hospital late on Thursday, because Georgann's vitals were not stable. Dr. Matthay told me to go home and get some rest; he would remain with Georgann the rest of the night.

I flew out of bed the next morning awakened by the slamming of the front door. I looked out of my bedroom window in time to see Kim dragging Gabby to the Blazer.

I noticed that Gabby was wearing long pants and a turtleneck which seemed strange, because it was exceptionally warm today. Why were they leaving so early? Was it to avoid me?

When I called the ICU, Dr. Matthay was still there. He told me that Georgann's vitals had stabilized during the night. I could drink my morning coffee with a little of peace of mind – until the phone rang again. It was my insurance broker. Kim Day rear ended another car with my Blazer the day before, and the driver of that car contacted my agent with a claim. Of course, since I had come home late last night, I didn't think to look at the Blazer. It was obvious now why Kim and Gabby left before I got up. I told the insurance agent to go ahead with the claim.

Betty came in about nine. "What are you doing here, Al? I thought you would already be at the hospital."

"Georgann had a rough night. Dr. Matthay stayed with her and sent me home. She's doing better now. I didn't get here until three this morning. I could use some more sleep before going back to the hospital later. Also, I want to be here when Kim brings Gabby home from school."

"I know she's Gabby's nanny, Al, but I don't like her."

"Neither do I." I told Betty about the car accident. "I want to confront her. Let's see how she gets out of this one."

I took a short nap; paid some bills, made a couple of phone calls and waited. When Kim and Gabby came in, Gabby ran up to her room without looking at me. I stood in Kim's way blocking her retreat to her room, "Why didn't you tell me you rear ended someone in my Blazer yesterday? Was Gabby with you?"

"Yeah, she was in the car. So what?"

"How is she? I can't have you driving my daughter around if you are going to put her in danger."

Strike me if I'm lying, but her answer to me was, "Kiss my ass," and she walked away. Lord knows I wanted to lose my size 12EE boot up her fat ass right then and there, screw the consequences. But, instead, I went to see how Gabby was doing.

I knocked on her bedroom door before going in. "It's me, sweetheart. Can I come in?"

"Sure, Daddy." I could tell she had been crying. She was sitting on her bed staring down at her feet.

"Kim told me you had a little accident in the car yesterday. Are you okay?"

"Yes, Daddy," she whispered.

"Why are you wearing long pants and a turtleneck? I thought you liked wearing shorts to school."

"Kim told me to wear them to hide the bruises. I was sitting in the front seat and not wearing my seat belt. When Kim hit the car in front of us, I flew into the dashboard."

"Bruises! What bruises? Show me your arms and legs!"

She pushed up her sleeves and pants. There were black and blues on her arms and legs.

"I'm okay, Daddy, they don't hurt anymore. Please, don't tell Kim I showed them to you. She'll be mad at me."

"I won't tell her, Gabs, but if anything else bad happens, you need to tell me. I won't say anything to anybody else unless you want me to. From now on, make sure you wear your seat belt and sit in the back seat." I gave her a hug and left her room.

I now knew why Kim made Gabby wear long pants and a long sleeved shirt to school that day – to hide the bruises. A person can take only so much, then something inside snaps. Already traumatized by Georgann's illness and worried about Gabby health, this off the leash nitwit, Kim Day, was putting me over the edge. I wanted to inflict severe pain on this woman, but if I went to jail, who would take care of Gabby? There was only Nicky or Marie and they were not options as far as I was concerned. I vowed to be more vigilant with Gabby until Melissa could take over.

Saturday, April 16 and Sunday, April 17, 1994

When I got home from the hospital Saturday morning, I found the house empty. Kim didn't work on weekends. She dropped Gabby at Marie's before going to wherever she went – in my Blazer. Nicky was not home either. Ask me if I cared.

I was standing in the front yard watching Brandy poop when the town Sheriff turned into my driveway. He got out of the patrol car, straightened his hat and walked up to me. "Are you Albert Volpe?" he asked.

"I am, officer, can I help you?"

"I think you need to help yourself first," he said handing me a piece of paper. Touching the brim of his hat, he said, "Have a nice day," before getting back into his patrol car and driving off.

It was a summons to appear in court on April 27th at 10:00 am. Nikol had filed a restraining order against me which stated that I threatened to kill her. The summons also said I broke her nose (the nose thing again) when she tried to call the police to have me arrested. In addition, the summons said she had proof that I had stolen two million dollars of Gabby's trust money. These accusations needed a diaper change having the stench of Marie written all over them.

Monday, April 18, 1994

Because I did not know exactly what a restraining order entailed, I thought it best to hire an attorney. I looked in the Yellow Pages for a Danbury law firm and chose Reifberg, Smart, and Donahue, because their ad said that one of their specialties was criminal law. I was able to make an appointment with Attorney Steven Smart for that afternoon.

I arrived at the law office on Sugar Hollow Road in Danbury fifteen minutes before my 2:00 appointment. I sat in the waiting room in anxious trepidation until the receptionist showed me into Smart's office.

Steven Smart had been with Reifberg, Smart, and Donahue for about eight years and was experienced in handling delicate domestic violence cases. After shaking my hand with a firm grip, he asked me to be seated. His easy smile did not mask the penetrating attention he afforded me with his hazel eyes. I sat on the edge of my seat as he read the allegations in the restraining order. For my benefit, he explained in simple terms that a restraining order was not a criminal charge; anybody could file a complaint against someone else. Nicky's claim that I threatened her with physical violence was relevant in the restraining order, but the accusation that I had stolen money from Gabby's trust was not.

The money steal may not be relevant according to Smart, but the fact it was put into the restraining order at all sent up a red flag. Marie's intended to use Nicky as a means to go after Gabby's trust.

Initially, Smart was reluctant to take the case, but, after much pleading on my part and taking a $1,000 cash retainer, he agreed to represent me for the upcoming court date. I did not mention my in-laws to Smart - no need to add to the fire that was beginning to burn hot in this bonfire of iniquity.

Tuesday, April 19, 1994 and Wednesday, April 20, 1 994

Tuesday – hospital all day. Wednesday was Gabby's fourteenth birthday. Betty, Sally, Josephine and Paul came to the house with cake and presents for Gabby. We set a place for Georgann at the table. We lit the candles and sang 'Happy Birthday'. Kim stayed in her room reporting everything to Donna who reported everything to Marie.

Thursday April 21 through Tuesday, April 26, 1994

All was quiet at my house the last few days. There were no more car accidents or fights. I ignored Kim and she ignored me, but she appeared to be taking care of Gabby – at least from what I could see. I checked out her bedroom and didn't find any more liquor bottles on the windowsill or empties under the bed. Apparently, she decided to behave herself – at least for the time being,

Nicky was staying with Marie.

Georgann was barely holding on. I was positive that it was only her will to live that kept her breathing. I spent most of my time at Georgann's bed-side going home only to shower and make sure Gabby was okay. I ignored the rest of the family.

10

Déjà Court?

Wednesday, April 27, 1994

Steven Smart and I met outside the courthouse. "Are you ready, Al? Make sure you speak only when the judge or I address you."

"I'm as ready as I'll ever be, but I can't guarantee I'll hold my tongue."

Judge T. Clark Hull, known for his sense of humor which at times masked his deep reverence for the law, was presiding. Although he retired from the Connecticut Supreme Court a few years before, he still served on part-time assignment as a state referee.

We went into the courtroom and took our seats at a table facing the judge. Nicky was sitting at a table on the left of us with her lawyer – some shyster Silvio hired whose fee he was most likely paying - I didn't bother to get his name. Marie seated herself on the bench right behind Nicky and the attorney. We remained seated as the judge questioned us.

Glancing at the restraining order, Judge Hull asked Nicky, "When did your father break your nose?"

She mumbled, "He never broke my nose."

"He never broke your nose, Miss Volpe? Then why is that a claim in the restraining order?"

"I don't know," said Nicky.

The judge turned to me, "Did you threaten to kill your daughter?"

"Your honor, I have barely spoken ten words to my daughter since we moved to Danbury let alone threaten her. I had a man-to-man talk with her boyfriend outside the house the other night. If Nicky was listening, she misunderstood me if she thought I said anything about a threat."

The judge asked Nikol, "Did your father directly threaten you, or did someone tell you that?"

Her lawyer whispered in her ear.

"I overheard him say it." Chuck had refused to come to court.

"But, did he directly threaten to kill you to your face?"

"No, sir."

"Why is an allegation that Mr. Volpe stole money from a trust included in the restraining order?" I cannot see that it has any bearing in Miss Volpe's request.

"My grandmother told me to include it," said Nikol

The judge sat back and let out a sigh. "I see no need for a restraining order, because none of the allegations made by Miss Volpe appear to have any corroboration. I can only recommend that the two of you stay out of each other's way. Dismissed."

I had no problem with his recommendation; I'd been staying out of Nikol's way for almost a decade.

Fifteen wasted minutes out of my life. That was that. A thousand dollars and my attorney never said a word. Little did I know this court event was only the beginning of me laying out big bucks for lawyers.

Marie and Nicky were standing in front of the courthouse when Smart and I came out. Marie approached me, "You got off this time, asshole, but don't count on your luck holding out. Come on, Nicky; let's get away from this gavone."

I turned to Smart. "Welcome to my life, Steve."

"I can see that your mother-in-law is trouble and has way too much influence over your daughter. I suggest you get an eviction notice and have Nicky removed from your house."

"I can't do that, Steve. Georgann would never forgive me if I turned our daughter out."

Thursday, April 28 through Friday, May 6, 1994

To spite me, Nikol taped her copy of the useless restraining order on the refrigerator. From that day forward, she and Kim began a crusade, independently and jointly, to seize every opportunity to demean, ridicule and harass me in front of Gabby.

Fatso Kim kept hitting me up for money like I was her personal piñata. She even told me that she lost the original $800 bonus check I'd given her and demanded a replacement. I told her she'd have to wait till I got the following month's bank statement in case someone else cashed the check although I already knew the check had not been cashed. I made her sign a paper saying she lost it.

Nicky, Kim, and Donna along with Marie's back-up mouth and Silvio's muscle had me roped in - the psychos were running the asylum. Donna tried to get rid of Betty by telling her that Gabby didn't want her around. Bless her big heart - Betty refused to be intimidated. She maintained her loyalty to me and Gabby. Unfortunately, these four harridans were so brutal to Betty that I finally had to tell her to stop coming to the house until Melissa Corsaro could take over for Kim.

If Nikol and Kim were cruel to Gabby, it was not in front of me nor where my CI Bob could witness it. But, deep down I knew it was happening.

As much as this knowledge burned me, I couldn't confront them; getting arrested by fighting with these shrews wouldn't help anyone, certainly not Gabby. I had to wait for Melissa to take over. Mostly, I put all my hopes into Georgann's recovery and return home to reestablish a nurturing, safe haven for Gabby.

Saturday, May 7 and Sunday, May 8, 1994

Georgann had been in a medically induced coma for over a month. Dr. Matthay and the Yale surgeons continued to perform medical miracles to keep her alive. No one else in the family came to the hospital since she was placed in a coma – she was of no use to them. They were too busy concocting schemes to grab control of Gabby's trust when, not if, Georgann died. I stayed at the hospital, steering clear of all of them.

After spending two straight days at Yale, I went home Sunday night to shower, change and sleep in a real bed. Nicky and Chuck were in Nicky's room, but the Blazer was gone.

I knocked on Nikol's door, "Where's Gabby?"

"I don't know and I don't care. Get away from me or I'll have you arrested."

I called Marie. As usual, Kim dropped Gabby off Saturday morning before running off to New York City (in my Blazer again) to attend a weekend head-banger concert. But, it was Sunday night, and Marie hadn't heard from Kim. She wasn't concerned; a nanny to the rich gets a pass.

"I'll take Gabby to school in the morning," she said.

"Marie, before you hang up, did the bruises on Gabby's legs and arms from the car accident heal all right?"

"What car accident?" Apparently, fearing Kim's revenge, Gabby told her grandmother that she had fallen down some steps at school. "What are you talking about?"

"No, Marie, she lied to you to protect that fat bitch. You know who I mean, the one with the impeccable credentials." I told Marie everything - the car accident, the lost bonus check, giving Gabby diet drinks, the use of my Blazer to go to New York, and Nicky and Kim making it impossible for Betty to stay on.

Marie went ballistic, "That fat, lying piece of shit porcacione. Wait till I get my hands on her!"

"Hang on, Marie; let me handle Kim, okay? I don't want her to make Gabby's life any tougher than it is. It's only until Melissa Corsaro can start in a few days."

"I'll stay out of it for now, but I'm keeping my eye on that pezza di merda."

Seeing my intro to pour gas on her flaming rage, I added, "I thought you made it clear to Nicky she wasn't to have any boyfriends staying at the house."

Marie stammered, "What the fuck are you talking about? She told me she hasn't."

"Then why is Chuck shacked up in her room right now?"

Amping up her rage to an ear splitting decibel, she shrieked, "That fuckin' bum Chuck! I told Nicky to get rid of him. He's a traitor. I'm calling her right now." Click.

I had a good laugh when I heard Nicky's phone ring. Moments later, Chuck blew out the front door. I know I was being petty, but it felt good having Marie vent her anger on somebody else for a change.

Monday, May 9, 1994

Kim hadn't come home Sunday night, but she picked up Gabby for school at Marie's house in the morning. Marie didn't say anything to her about the car accident, but I'm sure the icy stare she aimed at Kim's back as she walked toward my Blazer sent shivers through Kim. (I recalled vividly the first time I received Marie's eye stabbing in the back.)

I called Dr. Corsaro to confirm the date Melissa would be able to take over for Kim.

"She's coming home tonight, Al. She can start minding Gabby on Wednesday. She is really forward to it. How is Georgann doing?"

I told him that Georgann remained mostly stable in the induced coma and that Dr. Matthay was vigilantly monitoring her vital signs. I asked him to explain some medical terms Dr. Matthay used regarding oxygen absorption.

After giving me the dumbed-down version, he said, "I heard from a little birdie that Marie has been telling everyone who will listen that you are a gidrool, whatever that means. According to her, all you do is read your Bible while sitting on death watch at Georgann's bedside."

"You mean a vulture not a little birdie if it was someone in my family. What else has the birdie - I mean vulture - told you?"

He laughed. "What's this I hear about you stealing two million dollars of Gabby's trust? If I had that kind of money, I would build a high wall around my property and fill a moat with alligators to keep your family out."

"No wall or moat can keep out sewer rats. While I have you on the phone, do think it advisable to get Gabby some counseling to help her deal with Georgann's illness?"

"I think that would be a very good idea. I can recommend Dr. Mark Banshick in Katonah. He is a psychiatrist who specializes in child and adolescent therapy. I can call him and make an appointment for Gabby if that's what you want?"

"Thank you, I would appreciate that. Do you think that Marie and Nicky would benefit from counseling? Marie respects your judgment; she might listen to you. Why don't you give her a call? I give you permission to lie, but make sure you include that it's for Gabby's benefit and don't mention my name."

Corsaro laughed, "Al, they'd never go along with it. They're both beyond therapy's help."

I guess that was a reasonable assessment of the mental states of my mother-in-law and daughter.

Tuesday, May 10, 1994

I called Melissa at her home. "I can't tell you how happy I am that Gabby's care will be in your hands. I want you two to enjoy your time together. I'm giving your father three thousand dollars to dole out for Gabby's expenses and for your salary. If you need more, just ask. Betty will do the housekeeping, buy the groceries and make your meals. I'm also giving you the keys to the Blazer. Your job starts tomorrow. Your first duty is to pick Gabby up at school in your car and bring her home. After that, you can use the Blazer. I already told her you would be at the school and to look out for you. She is very excited."

"Thanks, Mr. Volpe. I know Gabby and I are going to have a ball. See you tomorrow."

As soon as I hung up with Melissa, I called Marie to let know that Melissa would be starting the next day. I didn't tell her I was giving Dr. Corsaro three thousand dollars for Gabby's expenses out of my pocket nor did I mention that I was scheduling counseling for Gabby with Dr. Banshick. I found that giving Marie too much information often backfired on me.

"I'm glad Melissa is starting tomorrow. She's a good girl. Nicky told me that she will be moving back to help Melissa with Gabby. What are you going to do about that fat pig, Kim?"

I found it hard to believe that Nicky was going to share in Gabby's care, but miracles could happen. I told Marie, "I'll take care of Kim tomorrow before Gabby and Melissa get here. Don't say anything to Donna or she'll warn Kim. I'll tell you everything when I'm done with Kim."

Marie actually whispered into the phone as if someone was listening on her end, "I won't breathe a word to that stupid woman I call my daughter. She and that piece of shit sit around all day drinking wine, feeding their fat asses, and holding each other's hands." I almost choked on the breath mint I had in my mouth. I couldn't believe my ears! Marie talking against one of her own! And to me, no less.

That morning, I drove to Yale more lighthearted than I had felt in weeks reveling in the thrill that I was finally getting rid of Kim Day. I called her from the hospital. "Meet me at the house tomorrow at one. I've got the $800 check to replace the one you lost."

I'd already stopped payment on both the old and new checks. Because Kim was such a wild card, I didn't trust her. I called Paul and Betty to ask them to be there when I confronted Kim. I needed witnesses.

To Betty, I said, "Betty, you're back on the payroll. Kim's leaving tomorrow, but she doesn't know it yet. Come to the house by nine tomorrow after she's left to take Gabby to school. Your first duty is to pack Kim's belongings and then sanitize her room."

Betty laughed, "I'll do that for free."

Wednesday, May 11, 1994

Betty arrived right on time with an obvious spring in her step. As we began to pack Kim's stuff in her luggage we found Georgann's jewelry she had stolen and hidden in a suitcase. I wasn't surprised but even though Betty knew Kim was a bad egg, she couldn't believe that she would steal from a woman who was in a coma!

When Paul arrived, we hauled Kim's belongings downstairs and put the stuff by the front door. I wanted to fling it all onto the lawn but that might have given me away before I had time to lay into her.

Betty began to clean the room "Don't bother washing the sheets and towels she used," I told Betty. "Throw them in the garbage." I refrained from adding that was where Kim belonged, too. After all, Betty was a Christian woman.

At one o'clock, Kim came bouncing into the kitchen fully prepared to beat me out of more money while taking the opportunity to deride me in the bargain. "Gimmee my money, dude," she bellowed.

I pointed to two checks sitting on the table, one for $200, her salary, and the other for $800 to replace the lost check. Kim made a grab for them, but I got to them first.

Holding up the checks, I said, "First, give me the car and house keys. You're fired. Your stuff is already packed and waiting for you by the front door."

"You can't fire me. It's Gabby's money that pays my salary. I'll sue, you creep. I'm going to call the cops."

"You do that, Kim," I said calmly. "That will give me the chance to tell them you fled the scene of an accident and to show them my wife's jewelry I found hidden in your suitcase. My witnesses here will back me up." Paul and Betty stood behind me nodding their heads.

Kim's face contorted turning an angry red. She threw the keys at me and grabbed the checks. "I'm going to tell Donna what you did," she growled, storming out of the kitchen.

"Be my guest," I answered.

From the open front door, I watched Paul throw her things into the back seat of her car while she sat in the driver's seat scowling. He barely closed the car door before Kim pressed hard on the gas pedal and screeched up of the driveway. Slowly, I closed the front door, leaned against it and breathed a hearty sigh of relief.

Once he made sure Kim was not coming back, Paul came into the kitchen.

"Betty, how about getting us a celebratory cup of coffee?"

"Coming right up, boss."

After Betty put a cup of coffee in front of Paul and me, he said, "Al, Josephine checked the references Kim provided to Donna - one was phony and the other came from a family who was looking to have her arrested for theft. She's some prize!"

"Impeccable," I said.

Betty almost choked on her coffee laughing so hard.

After Betty and Paul left, I called Marie to give her the good Kim news.

A few days later, I received confirmation from the bank that Kim had attempted to cash both $800 checks. I wish I could have seen her face when the bank told her the checks had been stopped. I let her keep the $200.

Melissa Corsaro moved in the afternoon Kim left. Finally, someone I could trust to care for Gabby. My relief was short lived.

The first week, Melissa was great with Gabby, but, as if hypnotized by the Svengali Marinos, she soon became a victim to this nest of vipers. Nicky was on summer break from teaching and had plenty of time to devote her attention to Melissa's education. As soon as Gabby was in bed, she would invite Melissa into her room for a relaxing glass of wine and fill her head with stories about what a lousy father and worse husband I was. On her first free weekend, after dropping Gabby at Marie's, Nicky took Melissa to a club where they partied until three am. Chuck introduced Melissa to a friend of his with whom she became immediately infatuated.

Poor, sweet Melissa succumbed to the dark side. Within weeks, chaos reigned again in my home.

11

Leap of Faith

It was now almost three months that Georgann lay motionless in a medically induced coma. During this time, I was still the only one who visited her. The doctors had pushed the medical envelope beyond all limits to keep her alive. Remarkable, to this date, Georgann was the only person who had ever survived a ruptured aortic aneurism into the lung. Even Dr. Matthay had no medical explanation for Georgann's continued survival given that her functioning lung continued to atrophy from the high oxygen concentrations. It was only a matter of time before her lung, arteries or heart would give out – odds were she would die in the coma.

With nothing to lose and with my permission, Dr. Matthay took a giant leap of faith. Over the next few weeks, he began to wean down Georgann's high oxygen concentration levels by small increments. Each time a lower tolerance failed, Georgann would lose vital signs. I would remain suspended in terror watching the doctors' work feverishly to bring her back, which they did - every time.

I rarely went home. To my detriment, I made the difficult decision to concentrate my rapidly diminishing energies on choosing Georgann over Gabby. Georgann's survival was our family's only hope. If Georgann wouldn't quit, neither would I - nor Dr. Matthay.

Sunday, June 12, 1994

Melissa was now disappearing for entire weekends to spend time with her new boyfriend. She brought Gabby to Marie who was only too happy to take care of Gabby from Friday afternoon to Sunday. Marie was so solicitous in allowing Melissa her me-time that she even brought Gabby home Sunday nights to save Melissa the trip. Usually, when Marie arrived, Melissa was already waiting for Gabby at the open door to welcome her home, but not this Sunday. Only Nicky was there.

"Where's Melissa?" Marie asked Nicky.

Nicky covered for Melissa who had not yet returned. "She just ran to the store for milk. She'll be right back."

For some reason, Marie believed Nicky. Silvio was waiting to take her out to dinner and she thought leaving Gabby with Nicky for only a few minutes would be okay. I guess Marie wasn't too good at taking her own advice where Nicky was concerned.

Fortunately, I chose this night to come home to shower and get a few hours sleep. As soon as I walked through the front door, I heard Nicky screaming and Gabby crying hysterically. They were in the living room. I ran into the room and was about to tell Nicky to shut up when she abruptly stopped yelling at Gabby to direct her vitriolic tongue on me. "Don't touch me," she said with a look of smug defiance on her face, "I'll call the cops and have your hauled away." Head up, she turned and went up to her room.

I put my arm around Gabby, "Are you okay, sweetheart?"

She pushed me away, "Leave me alone. I don't ever want to talk to you again." I watched her struggle up the stairs to her room.

What had I done to prompt such a response? She never talked to me like that before. Had the Marinos succeeded in turning Gabby against me, too?

I couldn't confront Nicky out of fear of incurring another restraining order so I called Marie. Instead of asking her why she left Gabby alone with Nicky, I chose to plead with her and Silvio to put a moratorium on the feud between us, because it was destroying Gabby.

Characteristically, she answered, "Go fuck yourself." In the background, I heard Silvio echo the same sentiment.

"I'm coming over as soon as Melissa gets here. We need to talk." I didn't give them a chance to say no. Fifteen minutes later, Melissa came in. I gave her strict orders to stay with Gabby until I got back.

I parked in the Marinos driveway. I saw the garage door open and went in. I knocked on the door in the garage that led into the kitchen.

Marie opened the door. "What are you doing here? Can't you get it into your thick head that we have nothin' to say to you?" She stood barring my way into the house.

I tried to stay calm, but my words came out in a screech, "Don't you have any respect for Georgann's wishes? She only wants us to get along, to be a family. She would be heartsick if she knew how badly Nicky treats her sister. Can't we call a truce for Gabby's sake?"

Silvio came from behind Marie, pushed her aside and shoved me out of the way before stepping into the garage. Leaning heavily on his cane, he walked over to his work bench, opened the top drawer and pulled out something I thought was the .38 caliber pistol I knew he kept there. I caught a glimpse of what he was holding just in time to throw my forearm up to divert the impact of the lead-filled black jack he was wielding to crack open my skull. He struck me a couple of times on my arm and neck but lost his balance when he thrust himself forward to put some weight behind the next blow. That gave me enough time to straighten up, push him against the wall and knock the blackjack out of his hand. He remained leaning against the wall trying to catch his breath, totally spent from the exertion of trying to kill me. I hoped he was having another heart attack.

Marie flew out the door, ran to where the blackjack had been flung and picked it up. She rushed at me swinging the blackjack wildly. I shoved her aside and out of the garage making a mad dash for my car. I jumped in, started the engine and threw it into drive. As I was pulling away, I looked in the rear view mirror to catch Marie running after me screaming at a high pitch. Her parting shot was to throw the blackjack hard enough to make a dent in the passenger side door. For an old lady, she had some arm.

I was shaking, because it sunk in that Silvio had tried to kill me! As soon as I was a safe distance from the house, I pulled over and lit a cigarette to calm down. As I sat smoking, a police patrol car flew by me in the opposite direction. Could it be heading to the Marinos? Was my heart attack wish to be granted?

I turned my car around to chase after the patrol car. I watched it go past their house and into the driveway next door. Realizing they had the wrong house, the police backed out into the street. Again, because I'm not very smart, I pulled up next to the patrol car and asked, "Are you looking for the Marino house?"

"Yes, sir. Do you know where it is?

"Yes, officer, follow me."

I led them to the Marino's driveway and turned in with the cruiser right behind me. I got out of my car and went over to the patrol car. I pointed to the house, "That's where Marie and Silvio Marino live." Innocently I asked, "Has something happened to them?"

"A woman called 911 to report that her husband had been attacked by a man who had forced his way into their house. Her husband tried to subdue the intruder, but when he saw that the intruder had a gun, he became frightened and he grabbed his chest as if having a heart attack falling onto the floor. The intruder must have panicked and ran away. 911 called an ambulance which should show up any minute." The officer finally realized he was giving up a lot of information to a stranger. "Hold on," he said, " who are you?"

"I'm the Marinos son-in-law. I was just on my way to visit them."

The officers went into the house. I leaned against my car massaging my neck and arm where Silvio struck me with the blackjack. Through the picture window in the living room I watched them talking to the Marinos. Marie was gesturing wildly and Silvio was lying prone on the couch. Before I could react, both cops rushed out of the house with guns drawn. They told me to turn around and put my hands on top of my car. I was frisked, handcuffed me and told I was under arrest.

Unceremoniously, they flung me into the back of the cruiser before heading to the Bedford police station. I figured I'd get to tell my side of the story at the precinct. Nope. I was fingerprinted and thrown into a cell so fast I wasn't given the courtesy to say a word.

As I sat alone in that dungeon, I had plenty of time to think. I recalled my mother's wise words, "Don't marry into the Marino family. They're no good." At this moment, I wished I had listened to her.

At three, the next shift came on. The Lieutenant on duty was reviewing the earlier shift's reports when he recognized my name. We'd met through my silk screening business in Katonah ten years earlier. He had commissioned me to do the lettering of t-shirts, caps, and jackets for his competitive shooting club. He knew the Marinos; too, by their mob connections, but he was not been aware they were my in-laws. He sent an officer to bring me up from the cell.

"Al, I'm surprised to see you here," he began. I stood in front of his desk my wrists handcuffed behind my back. Turning to the officer who had brought me up from the cell, he said, "You can take the handcuffs off Mr. Volpe, Officer. I don't think he's dangerous."

Once the handcuffs were removed, the Lieutenant motioned for me to have a seat in front of his desk. He gave me a wink. "I'm not so sure you aren't dangerous, Al. In the report from the arresting officers, Mrs. Marino told them you had a gun and fired at her and her husband.

"I'm surprised Silvio didn't make her shut up about a gun and shots fired. He is a convicted felon and knows guns are big cop issues they can't ignore. Besides, I did not have a gun." I didn't tell the Lieutenant that I kept my own .38 in the glove box of my car.

"I believe you, Al. She also told the police that you are her ex-son-in-law and have been harassing them ever since their daughter divorced you, because you blamed them for the breakup. When did you guys get divorced?"

"We are not divorced. Georgann's been in Yale Hospital since March in an induced coma after she suffered an pulmonary aneurism in one of her lungs. She's in very critical condition. Since I spend most of my time at the hospital, I am forced to leave my younger daughter - you remember Gabby - in the care of nannies and my mother-in-law. My older daughter wants no part in taking care of her sister. It's no mystery the Marinos have no love for me. I just wanted to get them to help me out by putting this family feuding aside until Georgann gets better. Instead of listening to me, Silvio attacked me in his garage with a blackjack." I showed the Lieutenant the bruises on my arm and my neck.

"You mean the same blackjack Mrs. Marino said was yours?"

"Yeah right, along with the gun. I didn't raise a hand to either one of them except to protect myself."

The Lieutenant looked down at the police report again and shook his head. He believed my side of the story, but the report couldn't be altered. I had to appear before the judge the next day.

The Lieutenant said, "Al, you're stuck. My advice is for you to get a good criminal lawyer to sort this out with the DA who will decide whether formal charges should be brought against you. In the meantime, I'll get an officer to drive you back to the Marinos to get your car. Don't have any contact with them." When the officer came to his office, the Lieutenant told him, "Go with Al to the Marinos and stay with him until he gets onto the highway. Make sure the Marinos don't come out of their house."

I thanked him before being driven back to the Marinos.

The house was pitch-dark when the police and I got there. The headlights from the patrol car shined a path to my Blazer. I got in the Blazer but when I started to move out of their driveway, I felt the car pull to the right. I pulled over to the side of the road; the patrol car right behind me. I saw in its headlights that my rear tire was flat. The cop helped me change it. As I tightened the lugs, he inspected the almost new tire. "Looks like you've been ice-picked."

Signature Marino. Unfortunately, Silvio must have recovered from his so called heart attack.

I didn't want to go home. Gabby wasn't talking to me, and I didn't trust myself not to have it out with Nikol or with Melissa for her negligence in her care for Gabby. I was again taking cues from the ostrich. I called Paul and asked if I could sleep at his house.

He opened the door with, "What did you do with the blackjack and the gun? How many shots did you fire? Why aren't you in jail?"

"What gun? What shots?"

"Donna called about two hours ago. She wanted to know if I had seen or heard from you - I guess to rat your whereabouts to the police. Marie told her you went to their house looking for a fight, because she left Gabby with Nicky for a few minutes until Melissa returned from the store. She and Silvio blocked your way into the house, but you pushed them aside and went in. You drew out a gun and pointed it at them. Oh yeah, you were also swinging a blackjack. You fired the gun at them and threw the blackjack but missed with both. Silvio grabbed his chest and fell to the floor apparently having a heart attack. When Marie ran to call the police, you scrammed. Where have you been all this time?"

"In jail." After I told Paul the real story, I asked him to accompany me to court the next day for the arraignment.

"Sure, Al," he said. "I'm going to start charging you chauffer fees every time I have to take you somewhere."

I was too tired to laugh.

Monday, June 13, 1994

I went before the judge and was charged with assault with a deadly weapon and home invasion. The judge released me on my own recognizance with a written promise to appear in court when the case was scheduled. Since the charges were in a New York jurisdiction, I needed to hire a New York lawyer to represent me. Steven Smart recommended White Plains criminal attorney Daniel Seymour. I was able to make an appointment for that afternoon.

Mr. Seymour was very tall and muscularly built. His fleshy face was framed by a head of thick brown hair he kept neatly trimmed. After seating me in front of his mahogany desk, he placed his elbows on the desk, held his long, tapered fingers in a teepee in front of him ready to listen attentively to my story. My guess was that he had already sniffed the cesspool stench of the mob, because he insisted on an up-front, $5,000 retainer. He probably thought I'd be lucky if I ever made it into court; better to collect his fee now.

On a more positive note, he said, "Al, it's their word against yours. Who's the jury going to believe - a convicted felon or you? My advice to you is to get character references from people you know for at least ten years both as a business and family man."

I couldn't help asking him as I did everyone, "How can Georgann's family act this way knowing she is fighting for her life?"

Mr. Seymour smiled at my naïveté. He was well acquainted with the kind of riff raff that were my in-laws. "Al, these people have no regard for family. I can name four million reasons why they want to get rid of you. I'm sure they've done a lot worse for a lot less. I'll get in touch with the DA. In the meantime, stay clear of the whole lot including Nikol. They've got restraining orders out against you. If you go near any of them, they'll try to pop you with another false arrest. Get those character references and be patient."

Josephine helped me draft a form letter requesting a character reference. She put her contact information on the letter adding that they could call her if they had any questions. She mailed copies of the letters to some of my friends, neighbors, and business associates in the area.

In the meantime, Paul's son, Angelo, a New York State Trooper, called the Bedford Police to inquire about the charges against me. He didn't get much actual information, but, off the record, the guys around the precinct were murmuring that the whole business sounded shady. It was common knowledge that Silvio Marino was connected; the cops were always on look out to catch him or someone in The Family doing something criminal. But, Silvio kept his illegal dealings under the bar, and, so far, the law had not been able to connect him to anything that was not legit. When the Marinos filed charges against me, it was the expectation on the part of the police that Silvio could be exposed to investigation into his mob dealings. Sometimes, Silvio was not as smart a hood as he thought he was.

Monday, June 20, 1994

I was sitting at Georgann's bedside trying to gain some solace from reading the Bible aloud to her when I heard a quiet voice at my side, "Are you Mr. Albert Volpe?"

I looked up to see a young, clean cut guy in Sergio Valente jeans standing in front of me. When I nodded, he held out his hand and motioned for me to take the paper he was holding. I thought it might be from the hospital administrator giving me an up to date account of Georgann's statement. As I soon as I took the paper, he said. "You've been served." (Not the right words, but I suppose he always wanted to say that.) It was a petition to have me removed as trustee for Gabby's trust. He placed another Removal of Trustees petition at the feet of Georgann's comatose body.

A smile still beaming on his stupid face he started to turn to leave. I jumped up and dragged him out of the room high fiving his head the whole time. He fell on his knees in the corridor. I called security and had him escorted out of the hospital with a warning not to return.

That afternoon, I brought the petitions to Smart's office in Danbury. I figured he should do something to earn the thousand bucks I already paid him. He looked over the petitions.

"The petitions assert that you stole two million dollars from your younger daughter's trust fund and that Gabrielle Volpe wants you as well as her mother removed as trustees. The petitions imply that Georgann was in full knowledge of the fraud. The only signatures on the petitions are that of Gabrielle Volpe." Smart held up his palm to me as I started to open my mouth to object. "Because the Marinos reside in New York, the petitions were filed in a New York State jurisdiction. As you know, I am not licensed to practice in New York. You will have to retain a New York attorney other than Seymour whose expertise is in criminal law to represent Georgann and you in this matter. I can recommend Harvey E. Corn. Corn is a top rated estate and trust litigation attorney. His office is on Third Avenue in New York City."

"I don't believe Gabby has any part in this bogus petition. She might hate me at this time, but she would never turn against her mother. I can only imagine what lies Marie is filling my poor daughter's head with for her to sign these petitions. If you think Corn is the best, I would appreciate you making an appointment for me as soon as possible?"

Smart called Corn's office and set up an appointment for 10:00 am the following day. That would make three separate law firms representing me at the same time.

Tuesday, June 21 to Thursday, June 30, 1994

I arrived promptly at ten for my appointment with Mr. Corn. The receptionist told me to go right into his office. After a bright 'good morning, Mr. Volpe', he asked me to have a seat in the leather chair in front of his desk. His engaging smile and kindly hazel eyes behind wire rimmed glasses made it hard for me to believe that this sweet looking man would be able to go against the Marinos.

Corn carefully examined the petitions before saying, "These are not legal documents, Mr. Volpe.They should not have been served on you and Mrs. Volpe. No agency can serve Removal of Trustees papers just by making a claim that money was stolen from a trust or by having a minor sign papers saying that she wants her parents removed as her trustees. New York law clearly states that there must be some legal reasons for the courts to remove a trustee such as mismanagement of the trust or misappropriating of trust property. To determine this, the court would order an accounting of the trust in order to establish whether there have been any discrepancies or improprieties in expenses made from the trust. A mere say so by your daughter who is a minor or by anyone else for that matter is not enough to remove you or your wife. By the way, where did they get the sum of two millions dollars as the amount you stole from your daughter's trust?"

Good question - seemed to be on everyone's mind.

"In 1992, Gabby was awarded a settlement for six million dollars in a malpractice suit. The trust shows that she only received $3,835,000 as her total settlement. The idiots, excuse me, my in-laws, didn't take into consideration that the attorneys who represented Gabby in the suit were entitled to receive one third of the settlement for their fees and legal expenses. Georgann and I were awarded $150,000 from the settlement for our pain and suffering – not two million."

Adjusting his glasses, Corn said, "It is difficult for me to believe that anyone could be so stupid or corrupt to insinuate that you stole your daughter's money before consulting an attorney who understood the trust system. In fact, I fail to see how any attorney would take such a case."

"Mr. Corn, you don't know how persuasive my father-in-law can be when it comes to money." I refrained from telling Corn about Silvio's Mafia connections; I didn't want to scare him off.

Looking at the petitions again, he said, "I see that the petitions request that you and Mrs. Volpe be replaced as trustees by Nikol Volpe and Marie Marino. I assume that Nikol is your older daughter, but who is Marie Marino?"

"Marie is Georgann's mother."

Shaking his head in disbelief he said, "These people are not only witless, they're insane. Who should I contact to obtain the trust information?"

I gave Corn the phone numbers for Mark Hollander and Tom Moore. They could provide him with all the information and documentation he needed concerning Gabby's trust.

"I will also get in touch with the attorney who served the original petitions to inform him that they are not valid. You and Georgann will probably be served Accounting of Trust petitions. Let me know as soon you get them. In the meantime, I will request the trust information from Hollander and Moore."

A few days after meeting with Mr. Corn, I was returning from a smoke break at Yale when the receptionist called me over to her desk. "Al, you need to contact the legal department."

"What for?"

"I was only told that you should call them as soon as you came in," she said handing me the phone.

She connected me to the legal department. I had been served the Accounting of Trust petitions Corn spoke about. I got a copy of the petitions from the legal department and sent them by FedEx to Corn's office. I put any further thoughts about the Marinos out of my head. I was paying my attorneys to deal with this scum – I needed to stay focused on Georgann.

By the end of June, Georgann's tolerances were holding at the lower life support concentrations with sustainable absorption levels. Nurses, doctors, receptionists, the parking attendants, Mrs. Thomas, Janice, Sofia, Father Valentine, and Ray, the maintenance guy, all held Georgann fervently in their prayers. Somehow, we all sensed a higher power was at work here – me the most.

Dr. Matthay was straightforward with me about his many misgivings over medical unknowns. If Georgann was brought out of her induced coma, would her one functioning lung, her heart, and arterial system be capable of sustaining the stress at awakening? Did Georgann still have brain function given that she lost vital signs so many times and her oxygen levels dropped drastically each time? Questions with no answers, but Dr. Matthay knew he had to take these risks if Georgann was to survive as anything more than a vegetable.

12

Miracle

Saturday, July 2 to Tuesday, July 11, 1994

On Saturday, Dr. Matthay came into the ICU at 1:00 to monitor Georgann's tolerance stats. I took the opportunity to go to the cafeteria to grab a sandwich. I was already down forty pounds from my usual two hundred ten. When I returned an hour later, Dr. Matthay was holding Georgann's hand. This was not unusual, because Dr. Matthay often held her hand when he spoke to her. I went to his side, and, to my astonishment, Georgann's eyes were wide open. I saw frustration on her face when she tried to speak but was not able to because of the tracheotomy.

Dr. Matthay asked her, "Do you know him?"

Georgann broke into a big smile, "Al," she mouthed.

Gently, I took her hand from Dr. Matthay, tears unabashedly flowing down my cheeks. I kissed her forehead feeling warmth I hadn't felt in months. I was transported to heaven. My Georgann had come back to me.

And yet, still another miracle - Georgann was alert and appeared to have no brain damage or memory loss. It was as if she had gone into a deep sleep that had lasted almost four months and awoke refreshed and ready to begin the day. I was overjoyed.

I hugged Dr. Matthay before turning back to Georgann. I said, "Dr. Matthay is God's medical miracle worker - your personal guardian angel who watched over you until you woke up."

Dr. Matthay humbly said, "Just doing my job, Al."

When Georgann gave me 'the look', rolling her baby browns I knew I wasn't dreaming.

Because Georgann wanted it, I gave permission for Marie to visit although it was against my better judgment. The first Monday Georgann was out of her coma, I was sitting by her side when Marie burst in.

"Georgann, my baby, my princess, God answered my prayers!" As soon as she saw me, she stopped in her tracks. "Georgann, I will not be in the same room as that man," she spit out pointing to me. "If you want your mother who loves you more than anything to stay then tell him to go." Dutiful as always, Georgann motioned for me to leave.

When Marie had the Removal of Trustees papers served, the odds had been in Marie's favor that Georgann would die in the coma or remain a vegetable if she did survive. Now that Georgann was neither dying nor mentally incapacitated, Marie was in a frenzy to hide all her traitorous deeds, but she couldn't do that with me looking over her shoulder. I had to go.

Sociopaths have no trouble twisting the truth. Marie's ritual of corruption was often wrong, but she was never in doubt. Add mob doctrine which dictates unrighteous authority can employ unrighteous deeds to take advantage of and eliminate rivals, and you have a terse but pretty potent description of the Marie's character. Taking in this two sentence narrative of Marie's mental instability, is it any wonder that she would resume her insidious campaign of slander, deception, and lies directed toward me to get what she wanted?

Marie began to set her sinister campaign in place. Before she made her initial visit to her beloved daughter, Marie's first order of business was to storm into Mrs. Scanlon's office to give her a copy of the police report stating that I was facing an assault with a deadly weapons charge in an attempt to kill them after invading their house. (Home Invasion Al) She told Mrs. Scanlon that I blamed the Marinos for instigating the divorce between Georgann and me and I was out for revenge. Marie had no doubt that I would be convicted of the felony and spend years in prison. It should be obvious to Mrs. Scanlon and everyone else that I was neither a fit parent for Gabby nor a suitable guardian of her trust. Therefore, my inevitable criminal prosecution and imprisonment gave the Marinos justification to initiate an action to have me removed as trustee and replaced by her and her granddaughter, Nikol, as co-trustees until Georgann was well enough to reassume guardianship. Enough said.

Mrs. Scanlon listened politely to Marie's ranting. She thanked Marie for the police report but refrained from making any further comment. Mrs. Scanlon and the ICU staff were well aware of the enmity between the Marinos and me. To avoid a possible confrontation between with the rest of my in-laws, Mrs. Scanlon gave the ICU receptionist instructions to warn me if any of Georgann's family signed in for a visit so I could leave the hospital by a rear exit.

I continued to spend my days and nights by Georgann's side. I never said a word to her about what had taken place during the months she was comatose: not about Kim Day - the nanny from hell - nor Nikol's abuse of Gabby, nor even about the Marinos campaign to take over Gabby's trust. Not only would that knowledge broken Georgann's heart, but it would have a negative effect on her recovery. Small credit to Marie, she kept her nefarious deeds to herself.

Although Georgann appeared mentally unimpaired, she was physically appallingly fragile. She continued to struggle to sustain tolerances at the lower life support settings. She was not yet out of danger and required constant monitoring by the ICU staff that was expertly trained in Georgann's specialized equipment.

Nicky continued to cause problems at home. My lawyers kept telling me to have her evicted, to get her out of the house for my own protection, but I couldn't chance her initiating another false arrest against me. Because I didn't want to leave Georgann alone for even one day; I stayed away from the house as much as possible. Attorney Seymour advised me to hire a security guard who would be there whenever I went home and to install a closed-circuit camera system to record any interactions I might have with Nicky. The cost of these precautions would have been too much for me to handle at the time; I just chose to stay away as much as possible

I left Gabby's care to Melissa and Betty during the week and to Marie on weekends. All three assured me that Gabby was doing fine. I prayed to God they were telling me the truth and taking good care of my baby. When I called the house, Gabby refused to talk to me. I just kept hoping that all would be put right once Georgann came home. God forgive me, I was not there for Gabby. In retrospect, of all the bad decisions I made in my life this was the worst.

While Georgann fought to sustain the lower support tolerances under the watchful care of Dr. Mathay, Marie continued her troublemaking tactics when she came to visit Georgann at Yale. She told Georgann that I never visited her when she was in the coma, because I was too busy gambling away Gabby's money and womanizing. That kind of talk from Marie did not shock Georgann; her mother never had a good word to say about me and Georgann knew they were all lies. But now Georgann was too weak to put up any fight to protect me or to be unaffected by her mother's lies; Marie was stressing Georgann to a breaking point. Marie even took down the pictures of Georgann, Gabby and me from the wall in Georgann's room and replaced them with pictures of just her and Georgann.

It was becoming increasingly harder for me to make excuses whenever Georgann asked why Gabby never came to see her or why her best friends, Sally and Sue, never called or visited. Marie told Georgann that I refused to let her friends visit out of jealousy and that I was the one who wouldn't allow Gabby see her mother. The truth was that Marie had made the usual threats of bodily harm to Georgann's friends and their families if she found out they tried to have any contact with Georgann. Marie told Gabby that her mother only wanted to see me and not her. Georgann was too frail do combat with Marie. I believed that any attempts on my part to keep Marie away would have further stressed Georgann. I just pretended that everything would be fine once Georgann came home rather than make any effort to stop Marie.

Ostrich Al strikes again

On July 8th, Daniel Seymour informed me that Silvio petitioned for a postponement of the home invasion hearing. Seymour would let me know when a new court date was set. "Get those references, Al," he said before ending the call.

That same day, Harvey Corn called. "Al, I reviewed the statement I received from Mark Hollander. He confirmed that the claim your in-laws made about you diverting two million dollars of the trust to an off shore account was false. Unfortunately, you still have to go through with the forensic accounting. I hope that once the accounting proves discrepancies do not exist in the use of the trust money, the Marinos will drop the charges."

I hoped he was right, but he didn't know this gang of reprobates like I did. After I hung up from Mr. Corn, I drove to Paul's.

After a hug, Josephine said, "Sit down, Al, I have some bad news for you. All the people we requested a character reference, to the very last one, apologized, expressed their condolences for Georgann, Gabby and you, but refused to submit a reference letter. They are afraid the Marinos would find out and go after them."

I got out my address book and gave Josephine fifteen new names of friends and business associates geographically outside the Marino sphere of influence. Josephine mailed out the new requests.

Wednesday, July 12, 1994

I went home for a change of clothes. When I opened the front door, I heard Gabby screaming, "Help! Help! Please, help me!"

Nicky and Melissa were in the downstairs bathroom doing each other's hair and didn't hear her screams. I flew up the stairs two at a time. Gabby was in the shower, unable to get away from the scalding hot water pouring from the shower head. She couldn't turn off the faucet or climb out of the tub by herself. I turned off the water, grabbed a towel, wrapped her in it and got her out of the tub. Melissa burst into the bathroom.

Gabby was scared; the water had turned her bright pink but she was otherwise unharmed.

"Why did you shower by yourself?" I asked.

"I didn't want to ask Melissa. She was busy with Nikol. They told me to go to my room and leave them alone. I thought I could do it by myself. I turned the faucet on but couldn't turn it off."

I was so angry with Melissa I could only sputter, "How could you let this happen to Gabby? You're supposed to be taking care of her."

"I didn't think Gabby would ever do such a thing. It'll never happen again, Mr. Volpe, I promise."

"I hope not, Melissa, for Gabby's sake."

I settled Gabby into bed before going to my room and shutting the door. Enough was enough. It was time to file an eviction notice at the Danbury courthouse giving Nikol thirty days to get out of the house.

Thursday, July 14, 1994

When I filed the eviction papers, I was told they would be served the following day. Because I wanted to be home when the sheriff served the notice, I cut my visit short with Georgann. Unfortunately, I was already too late. I was home by six. Nicky, Gabby and Melissa were sitting on the couch in the family room watching television. I started to go upstairs after nodding good evening.

Nikol jumped up and threw a crumpled piece of paper at me, "Take this and shove it up your ass. You can't evict me. This isn't your house."She had been served the eviction notice that afternoon. I continued to my room ignoring her, but she stayed right behind me.

"This is Gabby's house. Not yours. You don't have any rights here."

When she tried to follow me into my bedroom, I said, "Get out of my room."

"Not for long," she smirked sticking out her tongue before I shut the door in her face.

I showered, changed and lay down on the bed to try and get a few hours rest even though I knew I wouldn't be able to sleep. I heard a car pull into the driveway. I thought it might be Chuck who was still coming around although Marie had given him strict orders not to show up again. Since I was already fully clothed, I went downstairs to tell him to get lost. When I opened the door I was confronted by two police officers.

Not again!

Nikol, pushing me aside, ran up to them with the eviction order in her hand. "Thank God you are here, officers. Arrest that man," she said pointing at me, "He hit me and knocked me down, because I refused to get out of the house. This house belongs to my sister, not him. She doesn't want me to leave."

"I never touched her, officers. Ask my other daughter and Melissa who are in the house."

The officers looked at each other and shrugged before coming into the house. They questioned Gabby and Melissa separately. Nikol had told the girls to say they saw me hit her, but neither would lie to the police. After the officers admonished Nicky for wasting police time, they left. I'm sure Nicky was livid. I only hoped she didn't take it out on Gabby; Melissa was on her own.

Nicky did.

Friday, July 15, 1994

Marie and Melissa brought Gabby to Yale for the first time since Georgann came out of her coma. Gabby gave Georgann a note which read, "The house and the money are mine, not yours or Daddy's. I won't let you throw Nicky out. Tell daddy this is what I want." The three abruptly left without another word to Georgann.

Georgann wept.

Saturday, July 16, 1994 and Sunday, July 17, 1994

Georgann was slowly showing signs of improvement. No other visitors but me. She gave me the note from Gabby and questioned me with her eyes. I tried to keep all the troubles I was having with our daughters to myself; I did not want to inflict my pain on Georgann. My efforts were in vain: I had to tell Georgann the truth.

Georgann wept.

Monday, July 18, 1994

When I got home from the hospital, I received a notice that Nikol served me with a new restraining order. I would have to appear in court on Wednesday.

Tuesday, July 19, 1994

Hospital all day. I phoned Steven Smart from the pay phone in the lobby to request he represent me in court regarding the new restraining order. He agreed.

At 2:00, Marie made her motherly visit. I left the room as per Georgann's wishes and took a walk around New Haven to take the edge off my anger. I hoped that Marie cared enough about Georgann to realize that telling her about Nicky's restraining orders would affect her recovery. If Marie had, Georgann did not share it with me on the writing slate she kept by her side. I stayed late with Georgann to make sure everyone at home would be in bed when I got there. I had a fitful night worrying about the next day in court.

Wednesday, July 20, 1994

In court by 10:00 a.m. As before, Smart and I sat stony faced at the table as we listened to Nicky's lawyer read the allegations in the petition for the restraining order. He spoke as if he were addressing a jury with an opening statement. Marie sat in the back of the court room nodding her head and loudly uttering 'uh huh, uh huh.'

Judge T. Clark Hull was presiding again and stopped the lawyer in mid-sentence. "This is not the Supreme Court, Attorney Boombotz. (I never did get his name). You are here solely to request a restraining order not to plead a case." Essentially, if you're finished, sit down and shut up. Staring over his glasses, the judge asked Nikol, "Do you know that lady in the back?"

"She's my grandmother."

"She obviously has something to add to these proceedings. Would you like her to come forward to speak?"

My lawyer started to object, but I grabbed his arm whispering in his ear, "Let her talk, she's my best defense."

As soon as Marie stood in front of the judge, she waved the newspaper clipping of my arrest in Bedford. For his benefit, she included her usual tirade of abuse - I stole my daughter's trust money, I was a terrible cheating husband, blah, blah, blah.

Turning to my lawyer, Judge Hull asked, "Has Mr. Volpe been to trial for any of these accusations made by Mrs. Marino?"

"No, your honor."

"Mrs. Marino, would you say that if any man is guilty of such crimes that you say your son-in-law has committed, he should be locked away in prison for a very long time?"

Marie got excited. She did not realize the judge was being facetious. She cooed, "Oh, yes your honor, a very long time. I knew you'd see it my way."

If people in the courtroom had just been snickering they now began to laugh out loud. The bailiff trying to hold back his own snorts ordered silence. Judge Hull made no further comments to Marie before asking her to return to her seat. He did admonish her to be silent throughout the rest of the hearing.

"Just a moment, Mrs. Marino, I have one more question for you," said the judge looking at the charges. "It says that Mr. Volpe is your ex-son-in-law." He turned to Nikol, "How long have your mother and father been divorced?"

Nikol mumbled back, "They're not divorced."

Judge Hull shook his head before resting his chin on his hand. He asked me, "Do you have anything to say on your behalf, Mr. Volpe?"

I stood. "Your honor, these accusations are fabrications on the part of the Marinos and my older daughter to discredit me as trustee for my younger daughter's trust with the intent of having me removed so they could take over. I have never physically nor verbally abused my older daughter, and I am not divorced from my wife. Any criminal charges levied against me have yet to be addressed in a court of law." I sat down.

Judge Hull could not refrain from offering his opinion to the court. He stared directly at Nicky while speaking.

"I have little sympathy for anyone who uses the misfortune of another to exact financial advantage from that person. My compassion, in this case, is extended to Mr. Volpe whose wife is critically ill. That he must also deal, at this time, with the blatant attempts of the parents of Mrs. Volpe as well as the more heinous attempts, in my opinion, of that of his older daughter to wrest guardianship of his younger daughter's trust from her legal guardians is unspeakable. It is a sad thing for me to see a family so divided by greed. It would take ten judges half my age to sort out the dynamics behind their behavior. Unfortunately, I must issue the restraining order for the protection of all parties involved." Slamming down his gavel, Judge Hull rose and left the bench.

The only understanding Marie and Nicky came away with from the judge's words was that the restraining order was issued. They stood outside on the courtroom steps gloating as my lawyer and I left the building. Too fast for me to react, Marie ran over to me and kissed me on my cheek.

Oh, no, I knew what that meant.

13

The Trust Grab Heats Up

Thursday July 2, 1994 to Tuesday July 26, 1994

I stayed at Paul's to avoid Nicky as per Judge Hull's advice. Although I did my best to keep our family problems from Georgann, she was smart enough to pick up vibes from her mother, who visited daily, that she was up to no good. Georgann relied on past experience of how Marie acted out her animosity toward me to become even more concerned for my safety. Because she couldn't leave her hospital bed, Georgann's only alternative to protect me from her mother was to insist I never leave her side except when Marie was visiting.

Only one time when Georgann was asleep and Marie had already made her motherly visit, I thought it okay to leave her for a cigarette break and a short walk to stretch my legs. She woke, saw I was not there, looked around for a note from me, found none and buzzed for the nurse. Georgann's only method of communication was writing on the slate she kept at her bedside. On it, she begged the nurse to call Paul. I wasn't there. With mournful eyes and shaking hand, she wrote to have me paged in the hospital. I heard the page just as I was coming into the lobby. I rushed to her room and found Georgann severely agitated. I promised that I would never leave again without letting her or reception know where I would be. She sighed before giving me a small smile of relief.

The promise I made to Georgann was a small gesture if it eased her anxiety for me, but it gave me little consolation. The pressures I was dealing with from the family were trivial compared to Georgann's - I was not fighting to stay alive.

At least I didn't think so at the time.

Wednesday, July 27, 1994 and Thursday, July 28, 1994

During dinner Wednesday night, Paul said he had something special to give for me for dessert. Along with apple pie, Josephine brought out a manila folder full of letters. They were the responses from the second group of friends and business acquaintances from whom I had requested character references. They were overwhelming - fifteen out of fifteen glowing references. Over coffee, Josephine read each letter aloud; I was touched.

The next day, I delivered the character references to Daniel Seymour. He read each one before saying, "Al, these letters are going to show that if it comes down to your word or the Marinos, they lose."

"I hope you're right, Dan. I doubt Silvio could find even one person he didn't have to pay or threaten with pain of death to give him a reference."

Friday, July 29, 1994

Before I left for the hospital, I got a phone call from Mrs. Carmichael, a social worker with Danbury Child and Family Services.

"Mr. Volpe, Dr. Corsaro has registered a complaint with my office at the request of his daughter, Melissa. The complaint states that you, Mr. Volpe, have not provided the housekeeper or Melissa with enough money for their salaries or to purchase food and other items needed for the proper care of your daughter, Gabrielle Volpe. Gabrielle is your fourteen year old daughter and handicapped. Am I correct?"

"Yes, she is my daughter. She has cerebral palsy. Although I haven't spoken to Dr. Corsaro recently, I left three thousand dollars with him for Melissa's salary and for Gabby's care with the provision that if more money was needed, I would provide it. I pay the housekeeper separately."

She didn't respond to that. Instead, Mrs. Carmichael asked, "Did you go into the bathroom when Gabrielle was in the shower?"

I began to smell a big rat, and its name was Marie. "Why are you asking me about this? The report filed with the police explained the incident. I didn't realize that you were meant to get a copy of it."

She didn't answer the question. "At this time, my call is to make you aware of Dr. Corsaro's complaint and to solicit a statement from you. I have no other agenda in the matter. Thank you for your time." She hung up before I could ask any more questions.

It didn't take long for Marie to hire an attorney to handle the legal end of her scheme to take over Gabby's trust. A mob associate of Silvio's referred Marie to Nancy Boyle (not her real name). She was a Danbury attorney who had the reputation of being a barracuda divorce lawyer experienced in handling child custody matters. She was also not averse to using legal but dirty tactics.

Boyle was forty-seven; her short, fire hydrant body, although clad in designer suits, gave the appearance of a bulldog in drag rather than a trial lawyer. At first blush, Boyle bought into the Marinos claim that I was a low life piece of garbage. Corsaro's complaint with CFS constituted an emergency situation that laid the groundwork for Boyle to mastermind an ex-parte motion to have me removed as Gabby's custodian pending a formal hearing and to issue Nikol temporary custody of Gabby. An ex-parte motion provides an exception to the rules of due process allowing Nikol to petition the court without having to notify or serve the other parties involved - namely me and Georgann.

Once granted temporary custody, Nikol's eviction notice would be on hold until a formal hearing. The temporary custody would also give Boyle grounds to go to the Trust Court in Manhattan to petition that Nikol be given interim guardianship of Gabby's trust thereby removing me and Georgann completely from the picture. It was a masterful, sinister legal plan. Ex-parte is Latin for 'you're screwed, Al.' Of course, I was unaware of all this when Mrs. Carmichael called.

As usual, in her arrogance Marie overplayed her hand. On her own and without the knowledge of Boyle, she had called Mrs. Carmichael to insinuate that I had molested Gabby in the shower. When Boyle heard that Marie was shooting from the lip, she immediately put in a call to Mrs. Carmichael to urge her not to give any credence to Marie's abuse claim. Boyle offered up a lame excuse, 'Mrs. Marino is experiencing extreme duress over her daughter's illness which is clouding her judgment.' If Marie's accusation had been true, Mrs. Carmichael would be required to initiate my arrest on a child abuse charge. Boyle did not know that Mrs. Carmichael had already interviewed Nicky, Melissa and Gabby about the incident. They had all signed statements refuting Marie's claim. What Marie tried to pull with CFS should have landed her in jail. Too bad that didn't happen.

The complaint Corsaro's made to CFS on Melissa's behalf inferring I was not providing money for Gabby's care prompted me into action. It was time to fight back.

Instead of going to the hospital Friday morning, I picked up Betty. She was going to be my witness as well as take Polaroid pictures of what I intended to do. Back at my house, we took pictures of a fully stocked pantry and refrigerator holding up a newspaper to validate the date of each photo.

Melissa, Gabby and Nikol were there watching our every move without uttering a word. I had Melissa sign a receipt for the money she spent for Gabby's care and the salary she had received. There was still about fifteen hundred dollars left in Dr. Corsaro's care. I didn't understand why he failed to note that fact in his complaint to CFS. Again, I could smell Marie's paws in this pile of shit.

I tried to hug Gabby on my way out, but she pulled away from me. Betty and I left the house with no more than ten words said to either of us by my daughters or Melissa.

Before turning onto the street, I stopped to get the mail which had just been delivered. In the mail was the notice addressed to me for an interim custody hearing based on the ex-parte application Nikol had filed. The hearing was scheduled for the following week at the Probate Court in Danbury. What ex-parte application?

I headed to Smart's office after dropping Betty home. I needed some answers. I gave the notice to Smart along with copies of the character references Josephine had given to me. Smart explained that I was not required to be in attendance at the ex-parte hearing. If the judge had determined that an emergency situation was evident, I might have lost temporary custody of Gabby immediately. That not being the case, a formal interim custody hearing was scheduled for the following week. I stayed late at Smart's office strategizing and preparing for the hearing.

14

Custody Hearing 1

Saturday, July 30, 1994 to Thursday, August 4, 1994

I continued to keep a low profile by staying at Paul's at night and spending the rest of the time with Georgann. I was biding my time until the hearing.

Friday, August 5, 1994

Judge Dianne Yamin, elected Danbury's first woman probate judge in 1990, was presiding over the custody hearing. A court reporter was provided by the court to make a transcription of the proceedings. I had five of my character witnesses waiting in the Holiday Diner across the street from the courthouse in case they were needed. Smart and I were well prepared.

I was standing with Smart outside the court room when Marie, Gabby, Nikol, and Boyle got off the elevator. Initially taken aback at seeing me, Marie was quick to recover attacking me with her usual verbal harangue. Boyle shut her up fast. Boyle had not figured on me showing up at court - and with a lawyer. After she related all the Marino lies to the judge, she assumed it would be a quick no-questions-asked hearing before the judge appointed Nicky as Gabby's temporary guardian.

We entered the courtroom and took our seats at a large conference table. Already in the courtroom was Mrs. Silvert, the court appointed guardian acting on Gabby's behalf who, as a minor, could not represent herself. She sat on one side of Gabby. She was a tall, square shouldered woman in her late forties whose stern features softened only when she smiled and bent her head to talk to Gabby. Mrs. Carmichael from CFS sat on Gabby's other side. I was relieved to see that Mrs. Carmichael, in her sixties, held Gabby's hand like a loving grandmother. Nikol sat next to Boyle; Smart and I sat opposite them. Judge Yamin came in and sat at her desk in front of the table. The court stenographer was seated at a small desk by the table. A fuming Marie was asked to wait outside the courtroom. I was hoping my narrow-eyed stare directed at Nikol would unnerve, but she never once looked in my direction.

It was obvious by the look of alarm momentarily crossing Boyle's face that she had expected the hearing to be more informal. When Boyle learned that I had five character witnesses ready and waiting to testify on my behalf, and she almost wet herself.

Pulling herself together, Boyle presented Nikol's claims to the judge; the stenographer dutifully recorded every word. Here's the short list: I was an abusive father; an alcoholic; a gambler; and a womanizer; I had never been a decent husband or father; I hadn't worked for twenty years, because I lived off my wife's earnings and my daughter's trust from which I had stolen two million dollars; and, I had no friends, because everyone hated me.

Given my appalling character, Boyle asserted that it was evident I was morally unfit to be Gabby's guardian. It was unfortunate that Mrs. Volpe was physically unable to appear in court, continued Boyle, otherwise she would have corroborated Miss Volpe's claims. Furthermore, it was possible that Mrs. Volpe would never be able to care for her daughter given the severity of her illness. Therefore, Miss Volpe should be awarded temporary guardianship for her younger sister.

If this was tough for Gabby to hear, she made no sign.

Boyle first order was to question Mrs. Carmichael. She asked. "Can you address the complaint made by Dr. Corsaro on behalf of his daughter, Melissa, that there was no food or money in the house to pay Melissa's salary or to care for Gabby's needs?"

Mrs. Carmichael replied, "Dr. Corsaro phoned me at my office on July 29th to inform me that his daughter, Melissa, was concerned that the financial needs of Gabrielle currently in her charge due to Mr. Volpe's absence were not being addressed by Mr. Volpe. I told Dr. Corsaro that I would relay his daughter's concern to Mr. Volpe which I did by phone that day."

Boyle had no further questions for Mrs. Carmichael.

Smart spoke up. "Mrs. Carmichael, did you personally investigate the validity of Dr. Corsaro's complaint?"

"No. I was only required to make Mr. Volpe aware of the complaint Dr. Corsaro lodged against him. It was not up to me to determine whether the complaint was true or false. It is my understanding that is the reason for this hearing."

"You are indeed correct, Mrs. Carmichael." Smart brought out the dated photos that Betty and I had taken showing both refrigerators and our big pantry stocked to the brim. He also presented the signed and dated receipts I had obtained from Betty and Melissa verifying that payment for their services was current, and that they were aware that there was reserve money available if needed.

"As you can see by the photos and receipts, Mrs. Carmichael, Dr. Corsaro's complaint was unfounded. Mr. Volpe does not know the reason Melissa asked her father to call you." Mrs. Carmichael nodded and gave Gabby's hand a slight squeeze.

Given the evidence refuting Corsaro's complaint, Boyle hoped to deep silence Marie's other accusation that I had molested Gabby in the shower.

Smart pressed on. "Is it true, Mrs. Carmichael, that Mrs. Marino told you via a telephone conversation that Mr. Volpe entered the bathroom when his daughter, Gabrielle, was taking a shower with the intention of molesting her?"

Before she could answer, Boyle objected, "Your honor, Mrs. Marino has withdrawn that accusation."

"Mrs. Carmichael," continued Smart, "do you have something to add?"

"Yes, I do. Mrs. Marino did indeed call me to report this alleged incident with Gabby. Any accusation concerning the abuse of a minor is taken very seriously by CFS. It was my duty to follow up that charge. I personally went to Mr. Volpe's house and interviewed both of Mr. Volpe's daughters as well as Melissa Corsaro."

"What was your finding?"

"All three young women informed me that Mr. Volpe has never acted in any way inappropriately with Gabrielle. In fact, if he had not come home at that time and heard Gabrielle screaming for someone to help her, she would have been scalded in the shower, because she was unattended by either Melissa Corsaro or her sister."

Not only had another claim gone bust, but it was now evident that Melissa and Nikol were the guilty parties, not me. Boyle was running out of ammunition.

Judge Yamin thanked Mrs. Carmichael for her statement. Her furrowed brow and visible stiffening in her chair were signs that the judge was beginning to see a pattern developing.

Nikol was up next. It was Boyle's intention to portray Nicky and Gabby as loving sisters who were being exposed to a horrible, abusive father while their mother lay critically ill in hospital. Of course, after Mrs. Carmichael's account that there was no evidence to support the claim that I had ever abused or neglected Gabby, Boyle was disconcerted, but she had to press on in the same vein she had begun.

Boyle began, "Nikol's main concern is Gabby's welfare. She wants to protect her little sister from any further neglect by their father. For the past four months, Mr. Volpe has rarely been home claiming that he was at the hospital with his wife or staying with friends. He left the primary care of Gabrielle to Nikol."

As I sat there, my stomach began to churn because of the lies Nikol had Boyle believing. I looked over at Gabby who was sitting with her head bent down on her chest. Thank God Mrs. Carmichael still held her hand! The memory of what CI Bob told me the night he saw Gabby pleading on her knees, 'Please, Nicky, don't do this to Daddy,' and Nicky responding with, 'Shut up, you fuckin' little retard' filled me with misery.

"Nikol, how long have your mother and father been married?"

"I don't know."

I spoke up, "Twenty-eight years." Smart asked me to hush.

"How long have your mother and father been divorced?"

Nicky mumbled, "They're not divorced. My grandmother told me they were getting divorced."

It was obvious by the confounded look on Boyle's face that she had assumed Georgann and I were already divorced.

Boyle continued, "Miss Volpe, how often does your father drink? What does he drink and where, at home or in bars?"

Nikol became confused. She didn't know which question to answer first. Finally, she said, "I don't know," then blurted out, "He doesn't drink."

Boyle was squirming. Her examination was not going as she had expected. It was obvious that she had not prepared Nikol for testimony. Boyle decided to quit questioning Nikol.

It was Smart's turn to question Nicky, "To the best of your knowledge, Miss Volpe, did your father come home every night and sleep in the same room with your mother?"

"Not since my mother became sick."

"So, prior to your mother's hospitalization, your father was home every night?"

"I guess. I was away at college for several years."

"But, when you were home, as far as you were aware, was he there every night?"

"Yeah."

"Thank you. I understand that you attempted to place a restraining order on your father. The judge did not grant the order but suggested that he spend as little time as possible in your house to avoid any confrontations. Might that be the reason your father stays at his friends or at the hospital?"

"I don't know."

"Do you have personal knowledge of your father ever abusing your mother before your mother's illness?"

"I saw him push my mother once."

"When was that?"

"I don't remember. I was little. My grandmother told me he did."

"But, you have no personal knowledge he ever physically abused your mother."

"No."

So much for me being a lousy husband.

"According to your grandmother, you've been Gabrielle's main caregiver since your mother's illness."

Nicky nodded, "Yeah."

"Can you tell me the names of Gabrielle's therapists? Also, can you tell the court something about your sister's special needs?"

Nicky sat dumbfounded; it was obvious she knew next to nothing about Gabby's therapists, resources, or special needs. As far as she was concerned, it was Melissa's job to take care of the 'little retard.'

"I don't know any of their names or all my sister's special needs. I know she has cerebral palsy."

Smart went on, "You are also aware that your father hired a live-in caregiver and housekeeper to provide for Gabby needs since her mother's illness so that he could devote most of his time to be with her at the hospital. It was the caregiver and the housekeeper, not you, Miss Volpe, who were responsible for Gabrielle's main care. How many times did you take Gabrielle to her doctors and physical therapy appointments?"

"None."

"How many times did you make breakfast, lunch or dinner for Gabrielle?

"I got pizza a couple of times a week."

"Other than that?"

"None."

Smart let it drop. "I want to address Miss Volpe's assertion that her father has not worked for over twenty years. The fact is Mr. Volpe has owned a number of retail and wholesale clothing businesses both in The Bronx and in Westchester." He held up a 1972 clipping about Nikol's Tot Boutique with Nicky's picture as a baby. He held up another clipping dated 1985 of me hosting a charity fashion show and a more recent article showing me accepting a Chamber of Commerce business award in Katonah.

"Mr. Volpe sold his interests in the clothing stores three years ago at a considerable profit but retained his silk screening business. Were you aware of this, Miss Volpe?"

"I guess."

"Thank you, Miss Volpe, I have no further questions."

Boyle was not prepared to hear any of this. This custody hearing was supposed to be a walk in the park, a no questions asked, slam dunk custody grab. She now realized that she was basing her case on the pack of lies told to her by the Marino clan.

"Your honor, I want to address one last accusation presented by Miss Volpe which states that Mr. Volpe has no friends, because he is universally hated. This accusation may not have any relevance in these proceedings, but it does reflect on Mr. Volpe's character. I have a number of written character references I would like to introduce into the court record. Please take note of the letter from Mark Hollander, a vice president at Smith Barney. Besides given him an impeccable character reference, Hollander extolled Mr. Volpe's prudent overseeing of Gabby's financial security dealing with expenses charged to the trust. I also have five persons who wrote references waiting in attendance outside the courtroom should you require their statements."

Across the table, Smart laid out copies of the references portraying me as a different person than the one Boyle and her clients wanted the court to believe. The judge and scanned through the references while Boyle sat fuming like a bulldog in lipstick.

My attorney continued. "If the court permits, I would like to introduce some further evidence into the court record regarding Mr. Volpe's good character."

He removed a number of newspaper articles from his briefcase and placed them on the table for Judge Yamin to examine. The articles were about charitable events I had attended, press releases for the businesses I was involved in over the years, and my painting exhibition. Judge Yamin scanned the articles.

Smart went on, "Mr. and Mrs. Volpe are co-trustees of Gabrielle's trust. If Mrs. Volpe should succumb to her tragic illness, Mr. Volpe would remain sole trustee of their daughter's four million dollar trust. Nikol Volpe filed a Removal of Trust petition two weeks ago in New York and issued Mr. and Mrs. Volpe a subpoena to have both her mother and father removed as trustees and replaced by herself and Marie Marino. Mr. Volpe hired the law firm of Harvey E. Corn in New York to address the petition. Mr. Corn is has requested a forensic accounting of the trust."

Judge Yamin turned to Boyle. "Are you aware of this four million dollar trust fund and the Removal of Trust petition?"

Boyle snapped back. "Yes, your honor, but it is six million dollars, not four. It is my client's assertion that Mr. Volpe removed two million dollars of the trust illegally."

Silence stole the show. Judge Yamin realized there was a lot more going on here than a custody battle.

"I was not made aware that such a large trust was involved in this custody hearing nor of the allegation that Mr. Volpe illegally removed funds from it. To provide time for me to have this trust issue researched; I am going to adjourn today's hearing to continue at a later date"

Smart spoke up. "Your honor, before this proceeding is adjourned, I respectfully request that Sally Quinn be allowed to give a statement. Since Mrs. Volpe is hospitalized and incapable of speaking for herself, Mrs. Quinn, as her closest friend, asked that she be allowed to provide some insight into how Mrs. Volpe's might view this hearing."

Judge Yamin agreed.

Sally, who was waiting outside the courtroom, was called. She stated her name and address for the record. No one, including me, was prepared for what Sally was about to say.

"I have been Georgann's closest friend for over twenty years. She has honored me with her complete trust, and I have kept all her confidences. After Gabby was awarded a settlement in the malpractice suit, Georgann told me she made the decision to move to Danbury to remove Gabby from any negative influence her mother might have on Gabby. Georgann believed Mrs. Marino was the cause of her elder daughter's behavior problems and instigated the hatred Nikol exhibited toward her father. Georgann also blamed her mother for creating sibling rivalry causing Nicky's cruel treatment of Gabby, but Georgann could not find it in her heart to ask Nicky to move out nor was she able to keep her mother from interfering in her family's lives. Even with their faults, Georgann loved Nicky and her mother unconditionally - unfortunately to the detriment of her marriage. Marie put terrible pressures on Georgann to divorce Al, but she would not. Instead, Georgann made every effort to protect Al as best she could from the Marinos brutality."

Sally related the incident that occurred in St. Thomas just weeks before Georgann became ill. "Georgann was consumed with fear for Al's safety. She told me that her mother had gone completely overboard vowing to have Al killed if she didn't divorce him and get him off the trust. In the past, Georgann was able to resist her mother's persistent goading as just jealous rantings, but this time she took Marie seriously. She knew her mother and father had Mafia connections, and Georgann believed Marie's threat was not an idle warning."

Judge Yamin and Mrs. Silvert were astounded by Sally's narration. I think I saw their jaws drop - mine definitely did. I knew Marie hated me, but until this moment, I had not realized the intensity of emotional stress she was placing on Georgann.

Boyle cynically interjected, "You don't really think Georgann believed that her parents would have Al killed?"

Sally glared over at Boyle, "I know Georgann absolutely believed that her mother was capable of having Al killed or, at least, physically harmed if she didn't divorce him. Georgann was sick with fear. The first night she spent in Danbury Hospital, she called to beg me to watch over Gabby and Al until she got home. She made me and Sue, another good friend of hers, promise to never leave Gabby alone with her mother, Donna, or Nicky until then. Those were her very last words to me. I swear to God as my witness that I am telling the truth. To my shame and regret, Sue and I have not been able to honor Georgann's wishes. The Marinos threatened us and our families with harm if we went near Georgann or tried to contact her or interfere in any way with their relationship with Gabby."

The room was pin-drop quiet except for the faint clicking of the stenographer's typing. Judge Yamin and Mrs. Silvert were stunned to silence; Nikol tried to look bored; Gabby clutched Mrs. Carmichael's hand; and me, I grieved. I was totally unaware of how much torment Georgann had been suffering on my account. As long as the Marinos left me alone, I was fine. Again, readers, you are probably saying 'typical of Al the Jerk.'

Judge Yamin thanked Sally for her moving narrative of Georgann's confidences. She turned to Smart and requested him to provide her with information on Gabby's Trust as soon as possible. Judge Yamin also asked Mrs. Silvert to hire a forensic psychologist to interview Nikol, Gabby, and me. She had no jurisdiction to request that for Marie. Judge Yamin adjourned the ex-parte hearing with instructions that the hearing would reconvene in three weeks once she had examined the trust records and the psychologist's report.

Marie was waiting in the parking lot. She did not know what had taken place in the hearing, which, thank God, had backfired on her. Boyle's underhanded legal tactics and Marie's assertions didn't pass the smell test. I wished I was a fly on the wall when Boyle told Marie what had happened.

Splatt!

15

Marie's Revenge

I went directly to my house following the hearing. I figured that when Boyle informed Marie of the court disaster it would take a while for the screaming to stop and me enough time to gather the trust records Judge Yamin requested. My keys didn't open any of the three entry doors - the locks had been changed. I broke the glass on the back door to get in which triggered the alarm - my code didn't work - changed, too. The security company called on the alarm intercom asking for the password - also changed. When I couldn't give it to them, they called the police.

I waited in the driveway for the police to show up. The officers from the Danbury Police Department and I were on a first name basis by now, but, surprisingly, two officers I didn't know got out of the patrol car. They asked me for some identification. I showed them my license with this address and gave them an expurgated version of the ex-parte hearing initiated by Nikol and my in-laws to have me illegally evicted from the house. My family assumed the judge would rule in their favor and had already changed the locks and alarm codes without my knowledge. Once the officers ascertained that I had a legitimate reason to be there, they looked at each other, shrugged and handed me back my license - not police business. They left.

I called the alarm company from my car phone. Eddie, the owner, personally came to the house. He showed me the note allegedly signed by me which authorized the code number and password changes. Someone had forged my signature. I didn't have to wonder who since the new password was 'Marie'. How pathetic. Eddie hooked me up with new keys, but I told him not to change the alarm and password codes made by Marie. I didn't to alert my daughter and in-laws that I was aware of illegal actions nor did I want them to know that I could still get into the house.

I moved quickly. I wanted to go into the house, gather the financial records I needed and out before anyone showed up. I kept all our personal papers in a fireproof file cabinet in an upstairs bedroom I used as an office. I never thought to lock the cabinet and when I opened it, I found – nothing not even dust – wiped clean. All the files were gone. I took the time to search the rest of the house to see if anything else was missing. In my haste to get the files, I hadn't noticed that my paintings had been removed from the wall on the staircase. Searching the house further, I found personal items - even the

'Big Al' coffee mug Georgann brought back for me from St. Thomas - gone. I scanned through the family album we kept on the living room coffee table. My face had been ripped or blacked out of every photo. I recognized Marie's signature, because, twenty years earlier, she had cut out my face from our entire wedding album.

I wasn't going to take this lying down. After I locked up, I went to the police station and filed a report claiming destruction of personal property and theft of the legal documents. I didn't include in the report that I knew took them. No sense in giving Marie any warning. Then, I called Smart to inform him of the theft. He couldn't believe it. Maybe now the realization that the Marinos would stop at nothing to gain control of Gabby's trust was beginning to sink into his skull.

The Danbury police contacted the Marinos who, of course, denied any knowledge of the theft. Marie told the police, "The housekeeper and lots of other people have keys to the house. My granddaughters and I don't trust anyone who is friends with my criminal son-in-law so we changed the locks and the alarm code to keep those people out."

Those people! I guess she meant me and Betty, because we were the only ones who had keys. I waited until the next morning and made sure everyone was out of the house before going back to give it a more thorough once over. I didn't find anything else missing.

My ever-vigilant neighbor Bob called me on the house phone as soon as he saw my car pull into the driveway. "Al, I'm glad I caught you at home. Are you moving? I would hate to see you go."

"No, Bob, but I'm staying at a friend's until Georgann gets home. My in-laws and Nicky are not making it easy for me to be here. Why are you asking if I'm moving?"

"I saw a red van in your driveway yesterday morning. A couple of guys were loading stuff into it."

"It was my stuff, but it wasn't me who hired the van. Thanks for letting me know." Coincidently, my brother in-law, Dennis, owned a red van.

Saturday, August 6 through Wednesday, August 24, 1994

With the ex-parte hearing blowing up in her face, Marie's vengeance went into full swing. She recruited Silvio as her willing enforcer. Within days, all my new character references, as well as Dr. Corsaro, were threatened with physical harm to themselves and their families if they continued on my behalf. Although they all filed police reports nothing happened - Silvio was too mob wise to make explicit threats, and the police knew the Mafia had invisible fingers in many pies. Marie wanted to fire Boyle, who had been given a copy of the references, but could not; Boyle knew too much about Marie's illegal attempt to use the court system to get rid of me. Marie had no recourse but to keep Boyle as their attorney – with gag restrictions. To make sure Boyle kept her mouth shut, Nikol threw garbage on her lawn and threatened Boyle's daughter – again with no witnesses.

Melissa Corsaro used the excuse that she had to get back to college early and quit; she and her father bowed out of the picture. Dr. Banshek resigned as Gabby's therapist. Word was out; anyone who interfered with the Marinos grab for Gabby's money was a 'person who is a problem.'

With Melissa leaving, I had no choice but to ask Marie to care for Gabby full time. I knew Marie would threaten any nanny I hired, and I couldn't jeopardize the well being of another person. Again, for whatever virago she was to me, I could not deny that she was a very good grandmother. Also, Gabby made it evident that she preferred to be with Marie than with me. Unfortunately, Gabby living in New York removed her from Connecticut jurisdiction. This decision on my part to allow Marie to take Gabby to New York would eventually bite me hard in the ass.

Marie could not admit to Boyle that she had stolen the financial records. She insisted that I had taken the records to cover up a stolen money trail. Still, Marie was beside herself with fear that Georgann would find out what she'd done. She told Georgann," Al burned all of the trust files to cover his crooked ass. The judge froze Gabby's trust assets so he couldn't touch the money any more, but he's still got the two million he stole. They're gonna find out where he hid the money and when they do, the cops will arrest him and put him jail. I warned you years ago about that bum and that he would get caught one of these days."

Georgann told me that she even though she didn't believe a word of her mother's accusations, they had upset her. She knew I hadn't stolen even a penny from Gabby's trust. Her mother was lying, of course. It was the same deceitful fairytale Marie told to Georgann for the past three years only now, Georgann weak and unable to talk, was incapable of acting as my defender.

The following week, again without Boyle's knowledge, Marie brought the nephew of one of Silvio's Mafia buddies to the hospital. Marie told Georgann, "Mr. Bottigliere is a lawyer. He's gonna tell Mark Hollander to send some blank checks from Gabby's trust to the hospital for you to sign. I'm gonna need the money to take care of Gabby." Of course, that wasn't going to happen since the assets of Gabby's trust were frozen from everyone accessing them, but court orders couldn't stop Marie in her invariable ignorance from trying.

Since Gabby was no longer at my house, I had no reason to go there. Betty, bless her, took the animals home with her and came every few days to check on the house. CI Bob also watched the house. I stayed at Paul's when I wasn't at the hospital.

Marie kept my poor daughter cloistered in her house and never brought Gabby again to visit her mother. Georgann knew Marie was poisoning Gabby against me as she had done with Nikol but was powerless to do anything about it. If she wanted to keep her family together, she needed to stay alive and so did I. She still knew nothing of the Marinos efforts to take over Gabby's trust, and I wasn't about to tell her. That knowledge would only cause Georgann greater anxiety for my safety.

I was deeply troubled. How long could I keep up this charade? I actually entertained conflicting thoughts of suicide – a cowardly escape - and retaliation the Marino way. Only my faith in God and Georgann's need for me to be there for her kept these destructive thoughts in check.

In desperation to protect myself, I filed restraining orders at the Danbury Court Clerk's office against the Marinos and the Weigarts to keep them away from me. Unfortunately, the Sheriff's jurisdiction did not allow him to serve the orders in New York. He would have to wait to serve them when the Marinos and the Weigarts came to Danbury for the custody hearing on August 25th.

When I told Smart that Marie hired Bottigliere, he fumed. Watching Smart get upset was like watching a cartoon character on a sugar high - only with expletives.

Waving his arms in the air, he shrilled, "Those fucking people are insane! First, they get that Boyle broad to push to have you and Georgann removed as trustees. Now, this other shithead lawyer of the Marinos – if he really is one - tells Georgann that he represents her as trustee and demands she request Hollander to send blank checks to her room! Who the fuck is Bottigliere? I'm Georgann's lawyer. I represent you and Georgann in the trust removal proceedings - neither this jerk nor anyone else." Smart was really working up to a full blown rampage. He continued, "These fuckers aren't going to get away with this! You and I are going to Manhattan Probate Court tomorrow to get me legal power of attorney to administer the trust through a separate account until the settling of the forensic accounting. I'll be at your house by 7:30 tomorrow morning."

"I will do anything you ask as long as we leave Georgann out of it. I won't allow anything to upset her more than her mother is already doing brilliantly."

"She's still going to have to sign a statement giving me authority to administer the trust."

"Ok, Steve, I'll do it for Gabby's sake."

"Don't forget, Al, because she can't appear in person you will need to have two witnesses sign Georgann's statement in front of a notary to insure that it is a legal document."

I went to Yale as soon as I left Smart's office. I had to tell Georgann the truth. She was profoundly heartbroken but admitted we had no other choice if we were going to stop her family's take over. I outlined what Steve wanted her to put in the statement going over each point trying to soft soap it in an effort to keep Georgann calm. She became frustrated with me and grabbed the writing pad out of my hand. The following statement is Georgann's words exactly:

1. No one, including my parents, have any right to request an accounting or anything else regarding Gabby's trust … it's none of their business. They don't care about Gabby's welfare but are only interested in controlling her money.

2. My daughter, Nikol, isn't capable of running her own life let alone of being in charge of anyone else's.

3. There is no basis for any accounting or questioning the fitness of Al as trustee or guardian of Gabrielle. My mother is a troublemaker and my daughter, Nikol, is a product of her brainwashing.

4. We moved to Connecticut to prevent my parents from poisoning Gabrielle's mind, but obviously, we failed. They tried to get their hands on Gabby's money by asking for expensive watches, loans for illegal investments, or by using her trust to pay for vacations. They told Gabby that it was her money and her house, and that she didn't have to listen to her father.

This is my statement and my wishes. I'll have more to say when I recover. I love my parents very much and plead with them to stop this foolishness.

Signed: Georgann Volpe

Georgann handed me the pad, tears running down her face. I went to the reception desk and asked Mrs. Scanlon and the nurse at the desk to come into Georgann's room to witness Georgann's signature and to request a notary from the legal department. I held Georgann's hand as we waited for them to show up.

I read each point aloud and Georgann nodded in agreement. When I had finished the list, I gave the pad back to Georgann to sign. Once they heard what they were being asked to witness, both the nurse and Mrs. Scanlon bolted from the room before Georgann could sign the statement. With nothing to notarize the notary left, too. I don't know if the mad dash for the exit was out of fear of losing their jobs by getting involved in a legal issue that was not hospital business or out of fear of losing their lives because of the Marinos. All the pain Georgann suffered writing these hurtful words against her parents and daughter was for naught.

Smart and I went to the Manhattan Probate Court the next day with Georgann's statement anyway. Fortunately, the court accepted Smart's explanation that Georgann was unable to provide a witnessed statement because of her illness and allowed my signature as standalone. The court authorized Smart power of attorney to issue checks through a separate account from Gabby's trust as long as they were used solely for her expenses.

Marie was enraged that my attorney and not her bogus one obtained the right to issue checks from her granddaughter's account. She lost more than a legal battle. Not only was I not in jail, but Georgann was now fully aware of her mother's attempts to gain control of the trust. Marie decided that it was time for her to take matters into her own hands. Quoting from the Godfather movie, she said, "Fuck this legal bullshit. Just kill him!"

Once I was dead, Marie was confident she could win Georgann back to her sordid way of thinking. After all, wasn't Marie the most loving and caring of mother's to her princess!.

Silvio went along with Marie's conspiracy by throwing in some heavy muscle and a few bucks to contemptible lawyers to take pot shots at me. He figured I'd either run out of money defending myself, do something stupid, or be scared off. But, when that didn't happen, Silvio drew the line on Marie's insistence that only one solution remained – I needed to be dead, dead, dead. He didn't want to chance getting caught up in a possible murder investigation. Silvio was not about to spend his golden years back in Greenhaven U because of his crazy wife, four million or not. He put the word out - hands off Al.

Even Donna was alarmed by her mother's out-of-control behavior. She actually called Paul, "Tell Al to keep looking over his shoulder. My mother is berserk. She's cursing Silvio and Jimmy, because they won't put a hit out on him. She said she's going get someone on her own."

Over the years, I had become inured to Marie's threats, but this time it was different. When Georgann was well, Marie didn't have a chance at getting to Gabby's money nor would she risk losing Georgann's love if I came to harm. If Georgann died, I was the only obstacle standing in Marie's way to the pot of gold.

In those days, the streets of New Haven were a hotbed of drive-by shootings and muggings at night. It was a three block walk from the hospital to the dimly lit lot where I parked my car. I knew I would have been an easy target for a junkie or some bum to grab at $100 from Marie to stick a knife in my back. When I left the hospital at night, I stayed alert to everything around me, my head swiveling like a hoot owl. I walked in the middle of the street, never on the sidewalk or close to buildings; I carried a baseball bat. If a bum or panhandler came within twenty feet of me, I raised the bat in combat stance to threaten him off. I parked at the end of a row of cars in the lot so I didn't have to stand between parked cars. I never failed to check out the back seat before opening the driver's side door in case anyone was hiding there. I figured that if they were going to get me, it would be at night either in the street or in the dark lot.

All those years as Silvio's bag man had taught me something.

16

Restrained

Thursday, August 25, 1994

Paul and I sat with Smart in the clerk's office waiting for the second custody hearing to begin. Smart had subpoenaed Paul as a character witness just in case he was needed. I told my other character witnesses not to show up given the threats the Marinos made to them and their families, but Smart was armed with their sworn statements.

Boyle, Marie, Donna, and Nicky were standing together in the hall outside the court room when the Danbury Sheriff got off the elevator. He came into the clerk's office and over to me. When I pointed out the unholy threesome, he went up to them, identified himself and passed out the restraining orders I had filed. As soon a she saw what the paper was, Marie became so enraged she tried to slap the sheriff in the face. He managed to block her hand but couldn't stop her from pushing past him and rushing into the clerk's office to get at me. Paul and the sheriff pulled her off me before she could claw my face with her talons.

Boyle stepped in. Using the same sympathy ploy she had used on Mrs. Carmichael, Boyle pleaded Marie's case to the Sheriff (tiny violin).

"Mrs. Marino is devastated by her daughter's critical condition," Boyle began, "The trauma of having to go to court repeatedly in an attempt to legally protect her granddaughters from their abusive father is having a detrimental effect on Mrs. Marino's emotional state, and she cannot always control her actions."

I had to hand it to Boyle. She was so good at stirring up compassion for Marie's phony plight that the sheriff didn't arrest her on the spot. He allowed Boyle to take her to a bench in the hall. Marie went docilely – she knew how to act like a meek, old lady when it suited her.

Unfortunately, the sheriff also informed me that the hearing for the restraining orders I had taken out was scheduled for 11:00 am that morning and required my presence. Given the conflict, Smart went to Judge Yamin's office and was able to prevail upon her to postpone the custody hearing another two weeks.

Paul and I grabbed a coffee at Dunkin' Donuts before going to the hearing. Smart joined us. Marie, Donna, and Nikol (I starting referring to them as Moe, Larry and Curly) were already in the courtroom. A judge (loss of memory) other than Yamin presided over this hearing. He called my name, and I went in front of his desk. The judge asked me why I wanted a restraining order.

"Your honor," I said, "Three weeks ago during a court proceeding regarding custody of my younger daughter, Judge Yamin requested financial records concerning my daughter's trust. I went to my house to gather the financial records, but discovered that the door locks and alarm system code had been changed without my permission. I called the head of the security company who came to the house, let me in and gave me a new set of keys and the new password and alarm code. In the house, I discovered that all my financial records as well as personal property had been removed. My neighbor saw a red van pull up to my house the day before and watched two men load the van with items from the house. They had to have keys, the password and the alarm code to get into house. Coincidently, my brother-in-law owns a red van. Although I willingly gave care for my younger daughter to my in-laws in Westchester to allow me to spend time with my wife who is critically ill in Yale-New Haven hospital, they are not allowing me to contact my daughter nor are they taking her to the hospital to visit her mother. In addition, your honor, I applied for and was granted an eviction order to have my older daughter removed from my house over thirty days ago. She is still living there. It was she who authorized the changing of the locks and alarm code by forging my name."

Before the judge could ask the three stooges to respond to my narrative, they began mouthing off at him. Their barrage was unintelligible but loud, and he was unable to get them to shut up no matter how much he banged his gavel. Their protests pissed off the judge so much that he upheld my restraining orders barring them from the house. He ordered a police escort to accompany Nikol to the house and to supervise the removal of her belongings. He also ordered that Gabby be returned to Danbury. The judge slammed his gavel down, and with a nasty look at the unholy three, got up and left the courtroom.

Marie shouted after him, "Get back in here, you. I'm not finished." Too bad he hadn't heard her or she would have been charged with contempt. Another wish not granted.

The authority of judges and sheriffs meant nothing to Marie. Smart, Paul and I had just left the courtroom when Marie came charging out ready to curse and spit at me. She frightened my attorney so much that he scrambled into the elevator just before the door closed leaving me and Paul in the hall to fend for ourselves. Thank goodness the court security officers heard her screams and were able to restrain Marie long enough for me to escape intact. Paul and I didn't wait around to see what the cops did with her. Instead, we went directly to my house to wait for Nikol and the police escort. Ten minutes after we got there, the cops showed up, Nikol a few minutes later. They watched Nicky as she packed up her things; took her house keys and then gave them to me before following her car to the New York state line in Brewster. Not a word passed between Nicky and me. I called the security office to have them come and change the locks and security code.

What an insane day! Paul made coffee while I got some more clothes together to take back to his house. Even though the house was empty, I couldn't bear to be there alone. The house and the animals were in the capable hands of Betty.

Friday, August 26, 1994

Before going to Smart's office to discuss the postponed custody hearing, I stopped by Betty's to give her a new set of house keys and the security code. "You don't have to pick up after Nicky anymore – she's gone. Also, the Marinos won't be around to tell you how to do your job. I got them all slapped with restraining orders."

"That's a relief. What about Gabby? You know I would love to take care of her."

"You're a good person, Betty. When Marie brings her back to Danbury, I'll let you know. There is no one I would trust more than you to care for Gabby. The restraining orders should keep you safe." I hoped.

"I'll take care of her like my own granddaughter."

"I know you will, Betty." With the worry for Gabby's care off my plate, I headed for Smart's office.

Smart was still shaking from yesterday's events at court. His conservative New England law firm specialized in real estate closings, DUIs, wills, and simple probates. They were ill prepared to deal with the likes of my in-laws or with their corrupt lawyers. Although Smart had not yet received the Silvio Marino variety of encouragement to withdraw as my attorney, he (and I) knew it was only a matter of time. Fearful of future retaliation, he bowed out as my Danbury attorney. We settled our account, and shook hands as friends before I left his office with my legal records under my arm.

In my sinking canoe battling the rapids, I had no choice but to keep paddling. Fortunately, Smart, against his better judgment but feeling remorse for abandoning me, referred me to another law firm. At the time, Pinney Payne was the oldest and largest law firm in Danbury. I called and scheduled an informal meeting at a Chinese restaurant in Danbury with Attorney Chris Walters.

Over Moo Goo Gai Pan, Chris scanned the legal files I had brought with me. As we ate, I filled him in. I told him about Smart's gaining power of attorney for Gabby's trust to prevent the Marinos from getting access to the funds; about my criminal charges in Bedford handled by Seymour; about hiring Corn to oversee the forensic accounting of Gabby's trust; and about the Marinos practically kidnapping my daughter as part of their conspiracy to take over her trust. Even though everything I said was true, voicing it aloud sounded crazy even to me. I'm sure Walters questioned my sanity, but he said he would take the case anyway and represent me in the Connecticut custody matter.

The truth was beginning to dawn on Boyle. Before he backed out as my attorney, Boyle had phoned Smart to confide in him that she knew Marie's claim that I had stolen money from Gabby's trust was false. Although misled, Boyle was obligated to act on the behalf of her client by using any legal means available to her to remove me from the trust. How sad it must have been for Boyle (although my sympathy for her was minimal) to have to accompany Marie to the hospital to pressure Georgann into signing divorce papers.

"Sweetheart," Marie, crocodile tears and all phony compassion, said, "Al had the Danbury police throw Nicky and Gabby out of the house. I had to take them in, poor things. What kind of father does that to his own children? I don't know how you stayed married to that man all these years."

Georgann wrote, "I don't believe you, Mom. Al is a very loving father."

"That's what you think. He's nothing but a user. Boyle, show Georgann the restraining orders and eviction notice. He's got the house all to himself now so he can bring his bimbos there anytime he wants. Get rid of the bum, Georgann."

Boyle showed Georgann the court orders. Still, Georgann refused to sign divorce papers. When Marie's character defamation of me didn't work with Georgann, Boyle tried another approach.

"Mrs. Volpe, if you sign these divorce papers, Al won't be liable for your medical bills, because the Marinos will assume the responsibility. Besides that, my client is willing to offer Mr. Volpe a two hundred thousand dollar settlement once the divorce is final. Please believe me," Boyle leaned over and whispered to Georgann out of Marie's hearing, "it's the best thing you can do for Al. He'll have money to start over and no harm will come to him, I promise."

Still, Georgann refused to sign. Sometimes, the only defense is to lie still and remain quiet like a rabbit being hunted by jackals. I wouldn't have blamed her if she did sign just to stop their badgering, but Georgann was smarter than both these swine. Instead, to appease her mother, she signed a medical power of attorney making Marie her major health care agent. Removing me from that responsibility fed Marie's need to have some control over Georgann's life if not Gabby's trust. Also, Georgann was a pragmatist. She knew that I would never be able handle an end of life decision should it become necessary. Another bite-you-in-the ass decision, but this time it was going to bounce back on Georgann. (Spoilers)

Despite some street savvy, I was totally unprepared for the intricacies of the legal system in which I had become embroiled. I hung on to the naive belief that justice triumphed over evil, but the sewer rats that called themselves my family were gnawing off pieces of my heart. They could drag out their legal bullshit until I was financially drained. By taking Gabby to New York, they removed her from Connecticut's legal jurisdiction; I could do nothing to get her back other than file criminal charges in New York for kidnapping. More lawyers, more money. And, what good would it do? Even if she were returned to me, I knew the Marinos would threaten any caregiver I hired. Whose life would I be willing to risk for my daughter? More distressing to me was the knowledge that Gabby did not want to be with me. Without Georgann, this was more than I could bear. But, how much more stress worrying about me and Gabby could Georgann take? I had no answers; all I could do was press on and pray for Georgann's recovery.

17

Hearing 2

First three weeks of September, 1994

I had to tell Georgann that Gabby was being kept a virtual prisoner by her grandmother. Worse, it was Gabby who refused to see me or to even talk to me on the phone. Georgann's sorrow tore me apart.

Out of desperation, I asked Mrs. Carmichael for help. "Even though the court ordered my in-laws to return my daughter to me, they refuse and won't even let me speak to her. If they brought Gabby to Yale, I could have the order upheld. To prevent this, my in-laws are denying my daughter her right and need to see her mother. Georgann is so upset that it is affecting her recovery. Can't you do something to help me?"

"I'm sorry, Mr. Volpe, but CFS has no jurisdiction in Westchester. All I can tell you is that Gabby is being well cared for by her grandparents."

Small consolation.

I made an appointment with Mrs. Silvert to give her the updated information about the forensic accounting for Gabby's trust along with my new attorney's contact information. I wanted to get Mrs. Silvert on my side so I thought it couldn't hurt my case to bring along our family photo album to show her. Even though my face was blacked out, it was obvious I was the man in most of the photos. She scanned through the pictorial summary of my family's life together. She looked at photos of my daughters' births, their birthday parties, Christmases, vacations, pool parties, Nicky's dance recitals, teaching Nicky to ski, taking Gabby horseback riding, etc. - all revealing that I was an involved husband and father.

"These are lovely family photos, Mr. Volpe. Thank you for showing them to me, but I don't think they will have much bearing on your case. It is a shame they were ruined by the removal of your face."

"I can thank my older daughter and mother-in-law for defacing me. I do realize the photos aren't much help in my case, but I just wanted to show you than I am not the abusive, uncaring father my elder daughter and in-laws want you to believe I am. If the guardianship hearing is about Gabby's welfare, as her father, I believe that I am the best person to care for her. As convicted felons, I didn't think the court would consider awarding custody of a handicapped minor to families affiliated with Dennis Weigart and Silvio. Marino."

(Out of spite, I purposely let that last bit slip out.)

"What did you say? Your in-laws are felons? I had no idea. This sheds a new light on the custody proceedings. I will certainly take this information into consideration."

I gathered up my photo album, thanked Mrs. Silvert for listening to me and left humming a vengeful tune.

Monday, September 19, 1994

Judge Yamin was again presiding at the second custody hearing. In attendance were Walters, my attorney, Boyle representing Nicky, and Mrs. Carmichael and Mrs. Silvert at Judge Yamin's request. The stenographer Smart hired at the previous hearing was also present to provide a transcript of the hearing.

Marie was ducking CFS after Mrs. Silvert called to question her about my felonious relatives putting Marie on alert. She wouldn't chance bringing Gabby to Connecticut if there was any possibility that the court would enforce the order to hand Gabby over to me.

Judge Yamin began the proceedings. She asked Mrs. Carmichael for an update on the restraining orders issued the month before.

"On August 25th, Nikol Volpe was evicted from the house in Danbury and, since that time, only Mr. Volpe was has been in residence."

Judge Yamin asked, "Where is Gabrielle Volpe now living?"

Mrs. Carmichael replied. "Gabrielle was first living with her aunt and uncle, the Weigarts, but I believe she is now staying with her grandparents, the Marinos, in New York."

"Don't you know for sure? Aren't you in contact with CFS in New York?" Judge Yamin asked.

"No, your honor. We have not yet been able to establish a liaison with the CFS office in Westchester."

"Let me know as soon as you have, Mrs. Carmichael."

What a load of bullshit! At this point, I didn't care about order in the court and blurted out, "What good is a court order to have Gabrielle returned to her home in Danbury if it can't be enforced?"

"I understand your frustration, but as I told you, Mr. Volpe, CFS and the Danbury courts have no jurisdiction in New York," Mrs. Carmichael answered.

I pushed Walter's hand away and continued as my own counsel, "Gabrielle is either at the Weigarts or Marinos, right?"

"That's correct."

"I want to inform the court and you, Mrs. Carmichael, that both those households are headed by convicted felons. Doesn't that mean anything to CFS?"

Judge Yamin perked up.

Boyle objected, "You don't have to respond to that, Mrs. Carmichael. Mr. Volpe does not have the right to question you."

I was about to blurt out some more when Walters made me sit down before I was thrown out of the courtroom.

The judge upheld Boyle's objection and dismissed Mrs. Carmichael from the hearing. Boyle glared at me; I glared right back. She couldn't have me arrested for telling the truth.

Judge Yamin asked Mrs. Silvert if she had obtained the services of a forensic psychologist to interview Nicky, Gabby and me.

"I can recommend a very qualified psychologist whom I have worked with for several years." She handed Judge Yamin the psychologist's information. Judge Yamin approved her selection.

Judge Yamin continued, "Mrs. Silvert, what is the status of the forensic accounting of Gabrielle's trust fund?"

Mrs. Silvert replied, "Unfortunately, Judge Yamin, the accounting is going to take longer than expected. Since all the original records are missing, the transactions from the inception of the fund have to be reconstructed. Although Mr. Volpe's attorney, Mr. Harvey Corn, is pursuing the matter as expeditiously as possible, it may still take several weeks to compile the records."

"That is unfortunate, Mrs. Silvert. Please keep the court appraised of the progress of the accounting."

It was my attorney's turn.

"Before we precede, your honor," said Walters as he stood, "I would like the court stenographer to read back Nikol Volpe's statement from the first hearing to refresh our memories."

Nikol's inconsistent ramblings were read. To steal Boyle's thunder, Walters asked me, "Mr. Volpe, I understand that you were arrested in 1992 for assaulting your daughter Nikol and breaking her nose in the attack. Can you explain this incident?"

"There was no incident. I have never raised a hand to my daughter in anger. She does not nor has she ever had a broken nose. The x-rays my mother-in-law, Mrs. Marino, showed the police were taken prior to a nose job Nicky had when she was sixteen. No charges were ever brought against me, because Nicky would not corroborate Mrs. Marino's accusation."

Walters continued. "There are also assault with a deadly weapon and home invasion charges pending in Westchester against you. Can you explain those?

"My in-laws brought both charges against me, but they are false. I had no weapon, deadly or not, when I went to speak to them at their house. The doors were open to the garage. I went in and knocked on the door to the house. Mrs. Marino answered the door and told me to leave. I did not force my way into their house. I was about to leave when Mr. Marino shoved his wife aside to come into the garage. He went over to a work table and pulled out a blackjack. He attacked me with it but dropped it when I pushed him aside to run out of the garage to my car. Mrs. Marino picked up the blackjack and followed me out of the garage. She threw the blackjack at my car as I was driving away. There's a dent in the passenger side to show for it. The Marinos called the police who arrested me after the Marinos claimed I stormed into their house and fired a gun at them. No gun was found, because I did not have one. I was released by the Westchester police the same night. The pending criminal charges have been postponed twice, because my father-in-law, Silvio Marino, thought it inadvisable to perjure himself in court."

Boyle objected. "That is Mr. Volpe's opinion of his father-in-law and should not be considered in his testimony."

"Very well, Ms. Boyle, noted," said Judge Yamin.

Walters again. "Mr. Volpe, can you tell me something about your family life during your twenty-eight years of marriage to Georgann?"

I spoke for twenty minutes recounting our daughters' life-threatening illnesses, the malpractice suit, and many other occasions that illustrated that we were otherwise a close-knit, normal family before Georgann's illness. To my discredit, I did not mention the run-ins I had with Nikol. I wanted the court to believe I was the model father and husband.

Walters asked me to highlight my business career. I did so. He asked me to discuss the establishment of Gabby's trust. I gave the court a brief explanation of how the trust was set up.

Walter's asked, "Mr. Volpe, what do you believe will be the findings once the forensic accounting is completed?"

"The accounting will show that I never spent a dime of Gabby's trust money without the approval of the agency that oversees the trust. I swear I am telling the truth, and if Georgann was able to be here, she would back me up."

"Thank you, Mr. Volpe, for your frank answers. I have no further questions."

Boyle got up, and resorting to her killer divorce lawyer tactics, raised Nikol's claim that I was a womanizer who used every occasion to cheat on my wife.

(I, in my arrogance, (sorry reader) was positive that no one in my family knew anything about my infidelities.)

"I spent over twenty years in the woman's clothing business; my employees were women, most of the sales reps were women, my customers were women. I had friends in the business who were women. According to Marie Marino and my daughter that makes me a womanizer."

Boyle had nothing further to ask and sat down.

It was Mrs. Silvert's turn to question me on Gabby's behalf. She began. "Mr. Volpe, can you tell the court Georgann's current medical condition."

I related all the Georgann's medical details beginning with Danbury hospital to her current stay at Yale.

"Is it true, Mr. Volpe, that you spend a great deal of your time with Georgann?"

"The only times I leave Georgann's side is to go to court hearings, or to appointments with my several attorneys, or at home to shower and change.

"What about your daughter, Gabrielle? Doesn't she require special care? How did you justify your neglect if you spent so much time away from her?"

"Yes, Gabrielle is handicapped, but I do not feel I have neglected her needs. I hired a housekeeper and two live-in caregivers to assure that Gabby attended school, her resource sessions, and therapists. The first caregiver, Kim Day, was recommended to me by my sister-in-law, but she did not work out. The second caregiver, Melissa Corsaro, the daughter of Doctor Corsaro, is a college student who babysat for Gabby for many years and was like a big sister to her. I paid Melissa's salary out of pocket, not through Gabby's trust, and provided her with spending money for Gabby's care. I also gave Melissa the keys to Georgann's car to use to drive Gabby wherever she needed to go. Melissa had all my contact information if she needed to reach me. Unfortunately, she had to return to college early."

"Then what did you do, Mr. Volpe?" asked Mrs. Silvert.

"Mrs. Marino volunteered to care for Gabby in her home in New York until Georgann recovered from her illness. I had no other choice but to turn over Gabby's care to her grandmother. Gabby went to live with the Marino's prior to the court granting me restraining orders on the Marinos. Unfortunately, out of vengeance, Mrs. Marino has since taken it upon herself to prohibit Gabby from having any contact with her mother or me even though the court has ordered Gabby to be returned to me in Connecticut."

By the time Mrs. Silvert finished questioning me, she sounded more like my defense lawyer than Chris Walters. "Thank you, Mr. Volpe. Do you have any questions for Mr. Volpe, Ms. Boyle?" Boyle's puss said it all.

The Judge adjourned the hearing and scheduled the next one in three weeks time.

Tuesday, September 20, 1994 to October 11, 1994

Because I was still unable to get Gabby back from the Marinos, I spent night and day with Georgann. It wasn't always peaceful. A few times, Marie burst into Georgann's room unannounced just to scream her verbal cyanide at me. Georgann would frantically gesture her to get out. I resorted to calling security a couple of times to have Marie physically removed from the room because of her threats. If she were a man, I'd gladly have gone to jail for punching her lights out, but I did my best to maintain my cool for Georgann's sake.

18

Hearing 3

Wednesday, October 12, 1994

I was very confident that the third custody hearing would remove the veil of treachery that covered the Marinos naked trust grab conspiracy. Marie continued to ignore any efforts by CFS or Mrs. Silvert to contact Gabby. She knew these ladies were wise to her, but she also knew they had no jurisdiction in New York.

Having authority over Georgann's health care and cloistering our child in her house gave Marie power to bend Georgann to her will. Unwittingly, Georgann had given her mother everything she always wanted – her granddaughters' devotion and control over Georgann's life. Who needed me? Instead of 'Big Al,' I had become 'Redundant Al.'

Along with the stress her mother was putting on Georgann, the paranoia she felt for my safety consumed her. She feared the extent Marie might go to have me eliminated, and it was that fear that would lead to an unfortunate end. (Spoilers)

The forensic accounting was coming together. Although the theft of the financial records was a serious setback, I knew the final figures could not lie. Unfortunately, when Judge Yamin ordered the court to freeze Gabby's trust assets until a forensic accounting could be completed; I had to personally bear the full financial burden of the accounting, because I was no longer receiving a care-giving allowance. If the records hadn't been stolen from my house, the accounting would have taken about a week, costing maybe three grand. Now, having to subpoena all the documentation, it was taking months to retrieve years of transactional records. In the end, it cost me $34,000 in accounting and legal fees.

Marie's claim that I had stolen two million dollars from the trust proved to be another trumped-up story in a whole shopping list of falsehoods. Putting aside slander, libel, and character assassination, Boyle knew I was not going to be exposed as the lowlife crook Nikol wanted the court to believe. In addition, to Boyle's further mortification, the assault with a deadly weapons charge was proving to be unfounded. Where was the gun? And, the only fingerprints on the black jack belonged to the Marinos.

As attorney on record, Boyle had drenched herself in this stench of malicious prosecution and vexatious litigation en route to criminal fraud charges for the Marinos and for herself. She was now fully aware of the deep doo-doo in which she had embroiled herself by taking on the Marinos as clients. If Boyle was implicated as a knowing accomplice in their schemes, she might face the same disclosure leading to an indictment for the Marinos and her possible disbarment. She tried to persuade them to discontinue their groundless pursuit in an attempt to establish justification for their phony charges. The Marinos refused her council. The situation had gone too far for them to pull out now. They intended to tough it out.

The third custody hearing did not go as I had hoped. Instead of exposing the Marinos lies, Judge Yamin had called the hearing as a formality to schedule the agenda for the next hearing. Besides me and Walters, Nikol, Boyle, Mrs. Silvert and Mrs. Carmichael as well as the forensic psychologist were in attendance.

Judge Yamin asked Mrs. Silvert and Mrs. Carmichael if it were possible to obtain a written statement from Georgann regarding my administration of Gabby's trust. Even though I no longer had the legal right to assert any requests regarding Georgann's health, I had appealed to Mrs. Carmichael that Georgann might seriously suffer if she were requested to provide a second statement. With my wishes in mind, Mrs. Carmichael told Judge Yamin that, at this time, she considered it inadvisable to approach Georgann with such a request given her weak medical condition. Judge Yamin requested Mrs. Carmichael to obtain a statement from Georgann as soon as her condition improved.

Dr. Richard Foster, the forensic psychologist, provided Judge Yamin with a schedule for the interviews he intended to conduct with Nikol, Gabby and me. Judge Yamin said that she would schedule the next hearing once she received the evaluation of his findings.

Hearing adjourned.

Out of earshot, Boyle cornered my attorney in the corridor to offer the same incentive she had whispered to Georgann in the hospital. "My clients have authorized me to make a generous offer they believe Mr. Volpe would be foolish not to accept. If he signs divorce papers and resigns as trustee of Gabrielle's trust, they will give Mr. Volpe two hundred thousand dollars in cash and drop all charges against him. Discuss this with your client and let me know his answer by tomorrow morning. Here is my private number." She handed Walters a slip of paper, and, not waiting for his response, abruptly walked away.

Is this an offer I couldn't refuse? What am I in, a Godfather movie?

Walters knew I was financially and emotionally on the righteous side of losing. He asked me to follow him to his office so we could talk privately. As soon as we were seated at his desk, he took a deep breath before saying, "Al, your in-laws want to deal." He gave me their offer and waited for my answer without taking his eyes from my face.

I knew he wanted me to grab at this bone. The Marinos intimidated the hell out of him as they had with everyone who tried to help me. After all these years, I was impervious to their threats; love doesn't count cost. For thirty years, Georgann and I weathered everything life threw at us, because we did it together. The only blameless souls in this whole family of reprobates - me included in the number - were Georgann and Gabby; their love was pure. I could not turn tail and run abandoning them to who-knew-what fate. I knew Georgann would have wanted me to take the deal if it meant I would stay alive, but I was determined to see it through to the end. I could be as tough as the Marinos.

Walters continued to stare at me waiting for my response.

I said, "I want to talk to Boyle. Face-to-face. Set up a meeting."

Walters didn't try to convince me to change my mind. He phoned Boyle who must have been sitting on the edge of her seat waiting for his call, because she answered the phone before the second ring. They set up a meeting for ten the following morning at her office.

I stood, shook his hand, "See you tomorrow," and left.

Thursday, October 13, 1994

Walters and I got to Boyle's office fifteen minutes after ten to let her stew some more. We no sooner sat in chairs in front of her desk, and without even offering us a cup of coffee, she repeated the Marinos offer. It was evident she wanted to get this meeting over and us out of her office as fast as possible.

"Mr Volpe," she began in her most consolatory manner, "my clients are being very generous with their offer. You will never gain custody of your daughter, because she does not want to live with you. This is a good will gesture the Marinos are making to you, and I encourage you to accept it." Boyle knew that once she completed their bidding by getting me to take the deal, she would be done with the Marinos.

"Let me set you straight on one thing, Ms. Boyle," I said. "The Marinos don't know the meaning of 'good will' unless it was for their own good. Where are they getting this two hundred grand?" Boyle did not respond. I said, "First, get me a cashier's check for the two hundred thou authorized by Silvio Marino, then we'll talk." I was stalling for time.

Boyle snarled, "Are you calling me disingenuous?"

I smiled, "I'm not calling you anything, Ms. Boyle. I presume you know exactly what you are. Let's go, Chris." I got up and walked out of her office, Walters trailing behind me.

Awareness of the Marinos thug tactics was beginning to dawn on Walters; he was showing signs of running scared. I made an attempt to put on a fearless bravado for his benefit.

As soon as we got outside, I said, "These scumbags know they can't grab the trust as long as I'm still in charge. Who the fuck are they to demand I take their offer? Silvio may be Mafia, but he's not the godfather. I hope they rot in hell for what they're doing to Georgann and Gabby. As far as I'm concerned, those degenerates, including that viper Boyle, can stick their deal where the sun don't shine."

By the time I finished my rant, I think Walters was more afraid of me than the Marinos. Good.

Still, Walters tried, "Al, you don't need to decide now. All I'm asking is that you to give their deal some thought."

"You guys keep lawyering and let me worry about everything else. All you need to know is that I will show up in court when I need to."

19

Worse

Monday, October 17, 1994 to October 31, 1994

When Silvio postponed the trial in Bedford for the third time, the DA dropped all criminal charges against me. Silvio might be a thug, but he was savvy enough to stay away from legal proceedings if his illegitimate life might be exposed. He wasn't anxious to violate his parole. Never having my day in court cost me six grand for Seymour plus medical bills from Silvio's blackjack and the cost of repairing the dent in my car from Marie's killer right hand pitch.

I went to Seymour's office to settle my account. Before leaving, I asked, as I did with all my lawyers, how could people like the Marinos keep getting away with making false police reports and committing felonies with no consequences?

"Al, forget about it. Some people sometimes are above the law," was all the answer he would give me.

Somebody's pockets had been greased. Seymour knew about the two hundred thousand dollar payoff my in-laws wanted me to take, how, I never found out, but his parting words were to give me some free advice.

He walked me to the door, patted my shoulder and said, "Al, take their deal and disappear for awhile." He lowered his head as he shook it. Turning away from me, he went into his office and shut the door. I stared at the closed door a few moments before leaving.

The forensic accounting was finally complete. In forensic accounting jargon, the bottom line total of missing funds was nada - zilch - zippo – un gotz - zero. The auditors even made a note complementing me on the prudent investment strategies utilized in managing Gabby's trust. Call me naive, but I actually believed once the accounting proved my innocence, my in-laws would stop their attempts to get a hold of Gabby's money. What have I been saying over and over in this narrative? I was never very smart.

The one bright light in all this darkness was that Georgann was improving. Dr. Matthay was so encouraged by Georgann's progress that he was considering moving her out of the ICU to a step down unit.

A step-down unit is intermediate between that of an ICU and a normally staffed in-patient division. Matthay authorized personnel from the step down unit to familiarize themselves with Georgann's medical history and unique life support apparatus. Dr. Matthay's enthusiasm was contagious; I was psyched. Georgann was on her way to coming home.

Boyle was panicking; the trust grab was going to blow up in her face once the custody court examined the forensic accounting. During a visit with Georgann, Marie and Boyle again tried to pressure her into signing divorce papers. This knowledge that her parents had offered me two thousand dollars to get lost made Georgann more adamant than ever in refusing to sign divorce papers. She was so agitated by Marie's last visit that it triggered her life support alarms. Doctors and nursing staff rushed to her room throwing Marie and Boyle out.

It did not matter to Marie if she caused Georgann distress. Marie could never be accused of giving up easily, because she lacked even a scintilla of conscience. If Georgann would not divorce me, it was not beneath Marie to use Gabby as a tool to exert even more pressure on Georgann.

During her next visit, Marie whispered to her daughter in her most saccharine voice, "Georgann, sweetheart, Gabby doesn't even want to talk to Al over the phone let alone live with him. She says she is happy with me, because I love her more than her own father. If you won't divorce him, then ask the hospital security to stop him from visiting. If you do that, I can bring Gabby to see you. She won't set foot in the hospital if she thinks he might be here. Once Al is out of the picture, you can see your sweet baby."

(Reader, pay attention) Georgann understood the underlying threat in her mother's words - me out of the picture meant me dead. A predator's tactic is to isolate its prey before the final kill, and Marie was the leader of the pack. The Marinos had managed to alienate everyone who cared about Georgann or who was on my side. Whether sensible or not, fear for my safety was paramount in the decision Georgann made. She complied with her mother's request; she had me barred from visiting her.

The ICU staff could not understand why Georgann refused to allow me to visit given her prior fervent need to know exactly where I was at all times. The legal department told the hospital staff to stay out of it. This decision of Georgann's rendered her alone and helpless.

Although I was devastated because I could no longer visit Georgann, I knew her recovery hinged on her assurance that I was not in danger from her parents or from whomever her parents hired to do me harm. The Marino franchise of evil could put even the Pope in jeopardy of turning too many cheeks.

The Marinos continued to intimidate and goad me into doing something stupid. My friends warned me that I was setting myself up for a kill by living alone; they encouraged me to disappear for a while. I wasn't going anywhere. I wanted to be near Georgann even if I couldn't be with her. I took precautions to protect myself. I boarded up the downstairs front windows of the house; I didn't go out at night. If I went out at all, I made sure I left through the garage. When I returned, I opened the garage doors remotely and closed them the same way before getting out of my car; I carried a pistol on me at all times. I wasn't going to be an open target. Perversely, I almost wanted them to try to get at me so I could strike back. I couldn't go to jail if it was self defense, could I? Of course, Silvio would never deign to do the hit himself, but he knew plenty of thugs who would do the job for him.

My most ardent wish was that I could have protected Georgann in the same way I was doing for myself. Although she believed that giving Marie authority over her medical care was good strategy, that decision was about to backfire on her. Georgann didn't see it coming and neither did I.

Marie began an aggressive campaign to convince Georgann that she would go home quicker if she transferred to Gaylord Rehabilitation Center in Wallingford, CT instead of going into the step down program at Yale recommended by Dr. Matthay. Marie knew that Dr. Matthay was my champion; ergo he also needed to be out of the picture. As her care provider, Marie insisted Dr. Matthay transfer Georgann to Gaylord despite the doctor's insistence that this was an inadvisable move. Georgann's life support apparatus was highly specialized and required the maintenance of experienced technicians. Dr. Matthay was just wasting his breath. Marie won. Georgann convinced herself that she was on her way to full recovery and was so desperate to go home; she believed Marie was right and agreed to the transfer.

Marie had the legal authority. The hospital, whether out of fear of liability or perhaps after receiving a call from Silvio urging them to comply with his wife's (and his) request, advised Dr. Matthay to go along with her transfer. The transfer was scheduled for mid-November. As her physician, Dr. Matthay's final responsibility was to prepare Georgann for the move. That's all.

Again, I knew nothing about the transfer. I was unable to get any information from the hospital staff, because I was no longer the legal agent for Georgann's medical needs. Marie made sure I was blocked from all lines of communication with or about Georgann.

The predator's code: isolate before moving in for the kill.

Saturday, November 5, 1994

Five days went by with no word about Georgann. The Yale business office called this morning to inquire why the hospital was no longer receiving medical payments from me. I told the office manager I would come in the following day to straighten out the problem.

To spare myself the headache of keeping track of the payment transactions, I had given all hospital bills and insurance checks along with signed blank checks from my bank account to Josephine who would match them up and send them to the hospital along with my co-pay. But, since October, I hadn't received any more bills or insurance checks and was too preoccupied with the rest of my life to realize this. Josephine alerted me wondering why I hadn't given any further bills. Josephine and I both assumed that the health insurance had maxed out its million-dollar cap and hadn't gotten around to letting me know.

Since I was already going to Yale, I decided to phone Mrs. Scanlon. "Mrs. Scanlon, can you ask Georgann if I can visit her?"

Mrs. Scanlon, sounding very nervous said, "I'm not sure she will want to see you, but I will try. I'll call you back as soon as I speak with her."

Two hours later, she returned my call. "I'm sorry, Mr. Volpe, but your wife refuses to see you." She didn't take a breath before continuing, "Since I have you on the phone, the business office told me that you needn't come to the hospital tomorrow. As your wife's primary care agent, Mrs. Marino has accepted all responsibility for Georgann's medical bills."

What!

"Can you at least let me know how Georgann is doing?"

"I'm sorry, Mr. Volpe, but I can't give out patient information to someone who is not authorized. All I can say it that she is stable." That damn word again!

I was dumbfounded! How had all this happened in so short a time? I considered driving to New Haven, but what for? No one at the hospital would give me the time of day. To top it off, Marie had gone to my local post office and signed a change of address card rerouting all mail in Georgann's name to her. This included all the hospital bills and insurance checks. When I went to the post office, the postmaster told me what Marie had done is not considered a crime. Anyone can fill-out a change of address card without question to reroute another person's mail. It's hard to believe that someone could interfere with the mail without consequences from the federal government. Virtual head slap for being so brainless - again.

Thursday, November 17, 1994

If Georgann had not prevailed upon a nurse to mail a letter she had written to Frankie and Phyllis in Florida, I would never have known about her transfer to Gaylord. In the letter, Georgann asked Phyllis to pass the information on to me, but for my own safety she did not want me to visit her in Gaylord either, Georgann's last message for me - 'stay safe, home for Christmas, all my love.' (Spoilers)

Phyllis called me as soon as she received Georgann's letter. "Al, Marie had Georgann transferred to Gaylord Rehab on the fourteenth. She convinced Georgann she would recover faster if she was out of Yale. Al, Georgann was so desperate to get home, she agreed."

"Oh my God, Phyllis. This is the worst thing that could happen. She was doing so well at Yale."

"I know, Al. All we can do now is pray for her quick recovery."

"Yes, Phyllis. It's all in God's hands now. Thank you for calling me." Little did I know that the worst thing was yet to happen.

From that day on, I spent my days and nights fighting depression. I used my solitude to complete projects around the house I believed would please Georgann when she got home. I'd become so reclusive and despondent that my favorite cousin, Carol pleaded with me to stay with her and her husband, Raymond, in Yonkers over the Thanksgiving weekend. I went just to see some friendly faces.

Thursday, November 24, 1994

We were having our Thanksgiving dessert and coffee when the conversation turned to Georgann. We all wished she were here with us. I became so choked up; I could barely swallow a mouthful of my pumpkin pie.

Seeing my distress, Carol jumped up from the table. "I'm calling Donna. This has gone on long enough. Al deserves to know how Georgann is doing." Carol had been on friendly terms with Donna before Georgann's illness. When Donna answered the phone, Carol said, "Hi, Donna, happy Thanksgiving. We missed seeing Georgann this year and were wondering how she is doing. I haven't heard any news for some time. You know I love Georgann like a sister so please tell me." We couldn't hear what Donna was saying, but we saw Carol's face go pale.

I grabbed the phone. "Donna, you tell me right now what's happening or I swear, I'll come over there and wring it out of you."

"Don't tell my mother I told you, but Georgann's back at Yale. Her ventilator malfunctioned while she was at Gaylord. Al, she suffered a massive stroke. Georgann is brain dead."

"What are you saying, you nitwit. Georgann was doing great the last time I saw her. What happened?"

"I don't know, Al, but that's the story. My mother is going to authorize pulling the plug."

I dropped the phone, my knees buckling under me. As I started to black out, Raymond grabbed me before I fell. He hung up the phone.

"Sit down, Al," Carol said, "I'm calling Yale now and find out what's going on."

I sat with my head between my knees as Carol dialed the number. She asked to speak to someone in charge of Georgann's care and was forwarded to the ICU. Speaking to a nurse, Carol identified herself and said she was calling on behalf of Georgann Volpe's husband. They wouldn't give her any information.

"I'm going to Yale," I said trying to get up. Carol pushed me back down, "Tomorrow, Al. You can't do anything tonight. I'll call Paul and have him take you. You go to bed and try to get some sleep."

Sleep, right! I tortured myself all night with the insane belief that I was responsible for allowing my mother-in-law, a deranged psychopath, to decide the fate of Georgann's life. I should have done something, anything I could to protect Georgann even if it meant risking my own safety at the hands of the Marinos. As I lay there in the dark, pain and rage coursing through me, I realized that Marie had finally succeeded in destroying the one person we both loved most in our lives.

20

Heaven

Friday, November 25, 1994

Paul and I were at the front desk in the lobby of Yale New Haven by eight. Just as we were asking for the legal department, Marie and Nicky came into the lobby, saw me and began screaming like two hyenas. "Arrest him, he's not allowed to be here."

Rather than start a commotion, I grabbed Paul, "Let's go. I won't be able to see Georgann as long as they're here. Let's get some fresh air before we head over to the legal department."

The sight of Marie and Nicky turned my stomach so much that I puked in the parking lot. Paul and walked around for two hours before going back to the hospital. The front desk directed us to the legal department. There Paul and I were told by the receptionist that the department was closed until Monday because of the Thanksgiving holiday. She suggested I leave a voice message requesting the office to contact me when they returned on Monday. The receptionist dialed the number, handed me the phone and, to my surprise, a live voice answered.

"Good morning, you have reached the legal department at Yale New Haven Hospital. This is Mrs. Johnson speaking. How may I help you?"

"Mrs. Johnson, my name is Al Volpe. My wife, Georgann, is a patient of Dr. Matthay's. Can you spare me a few minutes to speak with you concerning her? I am in the hospital right now."

"You are fortunate I am at the office today. I only came in to catch up on some paperwork. I do recall a number of incidents regarding your wife and family. Tell the receptionist that it is all right to send you to my office."

Mrs. Johnson greeted us graciously. She was younger than I had expected given her position at the hospital. Although not quite forty, her gray hair was an indication that she had seen a lot of life. Casually dressed in jeans and a lilac sweater, she asked us to have a seat and offered coffee. My stomach was churning too much to think about swallowing anything but my own spit. Paul accepted her offer. Amenities over, I spilled everything.

"I was having Thanksgiving dinner at my cousin Carol's yesterday. She called Donna, Georgann's sister, to find out how Georgann was doing. Donna told her that my wife had been readmitted to Yale from Gaylord Rehab, because she had suffered a stroke and was brain dead. My sister-in-law is a nitwit. I need to find out firsthand what happened to Georgann. I had my friend, Paul, drive me here this morning. We were still in the lobby when my mother-in-law and older daughter came in. They screamed for security to remove me. I didn't think making a scene was a good move so Paul and I left the hospital. We returned a couple hours later and went straight to the legal department where the receptionist called you. I know I haven't the legal right, but I haven't had any contact with my wife since October. Please, Mrs. Johnson. I need to see Georgann. Can you help me?"

Mrs. Johnson stared at me for a few moments seeming to judge my sincerity. When she realized I was panicking and barely able to breathe, she stood up and walked over to a wall of file cabinets. She pulled out Georgann's file. Scanning through it quickly, she said, "According to our records, Georgann signed a formal statement in October prohibiting you from visiting her. In September, she appointed her mother, Mrs. Marie Marino, as her designated health care agent responsible for handling all her medical assessments including end of life decisions. In a meeting with the social worker in charge of Mrs. Volpe's case, Mrs. Marino said that you and Mrs. Volpe were divorced. Mrs. Marino did not produce the divorce papers, but she presented a police report stating that you were her ex-son-in-law. I am sympathetic to your plight, Mr. Volpe, but, since you are divorced you have no legal rights regarding Georgann."

I could not contain my anger. "Georgann and I are not divorced!"

She flushed, "What do you mean?"

I repeated, "Georgann and I are not divorced. There are no divorce papers. Marie Marino lied to the police in the report and she lied to you."

"What?"

I repeated almost shouting, "Marie Marino cannot produce any divorce papers because there aren't any! Georgann and I are not nor will we ever be divorced."

"Give me a minute," Mrs. Johnson said. She went back to her desk and picked up the phone to call the records department to request Georgann's complete file. We heard her say, "Fine. I'm not going to wait until Monday. I'm coming there right now to get it." She offered Paul and me coffee again before telling us to wait in her office until she returned.

Twenty minutes later, Mrs. Johnson was back pushing a big cart loaded with files. She slammed an eight-inch thick folder down on her desk and furiously began rifling through the documents. She pulled out the statements from the social worker and business office that referenced Marie Marino's alleged divorce papers. She read through the entire file before slamming it down on the desk again. She picked up her phone and called social services first, then the business office. All Paul and I heard her say after she asked about divorce papers was, "Uh huh, uh huh. I see. Thank you."

She carefully placed the phone in its cradle before turning to us. "Well, Mr. Volpe, good thing I was working this weekend. Although both social services and the business office have copies of the police report of the home invasion and weapons charges the Marinos filed against you, they have no record of divorce papers. I believe you may be correct, someone has perpetrated a fraud with Yale as its victim."

Mrs. Johnson got herself a cup of coffee, sat down, composed her face and folded her hands in front of her indicating that she was ready to give me her full attention. "I'm all ears, Mr. Volpe."

I related all the events that led to Georgann's decision to have me barred from visiting her leading up to Marie having her transferred to Gaylord Rehab. I included telling her about Gabby's birth and the trust settlement, my false arrests, and the custody hearings - the whole picture. Finished, I sat back and bowed my head; I was exhausted reliving all the wretchedness of those days as if it were yesterday.

Mrs. Johnson listened intently for the half hour I spoke. She opened the file again. "Besides your visits to your wife and from family members, the visitors log indicates that Mrs. Marino brought Attorney Bottigliere with her on a visit once in August. Also, twice in September she brought Attorney Boyle on a visit to Georgann. Are you or your wife a client of either of these lawyers?"

"No, we are not. Both were hired by Mr. and Mrs. Marino to pressure Georgann into signing divorce papers. Once Georgann learned from her sister that the Marinos offered me a two hundred thousand dollar bribe to get out of town or I would be sorry she refused to sign. As long we remained married, Georgann knew the Marinos wouldn't act on that threat."

"As horrific as that sounds, Mr. Volpe, I have no authority to address such an accusation. What would you like me to do?"

"All I want to do is see Georgann. I'm begging you, Mrs. Johnson, please take me to my wife!"

Mrs. Johnson took a few moments to give consideration to my request as she stared into my bereaved face. Without responding, she picked up the phone to call security. She informed them that she wished to visit Mrs. Volpe alone and to clear the room of visitors. Then, she called Dr. Matthay and asked him to meet us in Georgann's room.

Dr. Matthay was there when we arrived, but stood a few feet away from Georgann's bed. Mrs. Johnson and Paul also held back as I approached Georgann. They already knew.

I was feeling so light headed that I imagined I saw a string of little, golden angels circling above her beautiful face. I went to her, kissed her forehead and whispered how much I loved her. I could swear she smiled up at me. I was not ready to accept that Georgann had passed peacefully into God's hands two hours before. Again, my mother-in-law stole the last few moments I could have had to be with Georgann.

Dr. Matthay put his arm around my shoulders. He kept Georgann alive for months, working miracle after miracle, only to lose her in less than two weeks time at the inept hands of Gaylord Rehab. I pulled away from him. Crying inconsolably, I begged, "Please, Georgann come back to me. I need you." I couldn't catch my breath and started to black out. Dr. Matthay caught me before I fell. He held me up while Paul ran for a wheel chair.

Collapsed in the chair, I raised my right fist and swore, "Georgann, I couldn't save you, but, as God is my witness, I will do everything in my power to keep our precious daughter safe."

Paul took me home. He and Betty stayed with me round the clock for the next few days fearing that if they left me alone, I might kill myself. They needn't have worried. I had given my solemn promise to Georgann, and I would never forsake it.

Monday, November 28, 1994

Mrs. Johnson phoned early this morning. She offered her condolences again before asking how I was doing. "I'm sorry to bother you at this time, Mr. Volpe, but the hospital needs to know if you have made any arrangements for Georgann's remains."

"I haven't yet. I haven't been able to do more than grieve. I will call Clark Funeral Home in Katonah as soon as I hang up with you, Mrs. Johnson. I'll tell them to give you a call."

Not ten minutes after I got off the phone with Clark, Mrs. Johnson called back. I could hear panic in her voice. "Mr. Volpe, when I called you this morning, I was not aware that Mrs. Marino had already made arrangements to have Sisto Funeral Parlor in The Bronx pick-up Georgann's remains. They're at the hospital now."

"Do not release Georgann's body to Sisto's, Mrs. Johnson! I don't care what the Marinos say. As her husband, I have the legal right to decide which home should handle Georgann's funeral and that's Clark."

"Give me a little time to straighten this out with Sisto's, Mr. Volpe. I will get right back to you." What she really meant was to give her some time to call the Marinos.

I paced back and forth in the living room smoking one cigarette after another until Mrs. Johnson called me back. "I was too late to stop Sisto's from transferring Georgann's remains to their facility. They have already begun interment preparations. They assure me that if you allow them to complete their preparations they will bring her body to Clark for the funeral viewing no later than twelve noon on Wednesday."

I was too distraught to think otherwise, and, God help me, I agreed. I called Clark and gave them the new arrangements leaving it up to them to co-ordinate the details with Sisto's. Clark expressed concern over the provisions; it was not the usual protocol. I assured them it was my wishes and they acquiesced.

Tuesday, November 29, 1994

Donna called. She wanted to come by to get Georgann's clothes for the funeral. I said it was okay. I wanted to pump her for some answers.

She showed up a couple hours later. I took her upstairs to our bedroom and showed her Georgann's closet. As Donna went through Georgann's clothes, I offhandedly asked, although I already knew the answer, "Donna, why did Georgann consent to be transferred to Gaylord when Dr. Matthay planned to move her to a step down unit at Yale? I don't get it."

"Georgann wasn't thinking straight. My mother insisted on it against Matthay's wishes, because he was your buddy, not hers. My mother convinced her going to Gaylord was the best and fastest way for her to get home to Gabby." Donna, ignorant motor mouth to the end continued. "Al, you know my mother is after Gabby's trust. She tried to do it legally, but Boyle told her she didn't have a chance of winning once the forensic accounting got to court. Boyle warned my mother that she and my dad ran the risk of being charged with fraud. Boyle won't have to worry about that now since my mother withdraw her suit. You are aware, Al, that my mother has no intention of having Georgann's wake at Clark. She told me that the wake will be at Sisto's and, her words, 'If Al tries to stop it or show up, we'll be waiting.' See ya." She grabbed Georgann's clothes, ran down the stairs and out of the house before I could say another word.

Donna was not renowned for getting stories straight. I called Clark and asked to speak to the funeral director.

He said, "I'm afraid that your sister-in-law is correct. Sisto's is not releasing Georgann's remains to us. It's possible that you could take this to a magistrate, but by the time you resolve the issue, it'll be too late. Sorry, Al."

Marie could not leave Georgann in peace when she was alive nor let her rest in peace now that she was dead. She was not even allowing Georgann the dignity of a proper funeral surrounded by friends and family who loved her.

I did not go to the funeral. Being there would have erupted into a confrontation with Marie, and it would not have done Georgann's memory or Gabby any good. Carol went to the church service and to the cemetery where everyone ignored her. She thought it best not to attend the wake. Georgann is buried in Woodlawn Cemetery in The Bronx. This is what is inscribed on her tombstone:

MARINO
BELOVED DAUGHTER MOTHER SISTER AND AUNT
1944 GEORGANN 1994

Marie finally succeeded in erasing me completely from her daughter's life.

I arranged a beautiful memorial service for Georgann at Bright Clouds Ministry in Danbury. Over a hundred people showed up to demonstrate their love and respect for Georgann. I left a message on Donna's answering machine asking her to bring Gabby to the service. I never heard back from her.

21

Post Mortem

December 1994

Ignorance and evil never take a holiday. The seven deadly sins is a Marino to do list. Only days after Georgann's funeral, I got a call from my bank. Marie had gone to the branch manager and presented a false financial power of attorney along with Georgann's death certificate in an attempt to empty out our bank accounts. Since our accounts were in both our names, executing any transaction also required my signature. The bank manager refused Marie's request. As soon as she stormed out of the bank reeking vengeance on everyone within hearing distance, the branch manager called me.

"Do you know a Marie Marino?"

"She's my mother-in-law. What has she done now?"

"She tried to withdraw all the money in your accounts and have them closed. We told her it was not possible without your consent. Have you agreed to this?"

"No way! If she tries to do anything like that again call me. I will have her arrested on fraud charges."

The Marinos began a harassment campaign to force the Winig family out of our house in Purdys. It worked. Dr. Winig broke the lease and moved out. I didn't resent him for doing this; I knew how persuasive my in-laws could be. It was no use trying to rent the house again because whoever moved in would experience the same Marino welcome to the neighborhood. I put the house on the market.

Walters appeared to be in no hurry to speed up the forensic accounting to submit it to court during the next custody hearing. Each time we spoke, he urged me to take Boyle's deal which was still on the table. I told Walters 'no deal.'

"You do your job as long as I can pay you. Keep sending money from my account to the Marinos for Gabby's support. I may be prevented from having any contact with my daughter but be damned if anyone dares to call me a deadbeat dad."

The fourth custody hearing went nowhere. The upshot: the forensic psychologist's report was a waste of time; it confirmed what I and my in-laws already knew - I was a fit parent. Although the outcome of the hearing was in my favor, the court could do nothing to have Gabby returned to me, because she was living in another state. All that was left was to await the result of the forensic accounting. If it went in my favor, I would remain in control of Gabby's trust and remove the money reason for the Marinos to keep her.

Walters was my attorney, but he had also become a friend. He confronted me straight up with some harsh lessons in legal realities. He knew those jackals were tearing me to shreds mentally, emotionally and financially.

"Sadly, Al, I must make this our last meeting. I will be frank. You've got nothing to gain fighting these people. Maybe there are lawyers who will represent you as long as you have money to pay them, but I am not one of them. Don't go broke thinking you'll get justice. You and I know the custody hearings were all bullshit, but they're keeping Gabby in New York, and they're not bringing her back. Do you want to file kidnapping charges against Gabby's seventy-year-old grandmother? Because Gabby is living in New York, you'll need to hire New York lawyers to bring your case before the Superior Court in that state. More time, more money even if you can get a firm to represent you given the Marino connections. If Gabby hates you like your in-laws say, given the option she certainly won't choose to live with you. By the time the legal battle concludes Gabby will probably be eighteen. She will be in charge of part of her trust and financially independent. Wherever she decides to live won't be with you. As your friend, Al, my advice, take it or leave it, is to grab the deal and move on with your life before the Marinos shorten it."

"Please don't give up yet, Chris. Give me more time."

"Ok, I'll hang in a little while longer until the forensic accounting is completed." As a friend, Chris shook my hand. I left feeling more dejected than I have ever felt in my whole life.

Because I lost hope of ever getting Gabby back; I became a recluse. I barely left my house. I spent most of December reading the Bible enveloped in self-pity. From her place in heaven, I knew Georgann was saddened as she looked down upon me. I had not kept my promise to keep our daughter out of the hands of the Marinos. Tens of thousands of dollars for nothing! I would have spent a hundred times more than that if it meant that Georgann could rest in peace.

Still traumatized by Georgann's passing, the thought of never seeing our daughter again played in my mind like a frantic chorus of emotions. Without Georgann and Gabby, I was losing my will to go on. Although I continued to read and fill notebooks with unanswerable questions, the Bible gave me little solace.

If the forensic accounting should prove that I had illegitimately used funds in Gabby's trust, as sole trustee now that Georgann was gone, I would face criminal charges and forfeit guardianship. Nikol, and by proxy Marie, would take over as guardian of the trust. Should this happen, the following would be in my future: 1) since Gabby owned the house, per her request, I would be evicted; 2) no longer Gabby's guardian, I would lose the care giving allowance I received which Nikol would then assume; 3) having years before lost Nikol's love and respect because of Marie, I would now also be totally isolated from Gabby who no longer wanted anything to do with me; and, more importantly; 4) I would have failed in my promise to Georgann.

The projects I was working on for Georgann's homecoming were left uncompleted; I remained in deep depression.

Betty still came once a week to straighten up the house and make me some meals. Thank goodness she had adopted my pets, because I was unfit to care for them, too. One day, when vacuuming under the bed she found my loaded shotgun. Good Christian woman that she was, she chastised me, "Al, you're a child of God. It is against His will for you to do yourself any bodily harm."

"That gun is just in case I'm not a child of God, Betty. If I am, the Marinos aren't. I promise you that if I ever use the gun, it won't be on me."

January 1995

The New Year did not bring much good news. During the third week in January, Walters made a final call to me, "Al, I'm begging you, take Boyle's deal. Forget about the forensic accounting."

"What are you talking about? You said the forensic accounting was on my side."

"Yes, it is, but Al, I can't represent you anymore."

My heart sank. "Please, Chris," I begged, "We're so close. If I can't get Gabby back, at least I can prevent my in-laws from getting control of her trust."

"Al, I hope I can make you understand, you and/or the accounting will never make it into court. I can't put my family or my associates in jeopardy by catching a stray bullet meant for you. I'm sorry. It's over for me."

Obviously, Silvio convinced Walters that keeping me as a client was to his disadvantage. There's that offer again that Walters couldn't refuse.

"I do understand, Chris. I've lived with the way these thugs operate for thirty years. In their world, no one's life trumps money. I'm not going to give up yet. FedEx me my files and the forensic accounting. I'll try to get some other law firm to represent me."

I sat for days in complete despair mulling over why I shouldn't just cash it in, but then I felt Georgann's hand on my shoulder whispering sweetly in my ear, "Not yet, Al, not yet." I found a law firm in Manhattan whose specialty was trust agreements and made an appointment.

February 1995

The law firm (I won't even grace them with a fake name) had offices that overlooked the skating rink in Rockefeller Center. I was led into a conference room that was palatially paneled in rich, polished oak. A lawyer (who cares what his name was either) and an accountant were already seated in plush chairs covered in red velvet around a large table. They and the room smelled of old money. We were served tea from an antique, silver tea set, a uniformed hostess acting as mother. The lawyer and accountant scanned through the forensic accounting papers I had brought with me. Heads bent, they conversed quietly with one another for several minutes before turning to me.

"Mr. Volpe," the lawyer began, "My associate and I do not see any improprieties in the management of your daughter's trust account. We do not understand why an attempt is being made to remove you as trustee."

Before I realized I was sticking my foot in my mouth, I said, "My in-laws are corrupt people who do not see the law as an impediment to getting what they want."

"No one is above the law," he said, poor naïve sap that he was. "My firm will represent you in court for the forensic accounting. I just need to get a few more details from Mr. Walters before proceeding. I will get back to you in a few days." We stood, shook hands all around before the receptionist escorted me to the door.

A red flag should have gone up as soon as I heard him say he needed to talk to Walters. Sure as shit, a week later, my new law firm backed out of representing me in court. The arm of the Mafia is long and when it has a grip on your throat, you've breathed your last. There was no use trying to find another law firm to represent me; the same scenario would result forensic accounting be damned.

Upshot: No chance in getting Gabby back; no chance me making it to court alive; no fulfilling my promise to Georgann. No nothing. They won.

I gave up.

I took the cash deal.

The End (Maybe)

Epilogue

2017

In the prologue, I wrote that now that everyone was dead I could tell my story. I wasn't completely correct, just mostly correct. Of Marie's brothers, Crazy Vinnie died in 2002 having escaped capture by the FBI and the mob. Sonny, who suffered a few heart attacks, as of this date, is still making linguine with clam sauce for his family's Sunday dinner. Frankie slowly wasted away from cancer in a Florida nursing home while Phyllis is alive and well. Donna and Dennis continued to live in the house they were given by my in-laws enjoying each other's miserable company until Dennis died of throat cancer in 2015. Silvio died in 1996, killed by a fallen tree on the Saw Mill River Drive. It took the Jaws of Life to get him out. He was seventy-nine and probably never achieved 'made man' status in the Mafia since there were fewer than three hundred made men at his funeral. Marie Marino, nee Vingo, lived to see her two great grandchildren. She died in her own bed from complications of a stroke at eighty-nine surrounded by all her family outliving her Mafia princess daughter by eighteen years.

Nikol is married with two children - grandchildren I never met. Do you recall that in Chapter 26 in the Part One, I said I could not understand why Nicky hated me so much besides Marie's negative influence? Several years after Georgann died, I received a letter from Nicky. Apparently, Georgann knew about some of my lady friends, and, to my horror, made Nicky her confident. Georgann was forgiving, Nikol was not.

Gabrielle, my precious daughter, lived with her grandmother until Marie's death. She never stopped believing I was responsible for Georgann's death and hated me so much she preferred living with the housekeeper rather than with her father. Even though I tried many times to get in touch with her, she never spoke another word to me.

I was not always the most faithful husband, but I loved Georgann with my whole heart. I never remarried. I never loved another.

On Easter Sunday 2017, I died peacefully in my sleep of an aortic aneurism at age seventy-two. I hope I joined Georgann in heaven and not the Marinos in the other place.

The End - Really

Linda Robinson

Glossary of Mafia and Italian Slang

Agita – heartburn, indigestion
Associate – someone who works with the Family but not yet a made-man
Babbo - idiot
Bel l'Italia - beautiful Italy
Boombatz – a demented person
Bravisima bella – very good, lovely girl
Buffone – buffoon, bum
Buona Fortuna – good luck
Busta – money made from a wedding
Capisce – understand
Capo di capi – head of a Mafia family
Casus belli – an act justifying war
Che cozzo – what the hell
Cheroot - cigar
Chooches - meatballs; dummies
Dente di leone – lion's teeth, dandelions
Enforcer – Mafia member who handles those who don't abide by the rules;
Faccia brutta – ugly face
Family – organized Mafia clan
Finito – finished
Friend of mine – someone connected but not in the same Family
Friend of ours – a fellow made man
Gavone – uncouth pig
Gentile – refined status
Gidrool – ignorant, stupid bastard
Goombah - pal
Goumare – mistresses
Made-man – fully initiated member of a Mafia family
Making one's bones – personally killing someone for the Family
Mammalucco - idiot
Mangia bene – eat well
Non fa niente – it doesn't matter
Noogie – a light knuckle punch on the head
Nonna – grandmother
Nonno – grandfather
Omertá – Mafia oath not to put anyone or anything above the Family
Paisano – country man

Pasta e fagioli – pasta and beans
Pazza – crazy
Person who is a problem – a liability; someone who needs to be taken out
Pezza di merde – piece of shit
Polentone – polenta eater, someone from Northern Italy
Porcacione – big pig
Scaramouch – a clown
Schifosi – disgusting, loathsome, rotten men
Sfacim – scum; a wise guy, a member of the Mafia
Stronzi – turds
Stronziatini – bull shitters
Stunad – stupid person
Terrone – peasant, someone from Sicily
Testa dura – hard head, stubborn
Torrone – Italian candy
The bank – proceeds from illegal Mafia dealings
Una bella figura – making a good impression
Un gotz - nothing
Vig or vigorish – interest paid on a loan to a loan shark
Vino – wine
Wise guy – a person in the Mafia
Zio – uncle

Acknowledgements

This narrative of the marriage between Al and Georgann Volpe is almost too improbable to be believed, but Married to a Mafia Princess is truly a work of non-fiction. I spent countless hours with Al listening to him relate the history of his married life with Georgann as we consumed plates of spaghetti with clam sauce and many glasses of wine.

I want to thank my son, Daniel Robinson Esq. for his valuable legal expertise on all the court proceedings throughout the book. Thanks to my dear friend Michael Weingart who guided me through the chapter on Al's boot camp days. Caterina Proserpio, my friend for over fifty years, spent long hours editing the book guided by her muse, Rina Troletti. Stanley Diamond was a great help as my technical advisor. Also, thanks to my family and friends for their support. Wikipedia was my main source for information on the Five Families considered to be the Italian Mafia as well as for background information on the renowned people Al met throughout this true story

Special thanks to my sister, Rita, who said she heard Al's voice speaking to her in every word she read.

Al asked me to write his story in his words so that his daughters, Nikol and Gabrielle, would know the truth whether they chose to believe it or not. I did my best to honor his wishes. Unfortunately, Al never got to read his sad story.

I'll end with a quote from Voltaire Al wanted me to include in the book in deference to his love for Georgann.

"To the living we owe respect, but to the dead

we owe only the truth."

Linda Robinson